PARTIES AND PARTY SYSTEMS

PARTIES AND PARTY SYSTEMS

STRUCTURE AND CONTEXT

Edited by Richard Johnston
and Campbell Sharman

UBCPress · Vancouver · Toronto

23 22 21 20 19 18 17 16 15   5 4 3 2 1

Printed in Canada on FSC-certified ancient-forest-free paper (100% post-consumer recycled) that is processed chlorine- and acid-free.

Library and Archives Canada Cataloguing in Publication

Parties and party systems: structure and context / edited by Richard Johnston and Campbell Sharman.

Includes bibliographical references and index.
Issued in print and electronic formats.
ISBN 978-0-7748-2955-7 (bound). – ISBN 978-0-7748-2957-1 (pdf).
ISBN 978-0-7748-2958-8 (epub). – ISBN 978-0-7748-3084-3 (mobi)

1. Political parties. I. Johnston, Richard, author, editor II. Sharman, Campbell, author, editor

JF2051.P22 2015   324.2   C2015-905291-2
C2015-905292-0

Canada

UBC Press gratefully acknowledges the financial support for our publishing program of the Government of Canada (through the Canada Book Fund), the Canada Council for the Arts, and the British Columbia Arts Council.

This book has been published with the help of the University of British Columbia through the K.D. Srivastava Fund.

UBC Press
The University of British Columbia
2029 West Mall
Vancouver, BC V6T 1Z2
www.ubcpress.ca

Contents

Preface

This book has its origins in a conference to honour Ken Carty, and his impact on political science is visible at its every turn. Each contributor has close ties with Carty, and our emphasis is always on intellectual connections. Not that personal ties have been precluded; that would be unimaginable when dealing with someone as attuned to the personal as Ken Carty. Each contributor has something to say about parties and party systems. The full complement of contributors brackets the volume's key theme: the imperative for students of parties and students of party systems to learn from each other and to work together.

Parties and Party Systems follows two parallel arcs: (1) the study of parties and (2) Ken Carty's career. The parallel is no accident as Carty is one of the leaders in the comparative study of party organization. He came to UBC as a student of comparative politics, plunged into Canadian waters, made himself far and away the leading student of Canada's parties, and then took insights derived from the Canadian case back to the global stage.

Ken Carty has never lost his fascination with the grassroots. His UBC colleagues know that he reads a room better than anyone and that he has a bottomless archive of life stories. His first book, *Party and the Parish Pump*, exemplifies this. Who knew that it is possible to write the ethnography of the single transferable vote? *Party and the Parish Pump* remains one of the most distinguished contributions to the study of Irish politics. Ireland may also have been the perfect bridge to Canadian politics, at least as it was practised at the time. For decades, Carty has worked the rooms of Canadian parties, observing how national politics are articulated at the local level. Canadian parties are like cicadas, dormant except when they are called to reproduce – that is, during elections and the selection of leaders. This may explain why this journey led Carty back to the link between centre and periphery. Why would actors on the periphery spend their time advancing the interests of the centre? How can the centre keep its grip on the wheel? What implications does all of this have for overcoming – or failing to overcome – Canada's centrifugal tendencies?

Out of these questions grew Carty's intuition about parties as franchise systems. This idea was first put forth in his 2002 presidential address to the Canadian Political Science Association, an address that reminded his listeners of the charm and wisdom of Stephen Leacock. The idea went global with an article in *Party Politics,* and it complemented a Canadian theme that goes back to Carty's all-time favourite book, Siegfried's *The Race Question in Canada.* This is the idea of the brokerage party, a peculiarly fascinating one for Canadians. Brokerage is front and centre in *Parties and Party Systems,* with Carty once again leading the way. This book is intended to honour Ken Carty and, in doing so, it showcases yet another of his trenchant insights and may be the springboard to yet another decade of scholarship. No doubt much of this scholarship will be conducted by Carty himself.

Acknowledgments

Our contributors generated an amazing two days of academic exchange. But they were only some of the academic participants at this book's editorial conference. Several colleagues and students, past and present, served as discussants and moderators. We particularly wish to thank Nathan Allen, Gerald Baier, Donald Blake, Munroe Eagles, Lynda Erickson, Andrea Nuesser, Ben Nyblade, Netina Tan, Daniel Westlake, and Şule Yaylaci. A special role was played by John Aldrich and Matt Shugart, who embraced the task of summarizing the event and locating it in the study of parties.

Major financial support for the conference came from the Social Sciences and Humanities Research Council of Canada under workshop grant 646-2010-1054. Generous support also came from the Department of Political Science and the Centre for the Study of Democratic Institutions at UBC. Travel support for some participants was furnished by Carleton University, the University at Buffalo – The State University of New York, and the University of Calgary. Our host was Green College, surely one of the most blessed academic venues anywhere.

Parties and Party Systems could not have become a reality without financial and moral support from UBC Press. We are especially grateful for the professionalism and enthusiasm of the press's director emeritus, Peter Milroy, and our editor, the indefatigable Emily Andrew.

Finally, we must mention two contributors who could not make it to Vancouver: Peter Aucoin and Peter Mair. They were missed at the time. We miss them even more now.

PARTIES AND PARTY SYSTEMS

Introduction

RICHARD JOHNSTON AND CAMPBELL SHARMAN

The modern study of parties began with Duverger (1954), who offers an integrated account of their internal organization and their systemic relations with each other. But, over time, parties as organizations became a separate object of study from parties as systems. The next landmark in the study of parties is Sartori (1976), who unintentionally highlights this divide. Although the title of his book refers to both "parties" and "party systems," the focus is on the latter, and it is still the outstanding text in the field. If the study of party systems flourished in the following years, it did so by narrowing its focus to counting parties and then relating that count to electoral formulas, with Cox (1997) as the industry standard. This literature largely ignores what made Satori's work distinctively systemic: his analysis of the interaction between the number of parties and their ideological positioning. (A striking exception is Meguid 2008.) In this sense, the party system literature is stalled (Mair 2002; Wolinetz 2006). Satori's title includes the tantalizing "volume one." Volume two never appeared, however, and this missing volume might have done for the study of organizations what the existing one did for the study of systems. It is tempting to suggest, however, that the absence of the landmark volume liberated students of party organization to think for themselves. Certainly, the study of organizations seems to have flourished and to have outdone the systems literature in creativity and originality. It is time, as Bardi and Mair (2008) argue, to reconnect the literatures and to make students of organizations and students of systems talk to each other. Such an objective is a major inspiration for *Parties and Party Systems*.

Themes

Parties and Party Systems juxtaposes problems and analyses that should provoke further integrative thinking. It follows four themes: (1) brokerage across lines of division in society; (2) keeping the partisan team together in the face of the centrifugal pressures that necessitate brokerage; (3) the ensuing complications in principal-agent relations within parties; and (4) the institutional context, both as it constrains all the foregoing and remains quite fragile.

Brokerage as a type for either party organization or party system appears in neither Duverger nor Sartori. Indeed, the concept originates in the study of North American party organizations and seems to have a special attraction for Canadian scholars. But reflection on its morphology, bases, and organizational or behavioural entailments immediately takes us to the organization-system nexus. The brokerage party may be the organizational type for Satori's "polarized pluralism." It may also be a thing of the past. Students of Canadian parties were mesmerized from the start by the notion of brokerage. The Ur-text for Canada is André Siegfried's (1907, 113-14) *The Race Question in Canada*, and here is its primary claim:

> Aware of the sharpness of certain rivalries, they know that if these are let loose without any counter-balance, the unity of the Dominion may be endangered. That is why they persistently apply themselves to prevent the formation of homogeneous parties, divided according to race, religion or class – a French party, for instance, or a Catholic party, or a Labour party. The clarity of political life suffers from this, but perhaps the existence of the federation can be preserved only at this price.

The intuition is that Canadian party leaders sense that encouraging division would be fatal to the polity. Although avoidance of such division might seem to be nothing more than convergence of the parties on the median voter, as argued by Downs (1957), in fact most party systems exhibit non-centrist party positioning, with the middle commonly empty or occupied only weakly. So if it is true that Canadian parties (one of them, at least) straddle the middle of the policy spectrum, then there must be something about the Canadian case that privileges centrist parties as much as it does centrist voters. Whatever this is, it should have analogues in other systems with a dominant, centrist party.

Brokerage politics places a special premium on reconciling the need for a common message with the equally pressing need for mobilizing grassroots enthusiasm. But it does so as a polar case, not as something qualitatively distinct. The challenge of keeping the team together proves to be ubiquitous – but so are solutions. Indeed, the literature presupposes that these twin challenges exist in a zero-sum relationship. Reality may be more complicated – and more forgiving. Brokerage as a system challenges brokerage parties as organizations. Parties are required to balance national leadership – embodied either in a strong leader or a tight factional coalition – with a mobilizational requirement for local autonomy. As already noted, however, brokerage organizations may be a polar, but not a qualitatively distinct, case. All large parties face a coordination challenge – at least they do in parliamentary systems. And here lies a dilemma: MPs are at one and the same time servants of two masters – their local constituents and their leader. Inherent limits on legislative time make control of the agenda a central issue, and, in the Westminster context, the press of public business drives governments to discipline their followers (Cox 1987). Time pressure in Parliament can also bring opposition parties to see the logic of party discipline (Koss 2012). All this, seemingly, runs against the grain of local electoral mobilization. Both elements are central to the logic of parliamentarianism, yet they are obviously in tension with each other.

To date, the literature on parliamentary accountability has been preoccupied with how institutions moderate the trade-off (Cox 2006), in particular the extent to which electoral institutions permit local candidates to cultivate a personal vote (Carey and Shugart 1995). The argument presupposes that the need for cohesion follows from the core logic of parliamentarianism: the dependence of governments on majorities in the confidence chamber. Is it possible, however, that merely conducting elections suffices? The logic of elections – the requirement for party signalling and the maintenance of a "reputational premium" (Sniderman and Stiglitz 2012) – may be as critical as the logic of cabinet formation.

Whatever its source, the challenge of keeping the team together blurs lines of accountability – of principal-agent relations. In almost all of the literature, local MPs or candidates are agents, never principals (contra romanticized popular or journalistic notions of what parties should be). Carey (2009) alerts us to one complexity: that MPs serve two masters – the party leadership and their local selectorates. What matters for Carey is the relative balance between local principals and national principals. The suspicion lingers, however, that party leaders can use ostensibly independent selectorates to pursue ends they choose for themselves. Equally, we suspect that the real lines of accountability in local organizations do not routinely make the MP the servant of the local organization.

We think of principal-agent relations within parties as being conditioned by institutional context. This is the central intuition in Carey and Shugart (1995). The same is true for Carty (2004), who describes the adaptability of his "franchise" model (Carty 2002) to all spatially dispersed electorates with single-member districts. Is it possible, however, that the challenge of keeping the team together overrides variation in party structures and in the overarching institutional context? And institutions that seem to meet the test of time can crumble quickly. The literature on rational-choice institutionalism generally regards institutions as fixed precisely because they induce self-enforcing behaviour (Thelen 1999). Electoral institutions in particular are assumed to be changed only by external forces, basically by expansion of the franchise (Boix 1999). The rationalist literature has only begun to consider how institutional change might be generated from the inside (Greif and Laitin 2004). Historically, however, institutions can be at odds with each other and institutional change can be driven from within (Thelen 1999). Even adaptation at the margin can have massive implications.

Plan of the Book

In sum, parties live in two domains: (1) a public sphere constrained by partisan competitors, electoral rules, and parliamentary practice and (2) a private sphere created by a network of members and supporters, party officials, and elected representatives. This book brings together a distinguished body of research on both domains in order to integrate the study of parties as organizations with the study of parties as systems. The sequence of chapters is dictated by these four themes. However, as several chapters touch on more than one theme, the sequence is rough.

Brokerage

All parties face the structural problem of having to maintain the energy and responsiveness of a dispersed party membership without losing the central direction necessary for the party to succeed in winning government. In the Canadian context, to explain how this accommodation has traditionally been made by governing parties is to talk of brokerage politics – the idea that party leaders can engage the support of political interests in a regionally and socially diverse society through instituting a series of separate deals, each entailing a distinctive regional payoff. But Carty's innovative analysis in

Chapter 1 of this collection shows that the idea of brokerage parties only makes sense within a narrowly defined context. He argues that there can only be one brokerage party in each system at any given time since only one party can make credible claims to accommodate the range of competing interests across the whole electorate. The brokerage party in this sense spans sectional interests that "would otherwise provide the organizational basis for electoral division and enduring partisan alignments." This analysis means that, in Canada and elsewhere, a party relying on brokerage is bound to collapse once politics – whether from social or political change – becomes more ideologically polarized and the conditions for cobbling together a series of sectional deals disappear.

The implications of this analysis are further explored by Johnston (Chapter 2), who makes a powerful case for the critical role of Quebec in both the operation and the recent decline of brokerage politics in Canada. Given the need, since 1867, for the Canadian polity to encompass widely differing provincial communities, each with a distinctive political agenda, he examines how regional brokerage has provided an effective way of producing single-party majorities in the Canadian Parliament. A consequence has been that, through a combination of size and the disposition of electoral support since the 1870s, Quebec has become a regional "pivot" for gaining sufficient electoral support to form national governments. Like Carty's, Johnston's analysis implies that changing demographics and a move to more polarized party competition across Canada will undermine both the possibility of brokerage politics and the ability of Quebec to maintain a pivotal role in building national majorities.

The transformation from brokerage to a more ideological politics is illustrated by Stewart and Sayers (Chapter 3) in their study of the 2004 Canadian election. This marked the consolidation of the Conservative Party as a party defined by a distinctive set of social values rather than by the accommodation of diverse interests. All three chapters argue that regional variations in partisan voting across Canada will remain but that they will be driven more by differential support for sets of broad policy goals than by the aggregation of disparate regional interests.

Keeping the Team Together

But there is more to intra-party dynamics than brokerage, and, even for brokerage parties, there is the question of how central control of the party can be combined with the local organization required to select candidates and to mobilize supporters at election time. The variety of ways this linkage can be structured – and the corresponding variety of attempts at categorizing them – is dealt with in a masterly survey by Wolinetz (Chapter 4). His point of departure is the idea of the franchise party (Carty 2002, 2004), which enables him to describe the way in which party discipline in Parliament can co-exist with the much looser control that is in evidence when local candidates conduct their election campaigns. Candidates are franchisees of the party name but are responsible for their local election campaigns and, if elected, must either follow the party line in Parliament or lose their party franchise. Although originally developed to explain the operation of national parties in Canada, the idea of the franchise party has found much broader application. Wolinetz examines how this form of party structure fits with other families of party organization, and he looks at the implications for internal party operation.

The variety of relationships between leaders and the broader party membership is well shown in the following three chapters, each of which deals with a different political system. For Farrell, Mair, Ó Muineacháin, and Wall (Chapter 5), the concern is combining highly disciplined voting by members of the Irish Parliament with the dominance of local concerns for members. Part of the explanation for this disjunction can be found in the form of proportional voting used to elect members – the single transferable vote – which requires successful candidates to have strong community support in addition to party endorsement. Concentrating on servicing local communities has meant that members have little inclination to monitor the broader policies of the party leadership. The authors argue that, by contributing to the lack of effective scrutiny of government policy, what may have been a convenient working arrangement for both the leaders and members of governing parties can have dysfunctional effects on the parliamentary system as a whole.

A similar disjunction is examined by Hazan and Rahat (Chapter 6) in their study of Israeli parties. Both the attempt to broaden the party base in response to demands for greater inclusiveness and the attempt to democratize the selection process for candidates have the potential to weaken party unity. A more diverse party membership and a candidate selection process that is more open to factional competition can threaten the maintenance of the discipline required for effective parliamentary parties. Yet the authors observe that, as the price for achieving party coherence in Parliament, most parties have found a workable compromise by permitting limited dissent in some forums. Nonetheless, they stress that the compromises are fragile and that internal tensions remain a continuing challenge to the task of preserving party unity.

In their analysis of parties competing for representation in the European Parliament, Bardi, Katz, and Mair (Chapter 7) take a different tack. In dealing with complaints about the democratic deficit in the government of the European Union, some have suggested that the solution is to be found in the emergence of pan-European parties that will replace the present loose coalitions of national parties. But Bardi, Katz, and Mair argue that the absence of a single, system-wide set of parties at elections for the European Parliament is only a sign of failure if the goal is to replicate the executive-dominated parliaments that characterize member states. The more modest goal of mobilizing local support within member countries for cooperative ventures under the umbrella of the European Parliament should not be ignored – an example of a franchise party system with multiple franchisors.

The View from the Grassroots

Another virtue of Carty's franchise party model is that it encourages the study of local party workers and the critical role they play in the mobilization of electoral support. The following three chapters focus on the concerns of the franchisee and supporters: the view of the party from the perspective of the MP, the local campaign organizer, and the party member. Koop (Chapter 8) examines the informal resources that an MP can use to help with tasks expected of a local member, from recruiting constituency volunteers to fundraising and running the local election campaign. These are critical tasks, yet there are few inducements that the member can provide for volunteers. Koop shows the variety of ways in which an MP who is a skillful manager can use praise, gossip, and inside knowledge to keep party workers engaged and the local party association working effectively.

This theme is repeated by Cross and Young (Chapter 9), but their focus is on the ability of the candidate to adjust the local campaign to suit constituency expectations in the face of demands for policy consistency from the party's head office. They survey Liberal Party and New Democratic Party candidates to chart the variation in the mix of central and local influences at work in an election campaign. Like Hazan and Rahat (Chapter 6), Cross and Young point to the running compromise required to accommodate party diversity within the constraints of parliamentary unity.

Van Haute (Chapter 10) deals with party organization from the standpoint of the individual member. Much of the research on party membership concerns the reasons for joining the party and the changing profile of members; however, as Van Haute points out, there is little research on members' views of the party organization and why they stay or leave. With the general decline of party membership in established democracies, Van Haute calls for more research on the attitudes and aspirations of party members in order to gain a better understanding of the way party cohesion is established, maintained, and/or lost.

Institutions

To this point contributions have been concerned with the private sphere of party operation – that is, with the internal dynamics of parties as essentially voluntary organizations. But parties are increasingly subject to the constraints of government regulation, whether parliamentary, electoral, or financial. The following four chapters examine what is now an integral component of the Canadian party system: the rules imposed on parties as actors in the public sphere.

The problem for governments and parties alike is to know which issues can be dealt with by changing the rules and what the consequences of such rule change would be. This explains the ambivalence of parties towards institutional change, even though, as Courtney (Chapter 11) indicates in his magisterial summary, over the past fifty years the legal status and regulation of Canadian parties have been transformed. The growth of the regulatory regime surveyed by Courtney has been less the consequence of partisan initiatives and more the consequence of sequential responses to a series of alterations in the context of parliamentary politics, changing public expectations of the role of parties, and the intervention of the Supreme Court of Canada under the Charter of Rights and Freedoms.

The public funding of parties is a good example of the complex effects of rule changes and the mix of partisan advantage and public interest in considering electoral fairness. Aucoin and Bakvis (Chapter 12) examine the per-vote subsidy to parties introduced by the Liberal government in 2004 and its abolition by the Conservatives in 2015. As they note, this scheme, with its annual subsidy to parties based on actual votes cast in the previous election, looks like a scheme to cartelize political parties – to recognize parties as formal components of the governmental system. But Aucoin and Bakvis see the scheme and its repeal not as an even-handed response to competing views of the role of parties but, rather, as a partisan move by the government of the moment to reduce its chief rival's access to financial resources.

If these schemes for public funding of parties can be seen to have a partisan payoff, this has been less clearly the case in recent attempts at electoral reform. Sharman and Attanasio (Chapter 13) argue that a surge in proposals for electoral reform in five of Canada's ten provinces was driven by an attempt to increase confidence in the legitimacy of parliamentary government. This explains the unusual commitment, common to all proposals, to include the public in deliberations about electoral reform. In this context, calculation of partisan gain, far from driving the proposals, was the principal reason that governing parties shied away from implementing change.

Yet the key place of fair representation in maintaining a sense of legitimacy in parliamentary government is well illustrated by Cutler and Hooper (Chapter 14). Survey evidence captured during the 2005 and 2009 British Columbia referendums on electoral reform indicates that nothing undermines citizens' sense of involvement more than knowing that the voter's preferred party is a persistent loser at elections. From this evidence, government interest in electoral reform is justified even if governing parties cannot bring themselves to adopt it.

The Way Forward

The last chapter, by the editors, returns to the common themes of the book. It identifies commonalities and tensions among the chapters and shows how they unsettle common presumptions. It also identifies gaps. Few definite conclusions emerge, but then that was never the point. Rather, the purpose of *Parties and Party Systems* is to goad scholars into reconsidering their theories and into taking new directions in their empirical investigations.

References

Bardi, L., and P. Mair. 2008. "The parameters of party systems." *Party Politics* 14 (2): 147–66.

Boix, C. 1999. "Setting the rules of the game: The choice of electoral systems in advanced democracies." *American Political Science Review* 93 (3): 609–24.

Carey, J.M. 2009. *Legislative Voting and Accountability*. Cambridge: Cambridge University Press.

Carey, J.M., and M.S. Shugart. 1995. "Incentives to cultivate a personal vote: A rank ordering of electoral formulas." *Electoral Studies* 14 (4): 417–39. http://dx.doi.org/10.1016/0261-3794(94)00035-2.

Carty, R.K. 2002. "The politics of Tecumseh Corners: Canadian political parties as franchise organizations." *Canadian Journal of Political Science* 35 (4): 723–45. http://dx.doi.org/10.1017/S0008423902778402.

–. 2004. "Parties as franchise systems: The stratarchical organizational imperative." *Party Politics* 10 (1): 5–24. http://dx.doi.org/10.1177/1354068804039118.

Cox, G.W. 1987. *The Efficient Secret: The Cabinet and the Development of Political Parties in Victorian England.* Cambridge: Cambridge University Press. http://dx.doi.org/10.1017/CBO9780511571473.

–. 1997. *Making Votes Count: Strategic Coordination in the World's Electoral Systems.* Cambridge: Cambridge University Press.

–. 2006. "The organization of democratic legislatures." In *The Oxford Handbook of Political Economy,* ed. B.R. Weingast and D.A. Wittman, 141–61. Oxford: Oxford University Press.

Downs, A. 1957. *An Economic Theory of Democracy.* New York: Harper.

Duverger, M. 1954 [1963]. *Political Parties: Their Organization and Activity in the Modern State.* New York: Wiley.

Greif, A., and D.D. Laitin. 2004. "A theory of endogenous institutional change." *American Political Science Review* 98 (4): 633–52.

Koss, M. 2012. "The legitimate secret: The institutionalization of parliamentary agenda control in the United Kingdom and Germany." Presentation at the Annual Meeting of the American Political Science Association, New Orleans, LA, August 30–September 2.

Mair, P. 2002. "Comparing party systems." In *Comparing Democracies 2: New Challenges in the Study of Elections and Voting,* ed. L. LeDuc, R.G. Niemi, and P. Norris, 88–107. London: Sage.

Meguid, B.M. 2008. *Party Competition between Unequals: Strategies and Electoral Fortunes in Western Europe.* Cambridge: Cambridge University Press.

Sartori, G. 1976. *Parties and Party Systems: A Framework for Analysis.* Cambridge: Cambridge University Press.

Siegfried, A. 1907. *The Race Question in Canada.* London: Eveleigh Nash.

Sniderman, P.M., and E.H. Stiglitz. 2012. *The Reputational Premium: A Theory of Party Identification and Policy Reasoning.* Princeton, NJ: Princeton University Press.

Thelen, K. 1999. "Historical institutionalism in comparative politics." *Annual Review of Political Science* 2 (1): 369–404. http://dx.doi.org/10.1146/annurev.polisci.2.1.369.

Wolinetz, S.B. 2006. "Party systems and party system types." In *Handbook of Party Politics,* ed. R.S. Katz and W. Crotty, 51–62. London: Sage. http://dx.doi.org/10.4135/9781848608047.n7.

1

Brokerage Parties, Brokerage Politics

R. KENNETH CARTY

What impact does the character of individual political parties have for the style and shape of democratic politics? Thinking about this question is made more difficult by a proliferation of party types among scholars and by a confusion about the relationship between the kinds of parties that exist and the political dynamics of the party systems they construct. In no case does this seem so apparent as in accounts of the "brokerage parties" long described as practising a distinctive form of brokerage politics in Canada.

The very idea that Canadian party politics has assumed a special, or at least a distinctive, brokerage character is an old one. It is at the heart of Siegfried's (1966) masterful account of Canadian politics, an account written over a century ago. Yet, despite the regular description of Canadian political parties as unique organizations that practise a particular form of brokerage politics, little attention has been given to identifying what makes this type of party different from others or to what the consequences are when such parties organize a democratic political landscape.

But brokerage parties are different. And successful brokerage parties create a set of political dynamics that fosters idiosyncratic patterns of political competition and party life. This chapter explores these claims, drawing on both theoretical understandings of party organization and the empirical lessons of Canadian experience. This allows me to articulate just what it means to identify brokerage parties, to conceptualize their impact on a competitive party system, and then to compare the experience of a number of such systems across a variety of settings.

The Issue

In their sweeping characterization of Canadian national politics as a succession of "dynasties and interludes," LeDuc and his colleagues (2010, 33, 529–30) assert that the country's political life is dominated by the practice of "brokerage politics," a consequence of electoral competition between brokerage parties that have neither stable support bases nor differing ideological orientations. As pure office-seeking institutions, such parties are typically portrayed as particularly elastic versions of Kirchheimer's (1966, 184–92) "catch-all" parties and, in their more contemporary manifestations, cases of Panebianco's (1988, 262–69) "electoral-professional" party organizations. Wesley's (2009, 211–14) account of brokerage politics simply distinguishes it from "responsible politics" and argues that it is the consequence of a democratic electoral competition in which the major competitors are unprincipled catch-all parties.

On the one hand, it appears that brokerage parties – institutionally structured to represent a heterogeneous social base and to mobilize electoral support indiscriminately – are held to generate brokerage politics. But, on the other, it may be that it is the adoption of a brokerage approach to conducting national political life – the broad appeal to electors across the spectrum in terms of an accommodative policy package with something for everyone – that engenders brokerage parties. Is this a chicken-and-egg problem or simply alternate characterizations of the same phenomenon? Might it be that brokerage politics could be practised by different kinds of political parties? Does the existence of a successful brokerage party necessarily imply others of the same type? And does the presence of a brokerage party have recognizable consequences for the character and operation of its competitors in the wider party system? The literature on Canadian party politics, which makes so much of its brokerage character, is silent on these basic questions.

If the concept of a brokerage party is essentially the same as that of a catch-all party, then it is not clear what distinctive theoretical purchase it offers. However, if such parties are different from catch-all, or even from Koole's (1996) "modern cadre" party organizations, then we ought to be able to specify in what way they differ, to what end, and with what consequence. While the competitive dynamic between (at least) two catch-all parties is central to the operation of Kirchheimer's transformed party systems, it is not at all obvious that a brokerage party system requires two brokerage parties. Indeed, the most successful brokerage parties may persist precisely because they are able to deprive opponents of an opportunity to compete on comparable terms and so dominate their political systems. That raises questions about the essential dynamics, both short- and long-term, of brokerage systems.

Sorting out the distinctive features of brokerage politics thus seems to require that we begin by identifying what, if anything, is unique about a brokerage party and then by considering its impact on the competitive dynamics of a system. To do this, I start by juxtaposing the brokerage party – using the properties of the Canadian case as an empirical referent – against Kirchheimer's catch-all party, with which it is generally identified.

The Brokerage Party

In their straightforward and traditional account of a brokerage party, LeDuc et al. (2010, 33) define it as a political institution "hoping to put together a coalition of support across the entire electorate." Such a party does not see itself as constrained by past support or by specific groups in the society; indeed, its raison d'être is to act as a social and political broker capable of accommodating the competing interests of distinctive elements of the whole electorate. In this sense, the concept of brokerage extends beyond simple anthropological notions of skilful patronage management in the interest of accumulating and managing sufficient electoral support to form a government: it is about accommodating and integrating the social divisions that would otherwise provide the organizational basis for electoral division and enduring partisan alignments.

In modern theories of democratic electoral competition, political parties are recognized as the organizational instruments that articulate and institutionalize division – be it social, geographic, or ideological – and so structure choice and accountability. In sharp contrast, a brokerage party is conceived as one that seeks to reconcile the most fundamental divisions in the society: in so doing, it obfuscates and suppresses wider political conflict. In this sense, a brokerage party might be understood as a kind of anti-party, denying the reality of a political community's inherent political parts. This leads to a perception of brokerage parties as both unprincipled and shapeless. And it leads some to identify them as versions of the catch-all party that emerged in the modernizing social orders of postwar Western Europe.

In his classic account of the transformation of the party systems of Western Europe, Kirchheimer (1966) claimed that a new kind party had appeared, one marked by a number of distinctive elements. This catch-all party's electoral base was shaped and constrained by the identity of its historic core constituency; its origins and evolution lay in vigorous competition with other similar organizations; its mobilization appeal (what he called a party's "expressive function") was moderated and limited as ideology was eschewed; it commanded little loyalty from partisans who supported rather than belonged; and its evisceration of the role of party members represented the ultimate flowering of Michels's law of the oligarchical tendencies of organization (Michels 1966). Powerful and influential as this account is, little of it appears to resonate with the experience or practice of organizations like the Liberal Party of Canada, long described as the country's natural governing party and the archetypal brokerage party (Carty 2015).

One of Kirchheimer's critical insights is that catch-all parties emerged from earlier party forms as a competitive response to the successful organizational and behavioural adaptations of their electoral competitors (Kirchheimer 1966, 188).[1] Thus, in any individual polity, catch-all parties come in (at least) twos as their existence reflects a deliberate response to the competitive incentives created by a dynamic, similarly organized opponent. Brokerage parties face no such systemic imperatives. Typically created de nouveau by political entrepreneurs as polity-building instruments, their very success at incorporating a wide support base effectively constrains the capacity of opponents to replicate their formula. With limited alternate space available in the system, other parties are driven to mobilize pieces or interests in the electorate unreconciled to the broad accommodative package of the brokerage party. Thus successful brokerage parties typically stand alone, opposed by other kinds of parties in what predictably becomes an unbalanced and asymmetric competitive system. In Canada, over the twentieth century, the Conservatives were never able to match the Liberals' continuing ability to operate as a brokerage party.[2] They were left to operate as a sporadically competitive catch-all party that inevitably dissipated the oversized, unstable electoral coalitions it occasionally managed to mobilize.

Catch-all parties are compelled by the logic of their more limited electoral bases to restrain their mobilization appeals. There is no reason for brokerage parties to do this. Indeed, the very opposite is the case. With no simple, obviously defined constituency whose interests are immediately apparent, the brokerage party must be continually engaged in (re)creating its electorate by aggressively asserting its self-defined mission as representative of the entire community and as having a unique capacity to serve as the common political instrument of all. This same lack of a natural core consisting of those who belong to it means that the brokerage party must foster individual, as well as group, loyalties. This results in an indiscriminate approach to membership that is open to welcoming any and all former opponents or partisan agnostics into its structures and activities.

At the heart of a brokerage party's approach to politics is the construction of an accommodative bargain that defines its role in the system and encompasses its diverse electorate. Drawing on the Canadian case, LeDuc et al. (2010, 530) argue that this places "a great deal of emphasis on the role of the leader, whose job it is to act as the 'chief broker' among the many different interests and social groups" whose support the party requires. The general point is that, because it is required to do more than just represent and successfully communicate a partisan message, the party's leadership, however it is structured, becomes the locus of significant intra-party decision-making power. Although this can be a powerful centralizing force, the resulting strong leadership can also be fragile. Members or factions unhappy with their party's positions or activity know that attacking the leadership, rather than debating policy or strategy, is the most efficacious route to change. At the same time, brokerage party leaders are measured in terms of electoral success, so setbacks to party support levels can quickly lead to questions of the party's willingness to see them continue in office.

As an organization focused on mobilizing political support from a diverse and often internally contradictory electorate, brokerage parties need to find ways to penetrate and to engage the very different elements of their political community. While, on the one hand, this supports a centralization of power in the hands of a leadership that can broker and articulate widely acceptable policy bargains, on the other, it requires an organizational strategy that gives grassroots activists incentives and opportunities to be active participants in party life. For brokerage parties, the solution is a stratarchical structure that parcels out decision-making authority so that distinctive faces of the organization enjoy a significant degree of autonomy in areas, and on questions, relevant to them (Mair 1994; Carty 2004). In Canada, the brokerage party adopted a franchise system structure (Carty 2002); in other cases, institutionalized factionalism was a natural outcome. Whatever the form, this makes intra-party politics in the brokerage party much more open and contested than it is in the ossified hierarchical structures of the catch-all party, encumbered as it is with Michelian oligarchic organizations (Carty and Cross 2006).

On this account, brokerage parties are the antithesis of modern catch-all organizations.[3] Their claim to be able to represent all voters (typically in the name of nation-building or state-building), their accommodative style, their structure and internal party politics, and their dominant positioning in the party system mark them out as a unique type of democratic political party. And, as Bardi and Mair (2008, 148) note: "if there are different types of party, then there are also likely to be different types of relations between parties." For brokerage parties this is particularly the case given that, unlike catch-all organizations, they do not face their organizational equivalents in the competitive dynamics that mark their party systems. This leads us to the question of the characteristic features of the politics of a brokerage party system and its practice of brokerage politics.

Brokerage Politics

Brokerage parties, as a consequence of their need to appeal to a broad and relatively heterogeneous electoral base, have instinctively centrist political orientations. They argue that only they can reconcile the competing needs and demands of the political community. The assertion that their brokerage is necessary to defend the integrity of the wider political system amounts to a nation- or a state-building claim, depending on the historical context within which the party is constructed. Thus we find centrist brokerage parties in political systems in which the very construction (or maintenance) of a democratic electorate, or the institutional imperatives of state-building, are seen to be at issue.

These parties need to find and hold a political space that prevents them from being boxed into any place in the political spectrum that might constrain their ability to reach voters in all corners of the electorate. This is not to say that brokerage parties may not regularly enjoy disproportionate success among distinctive clienteles – for example, the Canadian Liberals were long preferred by Roman Catholics – but, rather, that they are positioned to bind the political interests of such groups to others in the electorate. Finding and occupying a centre among a mélange of partisan interests and claims is no easy task. In simple systems, driven by centripetal forces, the natural Duvergerian tendency is to squeeze the centre out; in multipolar systems, centrifugal dynamics can disadvantage centrality (compare Sartori 1976, chap. 10). This requires brokerage parties to set themselves apart from the normal competitive dynamics of representative politics, and it may well lead to Sartorian patterns of polarized pluralism.

Establishing itself as the centrist nation/state builder provides a brokerage party with a significant competitive advantage that, with political skill, can quickly be turned into long-term dominance. Thus brokerage parties are well placed to constitute the core of a distinctive form of a dominant party system. However, this advantage may dissipate over time if their very success then makes the existence or stability of the system less problematic. This suggests that brokerage parties are likely to suffer long-term electoral decline, with pieces of their initial dominant coalition falling to their political opponents. Dependent on the power to reward supporters who do not naturally belong to it, the brokerage party does not find it easy to sustain any prolonged period in opposition. Thus, despite the apparent hyper-stability implied by the strength and position of the core piece, brokerage party systems seem destined to disintegrate as their dominant party decays, ultimately to collapse or to be transformed into some other organizational form. This differentiates this form of dominant party system from those rooted in frozen partisan alignments (the classic case is the Swedish Social Democrats' long dominance of its party system) that may last as long as the form and balance of the social divisions underlying them persists.

The central democratic challenge of brokerage parties is to structure their internal organizational politics in a fashion that balances the interests of members and supporters with the demands for effective and responsive leadership. Given the brokerage party's long dominance of the polity, these internal party decision-making issues have a particularly significant impact on the democratic health of the wider system. There is no necessary leadership formula or mechanism that flows from the logic of brokerage per se, but the distinctive stratarchical accommodation made within any particular party will govern the pattern of government formation and shape the brokerage processes and trade-offs at the centre of the system's core policy and administrative accommodations.

Comparing Brokerage Experience

Canadian analysts have readily identified the Liberal Party of Canada as a brokerage party, perhaps the archetypical brokerage party. And the theoretical discussion to this point has drawn heavily on its experience. However, it is clear that Canada is not the only political system with a successful brokerage party and the distinctive politics that flows from its presence and

TABLE 1.1
Brokerage party systems

	Effective elective parties[1]	Election system[2]	Election wins	Time in office	Prime ministers	PMs duration (months)	PMs > 10 years
	n		%	%	*n*	*n*	*n*
Nation-builders							
Canada – Liberal	3.27	SMP	66	67	7	112	3
Ireland – Fianna Fáil	3.26	STV	76	73	7	104	2
India – Congress		SMP	67	79	6	95	2
State-builders							
Italy – Christian Democrat	4.26	PR	92	90	16[3]	31	0
Japan – Liberal Democrat	3.44	SNTV	89	93	22	28[4]	0

Note: Applies to Canada, 1920–2010; Ireland, 1927–2010; India, 1950–2010; Italy, 1948–92; Japan, 1955–2010.

1 Post-WW II averages; data from http://www.tcd.ie/Political_Science/staff/michael_gallagher/ElSystems/Docts/ElectionIndices.pdf. For an assessment of the Indian case, with considerable variance in its effective number of parties, see Nikolenyi (2008).

2 SMP = single member plurality, STV = single transferable vote, PR = proportional representation, SNTV = single non-transferable vote.

3 Several had more than one turn as PM; e.g., Andreotti had three terms forming six governments.

4 1960–72 = 6-year average; 1972–2010 = 2.2 year average.

success. A comparison with others, and the politics of the party systems they animate, illustrates the impact of a major brokerage party organization on the competitive dynamics of the wider system.

Several key features of the electoral politics and governmental leadership of five party systems dominated by recognizably brokerage parties – Canada (Liberal Party), Ireland (Fianna Fáil), India (Congress Party), Italy (Democrazia Cristiana), and Japan (Liberal Democratic Party) – are summarized in Table 1.1.[4] The longest-standing Canadian case is measured from the adoption of the (nearly) universal franchise, the Irish from the regularization of democratic politics after the Republic's post-independence civil war, and the other three from the establishment of a modern competitive party system in the aftermath of the Second World War. In each instance, a brokerage party arose to respond to the imperatives of integration, which required reconciling local political energies with national leadership.

In each case the brokerage party established, and sustained, a centrist orientation by positioning itself as the democratic instrument of a national political community. Three of the parties cast themselves as devoted to the primary task of nation-building. In Canada, the Liberal Party established itself as a preferred partisan instrument of francophone voters in the last years of the nineteenth century and then solidified its monopoly of that position during the First World War conscription crisis. As Johnston demonstrates in Chapter 2 of this volume, with Quebec as the pivot of national electoral politics the Liberals were left as the only party to bridge the two linguistic communities and thus to sustain the federation. In Ireland, Fianna Fáil cast itself as a national movement – more than just a simple political party – especially committed to articulating and defending the integrity of a republic struggling to emerge from British control. The Congress Party, in India, played much the same role as the popular instrument of that country's political independence. In the other two cases, Italy and Japan, the brokerage parties emerged as the principal state-building organizations of those working to construct and institutionalize a new set of political institutions in the aftermath of defeat in the Second World War. In both these cases the Cold War context played a considerable part in shaping the respective domestic party systems as the new brokerage parties were challenged to create and to organize an electoral instrument for a governing political class opposed by a much strengthened (socialist and communist) left.

All these brokerage parties were recognizably centrist organizations in the sense that they cast broad appeals aimed at attracting voters from across the political spectrum. All but the Japanese Liberal Democrats faced significant electoral opposition from both sides, although none of the systems was particularly balanced; the Liberals and Fianna Fáil confronted a comparatively weak left, while in Italy the left was stronger than the right. For all, their success was a function not only of their positioning but also of a splintered and variously organized opposition.

The evidence, both of the proportion of elections won and time spent in office,[5] reveals the extent to which these parties dominated their political systems. By these indicators the Canadian Liberals, although the oldest – by that measure perhaps the most successful of the brokerage parties – has been the least dominant, controlling its system for just two-thirds of the time. However, as with its counterparts in Ireland and India, a capacity to constantly reassert its capacity for nation-building brokerage ensured that it remained the central point of the party system, and occasional electoral defeats proved temporary. More striking, perhaps, is the comparatively greater electoral success and governmental dominance of the state-building brokerage parties. Both the Japanese Liberal Democrats and the Italian Christian Democrats (over their lives) enjoyed virtual monopolies (with control levels of around 90 percent) over their party systems. As primarily office-holding institutions, their focus on managing the machinery of government reinforced their centrist orientation and facilitated their capacity to continually mobilize a broad electoral base.

Electoral systems are held to shape the particular organization of party competition in the way they force political consolidation or permit electoral fragmentation. It is thus quite striking that these brokerage parties were able to establish their dominance and then thrive in a wide range of different systems, from the Italian postwar strongly proportional system, through the preferential ballot regimes in Ireland and Japan, to the majoritarian (single member plurality) systems of the more traditionally Westminster-style institutions in Canada and India. It was precisely their brokerage capacities and organization that allowed these parties to consolidate their electoral positions and to create a system of continuing one-party dominance, with all the policy and governance consequences that such regimes engender (Pempel 1990).

As a governing institution designed to accommodate rather than to articulate conflicting positions, the brokerage party requires a decision-making capacity to strike and enforce the necessary political and electoral bargains able to draw support from across the political community. The very earliest accounts of the Canadian brokerage party model point to the critical importance of the leader as organizational focus, electoral strategist, and policy adjudicator (Siegfried 1966 [1906]) – in LeDuc et al.'s (2010) terms, the person who acts as "chief broker." For the Liberal Party this meant adopting a practice of alternating between English- and French-speaking leaders who were freed from any direct parliamentary caucus accountability and so left to balance the hard inter-communal issues. That formula privileged long-serving personal leaderships – three of the leaders over the century served as prime minister for over a decade (four, if Wilfrid Laurier's dominance of the first two decades of the century are counted). As Table 1.1 indicates, the average Canadian Liberal leader enjoyed more time in office than did his counterpart in any of the other brokerage organizations.

While the Canadian party's core brokerage concern was to accommodate the country's two historic linguistic communities, each of the other parties wrestled with its own distinctive challenge. Necessarily they adopted particular approaches to the problem of leadership in a way that provided for the maintenance of their respective party's electoral coalition and its consequent control of the public agenda and government institutions. India's Congress Party responded to the realities of a deeply fragmented polity that threatened to splinter its base by adopting a dynastic model of personal leadership. Although the party produced six prime ministers over six decades, three came from the same family (father, daughter, and grandson) and a fourth held office on the nomination of the granddaughter-in-law: in total, the Nehru-Gandhi family has controlled the prime ministership for 90 percent of the time Congress has been in office.

If brokerage parties making essentially nation-building appeals have found it politically prudent to depend on stable, long-lasting leaderships that portray a consistent image and deliver an enduring message, quite the opposite appears to be the case when it is state institutions, as opposed to the political nation, that is at issue. Although both the Italian and Japanese brokerage parties also established dominant regimes – indeed more successfully if measured by time spent in office – they did so by adopting radically different approaches to providing for their organizations' accommodative leadership of party and state. By comparison with the other cases, they appear to have had a revolving-door style of party leadership, with individual party leaders spending comparatively short periods in office as prime minister.

This sharply different pattern reflects the adoption by the respective parties of a collective, rather than a personal, leadership rooted in and structured by the organizational factionalism that reflected the distinctive elements of their brokerage coalition. In their analysis of Japan's Liberal Democratic Party, Krauss and Pekkanen (2011) reveal how power in such a factionalized brokerage party is significantly more dispersed than it is in the more leader-centred versions.[6] Faction leaders take turns in the highest office – in the Italian case several had a number of turns – evidence that determining and managing the trade-offs implicit in the party's brokerage accommodations are not the prerogative of one chief but, rather, the responsibility of the wider institutionalized network that comprises the party's internal structure. As a consequence, individual prime ministers in Italy and Japan are among the weakest of any in the well-established parliamentary democracies, while, by comparison, their Canadian counterparts are rated the strongest (O'Malley 2007, 17). While brokerage parties may create similar centre-dominated electoral politics, they do not necessarily lead to similar patterns of governance. The business of government decision-making reflects the patterns of intra-party authority and competition structuring and animating the internal life of the dominant party.

If brokerage party structures are a natural organizational recourse of nation builders, or an institutional strategy of state builders, can such structures survive when either the political project itself succeeds or natural divisions in an established system emerge to foster adversarial as opposed to accommodative electoral politics? We have no theoretical expectations about the natural lifespan of particular party types.[7] However, it does seem reasonable to expect that brokerage parties may not be able to sustain their dominance from the centre indefinitely if the demand for systemic integration is no longer a major charge on the party system.

Figure 1.1 charts these brokerage parties' vote shares and makes it clear that they have all suffered a long-term secular decline in their electoral support: by mid-2011 only one – India's Congress Party – was in office. The Italian Christian Democrats disappeared with the collapse of a scandal-ridden party system after the country's 1992 election. The other four remain as active players in their party systems, although in two cases the parties have lost their easy dominance – evidence, perhaps, of their failure to operate any longer as genuine brokerage organizations.

Canada's Liberal Party lost its electoral hegemony over the country's French-speaking electorate in the 1980s when Quebec's position as the pivot around which government politics flowed ended (Johnston, Chapter 2, this volume). No longer being able, or perhaps even needed, to act as the political bridge between the country's two linguistic communities deprived the party of its distinctive historic mission and organizational imperative. This left the Liberals floundering in the face of an aggressive catch-all party on its right and a social democratic labour party on its left. The resulting squeeze produced a continuing drop in its vote share in four successive elections since 2000. In Ireland, Fianna Fáil's vote held up better (for longer) than did that of the other brokerage parties, but parliamentary arithmetic forced it into governing partnerships with other political parties from 1989 on. It took a catholic approach to its new situation, successively coalescing with a wide variety of different small parties from across the political spectrum, but this only indicated a new inability to stand above other parties as the embodiment of the Republic. The country's financial crisis led to its massive rejection in the 2011 election, leaving the party to rebuild without the advantages of office that, for so long, had allowed it to accommodate the representational demands of a parochial electorate. The recent experience of the Canadian Liberals suggests that the brokerage approach to political

FIGURE 1.1
Brokerage party vote shares

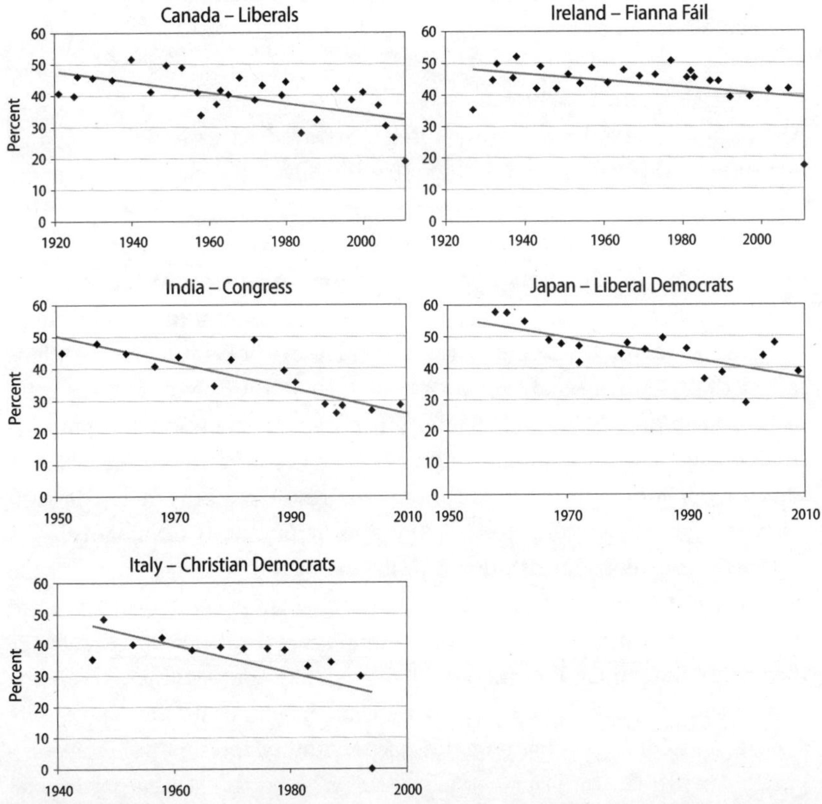

organization that sustained the party in office may prove to be a marked disadvantage in opposition.

Both the Indian Congress Party and the Japanese Liberal Democratic Party have also lost vote share over the last half-century, but neither appears to have yet been as displaced as the Canadian or Irish parties. The Congress Party, although badly beaten in India's 2014 general election, has so far survived periodic challenges to its dominance given its decided competitive advantage in a very fragmented electorate. The Liberal Democrats were defeated in 2009 but quickly returned to office in 2012 and remain the central player in what may be emerging as a competitive bipolar system.[8] Its strength is in its kōenkai organizations, which root the national party in networks of local politicians with long-nurtured patronage networks. Whether either or both of these parties will be able to sustain their position if over-all support levels continue to fall, and they can no longer govern as national brokers, is an open question.

From Organization to System

Although brokerage parties are often portrayed as essentially catch-all institutions, this theoretical and empirical analysis indicates that they are distinctive forms of partisan organization, with their own mobilization strategies and political orientations. It is therefore hardly surprising that their politics, and the party systems they animate, have a distinctive cast. Unlike Kirchheimer's (1966) dualistic catch-all systems of the United Kingdom or Germany, the competitive dynamics of brokerage party systems reflect the organizational imperatives of their dominant party. This privileges a form of political organization that seeks to smother and obfuscate fundamental social, economic, and cultural divisions as opposed to structuring open competition around them. The result is a prevailing centrism and the establishment of patterns of long-term, one-party dominance.

One of the central institutional problems of the brokerage party is the necessity of balancing the real intra-party tensions generated by the need for stratarchical organization and the imperatives for its leaders to manage the party's fundamental brokerage challenge. Its wider significance for the polity is the role that these same partisan leaders play as national governors and the consequent problem of elite accountability and renewal. The comparative evidence from our five cases suggests that brokerage parties can adopt a wide range of different solutions to the task of providing government leaders, each with immediate consequences for the organization and style of government decision-making. None escapes the problem that democratic accountability in the wider political system becomes subject to the relatively closed norms and practices of intra-party decision-making, depriving the electorate of a meaningful choice of its government's leadership.

As brokerage parties have no natural underlying electoral constituency they seem, inevitably, to be subject to the pressures of a steady secular decline in their support. This raises a difficult question: Why, if organizational decay and electoral disintegration is inevitable, is it so delayed and dominance so prolonged?[9] An answer would take us beyond the theme of this chapter (from brokerage party to brokerage party system) to wider issues of the relationship between brokerage politics and governance. As I have noted, brokerage parties' governing modes appear to reflect their internal decision-making structures and capacities. Being about nation-building and/or state-building, their long-term success appears to be rooted in their determination and capacity to use the institutions of the state to bolster their political position and to define their agenda in a fashion that privileges their centrist politics. In all the cases there is ample evidence that the ultimate result was the collapse of a distinction between politics and administration so that the parties became, in Whitaker's (1977) evocative phrase, simply their country's "Government Party." Brokerage party governments might retard their political decay through the aggressive and selective use of the distributive powers of government, but eventual administrative exhaustion and governance failures ultimately threaten to produce electoral collapse, heralding the end of the brokerage party and, hence, a transformation in the shape and content of subsequent party competition.

Notes

1 Duverger (1954) characterizes this response on the part of bourgeois parties as "contagion from the left"; Epstein (1967) argues that parties of the left were also subject to a "contagion from the right." For an account of these processes in terms of party models, see Carty (2013c).

2 The Conservatives had operated as a brokerage party in the first quarter-century of the Canadian state. Expelled from Quebec, they were replaced in this role by the Liberals in 1896 and left to continually struggle to find an organizational form that would make them competitive.

3 For a fuller theoretical account that elaborates the differences between catch-all and brokerage parties, see Carty (2013b).

4 For an assessment of the Irish case that draws on the arguments made here, see Carty (2013a).

5 Elections won is measured by whether the party provided the prime minister after the election; time spent in office is measured by the time during which a party leader held the office of prime minister.

6 For an analysis of how factionalism fragmented power in the stratarchical organization of the Congress Party, see Roy (1967).

7 Kirchheimer (1966) argues that parties transform themselves in response to their competitive environments, but the temporal dimensions of such processes are far from clear. The Lipset-Rokkan "frozen voter alignments" model implies that party systems may change if the system "unfreezes," although it is not clear what the implications of that would be for particular parties much less for distinctive types of parties.

8 The one previous interruption to the Liberal Democrats' long rule was a ten-month period in 1993–94 when the party briefly lost control of the government to what proved to be an unstable coalition of its opponents. On the shifting party system, see Krauss and Pekkanen (2011, 231–33).

9 I owe John Aldrich for this question. This last paragraph only hints at the direction of a possible answer, which is the subject for another paper.

References

Bardi, L., and P. Mair. 2008. "The parameters of party systems." *Party Politics* 14 (2): 147–66. http://dx.doi.org/10.1177/1354068807085887.

Carty, R.K. 2002. "The politics of Tecumseh Corners: Canadian political parties as franchise organizations." *Canadian Journal of Political Science* 35 (4): 723–45. http://dx.doi.org/10.1017/S0008423902778402.

–. 2004. "Parties as franchise systems: The stratarchical organizational imperative." *Party Politics* 10 (1): 5–24. http://dx.doi.org/10.1177/1354068804039118.

–. 2013a. "Fianna Fáil and Irish Party politics: A comparative analysis." A paper for the Irish Political Studies Association Annual Conference, Dublin, October 2013.

–. 2013b. "Has brokerage politics ended? Canadian parties in the new century." In *Parties, Elections, and the Future of Canadian Parties and Elections*, ed. A. Bittner and R. Koop, 10–23. Vancouver: UBC Press.

–. 2013c. "Party models and intraparty democracy." In *The Challenges of Intra-Party Democracy*, ed. W. Cross and R. Katz, 11-26. Oxford: Oxford University Press.

–. 2015. *Big Tent Politics: The Liberal Party's Long Mastery of Canada's Public Life.* Vancouver: UBC Press.

Carty, R.K., and W. Cross. 2006. "Can stratarchically organized parties be democratic? The Canadian case." *Journal of Elections, Public Opinion and Parties* 16 (2): 93–114. http://dx.doi.org/10.1080/13689880600715912.

Duverger, M. 1954. *Political Parties: Their Organization and Activity in the Modern State.* London: Methuen.

Epstein, L. 1967. *Political Parties in Western Democracies.* New York: Praeger.

Kirchheimer, O. 1966. "The transformation of the Western European party systems." In *Political Parties and Political Development*, ed. J. LaPalombara and M. Weiner, 177–200. Princeton, NJ: Princeton University Press.

Koole, R. 1996. "Cadre, catch-all or cartel? A comment on the notion of the cartel party." *Party Politics* 2 (4): 507–23. http://dx.doi.org/10.1177/1354068896002004004.

Krauss, E., and R. Pekkanen. 2011. *The Rise and Fall of Japan's LDP: Political Party Organizations as Historical Institutions.* Ithaca, NY: Cornell University Press.

LeDuc, L., J. Pammett, J. McKenzie, and A. Turcotte. 2010. *Dynasties and Interludes: Past and Present in Canadian Electoral Politics.* Toronto: Dundurn Press.

Mair, P. 1994. "Party organizations: From civil society to the state." In *How Parties Organize: Change and Adaption in Party Organizations in Western Democracies*, ed. R. Katz and P. Mair, 1–22. London: Sage Publications. http://dx.doi.org/10.4135/9781446250570.n1.

Michels, R. 1966 [1915]. *Political Parties: A Sociological Study of Oligarchical Tendencies in Modern Democracy.* Glencoe, IL: Free Press.

Nikolenyi, C. 2008. "Recognition rules, party labels and the number of parties in India." *Party Politics* 14 (2): 211–22. http://dx.doi.org/10.1177/1354068807085890.

O'Malley, E. 2007. "The power of prime ministers: Results of an expert survey." *International Political Science Review* 28 (1): 7–27. http://dx.doi.org/10.1177/0192512107070398.

Panebianco, A. 1988. *Political Parties: Organization and Power*. Cambridge: Cambridge University Press.

Pempel, P.J. 1990. *Uncommon Democracies: The One-Party Dominant Regimes*. Ithaca, NY: Cornell University Press.

Roy, R. 1967. "Factionalism and 'stratarchy': The experience of the Congress Party." *Asian Survey* 7 (12): 896–908. http://dx.doi.org/10.2307/2642533.

Sartori, G. 1976. *Parties and Party Systems: A Framework for Analysis*. Cambridge: Cambridge University Press.

Siegfried, A. 1966 [1906]. *The Race Question in Canada*. Toronto: McClelland and Stewart.

Wesley, J. 2009. "In search of brokerage and responsibility: Party politics in Manitoba." *Canadian Journal of Political Science* 42 (1): 211–36. http://dx.doi.org/10.1017/S0008423909090088.

Whitaker, R. 1977. *The Government Party: Organizing and Financing the Liberal Party of Canada, 1930–1958*. Toronto: University of Toronto Press.

2

Regional Pivots and Brokerage Politics

RICHARD JOHNSTON

As Carty argues in the first chapter of this volume, brokerage parties and brokerage politics appear when the central political challenge is building the state or the nation itself. By definition, brokerage parties dominate their system: if they are not dominant, they cannot offer the services of a broker. Indeed, success in brokerage is the very condition for longevity. But to say that brokerage is required is not to say that brokerage is inevitable. To get beyond a primitive functionalist account, we need to explore the mechanisms that enable brokerage's peculiar combination of one-party dominance and electoral incoherence. If exceptions are necessary to prove the rule, the end of Canada's brokerage era should help us understand how it lasted so long.

At the risk of oversimplification, the reason for both the persistence and the end of brokerage is Quebec. Over most of Canada's history, Quebec was the pivot for government. Before 1896, Quebec seats made the Conservatives the governing party for twenty-four of the first twenty-nine years after Confederation. Quebec's 1896 shift to the Liberals made that party more dominant than any comparable party in the Westminster world.[1] When the Conservatives occasionally attained power, Quebec was always at the cabinet table and usually opened the door. In the twentieth century, however, the Conservatives could never sustain their electoral coalitions. If the Conservatives' last experience, 1984–93, with a large bloc of Quebec seats, ended badly for that party, it also ended the Liberals' distinctive claim as managers of the nation-building task. Since 1984, the system has been sliding away from successful brokerage.

This chapter unpacks the dynamics of pivotal politics. It also speaks to debates about links between the electoral system and the party system (Cairns 1968; Johnston et al. 1992; Bakvis and Macpherson 1994). I start with an accounting framework that compares regions for their contributions to forming and blocking governing coalitions. This is not to say that only region matters in Canadian politics. But Quebec as a region had a distinctive place as the pivot, reflecting its electorate's collective ability both to coordinate electorally and to switch the direction of coordination at critical moments. At the same time, the presence of other considerations is implied by the general *lack* of coordination on the part of electorates in other regions. Then follows an analysis of mechanisms. Quebec's seat pattern is not an artifact of the electoral system. It is Quebec voters themselves who are distinct in coordination and mobility. Some of this distinctness is facilitated by a peculiar turnout pattern. The province's electoral distinctiveness reflects the Quebec voter's focus on defence of nationality. This, of course, defines the Canadian brokerage challenge.

Regions as Pivots

The essence of the pivot claim is as follows. It was almost impossible for a party to form a majority government if that party did not control a majority of seats in Quebec. As long as a party exercised such control it was next to impossible to push it from power: at most, the other party could form a minority government. But Quebec was not wedded to one party only: it could transfer its basic allegiance or administer short-term punishment. And, if it did so, the target party was bound to lose power. In short, it was claimed that a Quebec bloc was both necessary and sufficient for a party to hold power over the country as a whole. This section puts this claim to an empirical test.

First, however, some geographic arithmetic. Demographically, the fixed point for the regional basis of the Canadian party system has always been Quebec. This is shown in Figure 2.1, which portrays how a nineteenth-century two-and-a-half region game was transformed into a twentieth-century three-and-a-half region game. Ontario's relative shrinkage was dramatic: it went from holding over 40 percent of all seats in the nineteenth century to holding just over one-third in the twentieth. Also losing major ground was Atlantic Canada, whose share was cut roughly in half. These regions' loss of position mirrored the growth of the West, especially of the

FIGURE 2.1
Regional composition of the House of Commons

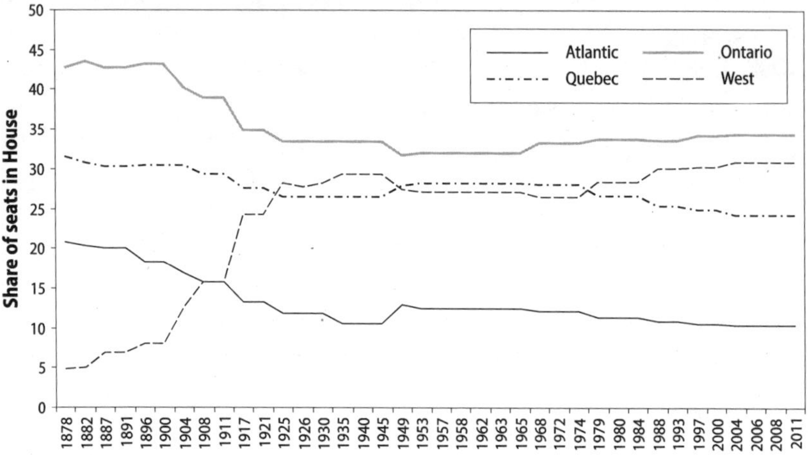

Prairie provinces. However, over the same period, Quebec's share shrank only slightly, and all along Quebec supplied 25 to 30 percent of all House of Commons seats.[2]

It was not enough that Quebec controlled a large share of the House of Commons. The West acquired a comparable share by 1921, and Ontario always had a larger one. The critical additional elements for Quebec were (1) concentration on one party and (2) mobility between parties. Concentration is anatomized in Table 2.1, which summarizes each region's pre-1993 role in building governing coalitions. Its basic currency is a major party's seats in a particular region as a percentage of all seats in the House of Commons. The focus is on instances in which a single region gives a party at least 20 percent of all House seats, such that the region, by itself, puts the party almost half way to a seat majority. As this was essentially never possible for Atlantic Canada, that region is excluded from the table. In Ontario and Quebec, according to Panel A, at least one party cleared this threshold over three-quarters of the time. In the West, a major party cleared the threshold only four times as this region has also been prime territory for minor parties.[3]

It is very common, then, for one or both of Ontario and Quebec to supply one party with big blocs of seats. Usually, Ontario does this simply because

TABLE 2.1
Regions as pivots in the old system, 1878–1988

	Quebec	Ontario	West (since 1908)
A. At least one major party > 20% of seats in House from this region (% of all elections)			
	77.4	77.4	16.7
B. Mean share of House from region in which at least one major party > 20%			
Advantaged party	23.6	24.0	22.7
Disadvantaged party	2.7	12.1	0.8
C. If major party's House share from province > 20%, does it form government (% of all instances)?			
Government	87.5	70.8	100.0
Majority government	70.8	58.3	75.0
D. If major party's House share from province > 20%, does other party form government (% of all instances)?			
Government	12.5	29.2	0.0
Majority government	4.2	25.0	0.0
E. If major party's House share from province < 20%, does it form government (% of all instances)?			
Government	26.3	37.8	45.5
Majority government	15.8	21.6	34.1

the province is big. In the nineteenth century, it was big enough, as Figure 2.1 implies, that it could sometimes give both parties a head start. The problem, of course, is that when both get such a start, neither is advantaged relative to the other. On average, as Panel B shows, when one party gets a big bloc from Ontario, the other party gets a bloc about half that size. In Quebec, in contrast, when one party gets the big bloc, the other party does not: on average, the disadvantaged party gets only one-tenth as many seats as the advantaged one. In one sense, the West is even more consolidated than Quebec: when one major party secures a 20 percent bloc, its advantage over its major-party rival is 20:1. But, as mentioned, a western big bloc materialized only four times.

Crossing the 20 percent threshold in any region is almost a sufficient condition for victory nationwide. Of the 24 times a party grabbed a big Ontario bloc, it formed the government 17 times, 14 with a majority. In the

West, the 20-plus beneficiary formed the government all 4 times, 3 with a majority. Of all regions, however, Quebec was most likely to have the condition both be fulfilled and be causally sufficient: of the 24 times Quebec gave a party a 20-plus bloc that party formed the government 21 times, 17 as a majority.

By themselves, however, such data are causally ambiguous. If a party sweeps the whole country, it will carry many seats in a region simply as a by-product, and in a big region this will be a big "bloc." So it is useful to look at what happens to the other party nationally when one party sweeps a region: How often is the region "rolled," as it were? The relevant data appear in Panel D.[4] Ontario was rolled more than one time in four, and to complete the indignity the party that lost Ontario usually won an outright majority nationwide. Quebec was rolled less than half as often, and only once did this yield a majority government.[5] So when a Quebec bloc participates in a government, it is rarely as a mere by-product.

Controlling Quebec is almost a sufficient condition for governing. Is it also a necessary condition? The answer to this lies in Panel E, which shows what happens when a party fails to extract a 20-plus bloc from a region. In the 38 Ontario instances, the party in question nonetheless won the country 14 times, 8 with an outright majority. The pattern for the West mirrors that for Ontario. For Quebec, the number of instances in which a party failed to get a 20-plus bloc was exactly the same as for Ontario. But when this happened, that party was the Canada-wide victor only 10 times, with a majority only 6 times.

Although the causal pattern is not airtight, it is nonetheless powerful. At any election, one party or the other typically extracted a Quebec bloc large enough to put it half-way to a majority. In these instances, the other party won almost no seats in the province. When this happened the lucky party would usually win nationwide. The pattern is not so stark for the other big regions, neither for internal consolidation nor for controlling the national result. The Quebec pattern is similarly sharp on the other side: just as Quebec can make governments, so it can block them. So, the claim stands: from 1878 to 1993 Quebec was regularly the pivot for government.

The claim is both strengthened and given nuance by rolling the pattern out over time, as in Figure 2.2. This figure plots each major party's share of all seats along with the share that the party brings in from each major region. For Canada-wide seats, the vertical scale (on the right side of each graph) spans seventy percentage points (10 percent to 80 percent). For seats from a specific region, the vertical scale (on the left) spans half that range, or

FIGURE 2.2
Regions as brokers of government

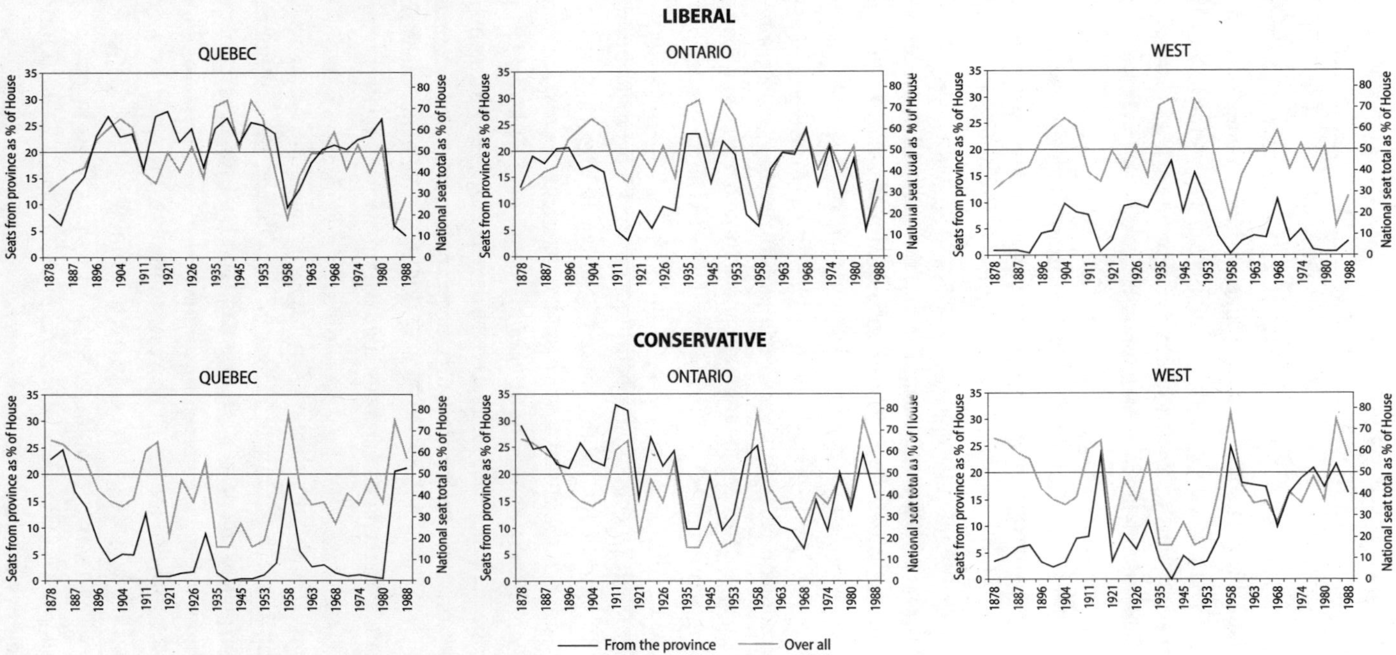

thirty-five points (0 to 35 percent). The reference line identifies a critical point on each scale, 50 percent for all seats and 20 percent for seats from a region. The former defines a parliamentary majority and the latter corresponds to Table 2.1's notion of a "big" bloc. A note of caution: because the region-specific plot spans half the range of the national plot, it can appear that the former accounts for all – or more than all – of the latter. This visual price seemed worth paying as juxtaposing the two lines clarifies their dynamic correspondence – or lack thereof.

For Quebec, the correspondence is close right from the start. The late-nineteenth-century rise of the Liberals from weak opposition to strong opposition to outright majority is almost exactly matched by the party's rise in Quebec. About two-thirds of the overall gain came from that province alone. Once the Liberals established their position in Quebec, they did not really surrender it for eighty-eight years, that is, until 1984. From 1896 to 1984, Liberal MPs from Quebec constituted more than 20 percent of the House in twenty of twenty-five elections. Of these, the Liberals lost only three.[6] But in the five elections in which its Quebec bloc dipped below 20 percent, the party lost four.[7] The pattern for the Conservatives is the mirror image of that for the Liberals: about three of every four Conservative seats lost between 1887 and 1896 were in Quebec. Between 1896 and 1984, the Conservatives were effectively shut out of that province. The Conservatives' median Quebec bloc constituted a mere 1.5 percent. The share was below 10 percent for twenty-three of the twenty-five elections. Of those twenty-three, the Conservatives lost seventeen. In only two of them did the party win Canada-wide majorities, and one of these (1917) was as part of a coalition. The other four yielded short-lived minority governments.

The Conservative Party's four Quebec pulses reinforce the main point. Although in the first three (1911, 1930, 1958) the resultant Quebec bloc was less than 20 percent, each represented a dramatic gain relative to preceding years, and the proportionate seat swing was much larger than the national one. In 1911 and 1930, the new Quebec seats made the difference between winning and losing. Only in 1958 were the Quebec seats, although a large bloc, surplus to the party's requirement. The 1984 surge, sustained in 1988, yielded a Quebec bloc exceeding 20 percent of the House, something that had last happened for the Conservatives in 1882. In 1988, the Quebec bloc once again made the difference between winning and losing.

Notwithstanding its bulk, Ontario rarely played so pivotal a role. The chronology for Ontario is more complicated than that for Quebec, and itemization lends to its clarity:

- Before 1935, Ontario resisted Liberal tides, typically to no avail. In the realignment that culminated in 1896, the Liberals' Ontario share shrank even as their national share grew. Instead, Ontario strengthened its commitment to the Conservative Party and maintained this position for the next fifteen years.
- The commitment did pay some dividend in the 1910s and 1920s as the truly massive Ontario Conservative consolidation in 1911 set the stage for a decade of rule even as the abject state of the Ontario Liberals after 1911 critically weakened that party when it returned to power in the 1920s.
- From 1935 to 1957, Ontario shadowed Quebec as a pillar of near-hegemonic Liberal rule. In those years, the Liberals' Ontario bloc exceeded 20 percent of the House three times and came close once. Ontario's flight from the Conservatives weakened that party nationally relative to the 1910s and 1920s. Even so, the Ontario Liberal bloc was never bigger than the Quebec Liberal bloc, and the Ontario Conservative group, although the weakest to that point in history, still constituted over half of that sad party's caucus. Ontario's dramatic swing to the Conservatives in 1945 did not dislodge the Liberals from power.
- From 1962 to 1993, Ontario supplied a critical short-term dynamic. More than any other region, Ontario dictated the Liberal margin, in particular giving or withholding majority status. After 1968, the trend away from the Liberals and towards the Conservatives, which set the stage for the 1984 Tory landslide, was mainly an Ontario phenomenon.
- For all that, Ontario still lagged behind Quebec with regard to influence. Before 1984, the trends just outlined did not drive the Liberals from power, with an exception that proved the rule in 1979. When the Liberals finally did lose it all in 1984, the swings in Quebec dwarfed those in Ontario. In 1988, Ontario regressed towards the 1980 baseline, only to be stymied by the Conservatives' immovable bloc in Quebec.

In sum, Ontario was often important with regard to dictating aspects of governance, especially the government's numerical strength. But the identity of that government was usually dictated by Quebec.

Typically, the West was a bit player. The region often opted out of the government game, and when it did play it backed losers. This is not to say that the region was always absent from the cabinet table, just that its presence or absence was not very critical to who was in control. As with Ontario, the story of the West benefits from being itemized:

- As the West gained political weight after 1896, it rallied to the Liberals. Certainly the region was more aligned with the governing party than was Ontario. What Figure 2.2 does not show, however, is that Atlantic Canada also became as one-sided as the West, and, notwithstanding the Atlantic region's relative shrinkage, it also grew as a component of the Liberal coalition. So the West was part of the governing coalition, but it was hardly pivotal to its creation.
- The West's desertion of the Liberals – for coalition in 1917 and for the Progressives in 1921 – critically weakened the party. Liberal recovery in the West over the 1920s helped restore the party to majority power. Once again, Liberal seats from the West outnumbered those from Ontario.
- After 1935, the West rallied further to the Liberals. Although the region never generated a 20 percent bloc, it came close to doing so twice. Like Quebec, the region was distinctive for shunning the Conservatives. However, in the major-party game the West was just one among many: in 1935, all regions moved towards the Liberals. For the next twenty-two years, Ontario supplied half again as many Liberal seats as did the West. Where the West was distinct in this period was in its commitment to third parties.
- In 1958, the region upped its commitment to the government game. Where in the preceding period, 44 percent of all Western seats went to third parties, for the next three decades that share was 23 percent. And the West rallied to one side: the dominant party typically receives six to seven times as many seats as does its major-party rival. Although the dominant party rarely exceeded the 20 percent seat threshold, it often came close. The kicker, of course, is that the dominant player in the region, the Conservative Party, was not the dominant party nationally. This was a recipe for frustration as one consequence of the West's return to national party politics was to increase Ontario's importance to the dominant Liberal coalition, even as it reinforced the pivotal role of Quebec.

Mechanisms

Quebec's status as the pivot for government rested on two things: (1) the concentration of its seats in one major party and (2) the mobility of that concentration between parties. What was the basis of this peculiar pattern in seats? Two possibilities exist and both could be operative:

1. The electoral system in Quebec could be singularly responsive, with a steeper seat-vote relationship than in other regions.

2. Vote shares themselves might be both more one-sided at each election and more variable across elections than in other regions.

This section shows that the vote-seat translation in Quebec is, if anything, less responsive than elsewhere. The burden of the province's distinctiveness falls on the voters themselves. Quebec seats came en bloc because Quebec voters acted en bloc. This points to a third mechanism:

3. Volatility on the scale exhibited in Quebec may require a peculiarly great role for turnout.

This sections works through the mechanisms in the order they have been introduced.

The Translation of Votes into Seats

We know that the first-past-the-post (FPP) formula magnifies both differences among parties and swings between elections. Further, the responsiveness of the formula rests on contingencies that can vary from place to place. It is natural to wonder if vote-seat translations are peculiarly efficient in Quebec. Cairns (1968, 67) hints at this:

> It is only at the level of seats, not votes, that Quebec became a Liberal stronghold, a Canadian "solid South," and a one-party monopoly. The Canadian "solid South," like its American counterpart, is a contrivance of the electoral system, not an autonomous social fact which exists independent of it.

If Cairns is silent on specifics in vote-seat translations, others are more explicit. Sankoff and Mellos (1973) argue that Quebec is indeed distinct, that the relative homogeneity (Montreal aside) of Quebec's geography enables modest vote flux to become immodest seat flux. Bakvis and Macpherson (1994) stake out a contrary position, and this section confirms their intuition. Indeed, if Quebec is distinctive for the vote-seat translation, it is for being relatively inefficient.

This is the lesson of Figure 2.3, which plots estimated seat-vote lines for the three big regions. The essential fact is that the Quebec line lies below the others for most of the range and below the West line for all of it. This makes Quebec more punitive than the West towards the smaller of the major parties. More to the point, however, it rewards strength less than

FIGURE 2.3
Seats and votes in the regions, 1878–2008

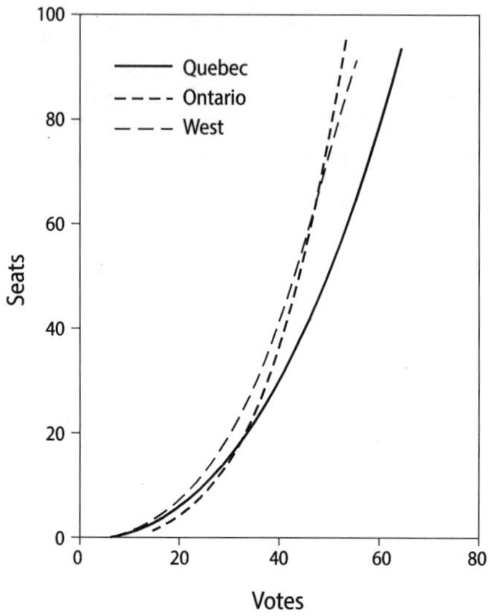

Note: Regression plots based on estimates in Table 2.2.

does either other region. If any region is an outlier, it is Ontario: the most punitive towards weakness and the most indulgent towards strength.[8]

Mobility in Vote Shares

Quebec's distinctive role must, then, stem from the volatility of its electorate. Circumstantial evidence and reflection on electoral history point to a distinctive pattern of volatility. Evidence from sample surveys indicates that, when class divisions emerge in Quebec voting, they are not expressed along the left-right partisan axis that characterizes the rest of Canada or, for that matter, most of the rest of the world. Rather, poor and unemployed voters tend to find their way to parties like Social Credit (Lemieux 1965; Pinard 1967, Table 1). Vote flux was characterized by reaction to the normal pattern of Liberal hegemony (Pinard 1971). Similarly, the policy differences that anchor electoral coalitions elsewhere in Canada are mirrored only weakly, if at all, in Quebec. Johnston (2008, Figure 2) shows that, in contrast to the rest of the country, federal party supporters in Quebec are essentially indistinguishable on a left-right axis. What sorts parties and their supporters is their degree of commitment to Quebec's specific interests. Johnston's (2008) evidence comes in a period when the Bloc Québécois anchored the pro-Quebec end of the distribution. In 1988, in contrast, the maximally pro-Quebec choice (for Quebeckers, not for the rest of the country) was the Conservative Party (Johnston et al. 1992, Figure 3.2). This divergence points to fungibility among federal parties, depending on how precisely the "national question" is framed. Most of the time, the Liberal Party controlled the pro-Quebec pole. Often, however, this was *faute de mieux*, as the other parties were actively hostile, or at best indifferent, to the interests of Quebec or French Canada. But the Liberal Party rarely adopted the position of Quebec's nationalist elites. An exception would be 1917, when conscription was the issue and the Liberal Party (minus many of its non-Quebec MPs, who had joined the pro-conscription Unionist coalition) adamantly opposed the measure. In other years, when the national question was activated, the Liberals temporized. In 1945, for instance, conscription was once again an issue, but this time it was the Liberals who introduced it, if only reluctantly. As in 1917, the Conservative alternative was even worse. In 1984 and, even more, in 1988, the Conservatives reached out to Quebeckers who, in 1980, had supported a move towards sovereignty; in doing so they outflanked the Liberals, who emphasized linguistic duality rather than the prerogatives of Quebec. One can spin further variants on stories like these, but the three examples make the point: (1) in 1917, all Quebec nationalists should rally to the Liberals; (2) in 1945, they should reject both federal parties, which they did in rallying to the Bloc Populaire Canadien; (3) in 1984–88, the Conservatives should be the preferred choice. Most of the time, however, national questions were dormant and the Liberals could be trusted, albeit without enthusiasm, to manage the shop.

And sure enough, vote shares are more mobile in Quebec than in any other region, with the partial exception of the West. Figure 2.4 captures the essentials of each party's pre-1993 vote in each region. For each region and party, distributions appear as kernel density plots, best thought of as smoothed histograms. The flatter the plot and the greater its range, the more variable a region's outcomes. Most striking is the contrast between Ontario and Quebec, especially for the Liberal vote. Where the Liberals' Ontario plot spans slightly more than twenty points, their Quebec plot spans more than fifty points. For the Conservatives, the contrast is not as stark, but it is nonetheless clear.[9] No less important, the provinces differ in the distributions' central tendency. In Ontario, the Liberals' historical advantage is modest. In Quebec it is huge.

The West is a partial mirror of Quebec. The Liberal distribution spans a smaller range than in Quebec but a larger one than in Ontario. The

FIGURE 2.4
Electoral volatility in the regions, 1878–1988

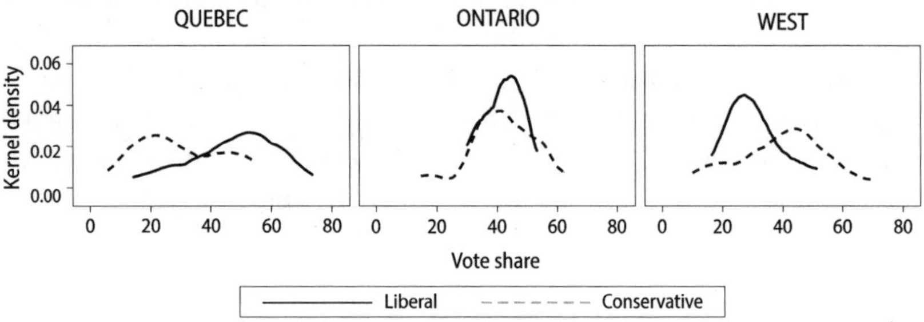

Note: Western data for 1908–88

Conservatives' distribution in the West is the most dispersed of all, more so even than in Quebec.[10] And, like Quebec, the West quite decisively favoured one party – the Conservative Party. But the gap between the parties' modes is smaller than in Quebec (partly as a reflection of the West's historic resistance to both parties).

Turnout and Liberal Domination

Recall from Figure 2.2 that vote and seat shifts in Quebec are not chronic; they are episodic. The big agenda shifts stylized in the preceding section are actually quite rare. In most elections, the Liberals would win and would do so with a solid bloc of Quebec seats. If 1917 was an instance in which the Liberals staked out a polar position – adamant opposition to conscription – more often the party hewed to a centrist position. More extreme positions were imaginable but, for one reason or another – usually because "national" questions were of low salience – nationalist elites in Quebec kept their heads down. When this was so, a large part of the Quebec electoral army was held, as it were, in reserve. This may have made turnout a key factor in Liberal success or failure.[11]

This section substantiates the above intuition. Turnout itself is not more variable in Quebec than elsewhere, but its flux translates very efficiently into shifts in party shares. Specifically, turnout surges are bad for the Liberals.

Table 2.2 connects Liberal vote shares in each region to turnout among registered voters. Alternative setups are imaginable, but the most economic focus is on the Liberal share of all votes cast.[12] As Quebec and Ontario are single-province regions, estimations are standard time-series

TABLE 2.2
Turnout and Liberal shares, 1904–88

	Quebec[1]		Ontario[1]		West[2]	
Turnout	*–1.06*	*(0.51)*	*–0.35*	*(0.27)*	*–0.45*	*(0.18)*
Intercept	130.44	(37.63)	66.21	(19.90)	63.08	(13.29)
R^2	0.26		0.42		0.30	
ρ	0.37		0.52		0.44	
N	25		25		96	

Note: Estimations for 1904–88 elections inclusive, except Alberta and Saskatchewan within West, 1908–88.
1 AR(1), Prais-Winsten estimation.
2 Estimated with panel-corrected standard errors, common AR(1).

setups. The West relationship is estimated as a time-series cross-section, with each province as a panel and standard errors corrected accordingly.[13] Estimation is for elections in the twentieth century only. In the 1880s and 1890s, franchise rules shifted and suffrage also varied considerably across provinces. By the early twentieth century, however, manhood suffrage or a close approximation prevailed everywhere (Elections Canada, n.d.). That women and certain ethnic and racial groups remained disfranchised does not matter for my purposes. The critical fact is that, by 1904, a form of mass politics was in place; subsequent enfranchisements did not alter the logic of mass campaigns and mobilization. Elections after 1988 are excluded, both as the party system changed (see below) and as the basis for turnout calculation shifted.[14]

And once again, Quebec stands out. Although the Liberal-turnout relationship is negative in each region, the link is two and a half to three times as strong in Quebec as elsewhere. Figure 2.5 completes the picture with scatterplots and fitted lines based on Table 2.2. In Quebec, although turnout values span only thirteen points, they map into a fourteen-point range of predictions for the Liberal vote. Only the West, with four provinces and ninety-two observations, produces a comparable range of predictions, but this is based on a turnout range of thirty-three points.[15] Obviously, much more is in play as even in Quebec turnout variation accounts for only one-third of the total range traversed by Liberal fortunes. But it seems reasonable to infer that the nearly one-to-one link between turnout and the Liberal share accounts for some of Quebec's differential volatility.

Of course, the link could simply be carrying causation in the other direction, where anticipation of a swing away from the normally dominant

FIGURE 2.5
Turnout and the Liberal share among voters, 1904–88

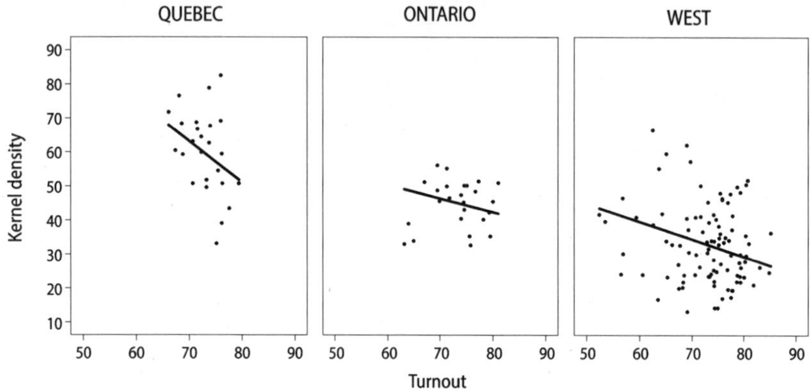

Note: Regression plots based on estimates in Table 2.3.

Liberals facilitates not just mobilization of former abstainers but also shifts among continuously active voters. We simply do not have the data to unpack the causal direction. But triangulation suggests that turnout played an independent role: (1) we know that Quebec is peculiar in the importance of province-specific considerations; (2) these considerations produce a higher level of indifference about the federal parties; and (3) this can facilitate both direct switching between the parties and selective turnout.

The End of Pivotal Politics?

In 1993, Quebec voters ceased to consolidate around a federalist alternative, and their return to the federalist fold in 2011 left them well short of pivotal status. Although the Liberals dominated the federalist side in the 1990s, their absolute share in Quebec was close to historic lows (although with a partial recovery as the decade advanced). In 2006, the Conservatives also staged a small recovery, and their gain in Quebec was the biggest single factor in their move from opposition to government. Consolidated or not, however, the total federalist seat share in the province ranged from about one-quarter to one-half, and averaged about one-third, of all seats. In short, Quebec no longer put a federalist party half way to a parliamentary majority. The 2011 election did return Quebec to the federalist fold, and it did so in a way that echoed the province's twentieth-century pattern of concentration and mobility. But this time the beneficiary was the NDP, which, notwithstanding Official Opposition status, still seems far from power (and seemed even further from power when Quebec voters were making the choice). Many of the seats in the NDP's large bloc were narrowly won, often with the help of vote splitting. This is a far cry from the twentieth-century pattern of unbalanced popular vote distributions.

Taking the years since 1993 as a whole, no one region controls the play. In some elections, virtually every province is pivotal, in the sense that withdrawal of its seats from government would hand power over to the other side or at least reduce a majority to a minority. If any region merits being singled out, the identity of that region shifts between decades. In the 1990s, that place was Ontario, which elected only Liberals.[16] Such is the bulk of the province that this put the party two-thirds of the way home. In the 2000s, the West was the key region in that it elected Conservatives to nearly three-quarters of its seats, which, in turn, put the party almost half way to a majority.

But this still does not describe pivotal politics on the twentieth-century Quebec model. True, Ontario was the most critical element in Liberal success in the 1990s, and Ontario's gradual withdrawal of support from that party helped pave the way for the Conservatives' rise to power. Aside from the extraordinary – and unsustainable – concentration on the Liberals in the 1990s, however, the Ontario story seems like politics as usual: once the Conservative Party got its act together, the more conservative parts of the province gravitated towards it. Vote swings between elections were modest, and there was no hint of a pan-Ontario coordination strategy. As for the West, the 2003 reverse takeover of the broader conservative interest by the regionally based Canadian Alliance put the region back into the major-party game and put a Conservative party by that name on the brink of power. And the West certainly seems like the rock on which the Conservatives' electoral coalition is founded. But the West's defection from mainstream politics in 1993 made as much sense for pivotal politics as did Quebec's defection in the same year. It is only in hindsight that the West's move makes any sense. The 2011 election yielded a Conservative governing coalition with almost equal contributions from the West and Ontario, with the West's component being modestly larger proportionally. But much of this was just a consequence of each region's sheer size. And in both regions, especially in Ontario, Conservative dominance was exactly the sort of "contrivance" that Cairns (1968) imputed to Quebec. In each region a significant number of seats are held by opposition parties, and this number will probably grow, especially in Ontario.[17]

Pivots, Brokerage, and National Unity

For more than a century, the electoral system and the party system successfully addressed Canada's most pressing problem of national integration. By virtue of the Quebec electorate's relative cohesion, its willingness to switch parties selectively but massively, and the FPP system's propensity to magnify differences and swings, French Canada was seriously represented in almost all winning coalitions. More to the point, Quebec votes pretty much made them winning coalitions.

Whether the beneficiary was the Liberal Party or the Conservative Party, its Quebec elements brought something distinctive to the table. As already hinted, the content of this distinctiveness varied with time. In the nineteenth century, the content was usually religious. In the first half of the twentieth century, the issue was Canada's relation to the external world as mediated by membership in the British Empire. In the second half of that century, the front shifted inside, to the place of French Canada in Canada and of Quebec in Canada (the two not being the same thing). Within periods, the relative appeal of the two traditional parties to Quebec's nationalist elites shifted. If the Conservative Party was unacceptable most of the time, the Liberal Party was unacceptable some of the time.

Sometimes, and to varying degrees, the positions of Quebec elites were incompatible – even incommensurable – with those of the rest of Canada. This put a premium on finesse and on agenda control, which, in turn, required distinctive organizational forms (Carty and Cross 2010). It is reasonable to ask, given the evidence presented in this chapter, if the Conservatives were as concerned or as able as the Liberals to create an organization adapted to the needs of brokerage. Then again, when the Conservatives did win, they assembled coalitions requiring even more brokerage skill than was typical of Liberal coalitions (Johnston et al. 1992). The infrequency and short life of most Conservative governments suggests that they did not succeed at this organizational task.

In any case, both the Liberals and the Conservatives may have lost the means, possibly even the will, to act as brokers. Since 1984, the Liberals have had only weak representation from Quebec, and they continue to be reviled by the province's nationalist elites, a legacy of Pierre Trudeau's firmly antinationalist stance. The Conservatives have a more equivocal relationship to those elites but now seem bent on severing it. Among federalists, this leaves the NDP. The party's new status may present the NDP with a brokerage challenge rather on the old model. Although NDP supporters in Quebec seem more federalist than the large residue of underrepresented Bloc voters, they seem less robustly federalist than Conservative and Liberal voters (Soroka et al. 2011, 73). But if the NDP faces an old-fashioned challenge in fitting its new coalition together, its pre-existing organization does not fit the model that Carty and Cross (2010) anatomized for the old parties. And there is a real prospect that the NDP will lose some of its 2011 gains back to the Bloc Québécois or to the possibly revived Liberals. None of this points to a consolidated Quebec electorate.

This is mostly speculation, however. Analysis of Canadian party organization is a task for others. The purpose of this chapter is to account for the electoral foundations – or entailments – of brokerage politics. Mostly, it describes precisely that, a politics centred on Quebec as the regional pivot for government. The special power of Quebec helps explain the special character of Canadian party organization. But Quebec no longer plays a pivotal role and seems unlikely to do so in the near future. Will the organization of Canada's major parties shift accordingly?

Appendix

The seat-vote relationship in Figure 2.3 is estimated as follows:

$$S_{it} = \beta\, V_{it}{}^{\rho},$$

> where: S_{it} is the i-th party's seat share at election t; V_{it} is the corresponding vote share; β is a "bias" parameter; and ρ is a "representation" parameter.

The nomenclature of "bias" and "representation" originates with King and Browning (1987), who focus on fair division of the vote between parties. In a pure two-party situation, where each party's vote and seat share are just the complement of the other party's values, β estimates bias as the departure from equal treatment, or the tilt off the 45° line. Bias is more easily grasped as the natural log of β, which centres the parameter at 0. The King-Browning framework can be adapted to estimate party-specific bias in a multi-party context (King 1990). Bias as such is not the issue in this chapter, however, as a given estimation incorporates data from both major parties. Instead, the coefficient of central interest is ρ. If ρ takes on the value of three, then the cube law (Kendall and Stuart 1950) holds. A ρ of one would indicate a purely linear relationship, as with a proportional formula. In general, the larger the value of ρ, the steeper the line in the middle of the vote-share distribution. The argument in Sankoff and Mellos (1973) implies that ρ should be bigger in Quebec than in the comparator regions.

TABLE 2A.1
Seats and votes, 1908–2008

	ln(β)	ρ	R^2	N
Quebec	−5.32 (0.52)	2.37 (0.14)	0.83	58
Ontario	−8.59 (0.72)	3.32 (0.19)	0.83	60
West	−5.33 (0.57)	2.46 (0.16)	0.80	59

	All parameters		ρ only	
Wald tests	χ^2	p	χ^2	p
All regions	5.79	0.0002	5.97	0.0031
Quebec v. Ontario	7.49	0.0009	11.72	0.0009
Quebec v. West	4.38	0.0148	0.16	0.6859
Ontario v. West	7.36	0.0010	10.24	0.0018

The estimation appears in Table 2A.1, along with Wald tests for regional differences in coefficients. Testing on both parameters indicates that each region is significantly different from the others. Focusing on the "representation" parameter, however, shows that Quebec is effectively indistinguishable from the West and that the outlier is Ontario. Ontario punishes weakness brutally yet responds dramatically to flux in the vote.

Alternative estimation strategies produce subtly different patterns but all concur: to the extent that Quebec is distinctive at all, it is not in the hypersensitivity of its electoral framework to small changes or differences in the vote.

Notes

1 Carty (Chapter 1, Table 1.1) shows that other brokerage parties are even more dominant than the Liberals, but none operates in a world of single-party governments only (at least not in recent decades).

2 Quebec's stability in the face of the rapid westward shift in the country's demography reflects the fact that the province had its own special weapon in the battle for regional advantage – an astonishingly high rate of natural population increase. After 1960, however, the Quebec birthrate plummeted, and it is now the lowest in North America. That shift combined with the province's relatively weak attraction for migrants accounts for Quebec's loss of ground since 1974. Indeed, Figure 2.1 masks rapid recent population shifts as various devices have come into play to maintain the representation of smaller and slow-growing provinces. How long the mechanisms can be sustained is a serious question.

3 The crudity of Table 2.1 masks near misses. Ontario gave over 17.5 percent of House seats to one party seven times, Quebec did so twice, and the West did so four times.

4 The data in the top row of Panel D are just the complement of the data in the top row of Panel C.

5 This was in the truly exceptional circumstance of 1917, when most Liberals in the rest of the country deserted their Quebec confrères.

6 One of the "victories" was in 1925, when the party continued in government even though the Conservatives won a nationwide plurality.

7 The exception is 1963, when the Liberal share just missed the 20 percent target.

8 Estimation is from a double-log setup, based loosely on King and Browning (1987), that has the virtue of forcing the seat-vote lines through the intercept. A detailed justification, along with comments on alternatives and a report of tests of distinctiveness between regions, can be found in the Appendix.

Three points about the data merit attention here, however. First, in contrast to most other presentations in this article, estimations include elections since 1988. The years since 1988 give us more observations near zero on both axes and help flesh out the bottom end, so to speak. Second, elections in which a party receives no seats must be dropped as zero cannot be converted into a natural logarithm, and even tiny tweaks off zero produce wildly varying estimates. We rely on true near-zero readings on the vertical axis to identify the low end, and, for this, post-1988 data are helpful. Third, plots for fitted lines give the appearance of truncation. At low values, this is because the plot is fitted to actual observations, and no vote percentage was as low as zero. At high values, no predicted values above 100 percent are plotted, and some of the very largest vote shares yield predictions above 100.

9 For both parties, overall vote variability, as indicated by standard deviations, was about twice as great in Quebec as in Ontario.

10 Standard deviations in the West are only slightly smaller than in Quebec.

11 Quebec voters also seem particularly responsive to whether or not a party leader is from Quebec (Lemieux and Crête 1981; Nadeau and Blais 1993), and before 1984 such leaders always were Liberals. If having a leader from the province induced higher turnout, this might depress the overall turnout-Liberal relationship.

12 The most conceptually sound approach arguably employs ratios of each party's share relative to a reference party (Katz and King 1999; Tomz, Tucker, and Wittenberg 2002), with the obvious denominator as the Liberal share. But this would require at least three estimations per region and rather complex periodization given the parade of niche parties and the late appearance of a party of the left. Simply focusing on the Liberals reduces the complexity without compromising comparisons across regions and, of course, follows from reflection on specifics of the Quebec situation.

13 Data in the multi-province regions are not merged as it seems unwise to throw information away. This logic does not apply for the seat-vote estimations in the preceding section because there the desire was to have seat numbers per election that were broadly similar across regions. For turnout and vote share, in contrast, the size of the provincial electorate should not matter.

14 Specifically, the change in voter registration made the denominator for turnout calculation generally suspect and especially bad in the transition years of the 1990s (Johnston, Matthews, and Bittner 2007).

15 Much of this range is cross-sectional; turnout is chronically lower in Alberta than in Saskatchewan, for instance. When data from the West are pooled into a regionwide estimate, with a single value at each election, turnout variation shrinks to the Quebec scale. The range for predicted Liberal shares also shrinks, and it resembles the Ontario pattern.

16 Of all Ontario seats in play from 1993 to 2000, parties other than the Liberals captured only five: one in each of 1993 and 1997, and three in 2000.

17 In the West, an opposition candidate (usually a New Democrat) finished within ten points of a Conservative victor in eight ridings and within fifteen points in another three. In Ontario, Conservative vulnerability is greater: twenty-one Conservatives won by fewer than ten points, and another six won by fewer than fifteen points.

References

Bakvis, H., and L.G. Macpherson. 1994. "Quebec block voting and the Canadian electoral system." *Canadian Journal of Political Science* 28 (4): 659–92. http://dx.doi.org/10.1017/S000842390001934X.

Cairns, Alan C. 1968. "The electoral system and the party system in Canada, 1921–1965." *Canadian Journal of Political Science* 1 (1): 55–80. http://dx.doi.org/10.1017/S0008423900035228.

Carty, R.K., and W. Cross. 2010. "Political parties and the practice of brokerage politics." Chap. 11 in *The Oxford Handbook of Canadian Politics*, ed. J.C. Courtney and D.E. Smith, 191–207. Oxford: Oxford University Press. http://dx.doi.org/10.1093/oxfordhb/9780195335354.003.0011.

Elections Canada. n.d. A History of the Vote in Canada (2nd ed.). http://www.elections.ca/content.aspx?section=res&dir=his&document=index&lang=e.

Johnston, R. 2008. "Polarized pluralism in the Canadian party system." *Canadian Journal of Political Science* 41 (4): 815–34. http://dx.doi.org/10.1017/S0008423908081110.

Johnston, R., A. Blais, H.E. Brady, and J. Crête. 1992. *Letting the People Decide: Dynamics of a Canadian Election*. Montreal and Kingston: McGill-Queen's University Press.

Johnston, R., J.S. Matthews, and A. Bittner. 2007. "Turnout and the party system in Canada, 1988–2004." *Electoral Studies* 26 (4): 735–45. http://dx.doi.org/10.1016/j.electstud.2007.08.002.

Katz, J., and G. King. 1999. "A statistical model for multiparty electoral data." *American Political Science Review* 93 (1): 15–32. http://dx.doi.org/10.2307/2585758.

Kendall, M.G., and A. Stuart. 1950. "The law of the cubic proportion in election results." *British Journal of Sociology* 1 (3): 183–96. http://dx.doi.org/10.2307/588113.

King, G. 1990. "Electoral responsiveness and partisan bias in multiparty democracies." *Legislative Studies Quarterly* 15 (2): 159–81.

King, G., and R.X. Browning. 1987. "Democratic representation and partisan bias in Congressional elections." *American Political Science Review* 81 (4): 1251–73. http://dx.doi.org/10.2307/1962588.

Lemieux, V. 1965. "Les dimensions sociologiques du vote créditiste au Québec." *Recherches Sociographiques* 6 (2): 181–95. http://dx.doi.org/10.7202/055266ar.

Lemieux, V., and J. Crête. 1981. "Quebec." In *Canada at the Polls, 1979 and 1980*, ed. H.R. Penniman. Washington, DC: American Enterprise Institute.

Nadeau, R., and A. Blais. 1993. "Explaining election outcomes in Canada: Economy and politics." *Canadian Journal of Political Science* 26 (4): 775–90. http://dx.doi.org/10.1017/S0008423900000470.

Pinard, M. 1967. "One-party dominance and third parties." *Canadian Journal of Economics and Political Science* 33 (3): 358–73. http://dx.doi.org/10.2307/139913.

–. 1971. *Rise of a Third Party: A Study in Crisis Politics*. Englewood Cliffs, NJ: Prentice Hall.

Sankoff, D., and K. Mellos. 1973. "La régionalisation électorale et l'amplification des proportions." *Canadian Journal of Political Science* 6 (3): 380–98. http://dx.doi.org/10.1017/S0008423900039998.

Soroka, S., F. Cutler, D. Stolle, and P. Fournier. 2011. "Capturing change (and stability) in the 2011 campaign." *Policy Options*, Institute for Research on Public Policy. June, 70–77.

Tomz, M., J.A. Tucker, and J. Wittenberg. 2002. "An easy and accurate regression model for multiparty electoral data." *Political Analysis* 10 (1): 66–83. http://dx.doi.org/10.1093/pan/10.1.66.

3

Barbarians at the Gate?

Conservative Identifiers and the Myths of Brokerage Politics

DAVID K. STEWART AND ANTHONY M. SAYERS

The story of Canadian politics since the electoral earthquake of 1993 has been the struggle to build a new Conservative party capable of challenging the Liberal Party. To some degree this story is about the value of brokerage over ideology and whether brokerage politics as practised by the Liberals is required for electoral success. In Chapter 1 of this volume, Carty notes that "Canadian analysts have readily identified the Liberal Party of Canada as a brokerage party, perhaps the archetypical brokerage party." The notion of brokerage parties dates back, at least, to the turn of the twentieth century and Andre Siegfried's analysis of Canadian politics. Such parties "are often to be found quite detached from the principles which gave them birth, and with their own self-preservation as their chief care and aim. Even with a programme, they continue to live and thrive, tending to become mere associations for the securing of power" (Siegfried 1907, 141–42).

In his analysis of brokerage politics Carty explains that it involves "the broad appeal to electors across the spectrum in terms of an accommodative policy package with something for everyone," and he goes on to state that "brokerage parties' political orientations are instinctively centrist." So powerful is this brokerage dynamic that it results in a form of party organization in which central and local components each adopt distinct functions and have limited interaction (see Johnston, Chapter 2, this volume).

The nature and role of brokerage parties – whether as description or myth – has been the subject of much debate in Canada, and the merger of the Reform/Alliance and Progressive Conservative (PC) parties in 2003 raises the question of whether the reunified right constitutes such a party. While their partisan opponents were clear that it did not and continued to emphasize their claim that the Conservative Party was out of the Canadian mainstream, we seek to explore this question by analyzing the attitudes of its supporters.

There is some evidence that the new Conservative Party is ideologically distinctive. During the 2011 election that resulted in a Tory majority government, the Canadian Broadcasting Corporation (CBC) *Vote Compass* provided visual indications of the differences between the Conservative Party and other Canadian parties. Based on responses to a series of statements, *Vote Compass* calculates a user's position in the political landscape and shows her or him the respective positions of the various parties running in the election.[1] The results placed the Conservatives alone in a quadrant signifying conservative social and economic policy preferences.

It is worth asking whether there ever was a relevant brokerage model to which the Conservatives could return. The Progressive Conservative Party had been, at best, largely ineffective at brokerage and was never able to convincingly speak to, or for, the significant francophone element of the country (see Carty, Chapter 1). We examine the brokerage potential of the "new" Conservative Party by looking at the proximity of the views of its identifiers to the Canadian mean and to those who identify with the clearly brokerage Liberal Party.

The notion that a brokerage style of politics is not firmly entrenched has much support. Carty, writing in 2006, notes that, despite the triumph of the centre and the Liberal Party, Canadians have been "trying to (or pretending to) practise brokerage politics without any genuine brokerage parties" (Carty 2006, 9). Indeed, Blake (1988) and Johnston (1988), in separate analyses, suggest that, in the dying days of the third party system, there were clear differences among Progressive Conservative and Liberal activists. Budge and Klingemann (2001, 24), in their analysis of party manifestos between 1945 and 1988, found that "the two major parties in the traditional Canadian set-up, Conservatives and Liberals, leapfrog and overlap quite extensively before 1974 but thereafter move clearly apart."

Cross and Young's work (2002, 859) suggests that differences between members of the various political parties have persisted. As well, Blais et al. (2002b), in an examination of voters in 1997, identifies clear attitudinal differences among those choosing different parties. However, there remained some indications that these differences were not as wide between the Liberals and the Progressive Conservatives as they were between the Liberals and the Reform/Alliance and New Democrats. As they conclude: "When it comes to ideology, then, there is little difference between [Progressive] Conservative and Liberal voters. In this sense, the portrait of the two parties as brokerage parties, competing for the median Canadian voter, remains intact" (Blais et al. 2002b, 195). It is important, however, to keep in mind that, at this point, the Progressive Conservative Party was a shell of its previous self and that it "was the more ideological members that left the Conservative party and joined with others to form the Alliance" (Cross and Young 2002, 859).

To capture shifts in partisan appeal consistent with strategies associated with brokerage politics, we focus in particular on changing orientations among Conservative identifiers across the four elections leading up to 2011. These are compared with Canadians generally as well as with those who identify with the New Democrats and Liberals. The comparison is operationalized using a recurring set of questions drawn from the Canadian Election Studies of 2000, 2004, 2006, 2008, and 2011. We focus on questions relating to two primary dimensions: social conservatism and individualism.[2] This is consistent with the approach of Budge and Klingemann (2001), which identifies economic orthodoxy, free enterprise, and traditional morality as elements of a right-wing focus. Following Blais, we limit our consideration of identifiers in the various elections to those who say they identify "very" or "fairly" strongly with a particular party (Blais 2005, 837). We also consider questions that tap attitudes towards Quebec, given that the divide between it and the rest of the country is considered to be the central driver of the need for brokerage politics.

We conclude that Conservative identifiers remain well away from the Canadian mean in these areas, even while the party has secured multiple election victories. There has been some moderation on social issues, where the average position in 2011 is the closest party identifiers have been to the Canadian mean across the period. The proximity of Liberal identifiers to the mean on both dimensions is relatively constant but has not protected the party from electoral setbacks. New Democrats are the reverse of the Tories, being on the other side and slightly farther from the mean. On the Quebec issue, Liberals have long been around the mean and were joined there in 2011 by New Democrats, with Conservatives continuing to be relatively distant.

As with the ancient barbarians, the success of the Conservative Party appears to result not from mimicking the once powerful but from remaining distinctive. Conservative victories have not flowed from the appropriation of the brokerage tradition but from collecting together identifiers whose attitudes are distinct from those of other parties and the mean position of Canadians.

Brokerage and the New Conservative Party

Brokerage politics has been seen as the defining feature of the Liberals, a party that Blais (2005, 821) describes as "one of the four most successful parties in contemporary democracies," dominating Canadian politics across the twentieth century. Given the current weakened state of the Liberal Party, whether or not the new Conservatives are a brokerage party has implications for the continued relevance of a party form that has been central to explanations of Canadian politics.

The unchallenged Liberal dominance in the 2000 election seemed based in part on the party's brokerage nature, its concomitant identification with core Canadian values, and its ability to present its major opponents as far removed from those values. The Liberal election strategy, as we shall show, involved demonizing its conservative opponents and implicitly, at least, presenting itself as the only party that could broker support across Canada. The Reform/Alliance was portrayed as a party at odds with the values of Canadians, despite, as Carty and colleagues show, efforts that had been ongoing to 1997 to make the party more moderate and attractive. As they note: "Since becoming the official opposition in 1997, the Reform party has tried to increase its appeal outside its original base of support by taking on the outward trappings of a traditional, ideologically flexible, party" (Carty et al. 2000, 220).

In a strategic move consistent with the effort of brokerage parties to portray themselves as indispensable to their country, the Liberals continued their efforts to polarize party politics, inviting Canadians to "choose your Canada," warning voters about Conservative hidden agendas, and depicting their opponents as "scary, right wing, and extreme." The Liberal Party was, in classic brokerage terms, "aggressively asserting its self-defined mission as representative of the entire community and as having a unique capacity to serve as the common political instrument of all" (Carty, Chapter 1).

The Liberal victory in 2000 was regarded by the party as a triumph, demonstrating that the efforts of the Reform Party to reconstitute itself as the Reform/Alliance and to present itself as a more pragmatic party were ineffective (see Ellis 2001, 76). The Reform/Alliance now seemed to recognize the point made by Blais et al. that "Canadian parties have been characterized as brokerage-style parties, taking middle-of-the-road and often fuzzy positions on most issues" (Blais et al. 2002b, 184). Successful Canadian parties were seen as moderate and pragmatic, and the Reform/Alliance Party was not seen in this light and, thus, not in the brokerage tradition. But successful Canadian parties went beyond pragmatism and moderation, as is indicated in Siegfried's description of non-homogeneous parties. As Carty and Cross 2006, 101) suggest:

> Each of Canada's major political parties has traditionally tried to include representatives of the country's distinctive social and demographic groups within their decision-making structures. This reflects a tradition of accommodating divergent political interests with the parties and not between them. The result is "big tent" parties charged with aggregating the population's diverse perspectives rather than sectarian parties representing narrow, parochial interests.

Conservative senator Hugh Segal (2006, 224) outlines this challenge: "The Tory question now is whether Conservatives are committed to actually being part of the political process as contenders as opposed to simply as participants. To be contenders, our vision must be larger than religious sectarianism, wedge politics, or the great luxury of perpetually outraged opposition." To some degree the origins of Reform/Alliance manifested a reaction against this particular view of party politics. Young and Cross note that Reform explicitly rejected the brokerage model and that the party was more ideological in its focus. Their work investigates "one of the recurring questions in the study of Canadian political parties: whether the parties that comprise the Canadian party system (and the system itself) are best described by the ideological or the brokerage model" (Young and Cross 2002, 553).

The Reform/Alliance experiment that helped sustain a decade of Liberal hegemony took a new direction in 2003 when the party merged with the Progressive Conservatives to form the Conservative Party. The new party astounded most observers by forcing the Liberals into a minority government at the subsequent 2004 election (Johnston, Chapter 2, this volume).[3] The election of 2006 saw the Conservatives themselves form a minority government, ending a streak of four successive Liberal ministries, including three successive majority governments.

Despite the change in government, "Canadians had no clear answer as to whether that election had brought an end to brokerage politics" (Brodie and

Jensen 2007, 49). The narrowness of the victory and its underlying electoral coalition left Leduc (2007) wondering whether the party could build a durable government and the degree to which the Conservatives were vulnerable to a reinvigorated Liberal Party. The 2008 election saw the Conservative Party retain its minority government (Gidengil et al. 2009, 1). The election of 2011 resulted in a majority Conservative government, consigning Canada's natural governing party to third place, with only a third as many seats as historic outsiders, the New Democratic Party. This appeared to answer some of the questions as to the viability of the Conservatives' coalition.

The failed Reform/Alliance efforts up until the 2000 election reflect an ongoing tension in Canadian party politics faced by new parties seeking electoral success. As Morton (1972, 161) writes in his review of the Progressive Party of the early twentieth century, "to compromise, no doubt is to corrupt, to corrupt the simplicity of principle, the clarity of policy, but if so, then all politics is corrupt and federal politics, the politics of vast sectional and communal aggregations especially. To this conclusion all purists, all doctrines, and all progressives must ultimately come or abstain from power." Successful parties have been willing to compromise while the less successful have focused on advancing a particular agenda. The implication is that brokerage politics begets success. It is to the degree to which this remains true for the new Conservative Party and, by extension, for successful Canadian parties more generally, that we now turn.

Partisan Competition in Canada from 2000 to 2011

Our analysis begins with the last Liberal majority victory in 2000. Blais et al. (2002a, 191) demonstrate convincingly that attitudes towards political issues affected vote choice in that election: "Those who believe in the virtue of the market tend to support right wing parties, and those who are more skeptical tend to vote for center or left-wing parties ... Canadian elections are ideological battlegrounds." Their analysis also carefully distinguishes between an economic and social right in Canada and an economic and social right elsewhere, suggesting that "most publics can be differentiated according to how conservative or progressive they are when it comes to a variety of matters that relate to so called 'family values'" (102).

In order to explore partisan competition from 2000 to 2011, we first created indices to capture elements relating to support for free enterprise and social conservatism. What we call our individualism index is constructed from answers to four statements: (1) "people who don't get ahead should blame themselves"; (2) "those who can't find work should move";

(3) "everyone, including the poor, benefits when business makes money"; and (4) "governments should do less to reduce the gap between the rich and poor." We score each respondent who agreed with the position "1" and those who disagreed "0." Our social conservatism index reflects positive responses to "Society would be better off if more women stayed home," support for the suggestion that abortions should be more difficult to obtain, and negative responses towards same-sex marriage. All these questions were asked in the first four election studies, but the last was dropped in 2011. These remain good comparative measures across the period.[4] If, for instance, a respondent's answers were all individualistic, she/he would score a 1 on the index, and if she/he gave no individualistic answers, her/his score would be 0.

We are most interested in the positioning of party identifiers relative to each other and the Canadian mean across the four elections from 2000 to 2011. By combining the data for each party and election and subtracting party scores from the mean of all respondents, we are able to locate the parties on these two dimensions with respect to each other and to the Canadian mean. The mapping of these data appears in Figure 3.1.[5]

FIGURE 3.1
Individualism and social conservatism: Positions of party identifiers relative to the Canadian mean, 2000–11

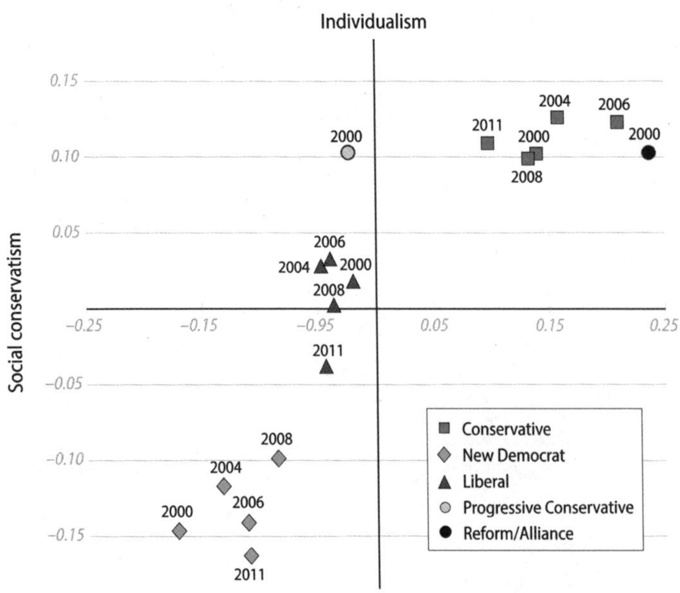

Figure 3.1 demonstrates the propensity of Reform/Alliance identifiers in 2000 to be socially conservative compared with other Canadians. Those who identify with the other parties were all below the scale's midpoint, while Reform/Alliance identifiers were almost two-thirds of the way up the scale. Consistent with the results found by Blais et al. among voters, PC and Liberal identifiers were almost indistinguishable on this dimension, and the PC identifiers were much further from their soon-to-be fellow partisans within the Reform/Alliance Party.

The challenge faced in uniting the right was exemplified by the positioning of the Progressive Conservative and Reform/Alliance voters in the 2000 election. We can clearly see in Figure 3.1 the proximity of PC and Liberal identifiers to the average Canadian on the social conservatism scale and the distance Reform/Alliance and NDP identifiers were from the mean on both dimensions.

The similarity between PC and Reform/Alliance identifiers on the individualism scale is also noteworthy and suggests that this is the area the new Conservative Party needed to emphasize in order to minimize internal tension. Blais et al. (2002a, 112) found that "Alliance and Conservative voters converged in their views about the market but then parted company when it came to social conservatism. On the latter dimension, Conservative voters were much closer to the Liberal voters than to Alliance voters." We artificially combined the PC and Reform/Alliance into a single Conservative category for 2000, and this combination was also above the midpoint on the scale, reflecting the greater number of Reform/Alliance partisans.

The individualism scale not only shows strong similarities between PC and Reform/Alliance identifiers but also rather modest differences between them and the Liberal identifiers. The New Democratic identifiers are the outliers on this scale, with a position much farther from the Liberals than was the Liberals' position from that of the Reform/Alliance. Liberal identifiers were almost equidistant between Conservatives and New Democrats, and the Liberal identifiers were closer to the Canadian mean than were those of any other party on both dimensions.

The 2004 election was quite a different contest: the Liberals and New Democrats had new leaders and the Conservatives had a new party, formed by the aforementioned merger between the Reform/Alliance Party and the Progressive Conservatives and led by the last Alliance leader, Stephen Harper. The merger was controversial. Stephen Clarkson (2004, 33), for instance, describes it as "a reverse takeover of the Progressive Conservatives." Former Reform/Alliance leader Harper had to deal with the aftermath of his

Reform/Alliance leadership race, in which his message indicated that "Canada was in need of a principled small-c conservative party that would not retreat from taking a more ideological stance on policy issues" (Ellis and Woolstencroft 2004, 76). In this environment the Liberal campaign again emphasized the Liberals' differences from the Conservatives, and "Liberal advertising took advantage of ... public doubts about the Conservatives – choose your Canada, voters were exhorted, not theirs" (Pammett and Dornan 2004, 22).

These concerns about where the Conservative Party was located were not simply held by partisans. A column by *Globe and Mail* columnist Jeffrey Simpson was entitled "A Conservative Wolf in Sheep's Clothing" and warned readers that the "Alliance dominated among candidates, organizers and Mr. Harper's advisors who are very, very right wing" (see Clarkson, 2004, 50).

The position of party identifiers on the individualism and social conservatism indices reveal relatively little change from the 2000 positions for the Liberal and NDP identifiers. As well, perhaps surprisingly given the view that the Reform/Alliance had triumphed in the merger, the Conservative identifiers appear to be quite similar in their positions to the artificial Conservative position we constructed for 2000. The new Conservative Party, at least in terms of values, appeared to have absorbed the bulk of the Progressive Conservative positions.

The Liberals hung on to a minority government in the 2004 election, but by 2006 Canadians were back at the polls, largely because the NDP was unhappy with the Liberals over health care issues (see Whitehorn 2006, 103). In between the two elections, according to Ellis and Woolstencroft, "the Conservatives made considerable movement to the centre of Canada's political spectrum ... They quelled many voters' anxieties by dropping the most problematic Reform-Alliance policies that had enabled their opponents to label them as extreme or harbouring hidden agendas" (Ellis and Woolstencraft 2006, 87). Pammett and Dornan (2006, 10) agree with this perspective, suggesting that the "Conservative party thus came more and more to resemble the old Progressive Conservative party." The Conservative campaign emphasized reforming health care and cracking down on violent crime as well as improving economic management and reducing taxes.

This did not dramatically change the Liberal campaign since "an area of Liberal strength that appeared to be intact was values. The Liberals felt that the morally and socially conservative positions taken in the days of the Reform and Alliance parties still lingered under the Conservative banner" (Pammett and Dornan 2006, 11). Clarkson (2006, 37) suggests that the

Liberals used "a negative ad campaign that would scare the public away from the Conservatives once again." This strategy of scaring Canadians away from the Conservatives could have the benefit of moving New Democratic supporters to the Liberals, and, indeed, when Buzz Hargrove of the Canadian Auto Workers endorsed Paul Martin it appeared that it might be successful (Clarkson 2006, 45). The New Democrats, however, campaigned with a focus on the Liberals – and a negative focus at that (Whitehorn 2006). Their message was essentially that the Liberals needed to be defeated, and they were willing to risk a Conservative victory to achieve that goal.

The partisan scores relating to social conservatism and individualism were very similar to those of 2004, although Canadians may have grown somewhat less socially conservative (even though the Conservative Party did not) due, in part, to changing views on same-sex relationships (Matthews 2005). As Figure 3.1 demonstrates, the patterns remain similar, with the Liberal identifiers closest to the Canadian mean and the Conservatives and New Democrats almost equally distant. The Liberal identifiers were closer to the New Democrats on social conservatism and to the Conservatives on individualism. To the degree, then, that the Conservatives could take social conservatism off the table, they might appear less threatening to these Liberal stalwarts. The positioning of party identifiers on these measures and placements largely replicates those of 2004, suggesting that, if the Conservatives had moved to the centre on policy and perception, the views of their base had not broadened and the positions of their key identifiers had not changed very much. This raises questions as to how far the party can go before these supporters start to defect (Downs 1957).

The Conservatives eked out a minority government in 2006 but found the ensuing Parliament to be unstable and, violating a commitment to fixed election dates, dissolved Parliament in 2008 in order to seek a majority. The period from 2006 to 2008 has been described as one of "incremental conservatism," and Dornan (2009) suggests that the Conservative government's record helped to undercut Liberal arguments about a hidden agenda, making it more difficult to forge an electoral alliance that could halt the barbarians' assault at the gate of majority government. The Conservatives attempted to present a more attractive view of Stephen Harper, putting him in sweaters, for instance, and portrayed themselves as the best party to manage Canada through an economic crisis (see Ellis and Woolstencroft 2009).

The Liberals were in an even more difficult position as they were unable to match the Conservatives in fundraising and, as Brooke Jeffrey (2009, 69) explains, the leadership race to replace Paul Martin "unfolded in obscurity, unknown to most of the electorate." The New Democrats campaigned differently in 2008. As Erickson and Laycock (2009, 98) note: "The party consistently portrayed itself as the principal opponent of the governing Conservatives ... From the first morning of the campaign, the New Democrats presented their leader, Jack Layton, as the main choice to replace the current prime minister." The NDP campaign emphasized that it was the Liberal Party that kept the Conservatives in power and that change required a vote for the NDP, not just a vote against the Conservatives.

The Conservative Party was able to increase its seat total, but the election proved disappointing nonetheless as the party failed to achieve its goal of majority government. Canadians, it seems, were still unwilling to see that much power in the hands of a Conservative government. Camped at the gates for three elections, with partial victories in 2006 and 2008, the Conservatives finally broke through to majority government in 2011.

The overall position of the three parties at the 2011 election remained consistent with that for earlier elections (see Figure 3.1). Despite some growth in the distance, the Liberals were closest to the Canadian mean on individualism and about halfway between the positions of NDP identifiers and Conservatives. New Democrats clearly replaced Conservatives as farthest from the mean on this axis, despite the distance increasing for the latter as well. The Conservative position on social conservatism moderated, leaving them slightly closer to, if on the opposite side of, the mean than New Democrats. Liberals and New Democrats retained positions similar to earlier elections, leaving Liberals closer to the New Democrats than to Conservatives. In sum, the Conservatives were able to secure re-election and a majority government even though on both axes their identifiers were farther from the Canadian mean than were those of the Liberals, and only modestly closer than those of the NDP, a party often derided as ideological.

It is not just responses relating to social conservatism and individualism that divide the parties. In an effort to broaden our understanding of the positioning of party identifiers, we spent some time mapping the positions of party identifiers on health privatization and law and order, issues that have popped up in most of the elections in this period and that, particularly in the case of law and order, add another right-wing dimension to the party positioning question (see Budge and Klingemann 2001). Essentially, the results for these questions replicate these measures, with the Liberal identifiers closer to the Canadian mean in all cases and the Conservative and NDP identifiers on different sides of that mean, usually quite far apart.[6]

To this point we have emphasized positions on economic and social issues in an effort to probe the centrist aspects of brokerage parties and politics. However, brokerage obviously goes beyond this, and one of its key aspects involves the integration of Quebeckers into Canadian political life (see Johnston, Chapter 2, this volume). More directly, Johnston speaks of the primacy of the Quebec issue, noting that, over most of Canada's history, Quebec was "the pivot for government."

The 1993 election left the old-line parties relatively uncompetitive in Quebec. From 1993 through 2008, the Bloc Québécois won a majority of the Quebec seats in the House of Commons. The Liberal majority governments of 1993, 1997, and 2000 were forged without a plurality of seats in Quebec, an unprecedented event as the Liberal dominance of the third party system rested largely on its virtual monopoly on Quebec seats. Most notions of brokerage refer to the measures taken to link the French and English portions of Canada. The Bloc's poor performance in 2011 and the New Democrats' success continued the pattern of Liberal and Conservative struggles in Quebec, although now with a potentially new dynamic.

Cross and Young (2004, 441) note the unique position of the Liberal Party on this dimension: "Only the Liberal party contains within it substantial numbers of members from both of Canada's linguistic communities. This signals an inability of the other parties to perform this accommodative function. In a country where political parties have traditionally played a significant role in bridging the divide between the two founding linguistic groups, this is a matter for some concern." Flanagan (2009, 101), in his account of the 2004 Conservative leadership race, acknowledges the weakness of the Conservative Party in Quebec, noting that, "even after the merger, there would be a large number of rotten boroughs, including most of Quebec." And he outlines the fears of the Harper team that a candidate from the PC wing might use this to secure election.[7]

We created a third index to explore attitudes towards Quebec. We considered whether respondents felt that more should be done for Quebec and how warmly they felt towards the province.[8] As is shown in Figure 3.2, Conservative identifiers, regardless of election year, recorded the lowest scores in this area, revealing the challenge faced by the Conservatives with respect to Quebec and suggesting that their identifiers are not particularly supportive or warm towards the only province with a French-speaking majority. In 2000, the PC identifiers were closer to the Liberals than they were to Reform/Alliance partisans on this dimension, and in 2004, the score of the new Conservative Party was lower than that of the artificial Conservative

FIGURE 3.2
Attitudes towards Quebec: Positions of party identifiers relative to the Canadian mean, 2000–11

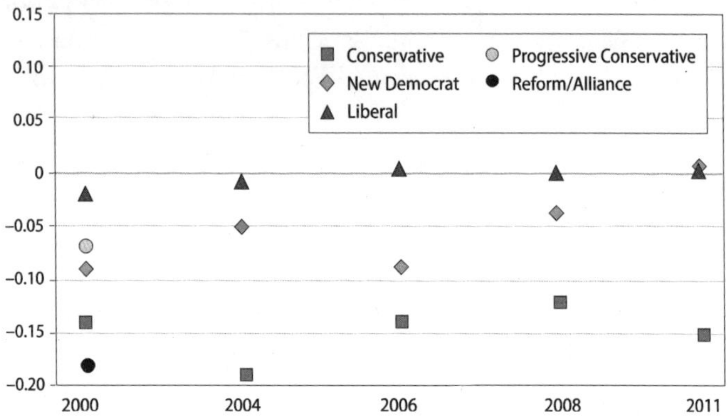

score in 2000. This may well have been due to an element of the PCs being lost in the transition. In three of the five elections, Liberal identifiers were at or above the Canadian mean in terms of being supportive of Quebec. Given the differences between Quebec and the rest of the country, this was not, however, something the Liberals could effectively exploit. New Democrats joined the Liberals, essentially at the Canadian mean, in 2011, evidence of their new-found relevance in Quebec. Conservatives were farther from the mean in 2011, consistent with their failure to gain traction in the province during the election.

The relatively low levels of sympathy for Quebec found among Conservative identifiers has not prevented the party from achieving power, an outcome that again focuses attention on the divergent patterns between Quebec and the rest of the country. This divergence was most prominent in 2011 when the Conservatives won a majority government, garnering almost 48 percent of the vote outside Quebec but receiving only 16.5 percent of the votes cast inside Quebec. This outcome suggests that, although the Conservatives may have attempted to reach out to Quebec, the party has much work to do in accommodating or attracting support in the province, providing another indication that the current governing party is not exactly a brokerage party. A long-term exclusion of the majority of Quebecers from the governing party and the growing divide between its supporters and the mean Canadian position on Quebec may have "incalculable consequences."[9]

The role of Quebec in Canadian electoral politics continues to evolve. For much of the reign of the third party system, the Progressive Conservative Party was not very successful in Quebec. Between 1963 and 1984, it never won more than eight seats in the province, and Joe Clark's minority government included only two MPs from Quebec. The exception was the Mulroney interlude between 1984 and 1988, when the party gained seat majorities in Quebec. This generally poor performance did not detract from the party's success in the rest of the country as, from 1958 to 1993, on only one occasion did it fail to secure plurality support outside Quebec. Success in Quebec was not uniformly required for victory; brokerage, if required at all, has been optional for the PCs. At the same time, despite its success until 2004, Johnston et al. (1992, 63) point out that "the Liberal party could no longer command regular pluralities anywhere outside Quebec," making it particularly vulnerable. Welding together electoral support inside and outside Quebec is now a rarity in Canadian electoral politics. Whether the success of the New Democrats in Quebec in 2011 indicates re-engagement by Quebeckers with a federal party that controls a stable national coalition remains to be seen.

Conclusion

There has been a major shift in patterns of party identification in Canada in the years following the Liberal majority of 2000. Blais et al. (2002a, 191) in their study of the 2000 election, suggest that "core values and beliefs had a substantial impact on vote choice and the implication of these findings is that ideas and world views played a major role in the 2000 election ... Canadian elections are ideological battlegrounds." This undoubtedly comforted the victorious Liberal Party, whose identifiers were much closer to the Canadian mean than were those of the Reform/Alliance and the NDP. The Progressive Conservative identifiers were quite similar to the Liberal identifiers, leading to speculation that a union of the right might not necessarily threaten Liberal hegemony.

The subsequent elections up to 2008 saw the emergence of Conservative identity as the plurality choice for Canadians (Gidengil et al. 2009, 5–6).[10] This move reflects a substantial growth from Reform/Alliance identification in 2000 and a modest growth over the combined PC Reform/Alliance identification. Over the same period, the percentage identifying with the Liberals has declined.[11] Not only the breadth but also the depth of identification with the Liberals shrank in that period, such that, while in "2000 the Liberals could command the loyalty of almost as many partisans as the other three parties combined ... By 2008, not only did the Liberals have fewer partisans, but they could not count on the loyalty of many of those who remained" (Gidengil et al. 2009, 9).

"The Liberals' claim to be Canada's 'natural governing party' has traditionally rested on the party's appeal to the median voter" (Gidengil et al. 2009, 5). There remains some basis for this claim, and if elections were decided by the proximity of a party's base to other Canadians it seems unlikely that the Liberal Party would be in such a precarious state. The Liberal strategy of making elections about Canadian values has lost its appeal, aided by the NDP's unwillingness to cede ground to the Liberals as the bulwark against the Conservative hordes.

Intriguingly, our artificial construction of the Conservative placement relative to the mean on economic and social conservatism in 2000 is very close to the placement of actual Conservative identifiers in 2008. The move from the Reform/Alliance into the Conservative Party shifted the balance of identifiers in the Conservative Party *somewhat* closer to both the middle and most Canadians. Nonetheless, they remained much farther from the mean than did the Liberal identifiers, which were balanced quite nicely between those of the NDP and the Conservatives. This safe middle ground did not save the Liberals either from an election defeat in 2008 or from the unprecedented loss in 2011, which has raised questions about the party's survival.

The growth in Conservative support has been noteworthy, but this has not been accompanied by a broadening of the party's base. The attitudes of Conservative identifiers with respect to individualism and social conservatism remain quite consistent over time. The Conservative growth appears to be based on the decision of more people with the same views to attach themselves to the party rather than on bringing in people with somewhat different views. However, as we pointed out earlier, those who identified with the new Conservative Party proved to be somewhat less socially conservative than their Reform/Alliance forerunners and somewhat more socially conservative than PC partisans. On Quebec, Conservatives remain far from the Canadian mean and the other two parties and not far from the Reform/Alliance supporters of 2000.

In 2008, the NDP and Conservative identifiers were about equidistant from the Canadian mean on our measures of individualism and social conservatism, albeit in different directions. Once again Liberal identifiers were much closer to the mean than were the identifiers of the other parties. This was largely true for 2011, with the exception that Conservatives were somewhat closer to the mean than New Democrats on both measures, particularly with regard to individualism. With respect to Quebec, New Democrats are no longer between the Liberals and Conservatives as they were from 2000 to 2008 but, rather, share the Canadian mean with Liberals. Conservatives, after a couple of elections in which they moved towards the mean, have now moved away. Because of their position on Quebec, the combined distance from the mean across the three issues is greatest for the Conservatives. It may not suit the Conservative Party to contest an election that revolves around Quebec's place in the federation.

In the aftermath of the 2011 election, *Toronto Star* columnist Chantal Hebert wrote that "Canadians turned their backs on more than a century of centrist elite accommodation ... and selected a Parliament where the populist right and the populist left will be going head to head for the first time ... There is less common ground between the current Conservative team and Jack Layton's NDP than there has been between any previous federal government and its official opposition" (*Toronto Star*, May 2, 2011). Although former Conservative strategist (and political scientist) Tom Flanagan predicts that the "median voter theorem" will lead to competition at the centre (*Globe and Mail*, May 4, 2011), former NDP leader (and political scientist) Ed Broadbent signalled that value competition is not going to disappear from Canadian politics. He talked about how the NDP is much closer to Canadian values than are the Conservatives, a factor that should enable it to improve its standing in future elections. In his words, "Frankly, I think, we represent the core values of Canadians better than do the Conservatives" (CBC, *The Current*, May 3, 2011). The evidence in support of this claim is far from overwhelming.

The question for the Liberal Party going into the future is whether this proximity to the mean can be exploited for electoral gain, allowing it to present the other two parties as far removed from the views of Canadians. If, as Flanagan suggests, the Conservatives will seek to move towards the centre in order to secure the median voter, and if the NDP is able to do this as well, the future for the Liberal Party is highly questionable (*Globe and Mail*, May 4, 2011). However, as Blais et al. (2002a, 17) note: "The parties' messages stem from a combination of ideological preferences and pragmatic considerations ... But politicians also have policy preferences. And they have to pay attention to party members, who often have strong ideological concerns." Our analysis suggests that it is not only members but also identifiers who have views that make movement to the centre challenging for both the Conservatives and the New Democrats – a move likely made even more difficult by the long-standing NDP tradition of grassroots participation in crafting policy positions.

Success for the Conservative Party has come despite identifiers retaining attitudes that once cast them as outsiders. The creation of the new Conservative Party in 2003 reflected neither a full-scale return of the dominance of the Progressive Conservative wing of the party nor the triumph of brokerage. The Conservative Party's identifiers in 2004, 2006, 2008, and 2011 were significantly to the right of the PC 2000 identifiers on measures of social conservatism, although on the individualism scale there is greater proximity. With respect to Quebec, our analysis raises questions about the ability and interest of the Conservatives in following a brokerage approach. Whitaker's argument that "the new Conservative party under Stephen Harper is not another Mulroney-type brokerage party; instead, it incorporates the conservative ideological drive of Harper's old party into a more flexible vote seeking organization" (*Globe and Mail,* May 16, 2011) is consistent with our analysis.

Carty, Cross, and Young (2000, 12 and 13) suggest that "one of the greatest electoral earthquakes ever recorded hit Canada in 1993" and that "national parties, national politics and national electoral competition no longer exist." The aftershocks of this earthquake have been far reaching, with subsequent elections exposing the weakness of Canada's once natural governing party and the mythologies of brokerage politics.

Notes

1 In 2011, *Vote Compass* explained its approach on its website in the following manner. First, a team of research assistants compiled all publicly available party texts relating to each statement. Second, analysts from the academic team then selected the most relevant texts and calibrated the party positions accordingly. Third, an intercoder reliability test was then run to ensure consistency across the academic team. Fourth, the parties were offered an opportunity to self-assess. Every party was provided with an advance copy of the survey and was asked to indicate its perceived position on each statement. Finally, where discrepancies arose between the party's self-assessment and the assessment of the academic team, the advisory board was asked to make a final ruling.

2 Data on the 2000, 2004, 2006, 2008, and 2011 Canadian elections are taken from the various Canadian election studies. The data were downloaded from the CES archive, hosted by the Canadian Opinion Research Archive. We thank Paul Fairie for his work on the data and its weighting.

3 See Flanagan (2009) for a discussion of the merger and the events leading up to it.
4 The components of these indices are somewhat comparable to those used by Blais et al. (2002a, 102–3).
5 This graph is based on the average percentage of Canadians taking the named position on each question in the scale and then calculating the difference from the average for party identifiers.
6 Our measures here identify those who favour having some private hospitals and those who favour allowing doctors to charge for services in 2000; however, in the next three elections, it was replaced by a question asking whether those who are willing to pay should get treatment sooner. With respect to law and order, a key component of Conservative platforms, and an area that would come to be associated with Conservative efforts to engage in wedge politics, we identified those who favoured dealing more harshly with young offenders and who favoured capital punishment. Finally, we looked at those who felt that only the police and the military should have guns. This did not fit well with the law-and-order measures, and we looked at it separately as the gun registry would become a recurring issue throughout this period.
7 These concerns flowed from the decision to have all constituencies weighted equally regardless of the number of members. This privileging of equality of constituency associations over equality of members was a major demand of the Progressive Conservative wing and a significant retreat from the Reform-Alliance model (Flanagan 2009, 99–102). Harper lost Quebec, receiving just 33 percent of the points from the province (132).
8 We scored those who gave Quebec a seventy or higher on the thermometer as pro Quebec as well as those who wanted to see more done for the province. In future versions it would be useful to split the analysis into Quebec and non-Quebec respondents, not only here but also on other measures.
9 These are the words Quebec premier René Lévesque used in 1981 to describe the agreement between the federal government and the other nine premiers to patriate the Constitution without the agreement of Quebec. Since that event, the Liberal Party has not won a majority of seats in the province that previously constituted its base.
10 Their data also reveal that party identification is less volatile than voting as almost a third of Liberal identifiers voted for another party in 2008 (Gidengil et al. 2009, 6).
11 Longer-term problems for the Liberals may relate to the loss of core support. "Catholics and minority voters have been the twin pillars of Liberal dominance, but their support is clearly crumbling" (Gidengil et al. 2009, 10).

References

Blais, A. 2005. "Accounting for the electoral success of the Liberal Party in Canada." *Canadian Journal of Political Science* 38 (4): 821–40.

Blais, A., E. Gidengil, R. Nadeau, and N. Nevitte. 2002a. *Anatomy of a Liberal Victory*. Peterborough: Broadview Press.

–. 2002b. "Do party supporters differ?" In *Citizen Politics*, ed. J. Everitt and B. O'Neill, 184–201. Toronto: Oxford University Press.

Blake, D.E. 1988. Division and cohesion: The major parties. In *Party Democracy in Canada*, ed. G. Perlin, 32–53. Scarborough, ON: Prentice Hall.

Brodie, J., and J. Jensen. 2007. "Piercing the smokescreen: Stability and change in brokerage politics." In *Canadian Parties in Transition*, 3rd ed., ed. A.G. Gagnon and A.B. Tanguay, 33–54. Peterborough: Broadview Press.

Budge, I., and H.-D. Klingemann. 2001. "Finally, comparative over time mapping of party policy movement." In *Mapping Policy Preferences: Estimates for Parties, Electors, and Governments, 1945–1998*, ed. I. Budge, et al., 19–50. Oxford: Oxford University Press.

Carty, R.K. 2006. "The shifting place of political parties in Canadian public life." *IRPP Choices* 12 (4): 3–13.

Carty, R., and W. Cross. 2006. "Can stratarchically organized parties be democratic? The Canadian Case." *Journal of Elections, Public Opinion and Parties* 16 (2): 93–114. http://dx.doi.org/10.1080/13689880600715912.

Carty, R.K., W. Cross, and L. Young. 2000. *Rebuilding Canadian Party Politics*. Vancouver: UBC Press.

Clarkson, S. 2004. "Disaster and recovery: Paul Martin as political Lazarus." In *The Canadian General Election of 2004*, ed. J.H. Pammett and C. Dornan, 28–65. Toronto: Dundurn Press.

–. 2006. "How the Big Red Machine became the little red machine." In *The Canadian Federal Election of 2006*, ed. J.H. Pammett and C. Dornan, 24–57. Toronto: Dundurn Press.

Cross, W., and L. Young. 2002. "Policy attitudes of party members in Canada: Evidence of ideological politics." *Canadian Journal of Political Science* 35 (4): 859–80. http://dx.doi.org/10.1017/S0008423902778475.

–. 2004. "The contours of political party membership in Canada." *Party Politics* 10 (4): 427–44. http://dx.doi.org/10.1177/1354068804043907.

Dornan, C. 2009. "The outcome in retrospect." In *The Canadian Federal Election of 2008*, ed. J.H. Pammett and C. Dornan, 7–15. Toronto: Dundurn Press.

Downs, A. 1957. *An Economic Theory of Democracy*. New York: Harper.

Ellis, F. 2001. "The more things change ... The Alliance campaign." In *The Canadian General Election of 2000*, ed. J.H. Pammett and C. Dornan, 59–90. Toronto: Dundurn Press.

Ellis, F., and P. Woolstencroft. 2004. "New Conservatives, old realities." In *The Canadian General Election of 2004*, ed. J.H. Pammett and C. Dornan, 66–105. Toronto: Dundurn Press.

–. 2006. "A change of government, not a change of country." In *The Canadian Federal Election of 2006*, ed. J.H. Pammett and C. Dornan, 58–92. Toronto: Dundurn Press.

–. 2009. "Stephen Harper and the Conservatives campaign on their record." In *The Canadian Federal Election of 2008*, ed. J.H. Pammett and C. Dornan, 16–62. Toronto: Dundurn Press.

Erickson, L., and D. Laycock. 2009. "Modernization, incremental progress, and the challenge of relevance." In *The Canadian Federal Election of 2008*, ed. J.H. Pammett and C. Dornan, 98–135. Toronto: Dundurn Press.

Flanagan, T. 2009. *Harper's Team*. 2nd ed. Montreal and Kingston: McGill-Queen's University Press.

–. 2011. "We don't need a centre party to prevent political polarization." *Globe and Mail*, May 4.

Gidengil, E., et al. 2009. "Anatomy of a Liberal defeat." Paper presented at the Annual Meeting of the Canadian Political Science Association, Carleton University, Ottawa.

Hebert, C. 2011. "No common ground left in the Commons." *Toronto Star*, May 2.

Jeffrey, B. 2009. "Missed opportunity." In *The Canadian Federal Election of 2008*, ed. J.H. Pammett and C. Dornan, 63–97. Toronto: Dundurn Press.

Johnston, R. 1988. "The ideological structure of opinion on policy." In *Party Democracy in Canada*, ed. G. Perlin, 54–70. Scarborough: Prentice Hall.

Johnston, R., et al. 1992. *Letting the People Decide: Dynamics of a Canadian Election*. Montreal and Kingston: McGill-Queen's University Press.

Leduc, L. 2007. "Realignment and dealignment in Canadian federal politics." In *Canadian Parties in Transition*, 3rd ed., ed. A.G. Gagnon and A.B. Tanguay, 163–77. Peterborough: Broadview Press.

Matthews, S. 2005. "The political foundations of support for same-sex marriage in Canada." *Canadian Journal of Political Science* 38 (4): 841–66. http://dx.doi.org/10.1017/S0008423905040485.

Morton, W.L. 1972. "The progressive tradition in Canadian Politics." In *Party Politics in Canada*, 3rd ed., ed. H. Thorburn, 318–23. Scarborough: Prentice Hall.

Pammett, J.H., and C. Dornan. 2004. "Election night in Canada: The transition continues." In *The Canadian General Election of 2004*, ed. J.H. Pammett and C. Dornan, 7–27. Toronto: Dundurn Press.

–. 2006. "From one minority to another." In *The Canadian Federal Election of 2006*, ed. J.H. Pammett and C. Dornan, 9–23. Toronto: Dundurn Press.

Segal, H. 2006. *The Long Road Back: The Conservative Journey, 1993–2006*. Toronto: Harper Collins Canada.

Siegfried, A. 1907. *The Race Question in Canada*. London: Eveleigh Nash.

Whitehorn, A. 2006. "The NDP and the enigma of strategic voting." In *The Canadian Federal Election of 2006*, ed. J.H. Pammett and C. Dornan, 93–121. Toronto: Dundurn Press.

Whitaker, R. 2011. "Is the government party over?" *Globe and Mail*, May 16.

Young, L., and W. Cross. 2002. "Incentives to membership in Canadian party politics." *Political Research Quarterly* 55 (3): 547–69. http://dx.doi.org/10.1177/106591290205500303.

4

Franchising the Franchise Party

How Far Can a New Concept Travel?

STEVEN B. WOLINETZ

The parties literature has no shortage of categories. Cadre, mass, and catch-all parties are standard fare. Joining them are variants denoting nearly identical types – elite parties, parties of mass integration, and electoral-professional parties. Even so, the numbers continue to grow: Katz and Mair (1995) added the cartel party, Koole (1996) the modern cadre party, Hopkin and Paolucci (1999) the business-firm party, and Carty (2002; 2004) the franchise party. The picture is no different if we consider designations for party families: Poguntke (1987) coined the new politics party and Kitschelt (1988) added the left-libertarian party while various authors added the new right party to standard varieties such as conservative, liberal, Christian democratic, social democratic, and communist parties.

Accumulating labels is no surprise. Comparativists need categories, and parties specialists have a long-standing fascination with change. Categories help make sense of change. New concepts are a mixed blessing, helping if they highlight phenomena missed using standard lenses but confusing if improperly applied or imperfectly integrated into earlier frameworks. Some extend earlier schemes, but others, like the business-firm party and the franchise party, are discrete or stand-alone categories. Typically, these function not as attributes whose variation we want to explain but, rather, as metaphors bringing common characteristics into sharp relief. Standing alone, they resemble ideal types divorced from the broader frameworks of which they should be a part. Discrete categories are useful if we want to draw analogies but problematic in systematic analysis. Missing is an indication of their range and variation: we need to know not only what something is when key attributes are present but also what it is not when they are absent.

This chapter examines Carty's franchise party. Initially advanced as a metaphor highlighting distinctive features of Canadian parties (Carty 2002), the franchise party can be interpreted either as a distinct type or as an optic focusing attention on the internal life of parties (Carty 2004). Arguing that stratarchical bargains exist in diverse settings, Carty suggests we view them as franchise systems. Prevailing models encourage us to think of power as zero-sum, but doing this blinds us to the disconnectedness that characterizes some parties. Viewing them as franchise systems brings key features into focus (Carty 2004).

Viewing parties as franchise systems highlights links between leaders and followers. However, not all parties are franchise parties. If the franchise party is to be more than an optic, functioning like night-vision goggles to bring certain characteristics into sharp relief, we need to understand both how forms of linkage vary and the conditions under which they occur.

What Is a Franchise Party?

Carty mooted the franchise party in 2002. The setting was the annual meeting of the Canadian Political Science Association, the occasion, his presidential address. Carty (2002) argued that Canadian parties were franchise parties and, in doing so, he drew on a familiar model. Franchise arrangements specify the terms under which owners operate local outlets of larger firms. Contracts typically specify the suppliers and ingredients to be used, the products and/or services to be supplied, and the standards to be maintained; however, they allow franchise owners to place a local stamp on the business. Franchising characterizes not only the ways in which fast food outlets expand their reach but also the relationship between local associations and parties at the centre. Although formally subject to the approval of the party leader, constituency associations are free to nominate whomever they please. Operating in a geographically diverse country, constituency associations can tailor candidates, points of view, and constituency-level campaigns to suit local tastes. Once elected, however, MPs are bound by strict party discipline.

Franchise arrangements allowed Canadian parties to cope with the environment within which they operated. According to Carty:

> The central linkage problem for Canadian parties is to respond to the imperatives of a competitive national system while incorporating the demands and energies of parochial supporters. The solution is an organizational form that best accommodates those tensions. Franchise systems are designed to do just that. They exist to maximize the efficiencies of scale and standardization while exploiting the advantages of local participation in the operation and delivery of an organization's product. Typically, a central organization operating under an established brand determines the products and sets standards for their production and labeling; designs and manages mass marketing and advertising strategies; and provides management help and training while arranging for the basic supplies needed by local outlets. For their part, individual franchises exist to deliver the product to a particular market. To do so, they invest local resources, both capital and personnel, in building an organization attuned to the needs and demands of the community they serve, and they are preoccupied with delivering the product to their market area. (Carty 2002, 730)

Widely understood, franchising captured key features of party organization in Canada. Carty (2004) extends the argument. The focus is not the franchise party but parties as *franchise systems*. Political scientists presume that parties are hierarchically structured, and, indeed, prevailing models indicate as much. However, these contain "discordant" elements: cartel parties have not only become more leader-centric but also give members greater voice in leadership selection (Katz and Mair 1995). Leaders are not only more prominent but also more vulnerable. Alternate approaches produce equivalent noise (Carty 2004).

Highlighting stratarchy, Carty suggests we think of parties as franchise systems. Parties have distinct levels operating more or less independently of each other. Stratarchical bargains reconcile the leader's need to act with the local association's demand for autonomy. Sometimes explicit, sometimes implicit, their content varies: although leaders determine positions and strategy, nominations and recruitment are either reserved for the rank and file or shared with intermediate levels. Arrangements can vary to accommodate different regions and preferences. Franchise arrangements provide not only an alternate set of lenses but also an antidote for the negative features of cartel parties: cartel parties marginalize members. Franchising narrows the gap: local parties have minimal influence on party policies but can choose their own candidates and tailor local campaigns to local interests (Carty 2004).

Focusing on their distinctive features, Carty adds the franchise party to the pantheon used to characterize parties. However, he tells us little about the circumstances in which franchise arrangements are most likely to occur. If the franchise party is to be more than a metaphor and franchise systems more than an alternate set of lenses, we need to know how they differ from other arrangements linking upper and lower echelons.

Approach to Viewing Parties

Parties are entities that must be constructed and maintained (see Aldrich 1995); however, more often than not we take them as givens. Thinking about parties as constructs directs our attention to aspects of them that we don't always consider. These include the resources upon which they draw and the relationships among their parts. Resources matter because they affect the kind of party that can be constructed. The classic class- and religion-based mass parties that Duverger (1954) describes drew heavily on trade unions or churches and the lay organizations built around them. Indeed, they would have been difficult to construct without them. In contrast, loosely organized cadre parties relied on personal connections, standing in the community, and, in Canada and the United States, newspapers that were part of a broader "family." However, the relationship also involved an element of reciprocity: newspapers supporting victorious parties could expect advertising revenue as compensation for their efforts. A core theme of more recent literature is the growing reliance of parties on public funds (Katz and Mair 1995). Parties, it is argued, distance themselves not only from their active members but also from society. Even if this is not regarded as an act of deliberate construction, agency is involved: parties in public office vote themselves the subsidies upon which they increasingly depend.

Viewing parties as constructs directs our attention to relationships between upper and lower echelons and among elements within them. The first is a vertical bargain linking upper and lower levels, the second a lateral bargain bringing together divergent ideas and interests. Vertical bargains allocate power among various levels of party organization.[1] Determining who decides what, they can be top-down (or strict or taut), with key decisions made at the top; looser, with key decisions either shared or dispersed among levels; or bottom-up and decentralized, with key decisions made at the base. Lateral bargains tap parties' ambition and reach – whom they represent and how they attempt to do so. Parties can be narrowly defined, representing a particular group or interest, or broadly defined, representing divergent interests. The former include class, religious, regional, and ethnic parties; the latter, the catch-all parties into which some of the former have transformed themselves as well as the broadly based aggregative parties found in the United States and, of course, the brokerage parties, mooted by students of Canadian politics as a distinctive Canadian type of party but shown to be more widespread than Carty (Chapter 1, this volume) originally thought. Arguably, the brokerage party is a distinctive form of aggregative party different not only from catch-all parties, as Carty points out, but also from other parties with broad lateral bargains. This is because it takes on systemic tasks such as holding a potentially divided country together. Such tasks loom large in the functionalist literature. However, they are typically thought not to be the task of a single party but, rather, of the party system as a whole (Almond and Coleman 1960; Almond and Powell 1966).

Vertical and lateral bargains are interrelated: looser vertical bargains go hand in hand with broader lateral bargains. Parties with broader lateral bargains often find it useful to maintain looser vertical bargains. Allowing divergence facilitates the inclusion of elements that might bolt if stricter control were enforced. One example is the Democratic Party in the United States: a loose vertical bargain allowed it to maintain a heterogeneous coalition that included southerners committed to segregation and northern liberals anxious to eliminate it.

Below we concentrate on vertical bargains. Teasing out vertical bargains, we focus not on the "official stories" used by Katz and Mair (1994) but, rather, on how rules and procedure play out in practice. Katz and Mair (1993; 1994) differentiated three faces of party organization. We combine party in public office and party in central office, referring to them as upper echelons, the leadership, or party top, and differentiate them only when necessary. Contesting elections and sparring while some govern and others oppose, parties must decide not only how they position themselves and whom they will nominate but also strategy and tactics and "brand control" – who is or is not entitled to speak for the party. These four activities provide benchmarks we can use to assess whether parties' "centre of gravity" is at the top, on the ground, or somewhere in between. Stratarchy is a key feature of franchise parties. It is also a concept that was dormant between its introduction by Eldersveld (1964) and its resurrection by Katz and Mair (1994; 1995). It is here that we begin.

Stratarchy

Impossible to find in most dictionaries,[2] stratarchy is readily understood. Lasswell and Kaplan (1950, 220) define it as a form of rule in which the ranks of those with power have been expanded to the point at which they resemble what is found in a republic. Stratarchy evokes images of stratified rock, and rule by layers piled one on top of the other. Eldersveld (1964) used it to characterize Wayne County parties. Wayne County included Detroit, several of its suburbs, and six congressional districts. Its Democrats and Republicans were organized at the precinct, ward, district, and county levels. Using structured interviews, Eldersveld found that Wayne County party organizations consisted not of smoothly operating hierarchies but, rather, of bailiwicks isolated from the layers above and below them: local officials were "little oligarchs" (408) who did not know what others were doing.

Political Parties: A Behavioral Analysis, received the 1965 Woodrow Wilson Prize for the best book on government, politics, or international affairs. A multifaceted study of local parties, their recruitment systems, and their leaders, it is remembered not for its ambitious methodology but for stratarchy. Stratarchy is one of four images that Eldersveld invokes to characterize parties,[3] but he discusses it only in two of twenty-two chapters.[4] Stratarchy entails "the enlargement of the ruling group of an organization, its power stratification, the involvement of large numbers of people in group decision-making, and thus, the diffusion and proliferation of control throughout the structure" (Eldersveld 1964, 99).

Drawing on Lasswell and Kaplan (1950), Eldersveld emphasizes the numbers involved in decision-making and "diffusion and proliferation of control" in a description that places greater emphasis on multiple centres of power than on organizations consisting of separate and autonomous layers. Denoting levels operating independently of each other, current usage differs somewhat from Eldersveld's.

Vertical Bargains and How They Vary

Franchising is one of several arrangements through which lower levels of party organizations are linked to upper echelons. If we want to know where the franchise party fits, we need to specify alternate ways in which parties link parties on the ground to parties at the top. Doing so is not as simple as it might appear. Party organizations are rarely as clearly articulated or closely connected as organization charts suggest; nor do they necessarily organize identically everywhere they operate. Nor are all key decisions necessarily made at the same level. Vertical bargains include some that are taut as well as others that are loose and disconnected (Figure 4.1) Below, we consider several varieties. Forms that are taut include strict hierarchies and bounded hierarchies; forms that are looser and less connected include

FIGURE 4.1
Vertical bargains: A preliminary view

Taut, hierarchical	Command and control, direction from above Low levels act in their own jurisdiction, keep centre informed Delegation from above, franchising
Looser	Cajoling and niggling Benign neglect
Disconnected	Minimal supervision

franchise parties, confederative parties, and clientelistic parties. Table 4.1 summarizes how these differ, and we explain them below.

Strict Hierarchies

Hierarchical parties require less explanation than do other forms of parties. Hierarchy is evident not only in organization charts but also in the ways in which some parties operate. Examples include most communist and early socialist and social democratic parties as well as others with unified top-down structures. Because some are more centralized than others, we differentiate strict hierarchies and bounded hierarchies. Strict hierarchies are highly centralized, with all power concentrated at the top. Bounded hierarchies are less centralized: rules and procedures introduce an element of accountability. Governed by democratic centralism and often Stalinist, most communist parties were top-down organizations in which leaders determined not only positions but also strategy and tactics. Recruitment was controlled from above. However, once positions were determined, others followed. Among larger Western European communist parties, only the Italian Communist Party (PCI) tolerated open debate on its party line (which became more prominent in later years) (Amyot 1981; Hellman 1988). In addition, advancement was controlled from above. Others, like the French Communist Party (PCF), were more rigid: only in brief periods was more open discussion permitted (Kriegel 1972; Jenson and Ross 1984). Although in theory democratic centralism should have been open enough to allow internal debate, in practice it was not. Using command and control from the centre, all were strict hierarchies. Moreover, if we take Michels (1962)

TABLE 4.1
Vertical bargains and the forms that they take

Vertical bargain	Characteristics	Examples
Strict hierarchy	Highly centralized: lower levels take direction from above Democratic centralism?	Former communist parties Some earlier socialist parties
Bounded hierarchy	Moderately centralized Organization is well integrated Leaders operate within framework of rules Exit as a further restraint Lower levels autonomous in own sphere, but keep higher levels informed	Contemporary social democratic parties Some Christian democratic parties Many liberal and conservative parties
Franchise parties	Stratarchical Stronger centre Lower levels autonomous and largely disconnected Operate within framework of rules and understandings Higher levels may intervene if these are violated	Liberal Party of Canada Progressive Conservative Party (federal) until 2003 New Democratic Party Australian parties Israeli parties
Confederative parties	Stratarchical Weak centre Lower levels separate and autonomous	Democrats Republicans EU parties Justicialists (PJ) Other Latin American parties?
Clientelistic parties	Characterized by unequal exchanges Centre negotiates with and plays off autonomous regional or local machines	Italian Christian Democrats (DC) before 1993 Socialists (PSI) before 1993 African parties

at face value, early socialist and social democratic parties were quite oligarchical. Although other studies of the early Social Democratic Party of Germany (SPD) (Roth 1984 [1963]; Hunt 1970) counter Michels's unrelenting portrait – there were factional conflicts that resulted not in one elite replacing another but, rather, in splits and schisms – parties like the SPD were nevertheless strict hierarchies.

Bounded Hierarchies

Few parties are as strictly controlled as are former communist parties. Many have a discernable elite and are controlled from the top. However, this often takes place under rules and procedures that are sufficiently democratic that they give rank and file and lower echelons a say in certain party decisions. This occurs not only because party laws require it – the case in more and more countries – but also because both members and attentive publics expect it. In an era of declining memberships, the threat of exit (Hirschman 1970) encourages leaders to pay attention to members and supporters (see Scarrow and Gezgor 2010). Whether this results in internal democracy is another matter. In practice, we should find give and take between lower and higher levels of party organizations held together not by threats of expulsion but, rather, by a sense of identity and of common purpose. Hierarchy is present, but, kept within bounds, it operates differently from the centralism that characterized communist and some early socialist parties. Because the extent of control is limited by nominally democratic procedures and because the threat of exit can be potent, we call these parties bounded hierarchies. Examples include contemporary social democratic and Christian democratic parties.

Few social democratic parties were as hierarchical as were communist parties. Nevertheless, believing they were engaged in a class struggle that dictated strict party discipline, many early parties were leader-centred. A hallmark of the Dutch Social Democratic Workers Party (SDAP) and the Netherlands Trade Union Federation (NVV), with which the former was intertwined, was that both were not only disciplined but also different from loosely organized antecedents, which veered towards anarchism. The Labour Party (PvdA) replaced the SDAP in 1946. In its first two decades, the PvdA maintained similar traditions of solidarity and discipline. Party statutes contained provisions for *royement*, or expulsion. Used primarily to prevent communist infiltration, these became a source of contention when a dissident faction, the New Left, challenged the party leadership in the late 1960s. Public attacks on the party leadership tactics violated PvdA norms and statutes. Because the dissidents represented elements that leaders hoped to attract and wanted to retain, they incorporated them rather than expelling them. One consequence of this was wider "space" for internal debate. Open criticism became more common, and New Left activists became part of the party leadership. A few years later, they found themselves under attack because they had become part of the party "establishment."

Bounded hierarchies can either be unitary or federal in formal structure. Parties in the Federal Republic of Germany mirror the structure of the state. Reflecting the Basic Law, parties operate under rules that are internally democratic. Federalism means that *laender* parties not only select candidates for provincial elections and determine with whom they will form coalitions but also construct party lists for *Bundestag* elections. However, decisions are taken within the bounds of collectively determined manifestos and with the knowledge – although not necessarily the explicit approval – of federal party leaders. Similar relationships exist between constituency associations and *laender* parties. (Detterbeck and Jeffery 2009).

Franchise Parties

Stratarchically organized, franchise parties are more loosely structured than are bounded hierarchies. Lower levels operate within bounds specified by party statutes and practices that have developed over time. As Carty (2002; 2004) argues, this results in substantial autonomy not only to designate candidates of their own choice but also in the way in which local- or district-level election campaigns are organized. If they are like Canadian constituency associations, local organizations become dormant between elections, but activity surges if the local nomination or the party leadership is at stake or an election is imminent. Communication between central party organs and parties on the ground should be less frequent in franchise parties than in bounded hierarchies. However, following Carty (2002; 2004), franchise arrangements should vary not only between parties but also, in some instances, within them.

Franchise parties disperse some power to the party on the ground; however, in parliamentary systems like Canada's, the party top determines strategy and tactics, policies and positions, and how the party presents itself on the national stage. This leaves only nomination and local positioning to the party on the ground. Allowing locals to nominate candidates of their choice makes franchise parties less centralized than bounded hierarchies but more centralized than parties in which the party top has even less control over strategy and tactics, positions, and how the party brand is used.

Confederative Parties

Confederative parties are less centralized than are franchise parties or bounded hierarchies. The locus of power is not the centre but, rather, the party at the local level or the regional level. Legislative caucuses are important, but key decisions about nominations and positions are made at lower rather than higher levels. Reflecting dispersion of power, the latter may vary from place to place. "Brand control" is minimal. Examples include not only American parties but also European Union parties and parties in some presidential systems.

The pre-1972 American parties were frequently characterized both as confederations of state and local parties and coalitions of divergent interests.[5] Before 1972, the principal task of each party's national committee was to call quadrennial national conventions, which, once convened, reviewed the credentials of the adopted platforms of state delegations and nominated presidential and vice-presidential candidates. Once these tasks were accomplished, the only jobs remaining were overseeing presidential election campaigns (a task taken over by candidate organizations) and routine housekeeping. Characterizing the national committees, the title of the first book to treat them systematically, Cotter and Hennessey's (1964) *Committees without Power,* aptly sums up their (absence of) power.

Changes to Democratic Party rules altered the balance among national, state, and local party organizations but not their confederative structure. Mandating the selection of national convention delegates in either primary elections or conventions open to party members, the new rules resulted in a rapid expansion in the number of states requiring primary elections (Shafer 1983). Curtailing the power of state and local party officials, this affected not only the Democrats but also the Republicans.

Hollowing out was offset by a counter-trend – bulking up (Katz and Kolodny 1994). In the late 1970s, the Republican National Committee (RNC) exploited direct mailing to raise money from individual donors. This was used to recruit first-time candidates and to support their election campaigns. The Democratic National Committee (DNC) followed suit. National committees transformed themselves from housekeeping organs into well-funded entities. Likened to super-PACs, the new-style national committees were able to recruit new candidates and provide them with financial support and campaign assistance (Cotter 1984). Parallel developments took place in both parties' House and senate campaign committees (Katz and Kolodny 1994). State and local party organizations lost power. In their place came candidates' campaign committees, political action committees, 527 organizations, and factions with varying degrees of organization. The latter include organizations like MoveOn.org (operating in the Democratic fold) and the Tea Party (operating in the Republican fold). Depending on the optic selected, both the Republicans and the Democrats could be regarded as either parties organized around multiple centres of power or containers for conflict over access to scarce goods – the right to use the party label, ballot access, and whatever loyal support the parties retain.

Without changes in formal structure, new-style national committees altered the balance between (1) state/local parties and (2) national parties. Differences between these two confederative parties and Canada's franchise parties are striking: parties in both countries have broad lateral bargains, but their vertical bargains are different. Although the McGovern-Fraser rules on delegate selection restricted the freedom of state and local parties, their obligations to the national parties are minimal. In contrast, as Epstein (1964) observes, Canadian parties are more disciplined. Moreover, brand control, absent in American politics, is prominent not only in Canadian parties but also in party government in Canada.

We know less about parties in other presidential systems. Operating for the most part in newer democracies, few have been studied in any detail. One exception is the Justicialist Party (PJ) in Argentina. Demonstrating how its less institutionalized structure allowed the Peronistas to shift from left-leaning populism to austerity in the 1980s, Levitsky (2003) describes a party with multiple centres. Operating within a federal presidential system, power is shared not only among provincial governors but also, lower down, by *punteros*. *Punteros,* or point men, derive benefits from officeholders and selectively distribute them to followers. This allows them to influence nominations and how the party operates. However, *punteros* are only one of several centres of power. Unions are another. Shifting from left to right, party leaders took advantage of the *Peronistas'* fluid, less institutionalized structures, drawing on different internal coalitions to make the change (Levitsky 2003). Although clientelism (see below) is prominent, so is confederative structure.

European Union parties are also confederative. At the top, we find the European parliamentary groups and the extra-parliamentary organizations linking them with parties in member-states. European parliamentary groups decide not only their positions on European legislation but also which member-state parties and which members of the European Parliament they will admit to their group. However, there is no party on the ground that is directly linked to European-level parties. Instead, affiliated parties decide whom they will nominate and the positions that they will take when they contest European elections. Although held in the same week, European elections are not only second order but also separate member-state elections that take place in close proximity to each other (Hix and Lord 1997; see also Bardi, Katz, and Mair, Chapter 7, this volume).

Clientelistic Parties

Clientelism can also have considerable impact. Linking local, intermediate, and higher levels through mutual but unequal exchanges, clientalism can pervade an entire party or only a part of it. Clientelistic bargains are likely when brokers – typically politicians with local or regional bases of support – interpose themselves between leaders at the top and populations dependent on government largesse at the bottom. Access to public resources enables intermediaries to act as brokers bartering support for benefits. Establishing bastions of power, clientelistic exchanges create fiefdoms within the larger organization. Examples include urban political machines that dominated some older American cities as well as parties in less developed societies and less developed parts of countries such as Italy.

Once entrenched, clientelism alters the internal distribution of power: lower levels may not only have to be consulted but may also exercise a veto over certain decisions. Power is dispersed but not in the same way as it is in franchise or confederative parties: in franchise parties, lower levels of party organization operate on the basis of grants or licences that can be withdrawn if upper echelons choose to do so. In confederative parties, lower echelons make key decisions as a matter of course. In contrast, if clientelism pervades, actors find themselves caught in reciprocal structures that are difficult, if not impossible, to dislodge.

Clientelistic parties confound attempts to array vertical bargains on a scale. We can consider them either as a distinctive form or as something that characterizes some confederative parties and, in some instances, franchise parties or even bounded hierarchies. Adding to the confusion is the possibility of asymmetry: clientelism can penetrate entire parties or, as both Italian and American parties demonstrate, be confined to certain regions or cities. Here, it is sufficient to say that it is an intermediate form, which concentrates less control at the top than does a strict or bounded hierarchy but more control than do confederative parties. In the latter, the centre is weak or non-existent. If this is the case, then the clientelistic party is an intermediate form that differs from the franchise party.

Categorizing parties is not very useful if the end result tells us little about the conditions under which different vertical bargains are likely to occur or what difference it makes. It is to these questions that we now turn.

Institutions and How They Shape Parties

Our classification does not constitute a comprehensive scheme but, rather, a device to help us think about the ways in which a party's upper echelons are linked to the party on the ground. Proposed categories need to be tested to determine how readily they can be measured and applied. Sketching vertical bargains, we have placed the franchise party within a broader context. Surrounding the franchise party with other ways of linking upper and lower echelons indicates that it is a concept that can travel – but not alone. We need to know more about the preconditions of different vertical bargains and what difference they make.

Determining this is not easy. Variants such as clientelism come with built-in explanations (e.g., the ability of politicians to skim patronage and to deliver it to dependent populations who can barter votes for benefits), and franchising can be thought of not only as a device for managing relations between the party top and the party on the ground but also as a tailor-made solution to accommodating difference in diverse societies. However, neither of these ways of viewing franchising explains why certain variants take root and others do not. Nor does the literature provide as complete an explanation as one might expect. It consists of two subfields: party organizations and party systems. Although intertwined, the two are analytically distinct. Only rarely do concepts such as brokerage party systems (see Johnston and Sharman, introduction and Chapter 15, this volume; and Carty, Chapter 2) or franchise party systems traverse both. Reflecting the relative ease with which they can be studied, the literature on party systems is better developed: how parties organize is not as well theorized as is how party systems develop or change.

As Ware (1996) points out, theories explaining how parties organize fall into three streams: electoral competition explanations, institutional explanations, and sociological explanations. The first regards party organizations – or, more typically, changes in party organization – as products of competitive dynamics. Not only Duverger (1954) but also Epstein (1967) and Kirchheimer (1966) maintain that changes in party organization result because parties in electoral competition imitate each other. Institutional explanations emphasize either the impact of state structure, electoral systems, or, more recently, election finance regimes and other forms of party law on party structure (or, in the case of Panebianco [1988], path dependency and the impact of early organizational forms). In contrast, sociological (or societal) explanations relate parties to broad stages of development and, in particular, to the resources available to them. Of the three, sociological explanations are the least persuasive. Although it is possible to relate clientelism to certain stages of economic development, parties are structures that are built through deliberate actions. Those who build them choose from available models or, in some instances, invent new ones (Aldrich 1995). Some form of agency is required. Sociological explanations help us understand settings in which parties emerge, the resources available to them, and the difficulties some encounter – but not the specific forms that parties take (Ware 1996).

In contrast, institutional explanations and explanations emphasizing party competition take us further. Parties organize around the electoral subdivisions of the state. Institutions matter because parties in liberal democracies are organizations engaged in electoral competition, whether for its own sake (in the case of vote-seeking parties), to seek certain policies, or to distribute and enjoy the spoils of office (Strøm 1990). However, how they do so depends not only on the resources available to them but also on the uses they make of them, how they respond to rules governing political competition, and how they solve the problems of enlisting participation and connecting different levels of organization. Of interest are not only electoral systems but also whether parties operate in unitary or federal and/or multilevel systems and in parliamentary or presidential systems. The parties literature focuses primarily on parties in unitary parliamentary systems. Today's universe is broader, but it has not been exploited to its full potential.

Institutions matter. If they did not, we would pay minimal attention to electoral systems or, more recently, election finance regimes and party law. Parties adapt to institutions because they help define the incentives that parties face when they contest elections. Only in party-state systems like the former Soviet-bloc countries have parties been strong enough to obliterate the impact of institutional structure. Whether a system is unitary, federal, and/or multilevel matters because it determines on how many levels parties can choose to compete. Unlike parties in Canada, parties in most countries contest two or more levels. In doing so, they have to figure out whether to organize separately for each level or, if they retain a unified structure, how to coordinate upper and lower echelons.

Presidentialism matters. Parties in presidential systems compete for a single indivisible office, and doing so encourages disparate forces to come together. Broader alliances improve the chances of finishing first. Moreover, presidential elections are single events, sometimes spread out over a short period if there is provision for a second ballot. Parties may find it useful to unite or to ally with others to maximize their prospects. However, once presidential elections are over, incentives to stay together can weaken or disappear. Staying together helps presidents get legislation approved, but, unlike in parliamentary systems, tenure in office does not depend on it (Samuels and Shugart 2010).

This suggests that there are relationships between types of political systems and the ways in which parties organize. It is no accident that our examples of parties with confederative structure include American parties, initially established in a federal and presidential system at a time when it was far more decentralized than is the case today, and European-level parties, operating in a multilevel system of governance that, at best, is partially integrated, with considerable power and fiscal weight remaining with the member states (despite the considerable powers of the European Commission in certain areas). Nor should it be surprising that Carty developed the franchise party while studying parties in a far-flung federation. His other examples include parties in Australia and Ireland: the former is federal but the latter is not. Australian parties operate in a country that is physically large but that lacks the strong regional tensions that Canadian parties encounter. Parliamentary systems can provide similar opportunities for parties that are cohesive but that want to vary local products to meet local needs and tastes. So can electoral systems that allow voters to focus on individual candidates. On the surface, Ireland is an outlier. So, too, is Israel, which Carty mentions. However, Ireland combines parish-pump politics and the single transferable vote – an electoral system that encourages competition within and between parties – with cohesive parties in Parliament. Franchise arrangements allow parties to reconcile the two.

Neither federalism nor presidentialism ensures that a given kind of party will appear. Parties are constructs that can be built in different ways. How they are built varies not only with time and place but also with party family. As we argue earlier, parties imitate each other, and initial organization shapes what comes later (Panebianco 1988). We mentioned that German parties are bounded hierarchies. This is not what we would have predicted if it was only institutions that mattered. Type of federalism and type of party matter as well: *Laender* governments are represented in the *Bundesrat,* which has an absolute veto over legislation affecting the *laender* and a suspensive veto over all other legislation. *Laender* elections are crucial because the

Bundesrat matters. If we add to this a party system that was initially deeply divided on religious and ideological grounds, and a mixed-member proportional electoral system that puts a premium on competition among party lists, it is not surprising that German parties are bounded hierarchies rather than franchise parties.

We cannot sustain general arguments on the basis of a handful of cases. There is enough here to warrant further investigation. Differently put, there is good reason to view the franchise party within a broader context and good reason, once we do, to investigate interconnections among formal institutions and forms of government.

Conclusion

One final question remains: Is there an ongoing tendency for parties to become more stratarchical and more like franchise parties? We can only offer a brief answer. Katz and Mair (1995) certainly thought that parties were becoming more stratarchical, and the diverse array of parties in which Carty and others have detected franchise-like features suggests as much. So does the very real difficulty that present-day parties experience in mobilizing and engaging prospective activists and supports. As Scarrow and Gezgor (2010) argue, parties draw more and more on fewer and fewer high-intensity supporters. In that many live busy lives, elements of slack will creep in. In most of Europe, except perhaps Scandinavia, the era of the mass party is past. However, this does not mean that all parties are franchise systems or that franchising is the best optic from which to view parties. This depends on what we want to know and what we want to do. Metaphors and optics like the franchise party or the brokerage party help because they bring key characteristics into sharp relief. However, systematic analysis requires classificatory schemes that differentiate and relate to other factors.

We still have to ask, "So what?" Carty (2004) argues that one reason to consider parties as franchise systems is that such parties allow a modicum of participation and control. Perhaps, but we also need parties that can balance demands for participation with effectiveness in government or opposition. Few do this as well as we might want. Nevertheless, most of us swear by Schattschneider's dictum, "No parties, no democracy" (Schattschneider 1942). How parties operate is an important piece of this puzzle.

Notes

1 Our use is different from that of Bardi and Mair (2008). Their focus is party systems: vertical divisions refer to party systems that are geographically distinct and that run

vertically in different parts of a country. Horizontal divisions refer to differences among party systems at different levels of government.

2 Stratarchy is, however, in the *Oxford English Dictionary,* which defines it as "the system of rule in army" and indicates that it is rare (*Oxford English Dictionary,* 2011).

3 The others were "the open accordion" to describe recruitment, "alliance of subcultures" to characterize the coalitional structure of the parties, and "multiple elites" to describe their leadership.

4 See Eldersveld (1964, 98–117, 378–408), "The Party Stratarchy" and "The Party as a Decisional System."

5 See, for example, Key (1964) and Ranney and Kendall (1956).

References

Aldrich, J.H. 1995. *Why Parties? The Origin and Transformation of Political Parties.* Chicago: University of Chicago Press. http://dx.doi.org/10.7208/chicago/9780226012773.001.0001.

Almond, G.A., and J.S. Coleman. 1960. *The Politics of the Developing Areas.* Princeton, NJ: Princeton University Press.

Almond, G.A., and G.B. Powell. 1966. *Comparative Politics: A Developmental Approach.* New York: Little Brown.

Amyot, C.G. 1981. *The Italian Communist Party: The Crisis of the Popular Front Strategy.* New York: St. Martins Press.

Bardi, L., and P. Mair. 2008. "The parameters of party systems." *Party Politics* 14 (2): 147–66. http://dx.doi.org/10.1177/1354068807085887.

Carty, R.K. 2002. "The politics of Tecumseh Corners: Canadian political parties as franchise organizations." *Canadian Journal of Political Science* 35 (4): 723–45. http://dx.doi.org/10.1017/S0008423902778402.

–. 2004. "Parties as franchise systems: The stratarchical organizational imperative." *Party Politics* 10 (1): 5–24. http://dx.doi.org/10.1177/1354068804039118.

Cotter, C.P. 1984. *Party Organizations and American Politics.* New York: Praeger.

Cotter, C.P., and B.C. Hennessy. 1964. *Politics without Power: The National Party Committees.* New York: Atherton Press.

Detterbeck, K., and C. Jeffery. 2009. "Rediscovering the region: Territorial politics and party organizations in Germany." In *Territorial Party Politics in Western Europe,* ed. W. Swenden and B. Maddens, 63–85. New York: Palgrave Macmillan.

Duverger, M. 1954. *Political Parties: Their Organization and Activity in the Modern State, with foreword by D.W. Brogan.* London: Methuen.

Eldersveld, S.J. 1964. *Political Parties: A Behavioral Analysis.* Chicago: Rand McNally.

Epstein, L.D. 1964. "A comparative study of Canadian parties." *American Political Science Review* 58 (1): 46–59. http://dx.doi.org/10.2307/1952754.

–. 1967. *Political Parties in Western Democracies.* New York: Praeger.

Hellman, S. 1988. *Italian Communism in Transition: The Rise and Fall of the Historic Compromise in Turin, 1975–1980.* New York: Oxford University Press.

Hirschman, A.O. 1970. *Exit, Voice, and Loyalty: Responses to Decline in Firms, Organizations, and States.* Cambridge, MA: Harvard University Press.

Hix, S., and C. Lord. 1997. *Political Parties in the European Union.* New York: St. Martin's Press.

Hopkin, J., and C. Paolucci. 1999. "The business firm model of party organization: Cases from Spain and Italy." *European Journal of Political Research* 35 (3): 307–39. http://dx.doi.org/10.1111/1475-6765.00451.

Hunt, R.N. 1970. *German Social Democracy, 1918–1933*. Chicago: Quadrangle Paperbacks.

Jenson, J., and G. Ross. 1984. *The View from Inside: A French Communist Cell in Crisis*. Berkeley: University of California Press.

Katz, R.S., and R. Kolodny. 1994. "Party organization as an empty vessel: Parties in American politics." In *How Parties Organize: Change and Adaption in Party Organizations in Western Europe*, ed. R.S. Katz and P. Mair, 23–51. London: Sage Publications. http://dx.doi.org/10.4135/9781446250570.n2.

Katz, R.S., and P. Mair 1993. "The evolution of party organizations in Europe: The three faces of party organization." *American Review of Politics* 14: 593–617.

–. 1994. *How Parties Organize: Change and Adaptation in Party Organizations in Western Democracies*. Thousand Oaks, CA: Sage.

–. 1995. "Changing models of party organization and party democracy: The emergence of the cartel party." *Party Politics* 1 (1): 5–28. http://dx.doi.org/10.1177/1354068895001001001.

Key, V.O. 1964. *Politics, Parties and Pressure Groups*. 5th ed. New York: Crowell.

Kirchheimer, Otto. 1966. "The transformation of Western European party systems." In *Political Parties and Political Development*, ed. J. LaPalombara and M. Weiner, 177–200. Princeton: Princeton University Press.

Kitschelt, H. 1988. "Left libertarian parties: Explaining innovation in competitive party systems." *World Politics* 40 (2): 194–234. http://dx.doi.org/10.2307/2010362.

Koole, R. 1996. "Cadre, catch-all or cartel? A comment on the notion of the cartel party." *Party Politics* 2 (4): 507–23. http://dx.doi.org/10.1177/1354068896002004004.

Kriegel, A. 1972. *The French Communists: Profile of a People*. Chicago: University of Chicago Press.

Lasswell, H.D., and A. Kaplan. 1950. *Power and Society*. New Haven: Yale University Press.

Levitsky, S. 2003. *Transforming Labor-Based Parties in Latin America: Argentine Peronism in Comparative Perspective*. New York: Cambridge University Press.

Michels, R. 1962. *Political Parties: A Sociological Study of the Oligarchical Tendencies of Modern Democracy, with an introduction by Seymour Martin Lipset*. New York: Free Press.

Panebianco, A. 1988. *Political Parties: Organization and Power*. New York: Cambridge University Press.

Poguntke, T. 1987. "New politics and party systems: The emergence of a new type of party?" *West European Politics* 10 (1): 76–88. http://dx.doi.org/10.1080/01402388708424615.

Ranney, A., and W. Kendall. 1956. *Democracy and the American Party System*. New York: Harcourt Brace.

Roth, G. 1984 [1963]. *The Social Democrats in Imperial Germany: A Study In Working-Class Isolation and National Integration*. Salem, NH: Ayer Co.

Samuels, D.J., and M.S. Shugart. 2010. *Presidents, Parties, and Prime Ministers: How the Separation of Powers Affects Party Organization and Behavior*. New York: Cambridge University Press. http://dx.doi.org/10.1017/CBO9780511780882.

Scarrow, S., and B. Gezgor. 2010. "Declining memberships, changing members? European political party members in a new era." *Party Politics* 16 (6): 823–43. http://dx.doi.org/10.1177/1354068809346078.

Schattschneider, E.E. 1942. *Party Government*. New York: Holt, Rinehart and Winston.

Shafer, B.E. 1983. *Quiet Revolution: The Struggle for the Democratic Party and the Shaping of Post-Reform Politics*. New York: Russell Sage Foundation.

Strøm, K. 1990. "A behavioral theory of competitive political parties." *American Journal of Political Science* 34 (2): 565-98.

Ware, A. 1996. *Political Parties and Party Systems*. Oxford: Oxford University Press.

5

Courting but Not Always Serving

Perverted Burkeanism and the Puzzle of Irish Parliamentary Cohesion

DAVID M. FARRELL, PETER MAIR, SÉIN Ó MUINEACHÁIN, AND MATTHEW WALL

Why is it that in some political systems legislators frequently vote against their own parties while in others such behaviour is very rare? Our starting point in addressing this topic is the work of legislative studies scholars who have theorized about the relationship between electoral system design and levels of cohesion in parliamentary parties (Bowler et al. 1999). The most comprehensive recent account of this subject is found in John Carey's notion of "competing principals" (Carey 2009, 17). Carey's approach is built upon the contention that all legislators in representative democracies are faced with a "structure of accountability" (Carey 2009, 14), which he discusses in terms of principals and agents. The accountability of an agent – in this case, a legislator – to a given principal, for instance, her/his party leadership or the voters in her/his constituency, is determined by the capacity of the principal to monitor the agent's behaviour and to consequently provide either rewards or sanctions for their actions.

Carey (2009, 17) argues that, where institutional design is such that "voters have the ability to reward and punish individual legislators directly," the structure of accountability will be one in which legislators are accountable to two separate principals: voters and party leaders. These competing principals can pull legislators in opposite directions. For instance, when legislation that involves the removal of a resource from a legislator's district is being considered, voters in that district may insist that their legislator oppose it. However, the same legislator's party leader may have a strong preference for the legislator to support the bill because it may be needed to implement a party's national-level policy (or it may have been agreed to gain concessions from a coalition partner in other areas). In such situations, when deciding how to vote, legislators are forced to choose between the desires of their competing principals.

Electoral system design has a significant role to play in determining the nature of the accountability structures encountered by legislators. At one extreme are closed list electoral systems in which the party leaders – or their proxies, party selection conventions – determine the electoral fate of parliamentary candidates by deciding on their ranking on the party list. Under such systems individual legislators are far more accountable to their party leaders than to the electorate. More open electoral systems lead to a situation in which, because they need to garner individualized support from voters, "legislators have reason to cultivate reputations distinct from their copartisans" (Carey 2009; note also Ames 1995; Hix 2004). One straightforward way to cultivate a distinct, and positive, local reputation is to vote against the locally unpopular party line. Carey's empirical examination of legislators' voting behaviour produces strong evidence to support the contention that open electoral systems encourage higher degrees of what he refers to as "legislative individualism" (Carey 2009, 160), in which legislators are more inclined to break with party ranks. This is manifested particularly in Carey's observation that legislatures elected by open list systems have lower roll call cohesion scores than do legislatures elected by closed list systems.

The Irish electoral system of single transferable vote (STV) proportional representation is about as open as an electoral system can be (Farrell and McAllister 2006). The incentives for personal vote chasing by legislators and parliamentary candidates that Carey and Shugart (1995; Shugart 2001) theorize as characteristic of open systems are at their most intense under STV, where each candidate competes for personal votes – that is, the candidate, not the party, is the object of electoral choice. As well as competing for individualized support with all other candidates in their district, many Irish politicians face competition from fellow party members. Moreover, under STV the mantra common to all proportional representation systems – that every vote counts – is taken to another level with the claim that every *preference* counts. It is hard to conceive of any other electoral system that could produce greater potential for legislators to be pulled in opposing directions by competing principals. Under STV the voter looms large in the life of a legislator, and, if anything, the party leadership might be expected to come a poor second. In return, the candidate looms large in the calculus of the voter: 58.7 percent of Irish voters in the 2002 Irish National Election Study cited the candidate as the most important factor in their first preference vote decision (Marsh 2007). Such a system appears to offer few incentives for party loyalty in legislative behaviour.

The Irish case, therefore, might be seen as providing the most likely case for testing Carey's competing principals theory: the quintessentially open electoral system of STV should produce ideal conditions for "legislative individualism." Simply put, Irish legislators, or *Teachtaí Dála* (TDs), should be especially prone to breaking party ranks. And yet the evidence of Irish legislative individualism fails to provide much support for this intuition – quite the reverse. As the leading authority on the parliamentary behaviour of TDs notes: "if anything, parliamentary party cohesion is even higher in Ireland than the European average" (Gallagher 2010, 202).

This leaves us with a paradox. Despite having one of the most open electoral systems in the world, Ireland's political class is among the most disciplined in Europe. As we shall see, the solution to this paradox lies in the separate worlds in which TDs and the party elites operate. Both operate on stratarchical lines – a style that is at the heart of the franchise model originally set out by Carty (2004) and that is reviewed by Wolinetz (Chapter 4, this volume).

We start by analyzing the extent of party rebellions in recent Irish history, confirming just how few cases there have been. We then examine how the parties enforce legislative discipline. This is followed by an analysis of a recent survey of TDs, which enables us to examine how legislators conceive of their representative role and how this enables them to maintain a balance between the competing principals of loyalty to voters and loyalty to party leadership. We conclude by offering some solutions to the aforementioned paradox – solutions that lend support to Carty's franchise party model.

The Irish Tradition of Parliamentary Party Discipline

Party discipline in Irish political parties has its roots in the strict discipline that Charles Stewart Parnell introduced in the Irish Parliamentary Party in the British House of Commons in 1885 – probably one of the first instances of disciplined parliamentary parties in the world (Farrell 1973). Party discipline quickly became established as a practice of party-affiliated TDs' behaviour following Irish independence in the 1920s (O'Halpin 1997). Discipline is enforced with high penalties for those who do not follow the party line, with the ultimate sanction being expulsion from the parliamentary party.

TABLE 5.1

TDs who have lost or resigned the party whip in Ireland, 1981–2010, by party, manner of whip loss, and readmission

		1980s	1990s	2000s	Total
Party	FF	7	8	9	24
	FG	8	2	0	10
	Lab	5	6	1	12
	Other	0	8	0	8
	Total	*20*	*24*	*10*	*54*
Way whip lost	Imposed	14	8	5	27
	Resigned	6	16	5	27
Gov/Opp	Government	12	13	9	34
	Opposition	8	11	1	20
Readmission	Yes	8	11	6	25
	No	12	13	4	29

Notes: Where a TD was readmitted after losing the whip and then lost the whip on a later occasion, this is counted as two separate instances. "Other" party category includes the Workers Party and the Progressive Democrats (both now defunct).

Source: Irish Times Historical Archive.

Just as in the UK House of Commons, the party officers charged with enforcing party discipline are known as the party whips (MacCárthaigh 2005). However, unlike the British case, where parties are prepared to make allowances for rebellious MPs for the sake of wider party unity (Cowley and Stuart 2003), in Ireland the rule is pretty simple and straightforward: rebellion usually means whip removal. There are very few cases of a TD who votes against the party being allowed to hold onto the party whip; indeed, the total number of cases in recent years are virtually in single figures, and these have typically taken place in exceptional political circumstances. The data reported in Table 5.1 cover the entire population of instances of Irish parliamentary party rebellion over the past thirty years.

There are just fifty-four TDs who lost the whip or resigned it voluntarily as a result of breaking with the party line in the entire period studied, representing a meagre 3.3 percent of the total number of TDs elected in that time frame.[1] There is an even split between voluntary resignation and expulsion from the parliamentary party. Overall, 63 percent of TDs who lost or resigned the whip were government deputies, while 37 percent were in opposition. This pattern is arguably what one would expect in a political system characterized by executive dominance: the voting behaviour of members of governing parties is far more consequential for voters and, hence, subject to greater scrutiny than the voting behaviour of opposition legislators.

Slightly more than half of our rebels (54 percent) were not readmitted to their original party. However, many TDs resigned the party whip and joined another party or formed a new party. There are twelve cases in which those who lost the party whip went on to join or form a new party. After this number is discounted we can see that only seventeen TDs, just under 32 percent of all those who lost or resigned their party whip, were not subsequently readmitted to any parliamentary party. Readmission to the parliamentary party is not a given following expulsion or resignation: TDs are required to reapply.

What these trends show is that Irish legislators are loyal followers of their parliamentary party leaderships, that voting cohesion is very high, and that the few cases of rebellion that occur are dealt with swiftly and summarily. Furthermore, the political system appears to be remarkably adept at avoiding situations in which TDs resign/lose the party whip due to a local issue. It may be the case that TDs are kept in line simply through the tendency of parties to remove the whip from all defectors. However, for this to be a credible explanation we have to see what happened to the subsequent political careers of those TDs who lost the whip.

What Are the Consequences of Losing the Whip?

To assess the electoral fate of parliamentary rebels we focus here on the electoral performances of those forty-one TDs who lost the whip and contested a subsequent election. We do so by calculating each TD's average share of the constituency vote in all elections before and after she lost the whip. We then subtract their pre-loss average from their post-loss average. Negative scores indicate that TDs won fewer votes in elections after losing the whip than they had before, while positive scores indicate the opposite. In Table 5.2 the differences between post-loss and pre-loss electoral performance are presented, and subcategories in which these differences were substantial are reported.

The results suggest that whip loss is not generally related to *any* discernible change in overall electoral performance. In fact, the average difference between pre- and post-whip-loss vote shares is just 0.86 percent of the constituency vote. We also performed a paired t-test and found that there is no statistically significant difference between the two vote shares (p-value = .1862).

TABLE 5.2
Percentage difference between pre-whip loss and post-whip loss electoral performance

	% difference in share of vote post-whip loss	*N*
All cases	−0.86	41
Party		
Fianna Fáil	−1.84*	15
Fine Gael	−4.72*	7
Government status		
Government	−1.65*	24
Readmitted?		
Not readmitted	−1.89*	20
Reason for loss		
Moral policy	−6.35***	5
Internal candidate selection dispute	−7.32**	2
Criticism of party leader	+4.36	2

* *p*-value < .1, ***p*-value < .05, ****p*-value < .01
Source: Irish Times Historical Archive.

When we disaggregate our data we can see that the circumstances of the whip loss matter. Table 5.2 shows that the support of one of the larger parties, and particularly of Fine Gael, can be crucial in determining one's chances of electoral success. Also, members of the larger parties, members of governing parties, and members not readmitted to the party all fare somewhat worse at the polls after having lost the whip than they did before.

Generally the electoral consequences of losing the party whip would seem to be minimal. But what about the subsequent career paths of those TDs who lost the party whip? Party leaderships control the career progress of TDs far more than they control the behaviour of the electorate. Therefore we may anticipate that the real sanction of whip loss will be the subsequent inability of TDs to win promotion, whether that involves being appointed to ministerial office, developing a political career in the European Union, or being compensated for loss of a Dáil seat by being appointed/elected to the Seanad, the upper house. Promotional paths are fully or partly controlled by party leaderships, and we would therefore expect them to be closed off to TDs who have lost the whip.

An examination of our fifty-four cases reveals that twenty (37 percent) went on to have subsequent careers beyond the backbenches, a figure that implies that the loss of the party whip meant the end of political career advancement for the remaining thirty-four (63 percent). The trends vary somewhat among the parties. Of the TDs who defected from the party whip when their party was in government, 75 percent did not enjoy career advancement, whereas this figure drops substantially for TDs who lost the whip while their party was in opposition. Party norms also seem to be a factor. As was the case with electoral consequences, rebels from larger parties did not do well in terms of career advancement, while members of smaller parties did.

In short, there are mixed messages regarding the consequences that TDs may experience if they dare to vote against the party whip. Generally they do not suffer electorally, though the reasons they resigned the whip or their party affiliation do have some bearing on how they fare electorally after the event. On the whole it would appear that the electorate neither rewards nor punishes dissent from their TDs. But party leaderships are a different matter. TDs' careers are affected, especially in the case of TDs from government or larger parties. However, some do enjoy subsequent promotion, indicating that legislative rebellion is not necessarily terminal for a TD's political career. As such, we cannot rely solely on the "tough consequences" justification to explain the low incidence of parliamentary rebellion in Ireland. We therefore turn to the views that TDs themselves take of their role in the Dáil.

Split Personalities?

A recent survey of TDs in the 2007–11 Dáil affords us an opportunity to examine possible explanations for the paradoxically high levels of parliamentary party voting discipline in Ireland.[2] Questions in the survey sought to assess the tensions between constituency-based and party-based or national representative roles. Table 5.3 reports the results of an item on the survey that required TDs to produce a set of transitive rankings of the various groups that they might represent. The "all-voters-in-the-constituency" option dramatically outperforms any of the others, receiving more than four times as many first preference rankings as the next highest placed option, which was also a constituency-based conception of representation. The supposed "competing principal" of TDs – differences between parties – was de-emphasized: party representation was the second lowest-rated representative role in the survey.

TABLE 5.3
Aggregate rankings by TDs of groups that TDs should "primarily represent"

Group	Average rank of importance	Number of number "1" rankings	Number of responses
All voters in the constituency	1.56	49	71
All those in the constituency who voted for the TD	2.77	11	62
All those in the constituency who voted for the TD's party	3.36	3	60
All voters in the country	3.37	10	64
All those in the country who voted for the TD's party	4.03	2	60
Members of a particular social group	4.89	3	59

Question wording: "There are different opinions about which people a TD should primarily represent. What is your opinion? Please rank all of the options below in importance: mark the most important as 1, the next most important as 2 and so on from 1 to 6. Note that some TDs gave multiple "1 rankings, which were counted in this analysis.
Source: TD survey 2010.

Given the strong constituency orientation expressed by TDs, the extent of observed legislative discipline in Ireland is remarkable. To investigate this further, a question in the survey presented respondents with the following dilemma: "How should a TD vote in parliament if there is a conflict of opinion between the party's supporters in the constituency and the party?" This survey question asks respondents to imagine a situation of competing principals. In such a case voting with the party line is likely to be a result of party discipline enforced by the party leadership. The information captured by TDs' responses to this question gives us an idea of the extent to which TDs choose the norms of party loyalty or legislative individualism in interpreting how to respond to the conflicting demands of their competing principals (Bowler and Farrell 1999).

The results indicate that a large majority of TDs feel that the party line should be followed: out of seventy TDs who responded to this item fifty-six (80 percent) indicated that the TD should vote according to the "party's opinion." We refer to these as *party loyalists*. Fourteen TDs (20 percent) responded that the TD should vote in line with the "constituency voters'" opinion. We refer to these as *legislative individualists*. While the legislative individualists are a minority grouping, their size is far greater than we would anticipate given the remarkably low levels of actual party indiscipline involved. This seems to indicate a considerable latent capacity for legislative indiscipline among Irish parliamentarians.

An analysis of the two groups' perceptions of the TD's representative role reveals that there is little difference between them. One might logically expect that legislative individualist TDs would be far more constituency-oriented generally than party loyalists; however, this is not the case, though there are some interesting differences between the groups in terms of the type of competition that they face in their constituency, their personal attributes, and their political careers. Table 5.4 presents the scores of each group in areas where they were found to differ from each other.

Intra-party pressures and electoral success both help to explain why some TDs purport to be legislative individualists. For all respondents we measured the number of co-partisans against whom they competed in their constituency in the 2007 general election and found that, on average, legislative individualists faced more opponents from their own party than did party loyalists. We also measured the electoral marginality of each respondent (the percentage of constituency quota received in first preference votes by the TD in the 2007 election). As we can see in Table 5.4, legislative individualists were typically more marginal than were their party loyalist colleagues, which suggests that those in marginal seats probably face stronger incentives to be responsive to their constituents. This finding, along with that on intra-party competition, suggests that the nature of the constituency-level electoral competition faced by TDs has a bearing on their inclinations with regard to which principal they should prefer.

In terms of TDs' characteristics, we found that the party loyalist group contains considerably more experienced TDs (with an average of 5.4 years more experience) than the legislative individualists. We would expect that those who have not profited from party appointments have fewer incentives to be party loyalists. To do this we created two measures. The first ascertained whether the TD held a position in the government, and the second measured whether the TD held any official position, such as committee chair or party leader. The difference between the two groups is statistically significant: unsurprisingly, there are more backbenchers among the legislative individualists. This tallies with what we would expect. TDs that do not owe offices they hold to the party leadership are likely to be more responsive to their constituents, something that is underlined by the fact that none of the ministerial office holders surveyed considered themselves legislative individualists.[3]

TABLE 5.4
Group averages and results of statistical tests for differences across groups comparing party loyalists to constituency loyalists

Variable	Average for party loyalists	Average for legislative individualists	Statistically significant difference?[1]
Constituency/electoral factors			
Intra-party competition	1.1	1.5	Yes, with 90% confidence
Electoral marginality	82.2%	70.8%	Yes, with 95% confidence
TDs' characteristics			
Experience (number of years in Dáil)	14.3	8.9	Yes, with 95% confidence
% male	78.6% (44/56)	92.3% (12/13)[2]	No
TDs' career status			
% position – backbencher	28.6% (16/56)	92.3% (12/13)	Yes, with 99% confidence
% position – executive	14.2% (8/56)	0.0% (0/13)	No

1 The significance test employed varies according to the nature of the variable being investigated. For continuous variables, *t*-tests were employed to test the hypothesis of a statistically significant difference between the two groups: experience and electoral success were analyzed using this approach. Ordinal variables were analyzed using the two-sample Wilcoxon rank-sum (Mann–Whitney) test: intra-party competition, and education were analyzed using this technique. The categorical variables (% male, % position – executive, % position – backbencher) were analyzed using chi-square and Fisher exact tests.

2 While 14 respondents gave the constituency loyalist response to the TDs' dilemma question, one of these tore the identifying number from their survey, and we were therefore unable to ascertain their gender, party, etc. Thus, for these variables, the individualist group has an *n* of 13.

Source: TD survey 2010.

Separate Worlds?

If the problem of legislative discipline can be cast in principal-agent terms, as Carey (2009) suggests, then two possible solutions to the puzzle of Irish party discipline can be suggested. The first is that the agent (in this case an individual TD) is able to respond to the competing demands of the party principal in the Dáil and to the constituency principal at home through obfuscation and shirking. That is, she tells one principal one thing and the other something else and assumes that nobody will check whether the two stories actually tally. This, however, is implausible. Not only is Ireland a small country in which, most famously, everybody knows everybody else and the parish pump dominates, thereby making it unlikely that two competing stories could survive for long, but there is also an increasing amount of very effective media scrutiny, and a large set of fairly rapacious political reporters who would quickly expose any attempt by TDs to deliberately pull the wool over the eyes of their party leader or their constituents. As such, obfuscation or deceit on the part of the TD is unlikely to work – at least beyond the short term.

The second and more plausible solution, and one that also might be used to question Carey's initial assumptions, is that, while there are two principals and just one agent, the two principals are not in fact in competition; rather, they exist in separate spheres, in which the terms of reference of the one are disconnected from those of the other. If the evaluations of candidates as individuals are largely divorced from their voting behaviour in Parliament then it becomes possible for the TD to satisfy both principals simultaneously. It is simply up to her, as agent, to find the time and organizational resources to respond to each.

The notion of separate spheres is at the heart of the franchise party model (see Wolinetz, Chapter 4, this volume), in which the lower level (TDs in this instance) can operate with substantial autonomy, in return for which the power at the centre determines strategy and tactics, policies and positions, and how the party presents itself on the national stage.

An argument for separate spheres has obvious traction in the Irish case (Carty 1981). On the one hand, there is clearly a national sphere in which parties as national organizations compete with one another at election time, publishing lengthy election manifestos, engaging in party leaders' debates on television, and promoting a national policy message and a national policy appeal. The differences between the parties competing at this level are not very pronounced, of course, and the policies of the mainstream parties usually come very close to one another in broad terms while differing in details or precise priorities. On the other hand, there is also competition in the local or constituency sphere, which is the second sphere that concerns us. Here also the competition revolves around valence issues, and even when policy differences between the parties or the candidates do become important, these are more likely to revolve around local concerns rather than around anything that might connect to the national sphere of competition. This is particularly so when the competition is between candidates of the same party since this will be depoliticized by definition.

In both of these spheres, and for the purposes of both principals, the TD is of course an agent. But since the spheres rarely connect – at least in policy terms – there need be no competition or trade-off between them. To work loyally as an agent for the constituency the TD must look after local representative needs and facilitate relations between local citizens and the state authorities. She must also seek to win public funding for local projects and to ensure that public benefits accrue to the constituency. Most of this work is particularistic and apolitical, in which, to recall the title of the classic study of localism by the late Basil Chubb (1963), the TD spends her local agency time "going about persecuting civil servants." Irish legislators face a huge volume of demands to act as brokers between citizen and state, and, according to Gallagher and Komito (2009), some 21 percent of the voting age population in Ireland have reported personally contacting a sitting TD between 1997 and 2002. Marsh (2007, 509) points out that responsiveness to such demands is essential to the electoral fortunes of individual TDs. He found that the selection of first choice candidates among Irish voters is dominated by evaluations of the candidate's individual attributes – that is, their reputation for being personally helpful to voters and active workers in the local area. Individual policy stances taken by candidates, however, are of only marginal significance to voters.

Table 5.5 reports the responses of TDs to two questions concerning their division of working time between "constituency-based," "Parliament-based," and "other" work. Their responses illustrate that, in terms of the way that they divide up their working week, the average Irish parliamentarian is about as far away as one can get from the ideals of (Dublin-born) Edmund Burke. While Burke pointed out to his constituents that "I could hardly serve you as I have done, and court you too" (Bromwich 2000, 217), Irish TDs in the 2007–11 Dáil appear to prioritize localized courtship over national-level political activity. Their self-reported estimates of how they divide their working time indicate that TDs spend considerably more time, on average, attending to constituency matters than to parliamentary work.

TABLE 5.5

TDs' responses when asked to estimate the percentage of their working week dedicated to constituency, parliamentary, and "other" activities

	Average % of workload spent dealing with activity	Total number of responses
Constituency-based work	53	74
Parliament-based work	38	74
Other activities	9	74

Source: TD survey 2010.

In many ways this is not surprising and is consistent with the evidence as described above.

To work loyally as an agent for the party principal, on the other hand, the TD must accept party discipline and obey the whips when instructed to go one way or another in the voting lobbies. But precisely because the two spheres are separated, the TD can be expected to face few if any problems in reconciling these roles. Since the policy choices faced in the Dáil lobbies usually pertain to national policies and will not impinge on local preferences, and since the local electorates have not been mobilized around national policies, any mandate received by the local TD is unlikely to have any relevance for these choices.

Following this reasoning and assuming that the two worlds do not connect it is then unsurprising that we see such high levels of cohesion and discipline in the Dáil: the existence of a detached local sphere ensures that the TD in the Dáil is unconstrained by a local constituency mandate. Basically, such a mandate does not exist, and the TD is effectively free to do exactly as she wishes within the national sphere, provided that she puts in long hours on the ground in her constituency. This also means that there is nothing to prevent the TD from following the party line and, thereby, gaining advancement. Rather than having two principals in the same sphere, which would be a problem, she has instead one principal in each of two spheres. Given enough time and energy the TD as agent can happily serve both.

That said, there are two points at which the worlds do connect. The first occurs when national policy has obviously unfavourable local repercussions, as, for example, when a party commits itself to reducing or reorganizing the resources available to the health sector at the national level, and when this spills down to a local hospital closure or to the transfer of hospital services to another constituency. In these circumstances principals clearly clash, and those TDs who have strong incentives to be attentive to their constituencies – and particularly those who have not been preferred in terms of ministerial/frontbench appointment by their party – may defect. The second point at which the spheres may collide occurs at the candidate nomination stage, when the party leadership exercises its right to determine the number of party candidates to run in the constituency and when this decision may work against the personal interest of a sitting or aspirant TD (see also Marsh 2000). In this case, however, the clash is not between competing principals since the voters are largely uninvolved at this stage but, rather, between the national principal and the agent who fears for the survival of her agency.

Conclusion

Irish politicians are at one and the same time excessively voter-oriented and excessively loyal to their party leaderships. Unlike their counterparts in other systems in which district-related issues can matter, there are very few instances in which Irish legislators rebel, and the few cases that do occur are dealt with ruthlessly by the party leaderships. Ireland therefore offers an important exception to the competing principals theory proposed by John Carey (2009), while also offering an important corrective to those party elites who steer clear of the STV electoral system on the grounds that it would make their lives as political leaders impossible. Indeed, in terms of party discipline and cohesion, Irish party leaders may have had it more easy than most.

However, this does not come without a cost. As long as the Irish TD takes as a major point of reference the local constituency, and as long as she continues to emphasize her role as a broker between individual citizens and the state apparatus, the party leaders in the Dáil will continue to have a relatively free hand in determining policy. This will certainly make their lives easier, but it comes at the huge cost of creating a substantial deficit in accountability and oversight, two of the functions that the legislature as a whole is expected to perform. Irish TDs are notoriously active and busy representatives, accessible to their constituents, and known personally to many of their voters. But precisely because their energies are channelled in this direction they are often passive as legislators and deferential as both backbenchers and oppositions. Within the Dáil, in other words, there is little sense of accountability or control, and there are very few real checks on executive autonomy (MacCárthaigh 2005).

The result is that, despite the existence of a relatively proportional electoral system and despite an institutional structure that is remarkably consensual in design, the practice of government in Ireland has become pronouncedly majoritarian, leading to the development of an executive, unchecked by Parliament, that has been allowed to fall far too easily under the influence of special interests and lobbyists. It is clearly much too farfetched to suggest that Ireland's ongoing economic crisis was the result of the localism and clientelism amplified by the STV electoral system or that electoral reform would therefore be the panacea for Ireland's present difficulties. On the other hand, by encouraging the Irish TD to focus on representation at the local level while remaining deferential to the leadership in the Dáil, the electoral system has helped to undermine any real sense of parliamentary accountability and has thereby enabled the government to have a freer hand than was or is desirable. As the present economic crisis takes its toll, it might be argued that effective local representation has come with a heavy national cost.

Notes

The authors' names are in alphabetical order. The data referred to in this chapter are from the Joint Committee on the Constitution's survey of Dáil deputies (Ireland, Joint Committee on the Constitution, 2010): we are grateful to the secretariat of the Joint Committee for granting us access to the data.

1 We allow each TD from each Dáil to be the basis of the analysis (not including the Ceann Comhairle, or speaker of the Dáil). There are ten Dálaí in the period covered by our analysis, leading to the following sets of TD numbers: 21st Dáil (1977), 147 (we include from January 1, 1981); 22nd Dáil (1981), 165; 23rd Dáil (February 1982), 165; 24th Dáil (November 1982), 165; 25th Dáil (1987), 165; 26th Dáil (1989), 165; 27th Dáil (1992), 165; 28th Dáil (1997), 165; 29th Dáil (2002), 165; 30th Dáil (2007), 165. This gives us a total of 1,632 TDs. Then, we take account of by-elections throughout this period, of which there have been twenty-three, leaving us with a grand total of 1,655 TDs in the period under examination. This gives a percentage of $^{54}/_{1,655}$ = 3.26 percent.

2 The survey of members of the Dáil was carried out as part of the Joint Committee on the Constitution's review of the Irish electoral system, which took place between September 2009 and July 2010. The survey was designed primarily to bring quantitative evidence to bear on the issue of the working practices of TDs and their opinions on the STV electoral system (Ireland, Joint Committee on the Constitution, 2010). The survey was implemented between October 2009 and January 2010. The response rate was 45.4 percent, with seventy-five of the 165 members contacted responding to at least some of the questions posed. A confidentiality agreement with the committee means that party breakdowns of responses cannot be provided.

3 It is worth noting that there were no statistically significant differences between the parties in terms of portions of constituency and party loyalists (this question was not asked of Independent TDs).

References

Ames, B. 1995. "Electoral strategy under open list proportional representation." *American Journal of Political Science* 39 (2): 406–33. http://dx.doi.org/10.2307/2111619.

Bowler, S., and D. Farrell. 1999. "Parties and party discipline within the European Parliament: A norms-based approach." In *Party Discipline and Parliamentary Government*, ed. S. Bowler, D. Farrell, and R. Katz, 208–22. Columbus: Ohio State University Press.

Bowler, S., D. Farrell, and R. Katz, eds. 1999. *Party Discipline and Parliamentary Government.* Columbus: Ohio State University Press.

Bromwich, D., ed. 2000. *On Empire, Liberty and Reform: Speeches and Letters of Edmund Burke.* New Haven: Yale University Press.

Carey, J. 2009. *Legislative Voting and Accountability*. Cambridge: Cambridge University Press.

Carey, J., and M. Shugart. 1995. "Incentives to cultivate a personal vote: A rank ordering of electoral formulas." *Electoral Studies* 14 (4): 417–39. http://dx.doi.org/10.1016/0261-3794(94)00035-2.

Carty, R.K. 1981. *Party and Parish Pump: Electoral Politics in Ireland*. Waterloo, ON: Wilfrid Laurier University Press.

–. 2004. "Parties as franchise systems: The stratarchical organizational imperative." *Party Politics* 10 (1): 5–24. http://dx.doi.org/10.1177/1354068804039118.

Chubb, B. 1963. "Going about persecuting civil servants: The role of the Irish parliamentary representative." *Political Studies* 11 (3): 272–86. http://dx.doi.org/10.1111/j.1467-9248.1963.tb00880.x.

Cowley, P., and M. Stuart. 2003. "In place of strife? The PLP in government, 1997–2001." *Political Studies* 51 (2): 315–31. http://dx.doi.org/10.1111/1467-9248.00426.

Farrell, B., ed. 1973. *The Irish Parliamentary Tradition*. Dublin: Gill and Macmillan.

Farrell, D., and I. McAllister. 2006. *The Australian Electoral System: Origins, Variations and Consequences*. Sydney: University of New South Wales Press.

Gallagher, M. 2010. "The Oireachtas: President and parliament." In *Politics in the Republic of Ireland*, 5th ed., ed. J. Coakley and M. Gallagher, 198–229. London: Routledge.

Gallagher, M., and L. Komito. 2009. "The constituency role of Dáil Deputies." In *Politics in the Republic of Ireland*, 5th ed., ed. J. Coakley and M. Gallagher, 230–62. London: Routledge.

Hix, S. 2004. "Electoral institutions and legislative behaviour: Explaining voting defections in the European parliament." *World Politics* 56 (2): 194–223. http://dx.doi.org/10.1353/wp.2004.0012.

Ireland, Joint Committee on the Constitution. 2010. *Results of Survey of Members of Both Houses of the Oireachtas: The Electoral System, Representative Role of TDs and Proposals for Change*. Dublin: Stationery Office.

MacCárthaigh, M. 2005. *Accountability in Irish Parliamentary Politics*. Dublin: Institute of Public Administration.

Marsh, M. 2000. "Candidate centred but party wrapped: Campaigning in Ireland under STV." In *Elections in Australia, Ireland, and Malta under the Single Transferable Vote: Reflections on an Embedded Institution*, ed. S. Bowler and B. Grofman, 114–30. Ann Arbor: University of Michigan Press.

–. 2007. "Candidates or parties? Objects of electoral choice in Ireland." *Party Politics* 13 (4): 500–27. http://dx.doi.org/10.1177/1354068807075944.

O'Halpin, E. 1997. "Parliamentary party discipline and tactics: The Fianna Fáil archives, 1926–32." *Irish Historical Studies* 30 (120): 581–90.

Shugart, M. 2001. "Electoral 'efficiency' and the move to mixed-member systems." *Electoral Studies* 20 (2): 173–93. http://dx.doi.org/10.1016/S0261-3794(00)00007-X.

6

Parties, Politicians, and Parliaments

The Impact of Intra-Party Democracy on Party Unity

REUVEN Y. HAZAN AND GIDEON RAHAT

Modern representative government has become party government, for good and for bad. Thus the basic precondition for the establishment, survival, and functioning of governments depends on the ability of the political parties to coordinate the behaviour of their elected representatives. The existence of noticeably "unified" parties is central to the theory and practice of democracy in general, and to parliamentary democracy in particular.

However, according to Bowler, Farrell, and Katz (1999), because this "hidden assumption" has reached normative status for a variety of scholars, its study is relatively underdeveloped. Scholars have good reason to stop treating parties as monolithic, unitary actors, for they evidently are not. This is particularly the case for those conducting research on intra- rather than on inter-party democracy. As Laver and Shepsle (1999, 24) declare: "We need a model of intra-party politics before we can develop a realistic model of interparty competition." Duverger (1954, 353) argues that representatives receive a double mandate: "Before being chosen by his electors the deputy is chosen by the party ... The importance of each varies according to the country and the parties; on the whole the party mandate seems to carry more weight than that of the electors."

This chapter addresses the relationship between intra-party democracy, which we define as the democratization of party selectorates in candidate selection, and party unity. Democratization of the party selectorate implies the widening of the body that selects the candidates who will subsequently become the party's candidates in general elections (Hazan 2002; Hazan and Rahat 2010; Rahat and Hazan 2006). Our focus is on the adoption of relatively inclusive selectorates, such as party members and supporters – more commonly known as (party) primaries – for selecting party candidates for the legislature. We argue that particular constraints are placed on the candidates based on the distinctive priorities of each selectorate. In other words, different selectorate priorities produce different candidates in terms of demography, stands, and behaviour. The main distinction here is between personal, candidate-centred responsiveness and a more collective, party-centred type of responsiveness. Best and Cotta (2000, 11) express this most appropriately: "Selectorates select candidates according to the result of complex choices considering the probable value of the contender's resources for electoral success, their ideological fit with and their practical function for the selectorates themselves and their likely loyalty, that is, their expected obedience to the implicit and explicit expectations of the selectors after becoming a parliamentary actor."

We look at party unity in terms of the party in Parliament. While parties are expected to present a coherent ideological image, party unity may result from the fact that party representatives enter Parliament with shared common policy orientations and thus behave cohesively, or it may result from the efforts of the party to overcome internal divisions and maintain policy consistency by imposing party discipline in order to coerce its representatives to vote in concert (Hazan 2003). Party unity, as it is discussed here, refers to the consistency with which party representatives vote as a bloc on the floor of Parliament.

The next part of this chapter argues that increasing intra-party democracy – an empirical trend in general and a particular feature of the "brokerage" party (Cross and Katz 2013; Carty, Chapter 1, this volume; Wolinetz, Chapter 4) – creates the problem of maintaining party unity. It explains that (s)elected representatives from parties that use inclusive selectorates are expected to behave more independently because of their need to be responsive to non-party actors (mass media, campaign professionals, heads of interest groups, and financial backers) who can help them get re-selected. The subsequent part presents four solutions to the problem of maintaining unity while using an inclusive selectorate. These are: (1) also involving more exclusive selectorates in the selection process; (2) sustaining a situation in which rhetoric is individualized but behaviour is still cohesive; (3) using patronage (when in government) and reforms (when in opposition) to maintain control over candidates; and (4) dividing functions (i.e., the members select, the party makes policy). In short, this chapter, as many others in this volume, addresses the theme of party unity. It posits that democracy within parties influences the effectiveness of parties in Parliament. And it asks if there might be a way to alleviate or even to solve this problem.

The Problem: Party Unity and Democracy within Parties

Bowler (2000) argues that the best explanation of party unity lies in nomination procedures in general and in who does the nominating in particular. We thus assume that the behaviour of elected representatives is significantly influenced by their desire to be re-selected, and in order to fulfill this goal, the agents – the party representatives – will try to satisfy their principals. One central – if not *the* most important – principal is the party selectorate. If party unity has a positive effect on re-selection, we expect the representatives to focus on party-centred responsiveness and to exhibit high levels of party unity. If, however, more individualistic behaviour is valued in order to be re-selected, then we expect the representatives to engage in candidate-centred responsiveness, which will lead to lower levels of party unity.

There are many actors towards whom politicians can, or should, demonstrate responsiveness. The notion of responsiveness is, indeed, based on a set of relationships between the people and their politicians, but one must take into account the fact that such relationships do not exist in isolation. There are additional important actors who must be considered. The main one is the political party, which we argue not only has a significant effect on politicians' behaviour but also can open or close the door to non-party actors who wish to play a role in the political game.

The party, as a collective, expects its candidates to work in concert. After all, this is the logic behind establishing a permanent organization. Candidate selection methods affect the balance of influence between party and non-party actors on the selection process, thereby affecting party unity. Different candidate selection methods will produce different groups of selectors to whom the politicians must be responsive, and they will either enhance or hamper the ability of the party to maintain its unity.

It should be stressed that the issue here is greater or lesser party unity. We expect parties with any selectorate, no matter how wide, to vote in a united manner across most issues. The reason is that the party "brand" name would lose any meaning if this were not the case. After all, in the eyes of the voters, a politician's belonging to a particular party leads to an identification with a set of specific stands and the expectation that the politician will vote together with fellow party representatives on most issues.

When the selectorate is highly exclusive – a party leader or the party elite – the main principal of the candidate in terms of candidate selection is partisan. That is, there is a single, cohesive intra-party selectorate that must be satisfied by the candidate's performance in order to ensure re-selection. In the case of a party leader, this selectorate is not merely partisan, it is the party ("I am the party"). In cases in which an elite is the selectorate – be it a nomination committee or a less formal group of leaders – it is very likely that the selected team represents, as a whole, the different groupings, camps, and wings that co-exist within the party. Thus, it is a more pluralistic game but one that is still contained within the party. Even when we get more inclusive, allowing party delegates to make the selection, we are still dealing with a partisan game. That is, while the party activists who play the main role in candidate selection may bring their affiliation (interest group or other) into the game, they are still part of a selected group, no more than a few thousand at most, and they are together a rather cohesive partisan whole. In addition, up to this level of inclusiveness, candidates can address their selectors, or at least a substantial number of them, directly, without the need for mediation.

Once we deal with thousands of party members (party primaries) or supporters, the game changes significantly.[1] The selectorate becomes a dispersed, atomistic, largely inactive and not well-informed crowd. In order to reach it, to capture its attention, candidates need to distinguish themselves from their fellow competitors. Unlike the case in which selection is strictly an intra-party matter, here the candidates need to send an explicit "public" message, one that will explain why they are better than their competitors even though they belong to the same party, adhere to the same ideology, and speak in the name of similar interests.

In order to successfully spread the word to the large, dispersed crowd, candidates require the assistance of mediators. While modern democracy is largely about politicians who are responsive to the people, this responsiveness can be mediated by either party or non-party actors. We argue that legislative unity is likely to be influenced by the way politicians respond to different selectorates: it is likely to be higher when they respond to party actors and lower when non-party mediators are involved. Facing a large and fluid selectorate, politicians will be responsive to those who can supply the resources, votes, and access to such a wide selectorate, and they will likely focus on at least four kinds of non-party mediators who can facilitate their link with the latter (Table 6.1): (1) the mass media, which supplies the candidates with an immediate and wide audience; (2) campaign professionals,

TABLE 6.1
Non-party mediators, their interests and impact on party unity

Non-party mediator	Interests of non-party mediator	Incentive(s) for candidate/ legislator to break party unity
Mass media	Newsworthiness	Gain exposure
Campaign professionals	Candidate re-selection	Stand out from intra-party competitors
Interest groups	Particular interests	Mobilize the group's support
Financial backers	Personal interests	Secure campaign funding

who advise and guide the candidates through the intra-party campaign; (3) leaders of various groups (such as unions), who supply the campaign with activists and mobilize groups of selectors; and (4) capital holders, who supply the necessary finances to reach a large selectorate (Rahat 2008). These mediators could promote different interests, or even interests that are at odds with those of the party, its ideology, or its leaders. As Narud, Pedersen, and Valen (2002, 227) argue: "The opening up of the nomination process gives other actors ... potential influence on the question of candidate selection." Ranney (1965) uncovered this more than fifty years ago when he pointed out that the primaries in the US empower the mass media and other non-party organizations to perform tasks that elsewhere belong to parties.

Non-Party Mediators

The Mass Media

If candidates satisfy the demands of the media for newsworthy items, they are likely to be rewarded with exposure to a large crowd that includes their potential selectors. One of the ways to become newsworthy – especially for individuals within a group who are interested in distinguishing themselves – is to announce a different opinion or to behave in a different manner. Hence, one of the ways for candidates and legislators to gain exposure is to break party unity.

Campaign Professionals

The people who are hired to promote the candidates are interested in making them prominent vis-à-vis their competitors. They are less interested in the party as such, in its image as a unified team, or in its success in the forthcoming general elections. Political consultants are primarily interested in the success of "their" candidate within the party – their reputation and remuneration depend on their candidate's success, not the party's. Therefore, they are likely to run a campaign that will distinguish their candidate from the other candidates, particularly when it comes to populist issues. They will also advise incumbent legislators to take actions that differentiate them from the others in their party for the sake of name recognition.

Interest Groups

The heads of interest groups can supply candidates with votes. They are able – or at least are believed to be able – to activate hundreds and even thousands of "their" people to register as party members, to mobilize them to show up and vote, and also to instruct them for which candidate they should vote. Later, if "their" candidate succeeds in being (re-)selected, they can pressure the candidate to "pay them back" even if their group's interest conflicts with the party program. That is, they can instigate a break in party unity.

Financial Backers

Those who contribute large sums to candidates enable them to communicate with the large, atomistic, dispersed and passive crowd that comprises an inclusive party selectorate. They are likely to be interested in getting a return for their investment. That is, they might expect their candidate to vote in line with their investments, and this might conflict with the party's policies.

Party Unity and Non-Party Mediators

All of these non-party actors have the potential to pressure candidates to behave in certain ways that might – and even sometimes must – conflict with party unity. The more inclusive the selectorate, the more these non-party mediators are needed by the candidate in order to appeal successfully to their selectors.

The idea that an inclusive selectorate leads to less party unity is exemplified by a comparison between the United States (US) and other established democracies. US primaries are the most inclusive selection method(s) in use – although they vary state by state – and, indeed, it is in the US that we find the lowest levels of party unity. As V.O. Key (1967, 452) puts it: "The nomination stage is the point at which party discipline can be applied most effectively. Yet the direct primary is a procedure not easily usable, either by the national leadership or by the voters of a district, for that purpose." The adoption of primaries thus led to a decline in party unity in the US (Crotty 2006).

Yet the US is different in that it is a presidential democracy,[2] while most other cases of established Western liberal democracies are parliamentary democracies (Lijphart 1999). One may claim that the different logics of these regimes explain these differences. While party unity can be helpful in presidentialism, it is not needed for the survival of the government; at the same time, party unity is a prerequisite in parliamentarism, and the survival of the government is based on unified parties. This conviction concerning candidate selection and party unity is expressed by Epstein (1964, 55) when he argues: "It appears illogical to combine primaries, intended to make legislators independent of party, with a parliamentary system that requires cohesive legislative parties in order to provide stable government."

Kristjánsson (1998, 177) claims that widening participation in the selection process in Iceland brought about a decrease in party unity: "The primary election period in Iceland, since the early 1970s, coincides with decreasing party cohesion. Increasingly, Icelandic political parties resemble umbrella organizations for individual politicians rather than highly disciplined organizations." In Israel, the overall tendency to democratize candidate selection methods has gone hand-in-hand with an increase in both the proposing and the passing of private member bills (Hazan 1997; Hazan 1999; Rahat and Sheafer 2007), along with other types of personalized behaviour (Dotan and Hofnung 2005) that damage party unity. A cross-national study of party unity in parliaments found that parties that use more exclusive and centralized selection methods behave in a more unified manner in Parliament (Sieberer 2006). Yet the difference is one between highly united parties and very highly united parties, not between united and disunited ones.

However, even in parliamentary democracies it seems that, for every case in which decreasing party unity can be explained by the democratization of the party selectorate (Iceland, Israel), there are counter-examples of parties that are able to maintain high levels of unity despite more inclusive candidate selection methods (Canada, Ireland – see Carty, Chapter 1, this volume; Farrell et al., Chapter 5).[3] As we will soon show, the problem we posit between intra-party democracy and party unity relates directly to the discussion of brokerage/franchise parties as one of the possible solutions.

If the logic behind the expectation that party unity will be lower when parties employ more inclusive selectorates is sound and simple, why is this not always the case? Why can we not show variation in unity levels despite differences in the extent of intra-party democracy? Apparently, parties are able to resolve this problem and (still) keep high levels of unity while they adopt inclusive selectorates. If we are right in arguing that intra-party selectoral preferences can work to hinder party unity – particularly when inclusive selectorates enhance the role of non-party actors – how can parties hold themselves together? We now turn to the ways parties cope with the problem that the use of inclusive selection poses for party unity.

Possible Solutions: How to Democratize and Maintain Party Unity[4]

Four solutions to the problem of keeping parties united while democratizing candidate selection can be suggested. We start with the claim that the linkage between inclusiveness and disunity is unavoidable and thus suggests that the solution is to involve additional selectorates in the process (Hazan and Rahat 2010; Rahat 2009). We continue with the proposal from one of the cartel party model initiators (Katz 2001), who argues that the problematic solution is two-faced: pretend to be responsive to external pressures in the public rhetoric while toeing the party line in legislative voting. We then turn to a solution that suggests that unity can be bought through patronage when in office and maintained by changing the rules of the intra-party game when in opposition (Bolleyer 2009). Finally, we look at the franchise party model (Carty 2004), according to which the solution is a division of functions: party members select, the national party leadership makes policy.

Solution 1: Involve Additional Selectorates

This solution looks at the political consequences of the democratization of candidate selection from a rather critical point of view. It recognizes that the democratization of candidate selection means the quantitative expansion of political participation and, as such, serves a democratic value. Yet, in terms of responsiveness – which is our focus here – intra-party democracy opens the door, as explained, to non-party actors and is thus likely to have a negative impact on party unity.[5]

The need of the representatives to ensure their re-selection in an inclusive selectorate causes a severe threat to party unity. Re-selection equals survival, and the threats it creates to party unity cannot be remedied by the conventional pool of disciplinary tools. Thus, this perspective argues that the solution lies in involving at least one party-oriented selectorate in the democratized selection process, along with the more inclusive selectorate. It follows the logic of Gallagher's (1988, 271) statement that, in order to maintain unity and party-centred responsiveness, "it may not matter much, in this sense *which* party agency selects candidates, but it does matter that *some* party agency selects them" (emphasis in original). Accordingly, the proposed solution is to involve a more exclusive selectorate – a nomination committee and/or party delegates – in screening the candidates prior to allowing the party members to select the candidates. The idea is that incumbent candidates who seek re-selection will understand that their candidate-centred responsiveness to those mediators who help reach the large crowd of party members during the campaign must also be balanced with party-centred responsiveness (Hazan and Rahat 2010; Rahat 2009).

The key here is not to allow the pathologies of one particular selectorate to monopolize candidate selection but, rather, to offset one selectorate by involving at least one other, forcing candidates to appeal to multiple selectorates. Indeed, in most of the empirical cases in which party members are or were involved in candidate selection in Western Europe, they were not the sole selectors (Hazan and Rahat 2010). This could explain why party unity was largely maintained in these cases while it declined in those in which party members or party supporters were the sole selectors, such as the United States, Iceland, Taiwan, and Israel.

Solution 2: Pretend but Behave

The cartel party leaders see the problems of party unity in managerial rather than in ideological terms (Mair 1994; Katz and Mair 1995; Mair 1997; Katz 2001). The cartel model requires that the party leadership be able to compromise across party lines and have enough space to manoeuvre when in government in order to cope with real world challenges, unlimited by constraints imposed on it by a group of ideological activists. In order to neutralize the party activists, party decisions (such as candidate selection) are opened up to the full membership.

The cartel party model guides party leaders to adopt a democratization strategy because it gives them greater leverage. The rationale behind this is that the less intensely involved rank-and-file party members are more likely to be swayed by such factors as name recognition and, hence, are more likely to take cues from the highly visible party leadership. Mair (1997, 149–50) explains this strategy: "the process of intra-party democratization is being extended to the members as individuals rather than to what might be called the organized party on the ground ... the 'ordinary' members, who are at once more docile and more likely to endorse the policies (and candidates) proposed by the party leadership and by the party in public office." The idea of direct membership votes in candidate selection is thus to give the leadership more influence in candidate selection – taking advantage of the iron law of oligarchy – in comparison to selection by delegates.

Katz suggests that one might describe the problem as the elected representatives having two masters: (1) the leadership of the party in public office and (2) the party on the ground (or a wing of it). The problem for the party leadership is to convince its representatives to opt for the first option rather than the second. A possible answer to the demands emanating from below (decentralized candidate selection) and from outside (democratized candidate selection), along with the pressure to sustain party unity, creates "a separation between the appearance and the substance of politics," which means that "there will be an increasing divergence between the rhetorical and the substantive behavior of MPs" (Katz 2001, 293). Thus the "image" of party unity is cracked, or even broken, as a result of the public expressions of intraparty opposition by backbenchers (and even by ministers); yet, at the end of the day, they all coalesce and vote in concert to maintain "substantive" party unity. Thus, the idea of allowing rhetorical freedom along with strong unity is to aid politicians in walking the tightrope of talking the talk of the representative of the party in public office while still walking the walk of the member of the party on the ground.

A recent study found that there is a significant gap between the "noise" that Israeli politicians make in the mass media and their actual voting in Parliament (Shapira and Rahat 2011). The study identifies the leading dozen media dissidents in the Israeli Parliament during 2009–10, those who were the most prominent in publicly expressing positions in opposition to their party and threatening to vote against it. These dissident representatives were located through an internet search using several expressions that showed their intent to breach party unity. The study looked at their voting patterns in general and, more specifically, on important issues (such as votes of no-confidence and the third readings of bills). The dissident legislators exhibited quite high levels of party unity rather than individualistic behaviour.[6] There were very few instances in which they breached party unity: in almost 99 percent of the cases they voted with their party, and on important issues they voted with their party 100 percent of the time (except for a single representative who voted on important issues with her party 98 percent of the time).

Yet this is only a partial solution as it is based on a fragile equilibrium and is hard to sustain for the long run, which is in line with Katz's (2001, 293) argument concerning "the self-limiting nature of the cartel party model."

Solution 3: Patronage and Reform

According to Bolleyer, increasing the inclusiveness of the selectorate, while keeping candidate selection local, creates a challenge for the party organization in its attempt to sustain party unity. "In a fully fledged cartel party, the party leadership is confronted with an increasingly incohesive parliamentary party composed of MPs over whose fate it has only limited intra-organizational control before they enter the public realm" (Bolleyer 2009, 565). The problem is that of ensuring unity when the selectorate is inclusive and decentralized. In other words, the principals in terms of re-selection are local party members rather than the national leadership of the party.

The solution to the problem of party unity is different when the party is in government than it is when it is in opposition. When the party is in government, political appointments and additional forms of patronage are used to ensure unity. The organizational vulnerability of parties can thus be overcome by the use of selective benefits, such as political appointments and patronage. When the party is in opposition, the leadership initiates reforms that aim to regulate organizational entry and grant some control to the central organization over the selection process. "In times of opposition the relationship between the leadership and the party as organisation changes since the infrastructure becomes a core source of control. Reform is one response to that, and the active implementation of party rules on the ground another" (Bolleyer 2009, 575).

Bolleyer demonstrates the validity of these claims by looking at the behaviour of the Fianna Fail in Ireland, which uses patronage when in power and internal reforms when in opposition to generate party unity. The Israeli case also provides support for these claims. The loyalty of representatives in the more cartelized parties in Israel (Likud, Labor, Kadima) was "bought" through an increasing number of ministerial appointments and other forms of patronage when the party was in government. Also, intra-party reforms are adopted most when the party is in opposition (Barnea and Rahat 2007). Yet the Israeli experience also demonstrates the limits of this solution. When Labor joined the Likud-led coalition in 2009 – claimed by many to be largely due to extensive patronage (five of the party's thirteen legislators were given ministerial positions) – discipline was attained only from those who were directly "paid" with ministerial positions, and for a limited period.

Solution 4: Functional Divide

The stratarchical model takes the internal party developments posited by the cartel party theory one step further. In order to understand party unity it functionally assigns distinct types of competences to different levels (Carty 2004; Carty and Cross 2006; Carty 2008; Carty, Chapter 1, this volume). This model declares that modern political parties are more leader-driven yet, at the same time, are internally democratic and have to compete in a more open electoral market with a less solid support base. Parties have thus become multi-level organizations in which the separate levels enjoy significant autonomy. In other words, parties have become something akin to federal systems, or a network of affiliated organizations.

Carty (2004) argues that parties have become a franchise system that couples the efficiencies of scale and standardization with the advantages of local participation in the delivery of the organization's product. There is no longer a zero-sum contest for power – power is broadly shared, but the autonomy of the different units is constrained by the interdependence of its parts. Carty (2004, 11–12) explains the economic analogy of a franchise to the political world and the multi-level stratarchical organization of political parties as follows:

> As a whole, the party embodies and sustains a brand that defines its place in the political spectrum and is the focus for supporters' generalized loyalties. Typically, parties' central organizations are responsible for providing the basic product line (policy and leadership) ... In office, the central party is likely to play the principal part in any governance responsibilities the party assumes. Local units, however they are defined (geographically or otherwise), more often provide the basic organizational home of most party members, and are typically charged with delivering the product, i.e., creating organizations that can find and support candidates as well as mobilizing campaigns to deliver the vote on the ground ... Once institutionalized, all elements must recognize their part and accept the power and role trade-offs as a necessary part of the bargain for making the party, as a whole, successful.

In other words, at the heart of the stratarchical party is a franchise bargain between the various levels over rights and duties. This is true when it comes to the selectorate level as well, as Carty (2004, 19) explains:

> Party selectors enjoy their powers only by virtue of the stratarchical distribution of authority within the wider party organization. Thus ... local party members know that the right to name their candidates is part of a more complex and encompassing franchise bargain in which [they] ... embrace the opportunities but accept the limitations.

Wolinetz (Chapter 4, this volume) suggests that franchise parties can be an antidote to the negative features of cartel parties. While the latter marginalizes members, the former allows them to choose their own district candidates and even to tailor the campaign to local interests; however, once the representatives are elected they are bound by strict party discipline. In Canada – upon which much of the stratarchical model literature is based – the parties allow local autonomy in exchange for national unity (Erickson and Carty 1991; Carty, Cross, and Young 2000; Carty and Eagles 2003; Cross 2004). That is, inclusiveness has not led to a decrease in party unity because the local selectorates choose candidates who will stick to the party line in the national legislature. Malloy (2003) adds that the volatile membership patterns associated with a more inclusive selectorate can actually work in favour of keeping elected representatives loyal since the unstable membership in the constituency means that dissenting representatives cannot count on retaining the support of the constituency organization if a challenger signs up more members. In other words, while the Canadian case shows a more democratized candidate selection process, this process is constrained by the particularly Canadian constellation of a parliamentary system with strong legislative incentives for unity, despite a lack of party cohesion. This constellation, coupled with the distinct geographically based distribution of party support in Canada and a complicated dissonant relationship between the national and the provincial parties, results in multi-level, autonomous, stratarchically organized parties.

In Ireland, also characterized by a highly candidate-centred electoral system and with strict party discipline, a similar arrangement exists. Party choices at the national level focus on national policies and do not impinge on local preferences, and local electorates are not mobilized around national policies. This means that Irish legislators are not constrained by a local mandate: they are free to adhere to party discipline in the national sphere provided they put in the time and effort required by their local constituency (Farrell et al., Chapter 5, this volume).[7]

The stratarchical party model thus argues that increasing inclusiveness need not impair the party's ability to remain unified. However, the party members' control over candidate selection is predicated by their willingness to avoid any attempt to influence the position taken by the parties on national policies. Members select and representatives follow the party line: the two do not have much to do with each other. As Sandri and Pauwels (2010, 1241) put it, "National elites are responsible for policy formulation, while local organizations are responsible for candidate selection." Or, to put it in terms of an ancient debate, stratarchical party selectorates choose trustees, not delegates. Thus the only way that party members can affect policies is through de-selecting their representative.

However, even Carty (Chapter 1, this volume) recognizes that in the brokerage party, intra-party politics are more contested and that the central institutional problem of the brokerage party is to balance intra-party tensions. The stratarchical arrangement, like that of the cartel party, might thus also be somewhat limited in its long-term applicability. As Carty (2013, 23) states: "To manage their system of stratarchical democracy successfully, the members ought to share an understanding of its basic intra-party trade-offs. Recent survey evidence suggests that they may not."[8] The difficulties of intra-party democracy, even in the stratarchical/brokerage party, are obvious – members may see leadership interference in candidate selection as illegitimate and also feel free to reject national policy positions adopted by their leaders. The challenges posed by intra-party democracy to party unity are evident here as well.

Conclusion

We supply four different solutions to the problem of maintaining party unity while using inclusive selectorates. However, these should not be seen as competing explanations. First, they could be more or less relevant in specific political systems and even for particular parties. These differences can be linked to variations in institutions (regime type) or in political culture. For example, involving additional selectorates in the process requires a long-term incremental approach to reform. This can explain why British parties involve several selectorates in their candidate selection process. Alternatively, the division of functions solution is more likely to work in decentralized systems and in decentralized parties (i.e., Canada) than in centralized systems. Second, the various solutions can work at the same time in the same system and even for the same party. The Israeli Likud seems to solve part of the problem of party unity through extensive nomination of ministers and deputy ministers and, partly, through allowing backbenchers to make a lot of noise while maintaining unity when it comes to voting in Parliament.

In summary, we argue that the more inclusive the party selectorate in the candidate selection process – intra-party democracy – the more it will produce incentives for individualistic behaviour in Parliament on the part of party representatives at the expense of party unity. The lack of significantly varying levels of party unity is due to the fact that parties have found several solutions to this dilemma and have, thus far, been able to balance increased participation with continued legislative efficiency. However, each solution is not a complete fix, nor is it a permanent one.

We should remember that unity is still the rule for political parties, and no wonder since this is the rationale for their creation and sustenance. Yet conflict is always there, within the party, and it must be regulated in order to keep party unity at a level that sustains the party's raison d'être. Inclusive selectorates make this conflict more explicit, and it is a challenge for the parties to regulate it if they wish to expand their internal democracy. If they do not, party unity will face a danger from within.

Notes

1 It should be clarified that differences within this category of "members" and even "supporters" can be substantial if parties raise significant barriers to becoming a member (or even to being considered a supporter who is eligible to participate in the selection of candidates). Yet, in almost all of the cases we know, parties try to recruit masses, focusing on quantity, and do not do much to ensure their quality as party members (Rahat and Hazan 2007).

2 In Mexico, also a presidential democracy, the adoption of primaries not only damaged party unity but also brought about the phenomenon of deserters who crossed from one party to another, together with their supporters, if they did not win the selection process in their original party (Combes 2003). Taiwan's experience with primaries, another presidential democracy, points to a similar conclusion. The primaries adopted during democratization led to more independent behaviour by politicians, thus eroding party unity even in the once-Leninist and disciplined Kuomintang Party, and, as a result, the party tried to move away from them (Baum and Robinson 1999; Wu 2001; Wu and Fell 2001).

3 A similar claim is made at the level of the electoral system: party unity is higher in those cases in which the electoral system does not allow voters to choose individuals and lower in those in which voters can cast an individual ballot (Carey 2009). Nevertheless, there are also known exceptions to this rule (i.e., Ireland with its personalized electoral system and extremely high party unity) (Farrell et al., chap. 5, this volume).

4 We thank Richard Katz, Nicole Bolleyer, and Ken Carty for commenting, elaborating, and expanding on what we define as their solutions. The interpretation, and especially the errors, are ours and ours alone.

5 Intra-party democracy also increases the quantity of participation but harms the quality of participation; limits the ability of the party to ensure that candidates will be representative in demographic terms; and produces limited competition (Rahat and Hazan 2007).

6 Putting aside the special case of the Labor Party, which was on the verge of a split.

7 However, they note that these two spheres – an unconstrained local mandate and adherence to party discipline at the national level – do connect, and even collide,

when it comes to candidate selection – that is when the party leadership exercises its right to determine the number of party candidates it will run in the constituency.

8 In the survey cited by Carty only 10 percent of the party members supported the stratarchical bargain, while the largest group (33 percent) opposed both aspects that define the stratarchical arrangement.

References

Barnea, S., and G. Rahat. 2007. "Reforming candidate selection methods: A three-level approach." *Party Politics* 13 (3): 375–94. http://dx.doi.org/10.1177/1354068807075942.

Baum, J., and J.A. Robinson. 1999. "Party primaries in Taiwan: Trends, conditions, and projections in candidate selection." *Occasional Paper/Reprints Series in Contemporary Asian Studies* 6 (155): 1–62.

Best, H., and M. Cotta. 2000. "Elite transformation and modes of representation since the mid-nineteenth century: Some theoretical considerations." In *Parliamentary Representatives in Europe 1848–2000: Legislative Recruitment and Careers in Eleven European Countries*, ed. H. Best and M. Cotta, 1–28. Oxford: Oxford University Press.

Bolleyer, N. 2009. "Inside the cartel party: Party organization in government and opposition." *Political Studies* 57 (3): 559–79. http://dx.doi.org/10.1111/j.1467-9248.2008.00741.x.

Bowler, S. 2000. "Parties in legislatures: Two competing explanations." In *Parties without Partisan: Political Change in Advanced Industrial Democracies*, ed R.J. Dalton and M. P. Wattenberg, 157–79. Oxford: Oxford University Press.

Bowler, S., D.M. Farrell, and R.S. Katz. 1999. "Party cohesion, party discipline, and parliaments." In *Party Discipline and Parliamentary Government*, ed. S. Bowler, D.M. Farrell, and R.S. Katz, 3–22. Columbus: Ohio State University Press.

Carey, J.M. 2009. *Legislative Voting and Accountability*. New York: Cambridge University Press.

Carty, R.K. 2004. "Parties as franchise systems: The stratarchical organizational imperative." *Party Politics* 10 (1): 5–24. http://dx.doi.org/10.1177/1354068804039118.

–. 2008. "Brokerage politics, stratarchical organization and party members: The Liberal Party of Canada." In *Partier og Partisystemer I Forandring: Festskrift til Lars Bille*, ed. K. Kosiara-Pedersen and P. Kurrild-Klitgaard, 301–13. Odense: University of Southern Denmark Press.

–. 2013. "Are political parties meant to be internally democratic?" In *The Challenges of Intra-Party Democracy*, ed. W.P. Cross and R.S. Katz, 11–26. Oxford: Oxford University Press. http://dx.doi.org/10.1093/acprof:oso/9780199661879.003.0002.

Carty, R.K., and W. Cross. 2006. "Can stratarchically organized parties be democratic? The Canadian case." *Journal of Elections, Public Opinion and Parties* 16 (2): 93–114. http://dx.doi.org/10.1080/13689880600715912.

Carty, R.K., W. Cross, and L. Young. 2000. *Rebuilding Canadian Party Politics*. Vancouver: UBC Press.

Carty, R.K., and M. Eagles. 2003. "Local conflict within national parties: The case of Canada." Paper presented at the Annual Meeting of the American Political Science Association, Philadelphia, United States.

Combes, H. 2003. "Internal elections and democratic transition: The case of the Democratic Revolution Party in Mexico (1989–2001)." Paper presented at the European Consortium for Political Research Joint Sessions of Workshops, Edinburgh, Scotland.

Cross, W. 2004. *Political Parties*. Vancouver: UBC Press.

W. Cross, and R. Katz, eds. 2013.*The Challenges of Intra-Party Democracy*. Oxford: Oxford University Press.

Crotty, W. 2006. "Party origins and evolution in the United States." In *Handbook of Party Politics*, ed. R.S. Katz and W.J. Crotty, 25–34. London: Sage. http://dx.doi.org/10.4135/9781848608047.n4.

Dotan, Y., and M. Hofnung. 2005. "Why do elected representatives go to court?" *Comparative Politics* 38 (1): 75–103.

Duverger, M. 1954. *Political Parties: Their Organization and Activity in the Modern State*. London: Methuen.

Epstein, L.D. 1964. "A comparative study of Canadian parties." *American Political Science Review* 58 (1): 46–59. http://dx.doi.org/10.2307/1952754.

Erickson, L., and R.K. Carty. 1991. "Parties and candidate selection in the 1988 Canadian general election." *Canadian Journal of Political Science* 24 (2): 331–49. http://dx.doi.org/10.1017/S0008423900005114.

Gallagher, M. 1988. "Conclusion." In *Candidate Selection in Comparative Perspective: The Secret Garden of Politics*, ed. M. Gallagher and M. Marsh. London: Sage.

Hazan, R.Y. 1997. "Executive-legislative relations in an era of accelerated reform: Reshaping government in Israel." *Legislative Studies Quarterly* 22 (3): 329–50. http://dx.doi.org/10.2307/440319.

–. 1999. "Yes, institutions matter: The impact of institutional reform on parliamentary members and leaders in Israel." *Journal of Legislative Studies* 5 (3–4): 301–24.

–. 2002. "Candidate selection." In *Comparing Democracies 2: Elections and Voting in Global Perspective*, ed. L. LeDuc, R.G. Niemi, and P. Norris, 108–26. London: Sage.

–. 2003. "Does cohesion equal discipline? Towards a conceptual delineation." *Journal of Legislative Studies* 9 (4): 1–11. http://dx.doi.org/10.1080/13572330420 00306227.

Hazan, R.Y., and G. Rahat. 2010. *Democracy within Parties: Candidate Selection Methods and Their Political Consequences*. Oxford: Oxford University Press. http://dx.doi.org/10.1093/acprof:oso/9780199572540.001.0001.

Katz, R.S. 2001. "The problem of candidate selection and models of party democracy." *Party Politics* 7 (3): 277–96. http://dx.doi.org/10.1177/1354068801007 003002.

Katz, R.S., and P. Mair. 1995. "Changing models of party organization and party democracy: The emergence of the cartel party." *Party Politics* 1 (1): 5–28. http://dx.doi.org/10.1177/1354068895001001001.

Key, V.O. 1967. *Politics, Parties, and Pressure Groups*. 5th ed. New York: Crowell.

Kristjánsson, S. 1998. "Electoral politics and governance: Transformation of the party system in Iceland, 1970–1996." In *Comparing Party System Change*, ed. P. Pennings and J.-E. Lane, 167–82. London: Routledge.

Laver, M., and K.A. Shepsle. 1999. "How political parties emerged from the primeval slime: Party cohesion, party discipline, and the formation of governments." In *Party Discipline and Parliamentary Government*, ed. S. Bowler, D.M. Farrell, and R.S. Katz, 23–48. Columbus: Ohio State University Press.

Lijphart, A. 1999. *Patterns of Democracy*. New Haven: Yale University Press.

Mair, P. 1994. "Party organizations: From civil society to the state." In *How Parties Organize: Change and Adaptation in Party Organizations in Western Democracies*, ed. R.S. Katz and P. Mair. London: Sage, 1–23. http://dx.doi.org/10.4135/9781446250570.n1.

–. 1997. *Party System Change: Approaches and Interpretations*. Oxford: Oxford University Press.

Malloy, Jonathan. 2003. "High discipline, low cohesion? The uncertain patterns of Canadian parliamentary party groups." *Journal of Legislative Studies* 9 (4): 116–29. http://dx.doi.org/10.1080/1357233042000306290.

Narud, H.M., M.N. Pedersen, and H. Valen. 2002. "Conclusions." In *Party Sovereignty and Citizen Control: Selecting Candidates for Parliamentary Elections in Denmark, Finland, Iceland and Norway*, ed. H.M. Narud, M.N. Pedersen, and H. Valen. Odense: University Press of Southern Denmark.

Rahat, G. 2008. "Entering through the back door: Non-party actors in intra-party(s) electoral politics." In *Non-Party Actors in Electoral Politics: The Role of Interest Groups and Independent Citizens in Contemporary Election Campaigns*, ed. David Farrell and Rudiger Schmitt-Beck., 25–44. Baden-Baden, DE: Nomos-Verlag

–. 2009. "Which candidate selection method is the most democratic?" *Government and Opposition* 44 (1): 68–90. http://dx.doi.org/10.1111/j.1477-7053.2008.01276.x.

Rahat, G., and R.Y. Hazan. 2006. "Candidate selection: Methods and consequences." In *Handbook of Party Politics*, ed. R.S. Katz and W.J. Crotty, 109–21. London: Sage.

–. 2007. "Political participation in party primaries: Increase in quantity, decrease in quality?" In *Participatory Democracy and Political Participation: Can Democratic Reform Bring Citizens Back In?*, ed. T. Zittel and D. Fuchs, 57–72. London: Routledge.

Rahat, G., and T. Sheafer. 2007. "The personalization(s) of politics: Israel 1949–2003." *Political Communication* 24 (1): 65–80. http://dx.doi.org/10.1080/10584600601128739.

Ranney, A. 1965. *Pathways to Parliament: Candidate Selection in Britain*. London: Macmillan.

Sandri, G., and T. Pauwels. 2010. "Party membership role and party cartelization in Belgium and Italy: Two faces of the same thing?" *Politics and Policy* 38 (6): 1237–66. http://dx.doi.org/10.1111/j.1747-1346.2010.00276.x.

Shapira, A., and G. Rahat. 2011. "Cohesion and personalization of Israeli politics." Paper presented at the conference on The Institutionalization of Political

Parties in Canada and Israel: Cohesion, Discipline and Personalization, Hebrew University of Jerusalem, Israel, June.

Sieberer, U. 2006. "Party unity in parliamentary democracies: A comparative analysis." *Journal of Legislative Studies* 12 (2): 150–78. http://dx.doi.org/10.1080/13572330600739413.

Wu, C.-L. 2001. "The transformation of the Kuomintang's candidate selection system." *Party Politics* 7 (1): 103–18. http://dx.doi.org/10.1177/1354068801007001006.

Wu, C.-L., and D. Fell. 2001. "Taiwan's party primaries in comparative perspective." *Japanese Journal of Political Science* 2 (1): 23–45. http://dx.doi.org/10.1017/S1468109901000123.

7

Towards a European Politics

LUCIANO BARDI, RICHARD S. KATZ, AND PETER MAIR

Although it is widely recognized that competition among political parties in free and fair elections is not by itself sufficient to ensure a democratic government, it is also widely accepted that such competition is a necessary component of democracy (Katz 1997, 3). As the competences of the European Union (EU) have expanded, and corresponding concern with the democratic deficit has grown,[1] attention to the two elements of this condition has also increased.

The question of free elections was first addressed in the institution of a directly elected European Parliament (EP). Simply electing the EP, however, proved inadequate in two respects. First, the adequacy of having a directly elected chamber depends crucially on the powers of that chamber – a purely consultative body (a talking shop) may be better than nothing, but it clearly is not enough. This problem has been ameliorated as the powers of the EP have expanded, although its authority still is not fully equal to that of the Council of Ministers. Second, even if the EP has powers formally assigned to it, it also needs to have a democratic mandate to use those powers and the organizational will to overcome the problem of strategic coordination among a large number of individual representatives. This problem remains significant.

In normal democracies, political parties play a central role in overcoming the second problem (Blyth and Katz 2005). On the one hand, by presenting the voters with a limited number of alternative visions or programs, parties in the electoral arena "channel currents of thought so as to promote the emergence of a sufficiently clear and coherent political will" (European Court of Human Rights 1987). In doing this, they make it possible for a party (or coalition of parties) with a majority in the parliament to claim a democratic mandate. On the other hand, within the parliament, parties provide the structure within which compromises can be negotiated and coalitions first built and then enforced.

In many quarters, the expectation was that direct election of the EP would lead inexorably to the creation of a European political space in which the practices of democratic party government as found in the member states would be reproduced at the European level. This clearly has not happened. There is instead continuing awareness of the inadequacy of the EP's powers – in particular of the fact that it has not "elected" and held accountable the European Commission and its president in the way that a national parliament elects the prime minister and cabinet. Although the role of the EP has increased under the Treaty of Lisbon, the initiative still lies with the national governments. If only the EP had the power to choose the president of the commission, so the argument goes, there would be a focus for the construction of real European parties. Each could either nominate its own Europe-wide candidate for the presidency or else join in a coalition with other European parties to support a joint Europe-wide candidate. If the popularly endorsed candidate were then elected to head the commission without the nomination or approval of the member governments, real Europe-level democracy would follow.

As all this suggests, the other side of the "democratic deficit coin" is the absence of real European parties and of a single European party system. We do not see the existence of fully developed party organizations, and even less do we see the current system of European party federations (which are only partially connected to party groups in the EP) as being synonymous with the existence of a single European party system. Against the background of this observation, in this chapter we ask whether it is realistic – and, indeed, whether it would even be desirable – to speak of the emergence of a supranational European party system.

Before we can begin to address that question, however, we first need to specify what a supranational European party system would look like. The second objective of this chapter is to assess the parties and party system of the EU as they/it currently exist(s) with regard to this standard. We then ask what institutional reforms might promote movement in the direction of a

European party system and how changes in the socio-political environment in which the EU exists might promote or retard such a development.

Finally, in imagining what a coherent European polity, with a true European party system, might look like, we consider the question of whether such a development would be an unmitigated improvement or whether, instead, there could be significant costs that might outweigh the benefits. In this regard, we start by observing that representative institutions – like both parliaments and parties – perform at least two complexes of functions. On the one hand, there are the functions of democratic governing, which is to say deciding on the course of policy and choosing and controlling an executive to carry out that policy (i.e., the formulation of a limited number of programs among which voters can choose and the construction of a majority to install and maintain an executive). On the other hand, however, there is the function of providing the conduits through which the rich variety of competing interests and opinions in the polity can be voiced between elections as well as within the context of election campaigns.

The conflict between these two sets of functions – one emphasizing compromise and simplification, the other emphasizing conflict and diversity – raises the possibility that a dramatic increase in the governing role of European parties as part of the development of a single European party system might come at the expense of representation of the diversity of European cultures, identities, opinions, interests, and desires. This potential trade-off is, of course, not unique to the EU: it is faced by every national system of representative government as well. The problem is, however, potentially particularly acute at the European level for a number of reasons, of which we here mention only two. First, there simply is more diversity to be represented at the European level than there is within any one of its component member states. Second, Europe does not have (or at least does not yet have) a reservoir of community identity comparable to that found in most individual states to mute the difference between winning and losing on any particular question.[2]

One could argue that, in other composite polities, the parties have effectively helped overcome the difficulties created by diversity, even if not necessarily by creating the conditions for building up a national identity but, instead, by "obfuscat[ing] rather than articulat[ing] interests, blur[ring] rather than sharpen[ing] divisions" (Carty 2006, 5). Canada, for example, in contrast with the United States, never developed a national "secular political culture," and one of the functions of the party system was "to foster a sense of national unity and of national being" by acting "as a broker of ideas, or of class and regional interests" (Meisel 1992, 329–30). Canada's "brokerage parties" were "typically created ... as polity building political instruments, their very success at incorporating a broad support base constrain[ing] the capacity of opponents to replicate their formula" (Carty, Chapter 1).

Whether the brokerage model is applicable to the EU is doubtful. Certainly the two largest Europarties, the European People's Party (EPP) and the Party of European Socialists (PES), are sufficiently broad-based and potentially pragmatic to satisfy the basic requirements of brokerage. In the Canadian experience, however, brokerage parties' pragmatism is brought out by converging nationally minded leaders' and provincial notables' power and (especially in the first nation-building phase of the country's history) patronage-seeking attitudes. Currently there is comparatively little power, let alone patronage, to be obtained at the EU level. Policies favouring individual member-states might be seen as the equivalent of patronage but, at the EU level, the interests of member-states can be very divisive and can reinforce the pro- and anti- EU political cleavage (Hix, Noury, and Roland 2007, 67). This is unlike what happened in Canada, where patronage became a means to cement provincial interests and national unity concerns. And the kind of coalitions that made the success of brokerage parties in Canada would not have to materialize in the EP but in the Council of Ministers, where Europarties hardly have any influence. The problem, then, becomes creating institutional arrangements whereby Europarties acquire some control of the EU executive. To expect them to act as brokers by simply exercising some sort of moral suasion over broad masses of voters would be unrealistic.

The Meaning of a European Party System

The first question is: "What does European party system mean?" We begin here with Sartori's definition: "Parties make for a 'system,' then, only when they are parts (in the plural); and a party system is precisely the *system of interactions* resulting from inter-party competition. That is, the system in question bears on the relatedness of parties to each other, on how each party is a function (in the mathematical sense) of the other parties and reacts, competitively or otherwise, to the other parties" (Sartori 1976, 44, emphasis in original). As this suggests, a party system is not defined simply by the existence of a number of parties but, rather, by the existence of a regular pattern of interactions among those parties. This, however, leaves a number of important questions to be addressed.

Competition or Cooperation

We normally assume that inter-party interactions will be competitive (as specified in Sartori's first sentence). Sartori's second sentence, however, talks about parties reacting to one another "competitively or otherwise." To what extent is institutionalized cooperation or collusion among some or all of the significant parties compatible with the idea of a party system?

A Uniform Cast of Characters

If we mean to talk about a (singular) European party system, to what extent must the pattern of interaction be uniform through the European political space, and what does uniformity mean? One sense of uniformity would involve the same set of parties interacting (particularly in the electoral arena) throughout the whole system. For a national party system, the simplest case would involve a single national election district, as in Israel: because there is only one district, the same parties appear on the same ballot throughout the country. The Netherlands comes close to this; however, although seats are allocated among parties as though the country were a single election district, it is in fact divided into twenty *kieskringen*, with the possibility that a local party might compete only in some – or that a national party might not compete in some – so that both the parties and the list of candidates for each party might not be uniform throughout the country. At the other extreme would be a "system" in which there were only district-level parties, approximated by Belgium, where Flemish parties only present candidates in Flanders and, hence, do not compete in the electoral arena with Walloon parties, which only present candidates in Wallonia. In this case, one might say that – at the electoral level – there are two regional Belgian party systems but no national system.[3]

Most real systems fall somewhere between these two extremes. In Canada, the Bloc Québécois only contests seats in one province. In the United Kingdom, it is only since 1974 that the three national parties have each had candidates in as many as 80 percent of the constituencies (Butler and Butler 1986, 226–28).

In Spain, in 2008 the PSOE fell seven seats short of a majority, while CiU held the balance with ten seats although it had only contested four of the fifty provinces. In Italy, the Lega Nord (sixty seats in the 2008 election and clearly an essential component of the Berlusconi coalition) only had candidates in the north. In Germany, although the CDU and CSU are in permanent alliance at the national level, they remain separate parties with distinct profiles: the CDU does not have candidates in Bavaria, and the CSU does not have candidates in the rest of Germany.[4]

While the Belgian example of two almost completely separate electoral party systems of nearly equal size is exceptional, it is exceptional only in degree. Especially if account is also taken of cases in which a major party does not contest every constituency, and of parties that win only a few seats without becoming relevant to national government formation, then the number of variations in the competitive constellations found in individual countries would increase, and the number of countries in which there was one uniform cast of characters would decrease.

What Is Uniform Interaction? Centralization of Control and Uniformity of Substance

Even if the same parties were competing throughout the system that would not, by itself, guarantee that the patterns of interaction among those parties would be uniform. On the one hand, given different interests in different places, the constant cast of characters may not emphasize the same issues in all parts of the polity. Even in single-district Israel, for example, one would expect different sales pitches to be aimed at voters in Jerusalem and voters in the agricultural areas of the coastal plain. Even more when there is the institutional separation of different electoral districts, parties may emphasize different aspects of their programs in different places.

On the other hand, institutional differences, such as differing district magnitudes, may create strategically different conditions that, in turn, mean differing patterns of interaction across the territory.[5] In multilevel political systems, there may be differences in patterns of coalition and opposition at the second tier that alter the terms of competition at the first tier. Differences in levels of support may make a party that is an important competitor in some areas essentially irrelevant in others. Although the same parties may be in competition everywhere, the way in which they relate to one another may still vary by locality.

Where Does the Interaction Take Place?

The discussion above focuses primarily on the pattern of interactions among parties in the electoral arena. More generally, however, parties also interact within Parliament, and between Parliament and the executive – especially in presidential systems, where there is a clearer demarcation between the legislature and the executive. Even within Parliament, bicameralism may result in different patterns of interaction in the two chambers.

In the Belgian case, it is easy to make the claim that there are separate Flemish and Walloon party systems in the electoral arena. Within Parliament, however, there are regular patterns of interaction that merge the two into a single system, in two senses. Most obviously, the parties need to form coalitions to support or oppose a cabinet; while these could, in theory, be based entirely on language, in practice that would be a recipe for disaster, and this then requires cooperation, and not just opposition, that spans the language divide. Even more, to the extent that coalitions are assumed to require both the Flemish and the Walloon party of a particular family (both socialist parties, or neither, for example), coalition policy (and common records in government or opposition) may force an element of patterned uniformity in electoral competition, even if the competitors are organizationally separate in the two regions.

If both chambers of a bicameral legislature were chosen by a highly proportional electoral system, and so could be relied upon to have the same partisan distribution of members, it *might* be reasonable to assume that the same patterns of party interaction would appear in both chambers. When the partisan balance differs significantly, however, so may the legislative party system. For example, between 1998 and 2001 the Australian Democrats (with nine seats out of seventy-six) held the balance between the two major parties in the Senate, although they had no seats at all in the House of Representatives. Of particular relevance to the idea that the EU has a bicameral legislature (EP and Council of Ministers), different voting rules and differing constituencies may produce differing patterns of interaction among the parties.

A third question is: Must the system-level (top tier) party system penetrate to (and presumably be uniform across) the subsystem level? In Britain or Germany, for example, subnational elections are frequently interpreted as second-order national elections, with strong implications regarding the popularity and strategic possibilities of the national parties. There is an expectation that inconsistencies of coalition policy or issue stands across the subnational units will be electorally costly at the national level – or that subnational coalitions can be used to try out possible changes in national strategy. For this to make sense there has to be a single party system that spans the different levels.

Canada represents the other extreme, with the provincial party systems essentially separate from the national. First, the parties themselves may be completely different: the Parti Québécois (the governing party in Quebec between 1976 and 1985 and between 1994 and 2003) and the Saskatchewan

Party (the governing party in that province since 2007) only exist in their own provinces. Second, even when parties of the same name exist at both federal and provincial levels, they may be separate organizations. Third, as surveys have shown, Canadian party identification among the electorate is often level-specific: a voter may identify with different parties at federal and provincial levels.

What Is Uniform Electoral Change?

Returning to the electoral arena, one indicator that a party system has become nationalized is uniformity of electoral swing: generally, the partisan balance moves the same way (and to the same degree) in all districts from one election to the next (Stokes 1967; Caramani 2004). While this would be strong evidence of a single uniform party system, in the sense that it is hard to imagine this kind of uniformity of outcome occurring unless voters were everywhere responding to the same combination of parties and issues, the converse is not so clear (Katz 1973). In particular, unless uniformity of party and issue competitors is combined with uniformity of socio-political environment, one might easily see the same parties taking the same stands throughout the system and yet obtaining diametrically opposed results. Racial politics in the United States in the 1960s provides a particularly clear example: when the Democrats under Lyndon Johnson became clearly identified with civil rights (in particular through Johnson's support of the Civil Rights Act, 1964, and then of the Voting Rights Act, 1965), there was no doubt that this national issue had a dramatic electoral effect. But while that effect was strongly in the Democrats' favour in the North, it dramatically weakened the party in the South. It is not just that the distribution of party supporters differs but that the reaction of party supporters to the same issue differs as well.[6] In the same vein, in Europe, social policies that would have been supported by Christian Democrats in Western Europe with no obvious electoral penalty (e.g., gender mainstreaming) might be expected to produce a quite different reaction in conservative Catholic Poland.

The EU Party System

It would be unrealistic to expect that a party system such as that of the EU, which stems from the combination of elements of the party systems of the twenty-eight member-states, would adhere to the single party system model. The task now is to assess the severity of the EU party system's departures from the model in terms of its expected role and functions. After all, the national examples we have seen indicate that distance from the model does not necessarily imply party system inadequacy.

The EU's Cast of Characters

Beginning our analysis of the EU party system with a survey of the uniformity of party actors, it might be argued that there is indeed a single cast of characters in the European party system. This is certainly what one would conclude by looking at the outcomes of EP elections, which reflect the existence of the same near-ubiquitous party families throughout Europe. In the EP returned by the 2009 elections, only 5 percent of all members of the European Parliament (MEPs) did not join any of the seven EP party groups and sat as non-attached. Moreover, of the five major groups, the Progressive Alliance of Socialists and Democrats (PASD) obtained seats in all member-states; the EPP included representatives from twenty-six of the then twenty-seven member-states; whereas Liberals (ALDE-ELDR), Greens, and the left (GUE-NGL), respectively, included representatives from eighteen, fourteen, and eleven member-states. In the latter cases the relative sparseness of individual country representation was due more to electoral thresholds than to absence from the electoral competition.

This seemingly positive picture is contradicted, however, by a number of other facts. The first is that the national delegations that make up the party groups originate from clearly distinct (organizationally and politically) national parties. This is evident in their histories, which in many cases long predate the foundation of the EU, let alone the foundation of its would-be party system. But it is also stated in the very document that establishes the existence of parties at the EU level. Regulation 2004/2003, the so-called Europarty statute, lists, among a series of requirements that parties must respect in order to acquire EU legal status and to obtain funding, that they demonstrate that their affiliates are present (and compete in elections) in at least one-third of the member-states. Such requirements would be unnecessary if it were assumed that, as was/is the case with most national counterparts, Europarties are created as central organizations that progressively establish local headquarters and federations.

Moreover, the structure of electoral competition in the member-states is more varied than seat apportionments resulting from electoral outcomes would lead one to believe. A couple of examples illustrate how significant these differences can be. The most relevant party "anomaly" in the 2009 EP elections was the absence of any party affiliated with the EPP in the UK electoral competition. While this is a new development, resulting from David Cameron's decision to revise the Conservative Party's European position (which had been within the European People's Party and European Democrats [EPP-ED] group), it is probably more than a temporary tactical adjustment. Another discrepancy reflects the difficulties experienced by the ALDE-ELDR in competing in important member-states like Austria, the Czech Republic, Hungary, Poland, Portugal, Greece, and Italy.

Limiting our discussion to the two of these countries that did not have postwar authoritarian experiences, the problem in Austria stems from the FPÖ's transformation, under the leadership of the late Jörg Haider, into a xenophobic formation, which made it incompatible with Liberal values. In Italy, the demise of the Republican and Liberal parties resulting from the Tangentopoli scandal was never compensated by the emergence of a new truly Liberal party, and the ALDE-ELDR group has included in succession the Lega Nord (also eventually expelled because of its xenophobia), the Democratici, the PPI, and, currently, Di Pietro's Italia dei Valori, none of which can be considered bona fide Liberal parties.

The British Conservatives also demonstrate the lack of unity and instability of Europarties in another way as they have been members of three different party groups in the course of the EP's elected history (the European Democrats, the EPP-ED, and now the European Conservatives and Reformists [ECR]). The number of party groups within the EP has varied, excluding the non-attached, between a low of seven in 1979, 2004, and 2009, and a high of eleven in 1989. While these numbers do not per se indicate the instability of specific groups, variations have also resulted from the creation and disappearance of the European Right, Forza Europa, Europe of Nations, and the Rainbow Group as well as from the consolidation of the Greens and Europe of Freedom and Democracy (EFD).

Finally, and perhaps most important, Europarties can differ in terms of their components' ideological and value orientations as well as in terms of their interests with regard to specific issues. All of these elements can have consequences for the uniformity of Europarties' policy positions. This is of great importance because of the provision in the EP's Rules of Procedure that political groups have to be formed according to their "political affinities." A group's political affinity is the result of political choices rather than legal requirements: groups remain free to set their own conditions for membership. Thus, an appreciation of the cohesion of the political groups can only be made empirically. A recent study (Bardi et al. 2010) analyzes EP group positions on the basis of two different data sources: the Euromanifestos issued by national parties for the EP elections and the self-placement of parties (EU Profiler data) on some well-known policy dimensions. The study's findings show that EP groups exhibit clear inter-party differences. For example, the liberal ALDE placed its strongest emphasis on market economy, the Greens on environment, the Communist GUE-NGL on welfare state expansion, the conservative ECR on law and order, and the EFD on Euroscepticism and restrictive immigration policies. The EU Profiler data clearly emphasize that the PASD supports liberal society and a stronger welfare state, while the EPP supports a more market-driven economic policy combined with a more traditional orientation towards social-liberal issues.

The picture is only slightly different if one looks at within-group cohesion and differences. Within-group cohesion is usually quite strong, indicating a potential for coherent transnational parties, but it does not apply to every issue area. For example, the EPP's position on socio-economic policies is right of centre and similar to that of the ECR, but some of its constitutive parties still stick to a centrist, if not slightly leftist, position. The PASD is the most cohesive of the three "historical" political groups. The classic literature on the EP groups has traditionally emphasized the relative ideological homogeneity of the socialists on socio-economic policies. The news is that now the PASD is also rather cohesively supportive of European integration. Finally, the ALDE-ELDR group is certainly united in its support for European integration, but it is more divided on socio-economic policies. Indeed, this is a classic problem for the liberals, who are traditionally divided into left- and right-wing components.

On a more general level, the findings on EP group cohesion are reasonably favourable for the prospects of EU democracy. The main political groups have cohesive and easily identifiable positions on left-right policies. And, among the smaller political groups, only the EFD shows a clear lack of ideological cohesion on the socio-economic dimension, but it is united by its strong anti-EU perspective. Political groups might then be able to translate this relative homogeneity into a concrete legislative agenda.

Candidate Selection and Centralization of Control

The selection of candidates is arguably one of the party functions that is most likely to produce tensions between different levels of authority (and power) within party organizations (see Hazan and Rahat, Chapter 6, this volume). A study of candidate selection procedures for EP elections could thus reveal how centralized Europarties actually are, depending on which level (national or European) plays a bigger role. Regulation 2004/2003 indicates the respective competences of the external organizations of EP Groups and Europarties and assigns the responsibility to campaign for and to conduct European elections to the latter. Europarties are often not directly active, however, since national parties act as the instruments through which they campaign. The selection of MEP candidates remains a prerogative of national parties, and yet it has outcomes that can have a decisive effect on the development of Europarties. That said, full transnationalization is unlikely to require wholesale uniformity in candidate selection procedures across all the national parties that are affiliated to a particular EP group or federation. Indeed, there is evidence from both Europe and North America that diversity in procedures is already tolerated within individual national parties. This diversity is likely to become even more pronounced with the development of "cartel" and "franchise" models of party organization (Katz and Mair 1995; Carty 2004; Wolinetz, Chapter 4, this volume).

National parties differ in their candidate selection procedures, depending on country or party family affiliation (Bardi et al. 2010, chap. 2). Candidate selection differences illustrate a lack of centralization of party authority and competences, which, in turn, could constitute an obstacle to effective transnationalization. If a pro-European approach in the selection of candidates is to materialize, it will most likely be at the national level rather than at the European level as the direct influence of the latter in national candidate selection is effectively insignificant – an example of the "functional divide" solution to combining partisan coherence with local participation suggested by Hazan and Rahat (Chapter 6, this volume; Bardi 2010, chap. 2). Even if nearly 20 percent of national parties have experienced some degree of interaction with the European level during the candidate selection phase, in only 14 percent of all cases has this been positively evaluated. It is hardly the case that dissatisfaction with the relationship between a national party and its corresponding Europarty can be considered as an element that advances the Europeanization process. Indeed, when only four national parties (2.8 percent) report clear and explicit consultations with, and direct involvement of, their European-level partner in the candidate selection process, it seems that the path towards effective transnationalization has only recently and timidly begun (Bardi et al. 2010).

The EU Party System in Different Arenas

EP elections are contested in a competitive manner by Europarties; therefore, we could perhaps recognize the existence of an EU party system in the electoral arena. But the important question concerns how European such competition really is. It is well known that electoral campaigns in EP elections are dominated by national issues and that, beyond rhetorical appeals, European themes and policies are completely neglected. The second-order nature of EP elections is often brought to the extreme when, as is often the case in Italy and France, political parties try out new electoral coalitions and strategies with a mind to the next national elections.[7] Whether the approach to EP elections is national or European, the fact is that EP elections are competitive, and so it is ultimately the (albeit composite) party system that characterizes them. Things are quite different if we consider different arenas. It could be argued that there are at least two other relevant arenas at the EU level: the EP and the Council of Ministers. In the EP we have a situation that is practically the reverse of that found in the electoral arena. At least on a formal level, the party system in the EP can be considered European in nature, as, technically, are its units, the EP party groups. But from a structural viewpoint the EP party system has always been cooperative rather than competitive. This characteristic is becoming progressively less pronounced as a result of new procedures for the appointment of the president of the European Commission and of increases in the EP's decision-making powers. It would be excessive, however, to claim that the EP party system is now competitive.

A party dimension seems to be altogether lacking in the Council of Ministers. The council remains the domain of intergovernmental decision making dominated by national governments' interests, where member-states' international status, prestige, and power count more than temporary ideological convergences among their leaders. If anything, party presences in the council reflect the continuing superiority of national parties (and their systems) over their European counterparts. When in government, national party leaders know they have much more effective means to influence EU policy making (in their national interest) in the Council of Ministers than they would in the EP as part of Europe-wide party groups.

The Transnationalization of the EU Party System

One final important aspect of the EU party system concerns the nationalization (in this case the "transnationalization") of parties and of the party system at the European level. According to Jones and Mainwaring:

> Parties and party systems vary significantly in the degree to which they are nationalized. By a highly nationalized party system, we mean one in which the major parties' respective vote shares do not differ much from

> one province to the next. In a weakly nationalized party system, the major parties' vote shares vary widely across provinces. The same logic applies to parties: highly nationalized parties have a relatively even share of the vote across different geographic units, whereas weakly nationalized parties have widely varying shares across geographic units. (Jones and Mainwaring 2003, 7)

Similarly, to be considered as transnationalized, the Europarty system and its units should present similar high levels of homogeneity in vote share distributions. Electoral data indicate that there is a low level of within-country and within-party homogeneity. Moreover, between-election swings are seldom uniform across member-states for parties affiliated to the same individual party groups.

Promoting a European Party System

The most obvious and effective way in which a European party system could be promoted is also the least feasible politically: to open the European executive, in whatever form, to electoral competition. With regard to promoting a European party system on the basis of a politically and electorally contested arena of executive power there are two options, neither of which is likely to be adopted. The first is to promote a presidential or semi-presidential system, in which the president of the European Commission becomes subject to popular election. The second is to stay with a parliamentary model, which would involve the EP electing and holding accountable the College of Commissioners. But while either might be beneficial to the promotion of a European party system, and might help to foster the democratic legitimacy of the EU, they would each require a substantial treaty change, which would be very unlikely to win unanimous approval by the member-states.

It follows that we need to consider modifying the conditions within the present institutional framework in a way that could enhance the profile of the transnational parties themselves and bring them to a stage at which they could at least engage in partial competition with one another (Bardi et al. 2010). This would not be enough to create a genuine and robust transnational party system, but it would come as close to that goal as current institutional circumstances permit. It would also require the transnational party organizations to become much more proactive and politically engaged than is currently the case. There are three areas of potential activity that might serve this purpose.

The first of these is potential involvement of the Europarties in the new European Citizens Initiative that is part of the Treaty of Lisbon. According to the provision in Article 11.4 of the consolidated version of the Treaty of European Union, no fewer than 1 million citizens from a significant number of member-states may petition the commission "to submit any appropriate proposal on matters where citizens consider that a legal act of the Union is required for the purpose of implementing the Treaties." Both the multinational and organizational requirements create opportunities for the Europarties to engage in the process and to be in more direct contact with the European citizenry. This would have two advantages for the parties: (1) it would facilitate their engagement with non-party actors and with organized civil society at the European level (since it is from these actors that the bulk of the proposals are likely to emanate); and (2) it could encourage a sharper profiling and a greater differential among the Europarties and, thereby, stimulate inter-party competition at the European level. This would not be competition for government and, therefore, would not offer a robust foundation for the emergence of the European party system, but it would help give shape to competing representative claims.

The second area for potential Europarty involvement connects to the new subsidiarity formula within the Treaty of Lisbon, whereby the time allowed for national parliaments to scrutinize commission draft legislation is raised from six to eight weeks and provision is made for one-third of these parliaments to object to a draft legislative proposal from the European Commission on the grounds of a breach of subsidiarity – the so-called "yellow card." A simple majority of parliaments can show an "orange card" to the commission, obliging it to refer their objections to the Council of Ministers and the European Parliament. This new provision clearly enhances the role of national parliaments in the EU decision-making process and, thereby, also has the potential to enhance the role of national parties and parliamentarians. But, given that the exercise of this provision is likely to require substantial coordination and cooperation between the national legislatures, we might also expect substantial Europarty involvement in the process. This is particularly so given that non-governing parties in some national systems might try to form blocking alliances against the Council or against the majority in the Council. To coordinate the activities of parties and MPs in at least nine, and possibly fourteen, national parliaments seems to lend itself to the employment of Europarty networks and communication channels. Moreover, this might also have a strong partisan component, thereby encouraging a sense of differentiation and competition. Given that elections in Europe tend to move in waves, currently favouring the centre-right, ten years ago favouring the centre-left, the party families tend to coincide with regard to incumbency and opposition, and, hence, coordination of parliamentary oppositions is likely to overlap with family identity.

The third area for Europarty involvement is possibly the strongest and most direct, and it has already been put in place in the 2014 EP elections. This involves the Europarties entering the European elections with their own candidates for the Commission presidency. As things formally stand, the president of the European Commission is nominated by the governments and elected by the newly elected EP. The EP is also required to give its approval to the Commission as a whole. This offers some degree of democratic accountability and transparency to the process of appointment, albeit in a very limited manner. In order to add a popular electoral dimension, in 2014 the five major Europarties – the EPP and the PES, the ALDE-ELDR, the Greens, and the EUL-NGL – entered the EP election process, putting forward at the same time their own candidates for the Commission presidency, which were backed by most of their national party affiliates (note Priestley 2010). The assumption was that the candidate proposed by the most successful Europarty would be nominated by the member-states' governments. Indeed Jean-Claude Juncker, the candidate designated by the EPP, the Europarty that obtained the highest number of votes Europe-wide, was eventually nominated by the European Council and elected by the EP. The elections thus conferred an indirect mandate on the new president of the Commission, boosting the democratic legitimacy of the system as a whole. It is less clear whether, as had been mooted by observers and commentators, Europarty competition acquired a genuine transnational patina. While all five Europarties were very active in their efforts to coordinate support for their candidates in each of the national settings, they also teamed up in collectively supporting Juncker through their members in the governments that formally controlled the nomination process in the Council of Ministers. In other words the old tendency to form consociational party blocks at EU level re-emerged when the Europarties once again were confronted with the need to assert their collective position vis-à-vis that of the member states. To be sure, the decision to designate Europarty candidates to the presidency of the Commission has not led to a fully fledged transnational party system; however, given the present institutional constraints and the fact that institutional reform by way of a new treaty is unlikely to be achieved in the foreseeable future, it has come as close to this goal as is currently possible.

Would a Single European Party System Be an Improvement?

As indicated above, parties serve a complex of functions in any democratic polity. In common with interest groups and the like, they provide a voice for opinions, interests, and preferences not just during election periods but also between elections. They *articulate* interests, and while they sometimes compete with non-party groups in an effort to serve as the favoured channel in this regard, they also often cooperate with these groups. Second, and again often in common with non-party groups, they serve as *intermediaries* between citizens and the state, representing citizens to the state and, in the case of the parties in particular, the state to the citizens. In the European case, this means that the parties, both at the European level and nationally, represent citizens to the European Commission, although, as a bureaucratic and formally non-partisan body, the commission itself has indicated a preference for interlocutors that come through civil society rather than through the parties (European Commission 2001). The parties also perform this representative role in the EP, where their position as intermediaries is effectively unchallenged. Third, and uniquely, parties *aggregate* these interests. They do this in three ways. First, they aim to produce comprehensive programs, thereby aggregating the myriad opinions, interests, and preferences of a diverse public and a diverse set of civil society organizations into a manageable number of alternative choices. Second, in forming legislative and governing coalitions, they aggregate this more limited set of choices into a single package that, in principle, can be said to command majority support. Third, they aggregate through governing, and through the occupation of public office, translating the aggregated preferences into public policy.

Parties perform both an expressive function and a governing function and, when in government, combine both at the same time. However, the combination of these two broad functions is not always comfortable. The articulation of interests requires diversity, whereas their aggregation requires coherence, and the trade-off is not always appreciated by those whose voice is intended to be heard. Representation as articulation often builds on local ties and local specificities, whereas aggregation, and particularly the translation of aggregated preferences into public policy, calls for centralized decision making. In the EU, a polity marked by pronounced national and regional diversity in political cultures and interests, these tensions are especially pronounced, and in that sense we might expect parties to function badly at the European level. Moreover, Europe does not (yet) have the degree of shared community identity or solidarity that might soften the difference between winning and losing, or that might encourage voters to accept the trade-offs that are required between articulation and aggregation.

In one important respect, however, the parties in Europe do have an advantage over those in the national systems of representative government. At the national level, parties in government are often pulled in different directions as they seek to respond to the demands emanating from the European level, while also trying to respond to the demands of their own citizenry (Mair 2009). This can eat into the capacity for representation, leaving the governing parties vulnerable to the politics of outbidding by their more populist opponents. This development may also be linked to the growing bifurcation in European party systems – between parties that claim to represent, but do not govern, and those that do govern, but find difficulty in being representative (Katz and Mair 2008).

The capacity of Europarties to represent is, in principle, unadulterated because there is no executive arena in which they compete for electoral support. This means that the EP is unique as the only Parliament in the EU in which the parties involved do not either form and sustain government or formally oppose it, and this also means that the parties in the EP are in a unique position (Mair and Thomassen 2010). They enjoy the capacity to represent citizens while being free from the constraint of governing. Although this reduces the pressure to aggregate the interests into a coherent program, and thereby undermines one of their core functions, it does encourage them to pursue more directly and less equivocally the articulation of interests. Given the diversity of interests in Europe today, this in itself is an important goal.

In sum, while the development of a real European party system within a traditional parliamentary setting might enhance accountability and responsiveness in the aggregate, it could come at the cost of the developing capacity of the parties to represent and articulate the diversity of voices that are found in the EU. One way in which this trade-off could be avoided would be by stepping away from parliamentary solutions and moving towards a sharper separation of powers, in which democratic accountability could be ensured through the direct election of the commission president, while interest articulation and representation would continue to be channeled through the EP itself. In other words, by promoting a fully presidential system at the EU level, something that is quite distinct from their own national traditions, the European parties might hope to achieve a capacity to articulate interests as well as to aggregate them, albeit in two different electoral arenas.

Appendix: Abbreviations

ALDE-ELDER	Alliance of Liberals and Democrats for Europe
CiU	Convergence and Union (Catalan nationalist electoral alliance)
CDU	Christian Democratic Union
CSU	Christian Social Union
ECR	European Conservatives and Reformists
ED	European Democrats
EFD	Europe of Freedom and Democracy
EPP	European People's Party
EUL-NGL	European United Left-Nordic Green Left
FPÖ	Austrian Freedom Party
PASD	Progressive Alliance of Socialists and Democrats
PES	Party of European Socialists
PPI	Italian People's Party
PSOE	Spanish Socialist Workers' Party
RPF	Rally of the French People
RPR	Rally for the Republic

Notes

Note from Luciano Bardi and Richard Katz: Peter Mair was a full contributor to the writing of this chapter, but due to his untimely death the very final revisions were made by us without the benefit of his wisdom. Any remaining errors are our responsibility alone. Authors' names are in alphabetical order.

1 For reviews of some of this literature, see Hix (2005, 177–79); Bellamy and Castiglione (2000); and Føllesdal (2006).

2 One could still ask how well existing Europarties already perform these functions. The answer is not very positive, not only because of limits posed by the current structuring and deficiencies of the European political system but also because of their own organizational inadequacies. See Bardi and Calossi (2009, 151–72).

3 This is a slight exaggeration, even at the electoral level, since parties based in both linguistic regions compete in the constituency of Brussels-Halle-Vilvoorde. For other senses in which it would be an exaggeration to say that there is no Belgian party system, see below.

4 Abbreviations for the names of parties are used in the text. For the full names see the appendix at the end of this chapter.

5 An example would be the different strategies of Spanish parties in large and small magnitude districts.
6 Obviously, this implies less than total homogeneity of preferences among a party's supporters: even if they agreed on many issues, Democrats were fundamentally divided on the question of race in ways that correlated with region.
7 See, for example, the case of the Italian Democratici and of Pasqua's RPF's challenge to the RPR in France, both in 1999.

References

Bardi, L., and E. Calossi. 2009. "Models of party organization and Europarties." In *Activating the Citizen: Dilemmas of Participation in Europe and Canada*, ed. J. DeBardeleben and J.H. Pammett, 151–71. London: Palgrave Macmillan.

Bardi, L., E. Bressanelli, E. Calossi, W. Gagatek, P. Mair, and E. Pizzimenti. 2010. *How to Create a Transnational Party System. Directorate General for Internal Policies, Policy Department C: Citizens' Rights and Constitutional Affairs*. European Parliament.

Bellamy, R., and D. Castiglione. 2000. "Reflections on the European democratic deficit." In *Democracy and the European Union: Integration through Deliberation?* ed. O.E. Eriksen and J.E. Fossum, 65–84. New York: Routledge.

Blyth, M., and R.S. Katz. 2005. "From catch-all politics to cartelization: The political economy of the cartel party." *West European Politics* 28 (1): 33–60. http://dx.doi.org/10.1080/0140238042000297080.

Butler, D., and G. Butler. 1986. *British Political Facts, 1900–1985*. New York: St. Martin's Press.

Caramani, D. 2004. *The Nationalization of Politics: The Formation of National Electorates and Party Systems in Western Europe*. Cambridge: Cambridge University Press. http://dx.doi.org/10.1017/CBO9780511616662.

Carty, R.K. 2004. "Parties as franchise systems: The stratarchical organizational imperative." *Party Politics* 10 (1): 5–24. http://dx.doi.org/10.1177/1354068804039118.

–. 2006. "The shifting place of political parties in Canadian public life." *IRPP Choices* 12: (4) 3–13.

European Commission. 2001. *Governance in Europe: A White Paper*. COM (2001) 428 final – Official Journal C 287 of 12.10.2001.

European Court of Human Rights. 1987. "Case of Mathieu-Mohin and Clerfayt v. Belgium," 2 March 1987, 9/1985/95/143, series A no. 113.

Føllesdal, A. 2006. "The legitimacy deficits of the European Union." *Journal of Political Philosophy* 14 (4): 441–68. http://dx.doi.org/10.1111/j.1467-9760.2006.00244.x.

Hix, S. 2005. *The Political System of the European Union*. New York: Palgrave Macmillan.

Hix, S., A.G. Noury, and G. Roland. 2007. *Democratic Politics in the European Parliament*. Cambridge: Cambridge University Press. http://dx.doi.org/10.1017/CBO9780511491955.

Jones, M.P., and S. Mainwaring. 2003. "The nationalization of parties and party systems: An empirical measure and an application to the Americas." *Party Politics* 9 (2): 139–66. http://dx.doi.org/10.1177/13540688030092002.

Katz, R.S. 1973. "The attribution of variance in electoral returns: An alternative measurement technique." *American Political Science Review* 67 (3): 817–28. http://dx.doi.org/10.2307/1958625.

–. 1997. *Democracy and Elections.* New York: Oxford University Press. http://dx.doi.org/10.1093/acprof:oso/9780195044294.001.0001.

Katz, R.S., and P. Mair. 1995. "Changing models of party organization and party democracy: The emergence of the cartel party." *Party Politics* 1 (1): 5–28. http://dx.doi.org/10.1177/1354068895001001001.

Katz, R.S., and P. Mair. 2008. "MPs and parliamentary parties in the age of the cartel party." ECPR Joint Sessions, Rennes.

Mair, P. 2009. "Representative versus responsible government." MPIfG Working Paper 09/8. Cologne: Max Planck Institute for the Study of Societies.

Mair, P., and J. Thomassen. 2010. "Political representation and government in the European Union." *Journal of European Public Policy* 17 (1): 20–35. http://dx.doi.org/10.1080/13501760903465132.

Meisel, J. 1992. "The stalled omnibus and the decline of party." In *Canadian Political Party Systems: A Reader*, ed. R. K. Carty, 328–50. Peterborough ON: Broadview Press.

Priestley, J. 2010. *European Political Parties: The Missing Link.* Brussels: Notre Europe (Jacque Delors Institute).

Sartori, G. 1976. *Parties and Party Systems: A Framework for Analysis.* Cambridge: Cambridge University Press.

Stokes, D.E. 1967. "Parties and the nationalization of electoral forces." In *The American Party Systems: Stages of Political Development*, ed. W.N. Chambers and W.D. Burnham, 182–202. New York: Oxford University Press.

8

Politicians and Local Party Organizations

A Delegation Approach

ROYCE KOOP

> The dominant Canadian party mould, cast in the first period, persisted: parties remained largely cadre-style organizations of electorally oriented local partisans gathered around a parochial politician and held together at the centre by leaders.
>
> – CARTY ET AL. (2000, 17)

The above quote nicely summarizes what party politics in Canada tends to look like on the ground: "local partisans gathered around a parochial politician." This chapter is about Canada's parochial politicians and the partisans that gather around them in the ridings, with particular emphasis on how we can understand the relationships between them. The issue is important given the crucial roles that political scientists in the so-called revisionist school are increasingly recognizing for local party organizations (e.g., Clark 2006). This literature emphasizes, for example, that well-staffed and well-funded local campaigns influence vote shares in individual constituencies (Denver and Hands 1997; Whiteley and Seyd 2003); and that effective local organizations, by keeping MPs informed of local service and allocative needs, assist them in the development of a "personal vote" (Price and Mancuso 1995, 218) by providing a sympathetic local face to parties in their roles as partisan "ambassadors to the community" (Scarrow 1996, 42–43). The question is: Given their benefits for incumbent MPs, what types of relationships do MPs maintain with their local party organizations and how can these relationships be understood?

I argue that the relationship between MPs and members of local constituency associations can be understood as a principal-agent relationship. MPs have a range of local goals and responsibilities that, due to time and specialization problems, they could not hope to accomplish themselves or by assigning them to their paid staff. This is especially true given that the constituencies in which MPs seek re-election are both populous (when compared, for example, to constituencies in the United Kingdom) and often composed of diverse and even conflicting interests. Instead, MPs delegate these responsibilities to members of their constituency associations. As in other principal-agent relationships, there are problems inherent to this arrangement. However, MPs are able to overcome these problems using a variety of managerial tools. MPs are not traditional managers and so are constrained with regard to the range of tools that they can use to minimize agency loss. This is compounded by the volunteer nature of constituency associations in Canada's loosely structured parties, where, as Carty (2002) points out, exit trumps voice and activists are likely to simply abandon their associations rather than be dictated to by a domineering MP. The tools employed by MPs to minimize agency loss are, therefore, distinctive: screening, selecting, and de-selecting personnel; monitoring and requiring reporting; and, most important given the volunteer nature of constituency association work, offering rewards.

The top-down application of principal-agent frameworks presented here – that is, MPs delegating responsibility to party members – is somewhat novel given that, in political science, principal-agent frameworks are typically formulated as bottom-up. This is true, for example, with respect to studies of democracy, in which citizens delegate responsibilities to elected officials; and party organizations, in which party members delegate powers to the leader in much the same way as shareholders delegate responsibilities to boards of directors (Koelble 1996). Other studies, however, apply principal-agent frameworks in a top-down manner – for example, studies of bureaucracy, in which the question is how elected officials can delegate responsibilities to civil servants while reducing agency costs (e.g., Brehm and Gates 1997) and studies of political parties in multi-level settings (van Houten 2009). It is the latter tradition that I follow in this chapter.

While I offer a deductive argument, I also draw on both unstructured and semi-structured interviews with thirty-eight sitting Canadian MPs and eight constituency association presidents as well as direct observation of constituency association executive meetings when MPs were in attendance. All MPs interviewed sat in the 40th Parliament. The MPs were recruited in order to maximize variation on a range of factors, including party affiliation, gender, number of terms served, the safety of their constituencies, and professional backgrounds. Twenty-one Liberal, ten Conservative, and seven NDP MPs were interviewed.

I build on Carty's work on franchise parties by both illuminating some of the inner workings of the local manifestations of Canadian political parties and, more important, considering the role of elected officials – MPs in this case – in the workings of stratarchically organized parties (for accounts of Carty's work in this area, see both Johnson and Sharman, introduction, and Wolinetz, Chapter 4, this volume). Franchise parties in Canada, Carty argues (2002, 739), produce incumbent MPs who are characterized by dualism: they are severely disciplined while in Ottawa to advance their parties' national brands but are dominant figures while in their constituencies, where they must develop and manage their own local franchises. Canadian scholars have tended to focus on the former role, but I explore how MPs interact with their local party organizations to maximize the possibility of re-election. By helping themselves, MPs help their parties, and the parties are well served by a caucus consisting of members whose eyes are firmly fixed on their own individual re-election prospects.

Principal-Agent Frameworks and Application to Political Parties

Principal-agent relationships occur when an actor (the principal) contracts authority over and responsibilities for one or more agents. Principals may delegate authority for a number of reasons, including to reduce risk (e.g., Epstein and O'Halloran 1999, 235); to improve the quality of decisions by delegating decisions to agents with unique knowledge and skills (Bendor and Meirowitz 2004, 294–95); and to gain a comparative advantage in terms of time. Contracting responsibilities produces an asymmetrical relationship, whereby agents as rational actors are assumed to maximize their benefits while minimizing their efforts. The result is agency loss. While it is sometimes assumed that principal-agent relationships are necessarily conflictual, this is not always the case (e.g., Bendor et al. 2001, 238–40), and, in fact, one way for principals to reduce agency loss is to recruit allies who share common goals with the principal.

Delegation frameworks have been extensively employed in political science, particularly in the study of bureaucratic management (e.g., Brehm and

Gates 1997; Huber 2000) and legislative politics (Cox and McCubbins 1993; Pollack, 1997). However, the study of party organizations and intra-party politics has generally been inductive in nature, with scholars observing particular parties in order to determine the development of new categories of party types (Wolinetz 2002). Deductive approaches to the study of party organizations, such as the application to them of principal-agent frameworks, have been rare.

There are, however, three notable exceptions. First, Koelble (1996) asks whether the principal-agent framework effectively summarizes intra-party relations within the German Social Democratic Party, the Spanish Socialist Workers' Party, and the British Labour Party. Koelble argues that party activists constitute principals who contract responsibilities to party leaders, with the implication that activists favour strict controls and screening whereas leaders favour maximum freedom. Second, Müller (2000) marshals a principal-agent framework to demonstrate how political representatives in European parties are held accountable for their actions. He argues that members of the party in public office in fact constitute agents provided with authority by the extra-parliamentary party organizations, which constitute principals. However, agency problems, including leisure shirking, dissent shirking, and political sabotage, all reduce the value of this relationship for the extra-parliamentary party. As a result, parties have developed both ex ante mechanisms (contract design and screening mechanisms) and ex post mechanisms (reporting requirements and institutional checks) to reduce these costs (Müller 2000, 322). Finally, van Houten (2009) employs a delegation framework to political parties in multi-level states. He argues that national party leaders act as principals who delegate responsibility for party business in the regions to subnational party units. Like Koelble and Müller, van Houten (2009, 145) outlines the intra-party institutional mechanisms that reduce the institutional agency costs associated with delegating power.

Why and How Do MPs Delegate Responsibilities to Constituency Associations?

Constituency associations represent the permanent organizational presence of Canadian parties in the constituencies. These organizations consist of three components: (1) the wider party membership in the constituency, (2) the small executive that is elected by party members at annual general meetings, and (3) the smaller number of officers (including the president, vice-president, treasurer, and secretary) that are also generally elected by local party members. The focus here is primarily on members of the association executives as these activists take on the roles assigned by MPs.

The services required by MPs can be divided into two groups: electoral and representational. Electoral services relate to the future re-election campaigns of MPs and Carty (1991) classifies them as incumbent support functions. They include membership maintenance, fundraising, and inter-election maintenance events that engage local partisans and keep them in contact with the MP (Koop 2011, 71). Representational functions include fulfilling the service and allocative requests of constituents, and demonstrating that MPs are aligned with the policy views of their constituents. In order to do this, MPs must find a way to determine their constituents' allocative and service needs.

However, MPs face both time and specialization problems in carrying out these tasks. As individuals, MPs cannot hope to find sufficient time to do this on their own, especially given the amount of time they must spend in Ottawa. As a result, they delegate many of these responsibilities to members of their constituency associations.

The first challenge is electoral in nature, and MPs cope with it by assigning a range of responsibilities for incumbent support functions to their constituency association executives. The classic way of doing this involves assigning committee chairs on the executive. Thus, it is common for an executive member to become the fundraising chair (although the executive treasurer will often take on this role). This chair is responsible for planning fundraising events or soliciting contributions from existing members, and the treasurer takes the opportunity of executive meetings to report on how prepared the association is for upcoming elections.

Membership chairs are also common on executives. These chairs are tasked with maintaining and expanding the party's local membership base. The result is that the chair will often either personally call lapsed members to invite them to renew their memberships or assign phone lists to local lieutenants. Membership chairs also organize renewal parties, where a number of volunteers meet to work their way through an accumulated list of lapsed members. Membership chairs also seek to expand the local membership by, for example, attending inter-election maintenance events and selling memberships.

Executive members also take on the role of events chairs or organizers for individual events. These executive members take responsibility for organizing inter-election maintenance events, which are designed not to raise money but, rather, to maintain linkages with the local membership, reach out to locals, and maintain the presence of both the MP and the party in the community. These organizers often hold barbeques and golf tournaments, picnics, or other public events at which the MP can speak and form a link with local charity groups in order to assist in local efforts. The well-attended annual picnic outreach event held by the Liberal constituency association in Don Valley East is an excellent example of such an event (see Koop 2011, 86).

In all these ways, executive members assist MPs in their electoral goals by maintaining electorally advantageous linkages with their communities. Members who take on these roles must have the time to carry them out, and, not surprisingly, they develop expertise in these areas. As a result, MPs can solve their time and specialization problems by delegating responsibilities to executive members.

The second challenge facing MPs is representational in nature. During their time in office, MPs carry out a range of service activities, including assisting constituents with requests and attempting to attract government funding to local projects. Such representational behaviours are important to building a reputation for service and for demonstrating allocative responsiveness to their ridings, which is the first step in constructing a local personal vote (Eulau and Karps 1977). Constituency service may therefore have indirect electoral benefits for incumbent MPs, and the MPs themselves know that failing to provide constituency service can be disastrous in future re-election campaigns (Docherty 1997, 173).

However, this raises an important representational dilemma: In ridings that are diverse in any number of ways, how can MPs hope to stay in touch with the concerns of myriad communities? This is a specialization problem: MPs cannot hope to be deeply enmeshed in each community in their ridings. They solve their specialization and time problems by delegating communication responsibilities to members of their constituency association executives.

In Canada, it is the constituency association executives who hail from their ridings' various geographical and/or cultural communities who are given the responsibility to maintain community contact. MPs use monthly constituency association executive meetings to collect the views of these executives on what is occurring in each of their communities, often using these blocks of time to keep ahead of emerging service and allocative needs. One MP succinctly expressed this function of the members of his association executive:

> They're a sounding board, they usually meet once a month and they always give you their views ... I always spend probably twenty minutes at every meeting asking, "Well, what are you hearing around town, what issues are you hearing about?" ... They'll tell you where the people are, what people are talking about, "that's not an issue," or "this is an issue" ... They'll give you specific examples.

Constituency associations assist MPs in their representational functions in other ways as well. Members of executives return to their own communities and brag about the service accomplishments of the MPs. By organizing inter-election maintenance events, association members provide MPs with opportunities to meet with constituents and to build up a reputation (albeit symbolic) for responsiveness. MPs will sometimes use their associations as focus groups to test policy ideas emanating from the centre and to determine how they can best be presented to local communities.[1] They can be expected to ensure that associations act in such a way as to deliver these benefits.

Agency Problems

It is to be expected that some delegation relationships between MPs and associations will break down. The result is agency costs. Following Brehm and Gates (1997, 50), I demonstrate in this section that executive members may either work in the interests of the MP or may engage in three behaviours – leisure shirking, competence shirking, and/or sabotage – that constitute agency problems for the MP and render the delegation relationship unsuccessful.

Members of constituency association executives may simply not do the best possible job for MPs, and information asymmetry – the problem in principal-agent relationships that occurs when agents possess more or better knowledge of the assigned tasks than do principals – means that MPs may be unable to immediately detect deficient work. There are two reasons for leisure shirking. The first is that members of constituency associations enjoy a certain local status that is not necessarily related to the quality of the work that they perform for the MP. The result is that executive members may enjoy their local status – particularly their perceived connection to the MP and his or her staff – without justifying that status by working on the MP's behalf. MPs are aware of this danger. "I do expect that if you're going to be on the board, you're on the board because you want to do something," notes one MP. "Not just say, 'look how cool I am, I'm on the board.'"

Leisure shirking may also result from the social goals of some executive members, which may be gained through sociability with other members and provide them with their most important rewards. While MPs may enhance this sociability, the members may get the rewards they need simply from interacting with one another, thus causing their actual work on behalf of the MP to become less important. This is one reason that MPs often favour the development of goal-oriented professional association executives (Koop 2010, 909–10).

The second source of agency costs for MPs is competence shirking, which occurs when association members take on roles on the executive that they are incapable of fulfilling. This is a problem in any volunteer organization, and we find it whenever members overestimate their abilities. Executive members, for example, may agree to accept the role of membership chair despite lacking the time to effectively maintain existing memberships, or they may agree to organize events despite little experience in doing so. The result is that these volunteers perform poorly in their roles, hurting the overall success of the delegation relationship.

Why do members assume positions that they are incapable of fulfilling? One reason is social status. It is very useful for MPs to encourage local elites to sit on their executives and to report on local happenings at executive meetings. It is also useful for these executive members to learn about local service and allocative needs in their communities and to pass this information along to the MP. The problem is that, in doing so, these agents may develop a sense of self-importance that ultimately works against the interests of the MP. This occurs, for example, when executive members promise residents that MPs can solve service and allocative problems when they may not, in fact, be in a position to do so. "Some of them run around in ... their village as the local MP," notes one MP. "We call them the mini MPs. So one guy in a fishing village who is the Liberal director, for him it's about the prestige, 'I'll talk to the MP about this.'" In this case, the MP received requests from executive members (1) to cancel a fine levied by Human Resources Development Canada against a constituent, (2) to cancel student loans, and (3) to secure employment in a local government office. He could provide no help in any of these cases and so was forced to tell the executive members to return to their communities with the disappointing news. Executive members may also commit the MP to allocative improvements over which they have no jurisdiction. The problem with these requests is that refusing them harms MPs' reputations for service and allocative responsiveness and ruins executive members' attempts to enhance their own local status. In this way, assuming difficult positions for status reasons often results in competence shirking.

Competence shirking also occurs in the realm of representation. MPs often rely on association members to collect and interpret local opinions on pressing policy issues. One difficulty with this, however, is that party activists are unlikely to hold the same opinions on issues as do the median voters in their communities, thus limiting the usefulness of their interpretations. Furthermore, association members may highlight issues that are of concern to them but not to the wider public. Agency costs necessarily result from MPs' privileging of information provided by co-partisans, and the challenge of lowering these costs is a difficult one.

The final source of agency costs for MPs is sabotage, which occurs when executive members work in ways that benefit them but that harm the interests of the MP. Sabotage is particularly dangerous when incumbent MPs are challenged for their local renominations as their challengers often attempt to swamp executives with friendly members. This occurs with some frequency in Canadian parties since friendly executive members, particularly the local president, can alter the arrangements surrounding nomination contests in order to favour one candidate over another (e.g., Cheng and Tavits 2011). In these cases, executives work in direct opposition to the MP, and the MP must attempt to overcome this disadvantage in subsequent renomination contests. One MP with whom I spoke, for example, encountered hostile executive members who provided no electoral or representational support as they were committed to his defeat in an upcoming renomination meeting. Following his successful renomination, the MP took specific steps to minimize agency loss by reducing the number of hostile members on the local executive.

How Do MPs Reduce Agency Loss?

What can MPs do to minimize agency loss? This is not a simple task as MPs are not traditional managers who can wield the full range of sticks and carrots. Drawing on the work of Müller (2000), I outline three mechanisms that MPs employ to minimize agency loss: (1) screening, selecting, and de-selecting personnel for the association executive; (2) requiring reports from the executive as well as monitoring outcomes; and (3) enhancing the rewards that activists receive from their participation.

Screening, Selecting, and De-selecting Personnel

The first way that MPs reduce agency costs is by playing a role in the selection and de-selection of personnel. One way they do this is by screening potential candidates who wish to sit on the executive. Executive members in Canadian parties are elected by the entire local party membership. However, MPs may review lists of locals who wish to run for positions and play a role in their election by endorsing certain candidates over others. This is an informal power, and MPs rely on their own influence to play a role in screening potential candidates.

Screening is a blunt approach and appears to be used sparingly. However, it is an effective way for MPs to ensure that only trusted local figures are installed on their executives. MPs appear to use screening more often in situations in which there is a danger of a rival's supporters swamping the executives as the first step to a successful local nomination challenge. In these cases, MPs are likely to take an assertive approach to screening potential executive members, although they may not be successful in doing so.

The second way that MPs reduce agency costs is by selecting personnel themselves. Executives are formally elected by local party memberships, but MPs may still play a role in encouraging trusted figures from the riding to run for election. An important reason for doing so concerns the desire to professionalize the executive. MPs prefer professional, dependable executives, and so they often recruit figures from the community who can be trusted to bring a deft hand to running the executive. Selecting personnel is a crucial prerequisite for the transition of sociable to professional executives under the guidance of incumbent MPs (Koop 2010, 909–10). By selecting members, MPs are able to reduce leisure shirking, in particular, on their executives.

MPs also select executive members in order to bring a more representative character to the executive. Recall that an important function of constituency association executives is to assist in the development of service, allocative, and policy responsiveness both by keeping the MP abreast of requirements in the communities of the ridings and by communicating the MP's accomplishments to constituents. MPs improve the ability of their executives to do this by encouraging residents of the riding's different communities (whether cultural or geographic) to get involved on the executive. The result is that the executive is able to more effectively assist MPs in their representational roles.

A crucial way for managers to minimize agency loss is by recruiting employees that share their own goals and priorities. If the priorities of both MPs and executive members align, then the potential for agency loss decreases (Müller 2000). The result is that MPs encourage citizens with goals common to theirs – namely, their own re-election and the representational achievements conducive to that goal – to sit on the executive. And the most common way that this manifests itself is for the MP to encourage figures from the prior nomination team – that is, people committed first and foremost to the MP – on to the executive.

Finally, MPs interfere in the composition of the executives in their ridings by de-selecting personnel. This is not a formal power held by MPs, but it can be exercised in exceptional situations. In these cases, MPs informally make it clear to executive members that they are no longer welcome on the executive. This occurred in one constituency when it became clear to an MP that an executive president coveted the local nomination and so was working to sabotage the functioning of the executive and, thus, the MP. The president was also a leisure shirker, who enjoyed the status of his role:

> I had to gas my last president ... He was the one who didn't do any work, liked it on the resume, and thought he could take over the association for his own purposes. I don't think so ... I hauled him in, sat him down, and I said, "I want your resignation on my desk as you walk out of here." And he provided it. There was a bit of fuss in the riding association that I was a little harsh, but when I was in Ottawa he tried to take over the riding association at an annual general meeting and tried to get rid of my key guy, my membership chairman, and you don't do that.

While the MP was not exercising a formal power, his status as a popular veteran MP provided him with the effective power to de-select personnel in appropriate situations, in this case when his association president was engaging in both leisure shirking and sabotage.

Reporting and Monitoring

The second method employed by MPs to reduce agency costs involves requiring executive members to report on their activities and by monitoring those activities. In doing so, MPs are able to ensure that executive members are meeting a certain standard, to praise executive members who are working hard, and to determine which executive members should be replaced. Indeed, the willingness of MPs to monitor creates an incentive for executive members to work hard in order to avoid disappointing the MP.

Reporting and monitoring take place within the context of constituency association executive meetings. There is wide variation in the frequency with which executives hold meetings, but executives with MPs tend to be professional and, therefore, hold monthly meetings (Koop 2010, 902–04).

There is also variation in the willingness of MPs to attend executive meetings: some never miss a meeting while others avoid them in order to not be perceived by the executive as domineering and controlling. If an MP is dissatisfied with the performance of his or her executive, attending executive meetings is a useful way of addressing this concern. MPs do not have to expend too much time or energy monitoring as they often attend executive meetings when in the riding even if there are no problems to address.

MPs expect information on the activities of the executive when attending executive meetings. The way that this typically takes place is as follows: the executive president goes around the table, with chairs of different committees providing reports on upcoming events, finances, membership, and local initiatives. Often, MPs interject in these proceedings to recognize the hard work of some members; in other cases, MPs interject in order to emphasize the importance of a particular project, the implication being that executive members should spend more time and effort on it. This is a process to which one MP referred as "bumping and nudging": lacking the tools of traditional managers, MPs can generally only state priorities and encourage executive members to meet them. Sitting around the table and receiving the MP's direct attention provides executive members with a powerful incentive to produce results. In this way, hands-on monitoring by MPs can reduce leisure-shirking behaviours.

Enhancing Rewards

The question, then, is: What carrots can MPs provide in order to enhance the rewards that activists receive for their participation? Before addressing this question, it is necessary to consider why activists continue to participate in constituency associations. Classic accounts of party members found in the "motivation theory" literature stress three such rewards: purposive (or ideological), solidary, and material (Clark and Wilson 1961; Ware 1996). However, motivations for initially joining a party may differ from motivations for continuing to participate, particularly as some benefits do not reveal themselves to activists until they are immersed in the organization (McCulloch 1990). Young and Cross (2002, 567), in their survey of Canadian party members, find that policy-related incentives continue to be important to maintaining membership in Canadian parties but that solidary motivations become important as well. In contrast, material incentives and the need to support the leader become relatively unimportant. In order to maintain participation, MPs must find ways of enhancing the solidary and ideological rewards that activists receive for their participation.

MPs draw on their positions as local elites and intermediaries between the local and central parties to reward solidary and ideological activists. Solidary activists are rewarded in three ways. First, they get to report on happenings from Ottawa, giving executive members insight into inside party business that they would not receive from the local news. One MP described how she does this at her executive meetings:

> I give really detailed reports about what's going on in Ottawa and I find that people really, really appreciate that. They want to know what's going on, they want to be a part of something, they want to know the backroom stories that they didn't read about in the [newspaper] and if that's the special thing that I can do, then that's awesome. That sort of feeling of inclusion is really important, that feeling of being a part of something.

Second, MPs reward solidary activists by emphasizing linkages between the central and local parties through bringing elites to the riding. In both these cases, solidary activists are given the impression that they are members of a wider team than that which exists within their own riding. This feeling of being "a part of the team" is important to solidary activists, and MPs can effectively enhance this reward.

Third, solidary activists enjoy social events in the riding since they involve interactions with other activists on their teams, and this encourages their continued participation. MPs can enhance this reward by planning additional events for local activists. The presence of the MPs themselves at these events further enhances their attractiveness as solidary activists relish the opportunity to speak with MPs outside the structure of official executive business. Many MPs with whom I spoke planned personal events designed explicitly to reward activists for their work, and they further improved rewards by holding these events at their own homes or cabins. It is important to recognize that these rewards are not generally available to activists in ridings without their own MP, which helps to explain why associations without MPs are smaller and less active than are those with MPs.

MPs also provide rewards to ideological activists. The first way that they do so is, as with solidary activists, by reporting on party business in Ottawa. In this case, they do this not to emphasize linkages between the local and national parties but, rather, to ensure local activists that the wider party is in fact fighting on behalf of the principles of the party – a particularly important consideration for Canada's old catch-all parties, in which ideological "believers" (to use Panebianco's term) may be disappointed by leaders' brokerage tendencies. Ideological activists may be sceptical of the party's commitment to a particular policy area when they arrive at executive meetings and then leave having been assured by the MP that the party is doing everything that it can.

The second way that MPs reward ideological activists is by encouraging local policy formulation processes. Canada's brokerage parties have particularly ineffectual policy formulation processes (Cross 2007, 425), so ideological activists may be dissatisfied with these roles. However, MPs can reassure them by encouraging them to continue, praising their work to other executive members and even sponsoring and speaking out in favour of their policy resolutions at party conventions. Some MPs appear to genuinely believe that local policy formulation processes are useful to the party; however, others are convinced that these processes are merely a useful way of maintaining the activism of committed party members. MPs encourage the continued participation of these members by supporting their policy formulation work.

An important point about the application of a principal-agent framework to political parties is that MPs and association members can both participate despite the fact that they have differing views of each other's roles. Ideological activists, for example, may see the association's role as providing policy ideas to the MP, who then carries these to the party centre, whereas the MP may see the association's role as providing representational and electoral support. By providing rewards to ideological activists, MPs can overcome the potential difficulties that may emerge from these divergent views.

Finally, while material and careerist rewards are relatively unimportant to sustaining participation in Canadian parties, there are undoubtedly activists who sign up seeking such rewards (e.g., Koop 2011, 54–58). This is because working on constituency association executives brings them into close contact with MPs on a fairly regular basis. However, my interviews provided me with little evidence that MPs use material or careerist rewards to sustain the participation of activists, at least in comparison with other rewards offered. They were more likely to complain about executive members hoping to extract favours. In terms of career rewards, for example, MPs can only offer positions to a limited number of loyalists, and these typically come from his or her nomination and campaign teams.

Discussion and Conclusion

The last section shows the steps that MPs take to reduce agency loss and, in so doing, to enhance the value of the principal-agent relationship. The extent to which MPs can do this, however, is shaped by their own abilities as well as by how receptive association members are to their efforts. First, MPs must be aware of the potential benefits of constituency associations and be willing to find a balance between reducing agency costs and alienating volunteers (who would likely rather leave than be dictated to). The key influence here appears to be time: MPs need time to learn about their associations – indeed, many MPs with prior experience in constituency associations have learned all they need to know by the time they are elected – and how best to interact with volunteer activists. Second, as has been hinted at several times, executive members must be receptive to the MP. Most appear to be receptive as, for the most part, their own goals coincide with the re-election goals of the MPs. And, over time, MPs' abilities to tamper with personnel selection will usually produce a cooperative executive. However, in other cases, as when a bitter renomination contest looms, executives may become hostile, and MPs must live without their electoral and representational benefits until the situation can be rectified.

The application of a principal-agent framework effectively captures the relationship between MPs and members of their constituency associations, and it illuminates the important and previously unrecognized role of MPs as local managers facing the difficult task of minimizing agency loss. However, one may ask whether using this framework is the most appropriate way of summarizing relationships between MPs and association members, especially since their reciprocal benefits suggest the existence of an exchange relationship (see Blau 1964). There are certainly elements of exchange involved in the relationship between MPs and their associations, and their ability to provide each other with reciprocal benefits addresses a potential problem, which is that these two actors may want very different things from their participation in the arrangement. Furthermore, the application of an exchange relationship framework suggests that MPs and activists may adjust their efforts to mirror the benefits each provides to the other (Homans 1958, 606). However, the informal power of MPs to remove members of their constituency association executives demonstrates that the power of MPs, though not total, overshadows that of association members. In other words, a principal-agent framework better summarizes the relationship between MPs and association members than does an exchange framework.

A next step for this research might include an examination of the conditions necessary for MPs to effectively manage their local organizations. Preliminary research suggests that MPs are better able to manage their local organizations when they bring both knowledge and skills to their roles. By "knowledge" I mean an understanding of how constituency associations function, particularly as volunteer organizations, and an appreciation of the individuals involved in the local party (which can be easily acquired by past participation in associations). By "skills" I mean the ability to be successful in volunteer management, which can be gained from previous professional experience in the not-for-profit sector. Understanding the conditions under which MPs effectively manage their local organizations may help to explain why delegative relationships succeed in some constituencies but fail in others.

Notes

I thank Erika Kirkpatrick for providing research assistance and gratefully acknowledge financial support from Memorial University and the Skelton-Clark Foundation at Queen's University.

1 I describe these representational functions more fully elsewhere (Koop 2012).

References

Bendor, J., A. Glazer, and T. Hammond. 2001. "Theories of delegation." *Annual Review of Political Science* 4 (1): 235–69. http://dx.doi.org/10.1146/annurev.polisci.4.1.235.

Bendor, J., and A. Meirowitz. 2004. "Spatial models of delegation." *Annual Political Science Review* 98 (2): 293–310.

Blau, P. 1964. *Exchange and Power in Social Life*. New York: Wiley.

Brehm, J., and S. Gates. 1997. *Working, Shirking and Sabotage: Bureaucratic Response to a Democratic Republic*. Ann Arbor: University of Michigan Press.

Carty, R.K. 1991. *Canadian Political Parties in the Constituencies*. Toronto: Dundurn.

–. 2002. "The politics of Tecumseh Corners: Canadian political parties as franchise organizations." *Canadian Journal of Political Science* 35 (4): 723–45. http://dx.doi.org/10.1017/S0008423902778402.

Carty, R.K., W. Cross, and L. Young. 2000. *Rebuilding Canadian Politics*. Vancouver: UBC Press.

Cheng, C., and M. Tavits. 2011. "Informal influences in selecting female political candidates." *Political Research Quarterly* 64 (2): 460–71. http://dx.doi.org/10.1177/1065912909349631.

Clark, A. 2006 "Local parties participation and campaigning in post-devolution Scotland." PhD diss., University of Aberdeen.

Clark, P.B., and J.Q. Wilson. 1961. "Incentive systems: A theory of organizations." *Administrative Science Quarterly* 6 (2): 129–66. http://dx.doi.org/10.2307/2390752.

Cox, G.W., and M.D. McCubbins. 1993. *Legislative Leviathan: Party Government in the House*. Cambridge, MA: Cambridge University Press.

Cross, W. 2007. "Policy study and development in Canada's political parties." In *Policy Analysis in Canada: The State of the Art*, ed. L. Dobuzinskis, M. Howlett, and D. Laycock, 425–42. Toronto: University of Toronto Press.
Denver, D., and G. Hands. 1997. "Challengers, incumbents and the impact of constituency campaigning in Britain." *Electoral Studies* 16 (2): 175–93. http://dx.doi.org/10.1016/S0261-3794(96)00065-0.
Docherty, D. 1997. *Mr. Smith Goes to Ottawa: Life in the House of Commons*. Vancouver: UBC Press.
Epstein, D., and S. O'Halloran. 1999. *Delegating Powers: A Transaction Cost Politics Approach to Policy Making under Separate Powers*. Cambridge, MA: Cambridge University Press. http://dx.doi.org/10.1017/CBO9780511609312.
Eulau, H., and P.D. Karps. 1977. "The puzzle of representation: Specifying components of responsiveness." *Legislative Studies Quarterly* 2 (3): 233–54. http://dx.doi.org/10.2307/439340.
Homans, G.C. 1958. "Social behaviour as exchange." *American Journal of Sociology* 63 (6): 597–606. http://dx.doi.org/10.1086/222355.
Huber, J.D. 2000. "Delegation of civil servants in parliamentary democracies." *European Journal of Political Research* 37 (3): 397–413. http://dx.doi.org/10.1111/1475-6765.00519.
Koelble, T.A. 1996. "Economic theories of organizations and the politics of institutional design in political parties." *Party Politics* 2 (2): 251–63. http://dx.doi.org/10.1177/1354068896002002005.
Koop, R. 2010. "Professionalism, sociability and the Liberal Party in the constituencies." *Canadian Journal of Political Science* 43 (4): 893–913. http://dx.doi.org/10.1017/S0008423910000740.
Koop, R. 2011. *Grassroots Liberals: Organizing for Local and National Politics*. Vancouver: UBC Press.
–. 2012. "Party constituency associations and the service policy and symbolic responsiveness of Canadian members of Parliament." *Canadian Journal of Political Science* 45 (2): 359–78.
McCulloch, A. 1990. "Joining a political party: A reassessment of the economic approach to membership." *British Journal of Sociology* 41 (4): 497–516. http://dx.doi.org/10.2307/590664.
Müller, W.C. 2000. "Political parties in parliamentary democracies: Making delegation and accountability work." *European Journal of Political Research* 37 (3): 309–33. http://dx.doi.org/10.1111/1475-6765.00515.
Pollack, M.A. 1997. "Delegation agency and agenda setting in the European community." *International Organization* 51 (1): 99–134. http://dx.doi.org/10.1162/002081897550311.
Price, R.G., and M. Mancuso. 1995. "Ties that bind: Members and their constituencies." In *Introductory Readings in Canadian Government & Politics*, ed. R.M. Krause and R.H. Wagenberg, 198–220. Toronto: Copp Clark.
Scarrow, S.E. 1996. *Parties and Their Members: Organising for Victory in Britain and Germany*. Oxford: Oxford University Press. http://dx.doi.org/10.1093/0198279183.001.0001.

van Houten, P. 2009. "Multi-level relations in political parties: A delegation approach." *Party Politics* 15 (2): 137–56. http://dx.doi.org/10.1177/1354068808099978.

Ware, A. 1996. *Political Parties and Party Systems*. Oxford: Oxford University Press.

Whiteley, P., and P. Seyd. 2003. "How to win a landslide by really trying: The effects of local campaigning on voting in the 1997 British general election." *Electoral Studies* 22 (2): 301–24. http://dx.doi.org/10.1016/S0261-3794(02)00017-3.

Wolinetz, S.B. 2002. "Beyond the catch-all party: Approaches to the study of parties and party organization in contemporary democracies." In *Political Parties: Old Concepts and News Challenges*, ed. R. Gunther, J.R. Montero, and J.J. Linz, 136–65. Oxford: Oxford University Press. http://dx.doi.org/10.1093/0199246742.003.0006.

Young, L., and W. Cross. 2002. "Incentives to membership in Canadian political parties." *Political Research Quarterly* 55 (3): 547–69. http://dx.doi.org/10.1177/106591290205500303.

9

Patterns of Party Recruitment and Campaign Individualization in an SMP System

WILLIAM CROSS AND LISA YOUNG

Politics, according to R. Kenneth Carty, is local. Writing with Munroe Eagles, he observes that geographic "constituencies, and the political organizations and processes that they frame, stand at the very core of Canada's political life" (Carty and Eagles 2005, 2). In his extensive work on the local dimensions of Canadian politics, Carty reminds us that it is a misnomer to speak of a single Canadian general election campaign. General elections in Canada occur at two different levels: (1) there is the national contest, dominated by the party leaders and reported on each evening in the television news broadcasts and, at the same time, (2) there are 308 individual contests being conducted in discrete geographic constituencies across the country.

In this chapter, we turn our focus to the key players in these local campaigns – the candidates – with a view to understanding the extent to which candidates differentiate themselves and their campaigns from the national party and its campaign. Building on earlier work that found considerable individualization – differentiation from the national campaigns at the local level in Canada – we focus here on the linkage between how candidates were recruited and their propensity to individualize their campaigns. Analyzing data from a survey of Liberal and NDP candidates in the 2008 federal election,[1] we find evidence supporting the contention that locally recruited candidates are more inclined to individualize their campaigns, while those recruited by the national party are more likely to run campaigns consistent with the messages of the national campaign. These findings speak to a tension between national and local parties in Canadian politics that may indicate an erosion of Carty's "stratarchical bargain" (see Carty 2002), in which the local party enjoys autonomy in matters of candidate selection and the national party enjoys autonomy in matters of policy. Locally recruited candidates appear more inclined to emphasize local issues and to run campaigns distinct from the national, while nationally recruited candidates – who should not exist in the context of Carty's stratarchy – are more inclined to emphasize the party over their own identity or local messaging.

The Local Campaign

Voters experience both the national and the local campaign. They watch the leaders' debates on national television; witness the internet, television, and radio advertisements produced and aired by the national parties; and view media coverage of the parties' policy platforms and the daily activities of their leading candidates. This air war is certainly significant, but it is not synonymous with the general election. Underlying the air war is the ground war fought in the 308 constituencies (Carty, Cross, and Young 2000). Local candidates campaign door to door in their districts, attend local events, and meet voters on street corners and subway platforms. Their campaign volunteers deliver locally produced messages to voters by telephone and through print materials created by the local campaign. Some voters will attend a local all-candidates' meeting to observe the candidates in person, and many will hear about these meetings through local media coverage, particularly outside large cities.

Most scholarly attention to campaigning in Canada has focused on the national campaign,[2] as this is understood to be the primary determinant of vote choice. Analyses of Canadian voting behaviour suggest that only about one in twenty Canadian voters base their vote on their views of the local candidates (Blais et al. 2003). Nonetheless, Carty and Eagles (2005) find that intense local campaign efforts can provide a party's candidate with a vote share premium. Coletto (2010, 216) concludes that candidate quality (prior political experience or a high-profile occupation) contributes to vote share. The local effects identified by these studies may have more to do with priming and turning out supporters than with converting sceptics. Nonetheless, parties expend a sizable portion of their campaign resources at the local level. As voter turnout has declined precipitously in recent decades, averaging in the 75 percent range for elections up to 1988 and in the 60 percent range for recent elections, efforts aimed at convincing one's supporters to vote, and then ensuring that they actually do so, are increasingly crucial components of campaign success and are largely local functions.

Despite media focus on the national campaign and compelling research indicating that the national campaign is the most important determinant of voters' choices, local campaigns remain vibrant. One indicator of this is total candidate spending. Carty and Young (2012) note that the Canada Elections Act allows a party's candidates to collectively spend $1.35 for each dollar the national party spends on its election campaign; in practice, most parties' candidates do not spend their total limit, so they collectively spend approximately the same amount as does the national party. Another indicator is the candidates' own reports of their local campaign effort. Analyzing data from our 2008 candidate survey, we have found that most candidates expend considerable effort in waging a ground campaign; there is, however, considerable variance in the strength of local campaign efforts as reported by candidates (Cross and Young 2011). Many candidates believe these local efforts to be critical to their chances of success. Collectively, candidates who responded to our 2008 survey believe a slightly larger share of their vote total results from their personal campaign than from their party's electoral efforts. This is inconsistent with the social science evidence relating to the determinants of vote choice in Canadian elections, but it gives an interesting insight into the candidates' perceptions of the significance of their local efforts and helps to contextualize the effort they expend on these endeavours.

The nature of campaigning is heavily influenced by the electoral system (Zittel and Gschwend 2008). Canada's single member plurality (SMP) system means that candidates win and lose based on vote totals in individual constituencies. Nationwide vote shares are largely irrelevant in these contests, particularly because of the regionalized patterns of support some parties garner. Thus, it is not unusual for two parties with similar vote shares to receive widely different numbers of seats in Parliament, depending on how efficiently the party's support is distributed. For example, the Progressive Conservatives and Reform Party received very similar vote shares in elections in the 1990s, with Reform winning more than twenty-five times more seats than the PCs in the 1993 election because of its concentrated support in one geographic area as contrasted to the PC's more geographically diffuse base of support. Even with a tradition of single party government, there is no guarantee that the party winning the most votes will form government. Parties are rewarded for an efficient distribution of their vote share that maximizes the number of constituencies in which they receive more votes than their competitors. Widespread voter popularity, not focused efficiently on a limited number of constituencies, regularly leaves some parties with far fewer parliamentary seats than their popular vote total would suggest. This, of course, encourages parties to focus on ridings in which they might finish first and thus add to their parliamentary representation. Even the small contribution that the local campaign effort makes to a candidate's vote share can determine the outcome in a closely contested constituency (Flanagan 2009; Marland 2011).

Canada's SMP electoral system also mandates that voters weigh many factors, both national and local, in determining their vote choice. Unlike their counterparts in presidential systems or those jurisdictions using some form of proportional representation, Canadian voters are unable to support a candidate from one party to be their local representative while supporting another party to form the government or to fill the top executive position. This makes it very difficult to definitively assess the comparative importance of each level of campaigning as undoubtedly both influence the single ballot cast by voters, though likely in ways not always apparent to either the voter or the political scientist.

All of this takes place in a party system with a tradition of stratarchical party organization (Carty and Cross 2006; Wolinetz, Chapter 4, this volume). The franchise bargain (see Carty 2002) structuring the relationships between local and national party organizations shifts over time and varies among parties. Nonetheless, the general contours have traditionally been described as a relationship in which local party activists exercise considerable discretion over candidate selection and the conduct of their local election campaigns. In return, the national party has near complete authority over policy determination and demands almost absolute party cohesion in Parliament. The salience of regional tensions and the emphasis placed on local representation has allowed Canadian MPs and candidates to negotiate some autonomy on local or regional issues but not on the national stances that comprise the core of parties' election platforms and legislative programs.

This stratarchical bargain raises questions regarding the nature of local campaigning. When local candidates produce pamphlets or advertisements for local media and knock on doors to talk with voters, are they delivering an individualized message or are they simply mimicking national messages and delivering materials prepared by the central campaign?

To understand the local dimensions of campaigning more fully, we undertook a survey of candidates in the 2008 federal election. Although all four major parties were contacted to participate in this survey, only the Liberal and New Democratic parties opted to cooperate with this research undertaking. Both parties sent letters of support and reminder mailings to the permanent addresses of their candidates, encouraging them to participate. The response rate for the survey was slightly greater than 55 per cent, with 170 NDP and 168 Liberal responses. Although candidate surveys sometimes suffer from overrepresentation of unsuccessful candidates, the proportion of respondents to our survey who were elected in 2008 (19 percent) matches the overall proportion of successful candidates from these parties. In terms of population density of the district, our respondents are almost equally divided in having contested constituencies they describe as primarily rural, suburban/small urban centre, and large urban centre.

Using our 2008 candidate survey data to explore this question, we find evidence of significant individualization of campaigning among Canadian general election candidates for the Liberal and New Democratic parties in the 2008 campaign. While there is a range in degree, candidates responding to the survey report considerable individualization of the campaign message, means, and organization employed by their campaigns (Cross and Young 2014). These differences can be attributed in part to characteristics of the party, noting a greater degree of individualization among Liberal candidates who were running under the banner of a party led by an unpopular politician (Stéphane Dion) with an unpopular platform. We also find that the characteristics of the constituency affect the degree of individualization of the local campaign, with a greater tendency towards individualization in rural electoral districts. In addition, the characteristics of the candidate herself affect the degree of individualization. Candidates who rate themselves as being more ideologically distant from their party and those who report being motivated to run for office because of particular policy concerns are all more likely to report raising local issues during the campaign. Candidates who live in the constituency in which they are running are also more likely to individualize their campaigns.

The importance of these candidate characteristics suggests that the way the candidate was recruited may be an important variable explaining the type of local campaign efforts waged. There are three primary modes of recruitment to candidacy in Canadian parties. Carty's stratarchical bargain would suggest that local party recruitment would be the most important form of candidate recruitment as local associations maintain considerable autonomy over the selection of the local candidate. Surveying Liberal and NDP candidates in 2008, we found that this is the most common form of recruitment, with almost four in ten candidates being recruited by a representative of the local party organization and another two in ten reporting being recruited by both the local and the national party organization (Cross and Young 2013). Given Carty's characterization of the stratarchical bargain in Canadian political parties, there is little reason to anticipate that the national party would play a role in candidate recruitment. In practice, however, there are some circumstances in which we would expect the national party to become involved in candidate recruitment. Where the local party is weak or non-existent, the national party might step in to find a candidate (Sayers 1998). When a high-profile individual signals that s/he is willing to run for the party, the national party may intervene to ensure that this individual finds a constituency in which to run. In addition, the national organizations of both the New Democratic and Liberal parties have been active in encouraging a diversification of their party's candidate pool, with an emphasis on recruiting more female candidates and candidates from other underrepresented socio-demographic groups. Candidates who report being recruited only by the national party comprise 15 percent of the respondents to our 2008 survey. Finally, some candidates are not recruited by any party representative or body but, rather, self-recruit or are encouraged to run by organizations outside the party. Candidates reporting no party recruitment comprise one-quarter of the sample (Cross and Young 2013).

Party Recruitment and Type of Campaign

An issue not raised in our earlier analysis is the relationship between the candidate's pattern of recruitment and the individualization of the campaign. We hypothesize that candidates recruited by the local party organization will run different types of campaigns as compared to those waged by candidates sought out and encouraged by the national party. Consistent with the stratarchical bargain outlined above, candidate recruitment and selection has been thought to be largely within the purview of local party associations. However, in the past two decades, the national parties have made significant incursions in this territory. Cross (2004; 2006) chronicles how national parties have increasingly involved themselves in the recruitment of local candidates, often in the face of significant opposition from local party activists. Our 2008 candidate survey results confirm this, showing that more than three in ten respondents were recruited by the national party, either exclusively or in addition to local recruitment. Although a higher percentage of candidates – six in ten – were recruited by the local party association, these numbers make clear that both levels of the party are actively engaged in the candidate recruitment business, a finding that has implications for our understanding of the parameters of the stratarchical bargain in Canadian politics.

Using data from our 2008 survey, we are able to test the proposition that local candidates will run more individualized campaigns, while nationally recruited candidates will be less likely to do so. Some candidates who responded to the survey reported having been recruited by both levels of the party. Because we are interested in how the types of campaigns executed by candidates recruited by the national and local branches differ, we exclude these candidates from our analysis. This leaves us with 133 candidates recruited exclusively by the local party and forty-six by officials from the national office. Much of the consideration is focused on the degree of individualization of the local effort. Candidates who are recruited by the national party we suspect are more attracted to the national brand and the party leader and thus are less likely to run individualized campaigns. Locally recruited candidates, we suspect, have stronger ties to their geographic community and are more likely to individualize their campaign appeals.

Before examining the relationship between party recruitment patterns and degrees of campaign individualization it is important to consider some of the characteristics of these two groups of candidates that might influence the nature of their local campaigns. In our earlier analysis, we found several differences between these two cohorts (Cross and Young 2013) although we did not extend it to consider whether the two groups of candidates ran different types of campaigns.[3] Consistent with the available evidence, we suspect that much of the individualization of campaigns that takes place in an SMP system such as is found in Canada relates to candidates emphasizing issues of local importance and their personal community involvement, so we first consider candidates' ties to their constituency and to civil society.

Perhaps the most striking finding is that eight in ten of the locally recruited candidates lived in the constituency in which they were seeking office as compared to 44 percent of candidates recruited by the national party. There are two reasons to expect that candidates running in the constituency in which they reside are more likely to individualize their campaign. First, as local residents, these candidates should be more familiar with local issues and the concerns of local voters and are consequently better able to shape their campaign message to reflect these local vagaries. Second, living in the same community, they are likely better known to voters and, thus, focusing on their personal accomplishments and views might resonate with their electors and provide a vote boost. Conversely, candidates living outside the district are unlikely to boast about this as it may result in a backlash from voters, who are often suspicious of candidates parachuted in from other communities.

Candidates recruited by the local party branch also have broader involvement in community activities and report that this involvement is an important factor in their decision to seek elected office. Candidates were provided a list of fourteen different types of community associations, ranging from sports clubs to service clubs to church and ethnic organizations. On average, candidates recruited by the local party association reported belonging to four of these groups compared with three for national party recruits. And, for six in ten of the local recruits, this community involvement was a very important factor in their decision to seek public office compared with 43 percent of those encouraged by the national party. That local parties are recruiting candidates with wider involvement in, and deeper commitment to, their community suggests that these candidates should be more likely to emphasize local needs and issues and their personal attributes in their campaign appeals.

How a candidate secures his nomination may also influence the type of local campaign he runs. If a candidate is challenged for the nomination, her path to victory typically involves encouraging large numbers of other local partisans (and friends and family) to join the party and to attend the nomination meeting (Cross 2002a; 2004). Nomination contests themselves are highly individualized. Survey data suggest that policy contestation among nomination candidates is very rare (Cross 2002a). Instead, these are generally personalized contests with candidates with stronger local ties and broader circles of contacts typically prevailing (Erickson and Carty 1991). Therefore it is expected that those who have to fight for their nomination will ultimately stage a more individualized campaign than do those who achieve the nomination by acclamation.

Increasingly, national party leadership has been involving itself in nomination contests and, in some instances, guaranteeing the position to a favoured candidate (Cross 2006). In these cases it can be expected that selected candidates have strong ties to the national party and leader and, thus, are less likely to individualize their general election campaign. While a large majority of nominations are won by acclamation, locally recruited candidates are more likely to have to compete for the right to run (18 percent versus 13 percent for those nationally recruited). And only slightly more than one-third of those encouraged by the local party had their nominations guaranteed by the centre compared with slightly more than half of those approached by the national party.

Propensity for individualization of campaigning might also be influenced by the degree of ideological coherence between the candidate and his party. Candidates who are more distant from their party ideologically might be more prone to emphasize their own issues and to downplay policy positions taken by the party. While there is not a large difference between the two groups of candidates in this regard, those who are recruited by the national party place themselves closer on a ten-point left-right scale to their party than do those encouraged to run by the local party. The latter group reports a median difference between candidate and party of 1.06 points compared with 0.96 for the prior cohort.

Candidates running in rural ridings might be more likely to individualize their campaigns. These ridings tend to follow municipal boundaries and often include stronger, more cohesive communities of interest as opposed to urban ridings, which may be comprised of parts of a large urban centre with no meaningful boundaries separating them from neighbouring districts. Local issues often do not correlate with a constituency's boundaries in urban areas, while they often do correlate in more rural areas. The data suggest that national parties are significantly more active in urban centres in terms of recruiting candidates. Four in ten candidates recruited by the local party contested a rural constituency compared with two of ten candidates encouraged by the national party.

These relationships all run in the direction of suggesting that there may be more individualization of campaigning among candidates recruited by the locals. The next section of this chapter directly considers this relationship between campaign individualization and patterns of party recruitment.

Candidate Recruitment and Individualization of Campaigns

Zittel and Gschwend (2008) contend that there are three components of election campaigns to be considered separately when measuring the degree of individualization of campaigns. These are a campaign's agenda, means, and organization. Each of these is addressed in turn.

In terms of campaign agenda we consider whether local candidates campaigned on issues that were "specific to [their] constituency and that were not raised by the national campaign." As illustrated in Table 9.1, local recruits were 7 percentage points more likely to have done so than were those recruited by the national party. The relationship was particularly strong, and

TABLE 9.1
Individualization of campaign by level of party recruitment (%)

	All candidates recruited		NDP recruited		Liberal recruited	
	Locally	Nationally	Locally	Nationally	Locally	Nationally
Campaigned on issues not raised by national party	68	61	66	42	71	82
Local campaign produced own advertisements	67	48	60	29	77	68
Local campaign created and maintained own web page	66	57	60	38	75	77
Central party notable campaigned for local candidate	43	50	48	63	37	37
Proportion of volunteers attracted by candidate	44	51	41	47	50	56
Proportion of volunteers long-time party members	51	31	54	27	47	35
Local campaign hired own campaign consultant	15	7	7	0	26	14
Proportion of local campaign funds from party	31	40	29	54	36	21

Note: Shading indicates significance at $p = .10$.

statistically significant, among NDP candidates. Candidates recruited by the national NDP organization appear more likely to rely on the policy positions adopted and emphasized by that level of the campaign. The pattern was reversed for Liberal candidates, possibly as a result of candidates trying to distance themselves from the Liberal Party's unpopular platform in 2008.

Having their own message, distinct from that delivered by the national campaign, appears to encourage local recruits to produce their own campaign materials. Slightly fewer than half of nationally recruited candidates produced their own campaign advertisements compared with two-thirds of those recruited by the local campaign. Local candidates were thus significantly more likely to communicate a distinctive message to voters and to produce their own advertisements rather than to rely on those produced by the party. This pattern is again particularly stark among NDP candidates: locally recruited New Democrats were twice as likely as those recruited nationally to produce their own advertising materials.

Consistent with this, locally recruited candidates were more likely than their nationally recruited colleagues to create and to maintain their own campaign web page, which they kept distinct from their party's page. Two-thirds of local recruits did so compared with 57 percent of candidates encouraged to run by their national party, with an even more stark, and statistically significant, difference among NDP candidates. It is likely that this, too, is related to the local candidate's desire to deliver a message somewhat distinct from that conveyed by her party. Producing their own web page provides these candidates with an additional medium for conveying their message separate from any sites run by the party.

As suggested at the outset, party leaders and other party notables travel the country during an election campaign visiting targeted constituencies and campaigning on behalf of local candidates. These visits, particularly by the party leader, are high-profile events and can be expected to attract significant local media attention. This, then, is an additional method of delivering a campaign message. These central party officials can be expected to deliver appeals consistent with the national party's campaign message. As shown in Table 9.1, candidates recruited by the national party were approximately 15 percentage points more likely to have had a party notable campaign on their behalf. As Table 9.1 also demonstrates, this difference is entirely the product of differences between locally and nationally recruited NDP candidates.

In terms of campaign organization we consider both the type of volunteers attracted to a local candidate's campaign and the source of their campaign funds. Many commentators on Canadian electoral politics have observed that candidates need money and volunteers to wage successful election campaigns (Carty and Eagles 2005; Carty, Cross and Young 2000). There are very few paid local party staff, which means that candidates are highly dependent upon volunteers. A campaign rich in one of these resources – money or volunteers – may be able to get by with a shortage of the other, but one with few of both will find it impossible to make a vibrant local effort. Candidates can draw their volunteers from one of two pools: (1) long-time party supporters who regularly work for their party's candidate and (2) their personal friends, family, and acquaintances who may be motivated to support the candidate even though they do not regularly volunteer for the party.

Overall, candidates reported that 47 percent of their volunteers were personal friends and supporters who "would not likely have volunteered if someone else was the candidate." There is a significant difference here between candidates recruited by the different levels of the party. Candidates recruited by the local party report that volunteers who are long-time party members make up a share of their total volunteer force that is almost two times higher than that reported by those recruited by the national party, and this is consistent across both parties. The difference is less stark, though still in the same direction, in terms of the proportion of volunteers who are personal supporters, with these comprising 51 percent of nationally recruited candidates' volunteers compared to 44 percent for local recruits. This is an expected finding as candidates recruited by the local party have deeper roots in the local association and are likely a more popular choice with local activists than are those who are recruited solely by the national party. In some cases, local party activists resent what they see as national-level intervention in candidate recruitment and selection, and this may result in fewer of them supporting national-level recruits.

The independent use of campaign professionals is not widespread in Canada. Overall, only about one in six candidates hired a campaign consultant to help with their local effort. This likely reflects the general reliance on the party campaign and the volunteer nature of local campaigns. Nonetheless, candidates recruited by their local party association were twice as likely as were those recruited by the national party to hire a campaign consultant. It is likely that these campaign professionals are hired to help the candidate craft an individualized campaign plan as those candidates wishing to mimic the national campaign would have no particular need to expend funds on a consultant.

In terms of source of campaign funds, nationally recruited candidates are more likely to be reliant on party funds than are local recruits. This, too, is not surprising. Locally recruited candidates, with their widespread local contacts, should be more able to raise contributions directly for their campaign and thus be less reliant on party funds. The national party may feel some responsibility to help fund the campaigns of those it recruited and this may help explain their higher reliance on party funds.

It is, of course, also possible that the national party recruits candidates in particular types of ridings in terms of competitiveness. The literature would suggest that these recruitments may take place primarily in two types of ridings. The first are ridings in which the party has little local organization and little chance for electoral victory. In many of these districts the parties find it difficult to find candidates, and the national party, wanting to ensure that it runs a full slate of candidates, will encourage someone to stand. These are what Sayers (1998) refers to as "stop gap" candidates. An example of this in the 2011 election would be the NDP's efforts to find candidates to stand in each of the province of Quebec's seventy-five constituencies. The party had never before won more than one Quebec constituency in any general election and had literally no local organization in dozens of ridings. The result was the conscripting of candidates who, in some cases, did not live in the province, had never visited the area in which they were to run, spoke little or no French, and did not campaign during the election. When the party leader's new found popularity in the province led to the NDP winning two-thirds of Quebec's seats, there was much public uproar over the lack of connection between many of these new parliamentarians and the communities they were elected to represent.

At the other end of the spectrum, national parties are thought to pay particular attention to candidate recruitment in those constituencies in which they are likely to finish first. The likelihood of electoral success encourages the party leadership to be interested in the identity of the local candidate as this individual stands a good chance of joining the party's parliamentary caucus and thus being someone the leader has to deal with on an ongoing basis.

The national party may also recruit candidates in ridings that appear highly competitive – that is, where it has a chance for victory but is in a tough contest with a competitor party. We know that the national parties focus their campaign efforts and resources on these constituencies in their attempt to maximize their yield of parliamentary seats (Cross 2004). Thus, if a party believes that the quality of the local candidate potentially adds a vote premium, the centre is likely to involve itself in candidate recruitment in these ridings.

These three hypotheses, then, make it unlikely that we would find a separate effect for competitiveness as the national parties tend to be involved in recruitment where they are electorally strong, where they are weakest, and

TABLE 9.2
Recruitment of candidates by national and local party branches by perceived competitiveness of district

	Candidate recruited by	
	Local party (%)	National party (%)
Thought I could not win	20	35
Thought it unlikely I'd win	37	24
Thought the race was wide open	29	20
Thought it unlikely I'd lose	12	20
Thought I could not lose	3	2

where they are in competitive contests with other parties. Table 9.2 illustrates that this is generally the case. Using candidates' subjective views of their chances prior to the campaign we find that both levels of the party are active in recruiting candidates in all sorts of races. Perhaps not surprisingly both are more active in recruiting candidates where the party is electorally weak. This likely reflects the need to actively encourage candidates to run in these areas in which the workings of the SMP electoral system result in their having little or no chance of getting to Parliament.

As illustrated in Table 9.1, there are differences between the Liberal and NDP pools of candidates on many of these measures. Liberal candidates were more likely to individualize their campaigns, particularly in terms of producing and delivering distinctive campaign messages. We suspect there are two reasons for this. First, theirs being a more ideological party (Cross and Young 2002), we expect NDP candidates to be more likely to centre their efforts around the ideological positioning of their national campaign. The Liberals, on the other hand, are a classic brokerage or catch-all party (Whitaker 1977; Wearing 1981). Consistent with this, our survey data suggest greater ideological diversity among Liberal candidates and a somewhat greater propensity for them to perceive a significant ideological distance between themselves and their party. This range in ideological perspectives among Liberal candidates likely encourages greater individualization.

The second factor is a more transient one relating to the specific dynamics of the 2008 campaign. Liberal candidates found themselves in a campaign led by an unpopular leader further weighed down by a platform with an unpopular central plank – the so-called "Green Shift." We suspect that Liberal candidates perceived their national brand to be unpopular and thus were more likely to attempt to distinguish themselves from the party's campaign by personalizing their local campaign efforts. This increased campaign individualization among Liberal candidates likely mutes any differences that may have otherwise materialized between those recruited by different levels of the party.

These differences between parties speak to the need to collect this sort of candidate and constituency-level data on a regular basis. Without similar data from several elections we are unable to determine whether there are real differences between the parties in terms of the likelihood of their candidates to wage individualized campaigns and whether differences between those recruited at different levels are party-specific or whether they reflect particular campaign dynamics.

Conclusion

This chapter is exploratory in nature. Inspired by the work of Carty to study constituency-based campaign dynamics, in earlier work we suggest that both national and local branches of Canadian parties are active in candidate recruitment and that each level recruits somewhat different types of candidates. We also identify a considerable degree of constituency-based campaign individualization in Canadian general elections. This chapter begins the task of bridging the different findings in the earlier work by asking whether candidates recruited by the local party run more individualized campaigns than do those encouraged to stand by national party officials. While not conclusive, the data suggest that this may well be the case as locally recruited candidates appear more likely to develop a campaign message distinct from their national party's appeal and to create their own means, through advertising and web pages, to deliver these messages. They are also more likely to hire their own campaign consultant to assist in executing their local campaign rather than solely relying on directives and assistance from their national campaign office. The 2008 data suggest these differences are mostly found in the NDP, but we cannot know whether the behaviour of Liberal candidates resulted from the particular circumstances they faced in that year's election or reflects deeper differences between the parties.

There is an ongoing tension in Canadian parties relating to the question of who has authority in local candidate recruitment and selection. Carty (2002) has long suggested that integral to the franchise bargain that structures Canadian party organization, locals have authority over personnel recruitment in turn for the centre demanding strong party cohesion inside Parliament. In recent years, this description has come under attack as national parties have clearly become more engaged in the recruitment of local candidates, though the data suggest that local parties remain more engaged in this activity. If, when the national party does involve itself, it tends to recruit candidates who are significantly more likely to rely on the national campaign and to run a local effort consistent with the themes established by it, this may have an important effect on the stratarchical bargain. This may be appealing to a national party that is concerned both with local campaigns deviating from their well-planned national appeals and with the possibility of MPs showing up after the election claiming a mandate based on their personal appeal and the distinctive messages upon which they campaigned. Party leaders concerned with maintaining control over their parliamentary caucus may find this worrisome, which may help to explain the increase in national party involvement in candidate recruitment.

As a construct, Carty's stratarchical bargain illuminates one of the central dynamics in Canadian party politics: balancing between local and national. The findings from this exploratory study suggest that even when recruitment is being done locally – as the stratarchical bargain suggests it should be – candidates craft some room to distinguish themselves, both in terms of their own individual attributes as local notables and in terms of crafting individualized messages that can co-exist with the national policy platform. A tacit acceptance of discussion of local issues – as distinct from deviation from the national platform and campaign – might best be understood as an element of the stratarchical bargain. The growing role of the national campaign raises greater questions for Carty's construct of party stratarchy. Certainly, there is a long history of national party incursions into the local privilege of selecting candidates, but evidence suggests that this tendency is increasing. If the national-local dynamic is, as Carty contends, a bargain between national and local, how much national incursion into local recruitment will be tolerated before the bargain collapses? Alternatively, is the increasing nationalization of Canadian parties an inevitable product of various trends towards party centralization and discipline? These are the rich questions of Canadian party politics with which Carty and his intellectual successors will grapple.

Notes

1 The Conservative Party of Canada (CPC) declined to participate in the survey. The reluctance of the CPC to allow its members and candidates to participate in academic surveys makes research focusing on Canadian political parties difficult.

2 There have never truly been national campaigns in Canada as parties have always run distinct French-language campaigns in Quebec, and, in recent elections, there has been a rise in regionalized campaigning orchestrated from the centre (see Cross 2002a).

3 It is important to note that, while this earlier article uses the same dataset as does this chapter, earlier categorizations are different as they do not remove candidates who are recruited by both levels of their party. Thus, for example, the category of candidates recruited by the local party association includes both candidates recruited solely at that level and those recruited at both the local and national levels. The analysis in this chapter includes only the first group.

References

Blais, A., E. Gidengil, A. Dobrzynska, N. Nevitte, and R. Nadeau. 2003. "Does the local candidate matter?" *Canadian Journal of Political Science* 36 (3): 657–64.

Carty, R.K. 2002. "The politics of Tecumseh Corners: Canadian political parties as franchise organizations." *Canadian Journal of Political Science* 35 (4): 723–45. http://dx.doi.org/10.1017/S0008423902778402.

Carty, R.K., and W. Cross. 2006. "Can stratarchically organized parties be democratic? The Canadian case." *Journal of Elections, Public Opinion and Parties* 16 (2): 93–114. http://dx.doi.org/10.1080/13689880600715912.

Carty, R.K., W. Cross, and L. Young. 2000. *Rebuilding Canadian Party Politics.* Vancouver: UBC Press.

Carty, R.K., and M. Eagles. 2005. *Politics Is local: National Politics at the Grassroots.* Toronto: Oxford University Press.

Carty, R.K., and L. Young. 2012. "The local underpinnings of electoral competition in Canada, 1979–2008." *Canadian Political Science Review* 6 (2–3): 227–36.

Coletto, D. 2010. "A Matter of Quality? Candidates in Canadian Constituency Elections." PhD diss., University of Calgary.

Cross, W. 2002a. "Grassroots participation in candidate nominations." In *Citizen Politics: Research and Theory in Canadian Political Behaviour*, ed. J. Everitt and B. O'Neill, 373–85. Toronto: Oxford University Press.

–. 2002b. "The increased importance of region in Canadian political campaigns." In *Regionalism and Party Politics in Canada*, ed. L. Young and K. Archer, 116–28. Toronto: Oxford University Press.

–. 2004. *Political Parties.* Vancouver: UBC Press.

–. 2006. "Candidate Nomination in Canadian Political Parties." In *The Canadian General Election of 2006*, ed. J. Pammett and C. Dornan, 171–95. Toronto: Dundurn Press.

Cross, W., and L. Young. 2002. "Policy attitudes of party members in Canada: Evidence of ideological politics." *Canadian Journal of Political Science* 35 (4): 859–80. http://dx.doi.org/10.1017/S0008423902778475.

–. 2011. "Explaining local campaign intensity: The Canadian general election of 2008." *Canadian Journal of Political Science* 44 (3): 553–71. http://dx.doi.org/10.1017/S0008423911000497.

–. 2013. "Candidate recruitment in Canada: The Role of political parties." In *Political Parties and Elections in Canada: A New Era*, ed. A. Bittner and R. Koop, 24–45. Vancouver: UBC Press.

–. 2014 . "Personalization of campaigns in an SMP System: The Canadian case." *Electoral Studies*. http://dx.doi.org/10.1016/j.electstud.2014.04.007.

Erickson, L., and R.K. Carty. 1991. "Parties and candidate selection in the 1988 Canadian general election." *Canadian Journal of Political Science* 24 (2): 331–49. http://dx.doi.org/10.1017/S0008423900005114.

Flanagan, T. 2009. "Campaign strategy: Triage and the concentration of resources." In *Election*, ed. H. MacIvor, 155–72. Toronto: Emond Montgomery Publications.

Marland, A. 2011. "Constituency campaigning in the 2011 Canadian federal election." In *The Canadian Federal Election of 2011*, ed. J.H. Pammett and C. Dornan, 167–94. Toronto: Dundurn.

Sayers, A.M. 1998. *Candidates and Constituency Campaigns in Canadian Elections*. Vancouver: UBC Press.

Wearing, J. 1981. *The L-Shaped Party: The Liberal Party of Canada 1958–1980*. Toronto: McGraw-Hill Ryerson.

Whitaker, R. 1977. *The Government Party: Organizing and Financing the Liberal Party of Canada, 1930–1958*. Toronto: University of Toronto Press.

Zittel, T., and T. Gschwend. 2008. "Individualised constituency campaigns in mixed-member electoral systems: Candidates in the 2005 German elections." *West European Politics* 31 (5): 978–1003. http://dx.doi.org/10.1080/01402380802234656.

10

Joining Isn't Everything

Exit, Voice, and Loyalty in Party Organizations

EMILIE VAN HAUTE

European political parties have been recruiting members for over a century. However, "parties without partisans" are now conceivable (Dalton and Wattenberg 2000). Clearly, parties are changing, whether they are mutating, adapting, or declining. This makes the study of party membership and its mechanisms, processes, and evolutions crucial. Besides, party membership is at the crossroads of two prolific fields in political science (party organizations and political participation). One would therefore expect to find an abundant literature on the topic. However, until recently, scholars have not devoted much attention to this phenomenon (van Haute 2009a).

The first developments concerned the general decline in party memberships, framed in the thesis of party decline. In return, this has made who joins political organizations a question commanding considerable attention. The work of Seyd and Whiteley is a turning point in this respect (Seyd and Whiteley 1992; Whiteley, Seyd and Richardson 1994). Since then, several scholars and teams have performed the same type of micro-level analysis in their national contexts.[1] Most of this literature is rather descriptive, with an emphasis on the socio-demographic and political profile of the respondents. When turning analytical, the literature is rooted mainly in the work on models of political participation: the resource model (Verba, Nie, and Kim 1978), the socio-psychological model (Finkel, Muller, and Opp 1989), and the rational choice model (Whiteley and Seyd 1996).

Today, we have a better picture of who joins parties, why they do it, and what opinions they hold. However, Heidar (2007) points out that our knowledge is still kaleidoscopic as the existing studies are generally of one party or one country. Very little comparative work has been done so far. I share this plea for more comparative work. However, I argue that it should take a step back from the theories of political participation. The dominance of the participatory approach to party membership leads to three main weaknesses.

First, because it is rooted in the theories of political participation, the existing literature on party membership does not contribute significantly to the understanding of parties as organizations. The focus is on the individual act of joining (Cross and Young 2008) and not on the relationship between the member and his/her party. Conversely, research on parties tends to focus on specific aspects of parties, generally along the lines of a functionalist divide (Dalton and Wattenberg 2000): parties in government, in the electorate, or as organizations (Reiter 2006). If the latter has known a theoretical revival in the mid-1990s with the cartel party thesis (Katz and Mair 1995), we still have little empirical evidence regarding what is happening in the black box of party organizations.

Second, the contribution to the knowledge of political participation is in itself limited due to the survey method used to collect data. At most we can say that we know more about ex post reconstruction of the motives to join than about the process of joining itself. Indeed, the surveys are aimed at members who joined on average a long time ago.[2] Studies have shown that the longer the retention period, the higher the expected bias due to respondent recall error (Biemer et al. 2004, 134).

Finally, the existing literature based on explanatory models for joining could be compared to fairy tales. We meet the characters (the individual members and the parties), get to know them, learn how they met, fell in love, and got engaged. But these studies too often end on a "happily-ever-after" note. As with fairy tales, some fundamental questions are left open: What happens after the engagement? Do they remain faithful to each other? Do they face crises? How do they cope with these tensions? Does the story end in a divorce?

The reference to romance and fairy tales is seemingly trivial. However, it emphasizes the fact that party membership can and should be studied with theoretical frameworks other than those of political participation. The latter do not shed light on what happens inside the parties once members have joined. Yet parties as membership organizations often face the difficulties of maintaining internal cohesion and discipline. This is especially true in big tent parties such as brokerage parties, which aggregate disparate and heterogeneous groups and in which the various layers are characterized by their autonomy. Inclusiveness and stratarchy can generate centrifugal effects and make it more difficult for parties to achieve cohesion. When facing that coordination challenge, parties – and brokerage parties especially – have to manage to balance the interests of the members with the imperative of an effective central leadership. According to Carty (Chapter 1, this volume), this is done via an indiscriminate approach to membership and by fostering individual and group loyalties.

Party membership studies have yet to better capture this idea of relationship between the members and the party, these questions of loyalty, dissatisfaction, doubts, and/or criticism. In order to do this, I propose using new theoretical tools to better understand membership satisfaction, loyalty, and the mechanisms through which party members renew their membership, decide to stay with the party organization, or decide to leave it. These processes and concepts are surprisingly close to Hirschman's model of exit, voice, and loyalty (Hirschman 1970). I discuss how Hirschman's model can be mobilized to analyze party members and their relation to their political party. In order to do this, I first explore Hirschman's contribution and its consecutive applications in various fields in social sciences, including political science. I then offer arguments regarding why and how to apply Hirschman's model to the study of party membership and party organizations.

Hirschman's Model and Its Possible Applications

Hirschman's model for measuring consumer reaction to decline in quality – exit, voice, and loyalty – has proven fruitful in various domains but has never been thoroughly applied in political science. Startlingly, its more obvious application to party organizations has been neglected. However, I think it offers fertile ground for studying (dis)satisfaction among party members, their reactions to dissatisfaction, and the nature of intra-party participation.

The main thesis developed in Hirschman's (1970) *Exit, Voice and Loyalty: Responses to Decline in Firms, Organizations, and States* suggests that exit and voice are the two consumer reactions to a reduction in the quality of a product provided by an organization. The choice between exit and voice entails, partly, a rationalistic decision whereby individuals evaluate the costs and benefits of their actions according to their own interests. But it is also influenced by a third concept, "loyalty," which would prevent consumers from leaving the organization.

Barry (1974) refers to Hirschman's book as the only one to rank with Downs's *Economic Theory of Democracy* (1957) and Olson's *Logic of Collective Action* (1965). According to Barry, Hirschman stretched the economic approach beyond its conventional topics, attained an "ecumenical spirit," and opened new horizons for research. Each of the three concepts utilized in his model appeals to a specific domain. Economic analyses concentrate on "exit" – customers ceasing to buy a product or employee turnover in firms. The study of "voice" opens the political dimension of the model (Kolarska and Aldrich 1980, 42), while the study of "loyalty" opens the socio-psychological dimension. Therefore, it is not surprising that the model has been used in various fields of research.

The social-psychological literature uses Hirschman's work to study interpersonal and intergroup relations (Dowding et al. 2000). Research looked at dissatisfaction in social relations at work, in groups, or in couple relationships. The main contribution of these studies is the addition of a fourth concept to the exit, voice, loyalty model: neglect, defined as (1) adopting a negative attitude towards the partner relation and (2) entailing the idea that responses to dissatisfaction can be constructive/destructive or passive/active. These studies conducted empirical tests of the model and combined various methodologies, including surveys and role-play. Their main weakness is a lack of theoretical discussion. Loyalty is seen as one of four forms of behaviour, and exit and voice are conceived as mutually exclusive – something that is questioned in other works. Finally, these studies rely mainly on cross-sectional analyses that do not adequately address the problem of temporality, and they investigate reported behaviour rather than actual behaviour.

In the labour economics and management literature, the application of Hirschman's model uses only the concepts of exit and voice. The focus is on the trade-off between exit and voice, and little room is dedicated to theoretical debates. Overall, the accent is put on exit (turnover in firms), and voice is mainly seen as collectively expressed through unions. The main interest of these studies lies in their "considerable statistical sophistication" (Dowding et al. 2000, 486). In the same vein, marketing and psychologists focus on the relation between consumers and producers. Again, the main focus is exit and the impact of market competition on the decision to exit. Urban studies also focus on exit, defined as the decision to move (Dowding et al. 2000). Their contribution is to introduce longitudinal approaches through data collected on both intention and realization. They were also the first to emphasize the richness of voice and the difference between private voice and collective voice.

Political scientists have largely ignored Hirschman's model. This is surprising given that Hirschman applied his model to political phenomena in two of his chapters. In one he attempts to explain the failure of the dissident members of the Johnson administration to resign and to denounce the Vietnam War as due to "excessive loyalty"; in the other he applies his ideas to party competition in the United States. Indeed, some work in comparative politics does use Hirschman's model, but, according to Dowding et al. (2000), this is done merely to give a name to the process. There is no rigorous testing of models, as is the case in other fields. Some comparative studies focus on the role of state repression in the choice between voice and exit (Lee 1992; O'Donnell 1986; Scott 1986; Hirschman 1993; Colomer 2000; Pfaff and Kim 2003; Gehlbach 2006). Others are interested in the role of socio-economic status (Ross 1988) or institutional variables (such as type of regime) (Clark, Golder, and Golder 2006) in explaining the choice between modes of participation. Others analyze the effect of foreign aid, inequality, economic development, natural resources, and/or authoritarianism on democratic transition (O'Donnell 1986). Finally, Weber (2009) uses the model to explain voting behaviour through the electoral cycle to explain the "second-order" effects in elections to the European Parliament.

There are few applications of Hirschman's model to party organizations. Eubank, Gangopadahay, and Weinberg (1996) look at the decline of Italian Communism and the role of loyalty in the reform proposals. In the same vein, Salucci (2008) explores the breakup of the democratic left party (Democratici di Sinistra) in Italy in 2007 through direct interviews with the party leaders. Others have used the model to study the behaviour of parliamentarians (Kato 1998) or party leaders in one-party hegemonic regimes (Langston 2002).

Several chapters in this volume make use of Hirschman's concepts. The contribution of Farrell et al. (Chapter 5, this volume) may be considered as a soft application of Hirschman's concept of loyalty to the study of party discipline among Irish MPs. Hazan and Rahat (Chapter 6, this volume) do the same when analyzing the negative impact of intra-party democratization – the increased inclusiveness of the selectorate – on party unity. Koop (Chapter 8, this volume), by looking at the interaction between MPs and their local party organization, considers how parties address the challenge of coordination. However, these contributions tend to focus on party elites rather than on party members. For this reason, I shift the focus back onto party members and offer some suggestions on how to apply Hirschman's model to the study of membership organizations.

Decline in Quality: Dissatisfaction among Party Members

Parties are not homogeneous entities, and it seems inevitable that some events or leadership decisions will create dissatisfaction among the membership (van Haute 2009b). If not completely ignored, dissatisfaction is rarely investigated. However, understanding dissatisfaction is crucial when considering the coordination imperative that parties face. Especially in the case of brokerage parties, unmasking the dynamics of membership (dis)satisfaction and its consequences for intra-party participation is critical to grasping the process leading to their survival or disappearance. In this sense, Hirschman's model is an interesting starting point. Exit, voice, and loyalty are conceived as various reactions to a decline in an organization's quality of performance.

The notion of decline in quality is rather vague. Few applications of Hirschman's model discuss this concept; rather, they tend to focus on the reactions to decline, taking decline itself for granted without defining or measuring it. Most of them assume a tangible and objective decline in quality. However, one can assume that consumers will not react to some objective decline in quality but, rather, to their perception of such decline. In other words, it is the perception of decline that matters. Hirschman (1970, 48) suggests that consumers have different ways of evaluating decline in quality, depending on their criteria of evaluation. In labour economics, the perception of decline is often equated to job (dis)satisfaction.

With regard to party organizations, I am not interested in some objective decline in quality of the performances of the party; rather, I am interested in party members' perception of a decline in quality because this is what could trigger their reaction. Evidence shows that party members do display such perception of decline. For example, among the Belgian French-speaking socialists (PS), 46 percent of respondents thought that the party had abandoned its principles, 20.5 percent thought that party members did not have a say in the decision-making process, 8.7 percent thought that the party did a bad job when in power, and 5.5 percent were not satisfied with the leadership of the party. In Canada, 34.5 percent of party members (Progressive Conservatives, Liberals, Canadian Alliance, New Democrats, and Bloc Québécois together) thought that the leadership did not pay enough attention to ordinary party members (van Haute and Carty 2012). In the same vein, van Haute and Carty show that political parties host a number of "misfit" members who, on a left-right scale, position themselves as being at odds with their party.

So far, membership surveys have provided only impressions of dissatisfaction. We suggest that such surveys should measure dissatisfaction in a systematic and coherent manner. One way to do this is to rely on such tools as the job descriptive index, the job in general index, or the job diagnostic survey. These indices combine multiple dimensions and indicators, such as satisfaction with leadership, nature of specific tasks, relation with co-workers, role of supervisors, person-environment fit, promotion opportunities, compensations and benefits, and so on (Bateman and Organ 1983; Mayes and Ganster 1988). Applied to membership (dis)satisfaction, these indices could tap such facets of satisfaction as:

- satisfaction with collective goals (overall project, ideological orientation of the party)
- satisfaction with material benefits (promotions and pay)
- satisfaction with interactions with co-workers (social interactions)
- satisfaction with the leadership
- satisfaction with the functioning of the organization (role granted to members, rights and obligations)

Analyzing the decline in quality of party membership via dissatisfaction would shine new light on intra-party life and dynamics.[3] One interesting question raised in this respect concerns the origin of dissatisfaction. Barry (1974) argues that a decline in quality of performance is not enough and that the central point is the possibility of improvement – that is, the belief that the organization can do better. However, Birch (1975) argues that the possibility of improvement is always present and that the real question is why quality suddenly becomes problematic. Applied to party organizations, the question would be: Why, at some point, do certain party members become dissatisfied with their membership? The literature provides hypotheses concerning the reasons for growing dissatisfaction (Birch 1975; Bajoit 1988).

Dissatisfaction can plant its roots in a relative decline in quality: a new contender appears on the market with a higher-quality product or a better job offer or an old rival improves its offer, making the organization's own offer look less appealing. In this case, it is the comparison with the existing market that generates dissatisfaction. Party members compare their current situation to their potential situation in other parties. Dowding et al. (2000) points out that this process depends on the nature of the firm and that competition would be less fierce between purposive organizations. This means that researchers must take into account the context within which parties and party members play. Parties are not islands and should not be studied as such.

Dissatisfaction can be related to an absolute decline in quality – that is, to an organization's diminishing performance. When this happens, the organization is not able to maintain an equilibrium between employee costs and employee benefits. Growing costs and diminishing benefits trigger dissatisfaction. Clark, Golder, and Golder (2006) provide examples of this kind of situation. Say a state introduces new taxes, devalues its currency, or passes new rules about public schools. This can affect the equilibrium between costs and benefits for citizens and, thus, generate dissatisfaction. The same reasoning can be applied to political parties. The party can face problems in maintaining the equilibrium between payoffs to members and costs of membership. It can raise its fees or simply cease to provide the same upward mobility as before (Bajoit 1988, 337). It can reduce the fit between the member and his or her environment and increase the difference between the wants of the members and the perception of what is available (Mayes and Ganster 1988), thus generating dissatisfaction. One critical moment for parties occurs when they move from government to opposition and lose part of their capacity to provide material benefits. The Belgian French-speaking Green Party (Ecolo) experienced this after its first experience as government. Its membership grew to 28.3 percent in 1999, after it first achieved power at the federal level, but it fell after the party returned to the opposition benches in 2003 (Delwit and van Haute 2008).

Finally, agenda setters, or "agitators," can initiate or facilitate the perception of decline. They provoke the desire for improvement. For example, among the Belgian Dutch-speaking Liberals (VLD), the former professional judoka Jean-Marie Dedecker stirred dissatisfaction among the grassroots by pushing for a clearer right-wing position on economic issues. This might be the reason for the high percentage of misfits in the party at the time this survey was conducted (see Table 10.1).[4]

Responses to Dissatisfaction

As I have shown, the existing literature on party membership relies mainly on theories of political participation. Membership surveys provide data on reasons for joining and on intra-party participation. They give us an idea of

TABLE 10.1
Party members: Perceptions of self and party (%)

		Congruent/Perfect fit	Misfits	*N*
Canada	CA	44.3	7.5	961
	PC	29.7	20.7	784
	Liberal	32.3	17.4	815
	NDP	24.2	25.0	575
	BQ	41.7	15.7	362
Belgium	VLD	45.8	19.3	404
	CD&V	52.2	12.5	510
	PS	42.8	22.9	783
	Ecolo	46.7	12.5	1,001
Total		39.8	16.5	6,195

Source: Party membership surveys (www.projectmapp.eu)

the intensity of participation (Whiteley and Seyd 2002), the amount of time that members dedicate to party activities, and their attendance at party meetings and congresses. However, surveys do not provide information on the *nature* of intra-party participation: What do members actually do when they participate in a meeting? Do they attend silently? Are they intervening in debates? So far, surveys are silent on this essential aspect of intra-party dynamics.

Hirschman's model of the consequences of dissatisfaction in organizations provides another avenue for research, emphasizing the role of loyalty and the forms that the responses to dissatisfaction can take. One cannot study responses to dissatisfaction without discussing loyalty, a concept that is highly ambiguous in Hirschman's work. Sometimes loyalty is depicted as an attitude, influencing the choice between voice and exit (Boroff and Lewin 1997); at other times it is described as a form of behaviour and as a distinctive response to dissatisfaction. This has been the source of continuing debates in the literature. Besides this, loyalty is a value-laden term, related to such ideas as constancy, fidelity, devotion, attachment, sense of belonging, and/or affection (Graham and Keeley 1992). I agree with Dowding et al. (2000), who suggests that loyalty should be seen as an independent psychological variable, an attitude linked to identification (Campbell et al. 1960) built on past investment, personal history, and social capital, and reinforced by social groups. This identification, this sense of attachment, can be directed towards the product (i.e., brand loyalty) or the organization or at least part of it (i.e., group or subgroup loyalty).[5] Group membership becomes part of individual identity, while party identification becomes part of self-identity. For this reason, loyalty should not be treated simply as a possible reaction to dissatisfaction but, rather, as something that can influence the choice between possible reactions.

The range of possible reactions to dissatisfaction has also been heavily debated. Hirschman's model presents a choice between voice and exit, or fight versus flight. According to Barry (1974), the first choice is between exiting and staying, the second between voice and silence, thus broadening the model to four possibilities (exit and voice, exit and silence, staying and voice, staying and silence). Rusbult et al. (1988) propose to differentiate constructive and destructive reactions to dissatisfaction, which we tend to think cannot apply to exiting because the act of exiting destroys the individual's relationship with the organization. Dowding et al. (2000) add yet another nuance when they distinguish individual and collective reactions, which is crucial for purposive and collective organizations such as parties.

Applying types of response to dissatisfaction with party organizations enables a more effective analysis of the dynamics of party life. It shifts the research away from the analysis of the intensity of intra-party participation and brings it closer to the study of the nature of participation and the variety of intra-party behaviours.

A first type of response to dissatisfaction is to exit the organization, according to Barry's (1974) revision of Hirschman's model. Applied to political parties, the choice to exit is binary:

1. *Exit and voice:* the individual (or subgroup) breaks the relationship and retreats from the authority in a vociferous manner. This is combined with attempts to convince others, with confrontation with the leaders, and so on. Examples of individual exit/voice include party officials resigning in protest or an ordinary member making angry comments, leaving a local meeting, and slamming the door. Vociferous collective exit can be associated with party splits, such as when a subgroup decides to leave the party. One can think of multiple cases of such splits (e.g., the UK case in which four senior Labour Party figures decided to split from the party) (Mair 1990).
2. *Exit and silence*: the individual (or subgroup) breaks the relationship quietly. Kolarska and Aldrich (1980) emphasize that this reaction might

TABLE 10.2
Typology of intra-party responses to dissatisfaction

	Voice	Silence
Constructive	Stewardship	Resignation
Destructive	Sabotage	Neglect

have contradictory consequences since the reason for exit may remain undetected for some time, meaning that the discontent would not spread and mass exit would be delayed. Examples of individual exit/silence include party members who do not renew their membership and party officials who retire from politics. Collective exits are more noticeable, and they seldom pass unremarked. Voerman and van Schuur (2011) show that exit/silence is a common phenomenon in Dutch political parties. In 2008, in the Netherlands, 29,295 members decided not to renew their party membership, whiles 21,005 new memberships were recruited, leaving the country with a negative balance of 8,290 members.

The choice to stay in the organization paves the way for a variety of intra-party behaviours on the part of dissatisfied members. I argue that staying can be associated with four different types of behaviour within a voice/silence and constructive/destructive framework. These are listed in Table 10.2.

1. *Stewardship:* the individual (or subgroup) decides to voice dissatisfaction to improve the relationship and to suppress discontent. Bajoit (1988) explains this behaviour as a mix of conviction and vigilance. In a party organization, stewards would, for example, make suggestions, develop arguments for change, participate in the decision-making process, and express principled dissent (Gorden 1988, 285). Among the members of the Belgian French-speaking socialist party (PS), 17.7 percent admitted that, when they intervene in a local party meeting, it is usually to make constructive suggestions; 82.3 percent said that they only occasionally or rarely intervene in such a way.
2. *Sabotage:* the individual (or subgroup) decides to use voice to criticize. To clearly distinguish sabotage from stewardship, we have to look at the content of the behaviour and not at the intention of the actor. Sabotage would include complaining to other members, duplicitous behaviour, verbal aggression, and bad-mouthing.[6]

Laver (1976) links collective voice with consumer associations; Spencer (1986) links it with unions. They both consider collective voice as something that could reduce (or delay) exit but that could also lead to increasing friction if the organization does not appropriately respond to criticism. In a political party, collective voice can be related to factions and factionalism (Close 2011).

Voice can be expressed horizontally (among equals at the local level) or vertically (local members talking to superiors or party leaders), and it can be expressed inside or outside party channels.

3. *Resignation:* the individual (or subgroup) decides to endure and accept the situation passively until things improve. This entails tolerance, patience, and faith (Graham and Keeley 1992, 194). In an organization, it translates into such behaviours as attentive listening, quiet support, unobtrusive compliance (i.e., self-censorship), and cooperation (Gorden 1988, 285). Gorden underlines that too much team spirit might have negative consequences for organizations. "Groupthink" can favour cover-ups or the suppression of individual critical thinking. Hirschman stresses the necessary balance between voice and silence in any given organization. Resignation would moderate the effects of voice (i.e., stewardship or sabotage), but it should not be too strong or it will compromise and degrade the effectiveness of the organization (Farrell 1983).
4. *Neglect:* the individual (or subgroup) decides to wait until things fall apart (Rusbult and Zembrodt 1983). In an organization, this translates into behaviours such as absenteeism, virtual withdrawal, calculated silence, or apathy. It can be summarized by such comments as: "I just work here" (Gorden 1988, 285).

These various reactions to member dissatisfaction can be sequential or synchronic (Laver 1976, 469; Withey and Cooper 1989). They are certainly not mutually exclusive (Dowding et al. 2000, 491).

I do not claim that these types of behaviours are a party's only options. For example, certain behaviours associated with satisfaction – compliance, dependability, and cooperation – could be investigated further (Bateman and Organ 1983). I am concerned with possible responses to party members' perception of decline in quality. The notion of perception is crucial because decline can go unnoticed as a result of inattention, selective perception, or a cult-like belief in leaders coupled with a diminished sense of individuality (Graham and Keeley 1992, 194). If organizational decline is unnoticed, there is no dissatisfaction and, therefore, no reaction.

Conclusion

Literature on party membership focuses on the question of who joins parties and why. However, party membership studies shed little light on what happens inside the parties once members have joined. These studies need to better capture the relationship between the members and the party. Parties are not homogeneous entities, and we know that they often have difficulty maintaining internal cohesion and discipline. This is especially true of big tent parties such as brokerage parties, which bring together disparate and heterogeneous groups and in which the various components have a substantial degree of autonomy. Unmasking the dynamics of membership (dis)satisfaction and its consequences for intra-party participation is crucial to better understanding the capacity of parties to coordinate and discipline themselves. However, dissatisfaction is rarely investigated in studies of party membership.

In order to shed light on questions of loyalty, dissatisfaction, doubts, and criticism, I offer some new theoretical tools inspired by Hirschman's notions of exit, voice, and loyalty (1970). I discuss how this model can be used to analyze party members and their relation to their political party, and I conclude by offering further suggestions for party membership research.

My first suggestion is methodological. I argue that, in order to go beyond the traditional questions of who joins parties and why, we have to investigate the relationship between members and their parties. Relationships are dynamic, and their evolution needs to be monitored. However, existing party membership studies rely mainly on cross-sectional survey data. Research in other fields shows that longitudinal (panel) surveys and experimental studies contribute significantly to our knowledge of dynamics and processes. For this reason, I make a strong plea to apply such studies to parties and their memberships.

My other two suggestions are theoretical. The first is concerned with measuring and understanding dissatisfaction among party members. We know very little about this phenomenon and its consequences for party organizations. What we do know is that parties are composed of heterogeneous groups guided by various interests. This is even more the case for brokerage parties. One can assume the choices and decisions made by the party leadership do not always please the grassroots. Maintaining central principles without losing grassroots support is a constant challenge for parties, especially for brokerage parties. My suggestions for measuring (dis)satisfaction, as well as my hypotheses regarding why certain parties face higher levels of grassroots dissatisfaction than others, should be useful here.

My second theoretical suggestion concerns investigating the nature of intra-party participation rather than its level of intensity. We know that party members are not all active and participating. Whiteley and Seyd (1998, 115) show that, between 1990 and 1994, in an average month, "the mean number of hours worked in the case of Labour fell from 1.96 to 1.89, and the mean number of hours for the Conservatives from 1.44 to 1.40." What we do not know is what kind of behaviour party members adopt when engaging in party activities. I argue that such knowledge is crucial if we want to understand intra-party dynamics and their consequences for party organizations. Whether active members engage mainly in stewardship or sabotage, or whether passive members evince resignation and neglect, may have drastic consequences for the fate of the party organization and its capacity to take on the challenge of coordination.

By shifting the focus from the act of joining a party to the relationship between parties and their members, we could shed more light on the coordination challenge (i.e., the challenge of maintaining internal cohesion and discipline) that all parties must face. By doing so, we can better understand membership (dis)satisfaction, change in membership numbers, the nature of intra-party participation, and the survival or decline of parties.

Notes

1 See special issue of *Party Politics* on party members (July 2004): 10 (4).

2 For example, in Canada (Blake, Carty, and Erickson 1991; Cross and Young 2004), the data show that respondents joined their party on average 23.9 years ago for the New Democratic Party (NDP), 21.6 years ago for the Progressive Conservative Party (PC), 18.2 years ago for the Liberal Party, 9.2 years ago for the Canadian Alliance (CA), and 7.0 years ago for the Bloc Québécois (BQ). In Belgium, the surveys show that members joined their party on average 24.8 years ago for the Dutch-speaking Christian Democrats (CDandV), 19.7 years ago for the Dutch-speaking Liberals (Open VLD), and even 29.5 years ago for the French-speaking socialists (PS).

3 In Chapter 6 (this volume), Hazan and Rahat show that parties adopt internal reforms to enhance satisfaction and to avoid party disunity. Parties developed patronage in order to provide material benefits to certain party members, and they increased the inclusiveness of their selectorate in order to maximize satisfaction with the functioning of the organization.

4 Dedecker ended up leaving the VLD and created his own party (Lijst Dedecker) in 2007, a few months after the survey was conducted.

5 In the case of political parties, the loyalty towards the party can be supplemented or challenged by subgroup loyalties, or factions, whether they are geographically or ideologically based (Close 2011).

6 In Chapter 8 (this volume), Koop stresses how executive members of local party organizations direct a similar type of behaviour towards local MPs.

References

Bajoit, G. 1988. "Exit, voice, loyalty ... and apathy: Les réactions individuelles au mécontentement." *Revue Francaise de Sociologie* 29 (2): 325–45. http://dx.doi.org/10.2307/3321910.

Barry, B. 1974. "Review article: Exit, voice, and loyalty." *British Journal of Political Science* 4 (1): 79–107. http://dx.doi.org/10.1017/S0007123400009376.

Bateman, T.S., and D.W. Organ. 1983. "Job satisfaction and the good soldier: The relationship between affect and employee 'citizenship.'" *Academy of Management Journal* 26 (4): 587–95. http://dx.doi.org/10.2307/255908.

Biemer, P.P., R.M. Groves, L.E. Lyberg, N.A. Mathiowetz, and S. Sudman, eds. 2004. *Measurement Errors in Surveys*. New York: Wiley. http://dx.doi.org/10.1002/9781118150382.

Birch, A.H. 1975. "Economic models in political science: The case of 'exit, voice, and loyalty.'" *British Journal of Political Science* 5 (1): 69–82. http://dx.doi.org/10.1017/S0007123400008048.

Blake, D., R.K. Carty, and L. Erickson. 1991. *Grassroots Politicians: Party Activists in British Columbia*. Vancouver: UBC Press.

Boroff, K.E., and D. Lewin. 1997. "Loyalty, voice, and intent to exit a union firm: A conceptual and empirical analysis." *Industrial and Labor Relations Review* 51 (1): 50–63. http://dx.doi.org/10.2307/2525034.

Campbell, A., P. Converse, W. Miller, and D. Stokes. 1960. *The American Voter*. New York: John Wiley & Sons.

Clark, W.R., M. Golder, and S.N. Golder. 2006. "Power and politics: Exit, voice, and loyalty revisited." Paper presented at the Annual Meeting of the American Political Science Association, Philadelphia.

Close, C. 2011. "Le factionnalisme partisan: Imbrication ou concurrence des loyautés?" Paper presented at the 4ème Congrès international des associations francophones de science politique, Brussels.

Colomer, J.M. 2000. "Exit, voice, and hostility in Cuba." *International Migration Review* 34 (2): 423–42. http://dx.doi.org/10.2307/2675908.

Cross, W., and L. Young. 2004. "The contours of political party membership in Canada." *Party Politics* 10 (4): 427–44. http://dx.doi.org/10.1177/1354068804043907.

–. 2008. "Factors influencing the decision of the young politically engaged to join a political party: An investigation of the Canadian case." *Party Politics* 14 (3): 345–69. http://dx.doi.org/10.1177/1354068807088126.

Dalton, R.J., and M.P. Wattenberg, eds. 2000. *Parties without Partisans: Political Change in Advanced Industrial Democracies*. Oxford: Oxford University Press.

Delwit, P., and E. van Haute. 2008. "Greens in a rainbow: The impact of participation in government of the Green parties in Belgium." In *New Parties in Government: In Power for the First Time*, ed. K. Deschouwer, 104–20. London: Routledge.

Dowding, K., P. John, T. Mergoupis, and M. van Vugt. 2000. "Exit, voice and loyalty: Analytic and empirical developments." *European Journal of Political Research* 37 (4): 469–95. http://dx.doi.org/10.1111/1475-6765.00522.

Downs, A. 1957. *An Economic Theory of Democracy*. New York: Harper.

Eubank, W.L., A. Gangopadahay, and L.B. Weinberg. 1996. "Italian communism in crisis: A study in exit, voice and loyalty." *Party Politics* 2 (1): 55–75. http://dx.doi.org/10.1177/1354068896002001003.

Farrell, D. 1983. "Exit, voice, loyalty, and neglect as responses to job dissatisfaction: A multidimensional scaling study." *Academy of Management Journal* 26 (4): 596–607. http://dx.doi.org/10.2307/255909.

Finkel, S.E., E.N. Muller, and K.-D. Opp. 1989. "Personal influence, collective rationality, and mass political action." *American Political Science Review* 83 (3): 885–902. http://dx.doi.org/10.2307/1962065.

Gehlbach, S. 2006. "A formal model of exit and voice." *Rationality and Society* 18 (4): 395–418. http://dx.doi.org/10.1177/1043463106070280.

Gorden, W.I. 1988. "Range of employee voice." *Employee Responsibilities and Rights Journal* 1 (4): 283–99. http://dx.doi.org/10.1007/BF01556937.

Graham, J.W., and M. Keeley. 1992. "Hirschman's loyalty construct." *Employee Responsibilities and Rights Journal* 5 (3): 191–200. http://dx.doi.org/10.1007/BF01385047.

Heidar, K. 2007. "What would be nice to know about party members in European democracies?" Paper presented at the European Consortium for Political Research (ECPR) Joint Sessions of Workshops, Helsinki.

Hirschman, A. 1970. *Exit, Voice, and Loyalty: Responses to Decline in Firms, Organizations, and States*. Cambridge, MA: Harvard University Press.

–. 1993. "Exit, voice, and the fate of the German Democratic Republic: An essay in conceptual history." *World Politics* 45 (02): 173–202. http://dx.doi.org/10.2307/2950657.

Katz, R.S., and P. Mair. 1995. "Changing models of party organizations and party democracy: The emergence of the cartel party." *Party Politics* 1 (1): 5–28. http://dx.doi.org/10.1177/1354068895001001001.

Kato, J. 1998. "When the party breaks up: Exit and voice among Japanese legislators." *American Political Science Review* 92: 857–70. http://dx.doi.org/10.2307/2586308.

Kolarska, L., and H. Aldrich. 1980. "Exit, voice, and silence: Consumers' and managers' responses to organizational decline." *Organization Studies* 1 (1): 41–58. http://dx.doi.org/10.1177/017084068000100104.

Langston, J. 2002. "Breaking out is hard to do: Exit, voice, and loyalty in Mexico's one-party hegemonic regime." *Latin American Politics and Society* 44 (3): 61–88. http://dx.doi.org/10.2307/3177047.

Laver, M. 1976. "Exit, voice, and loyalty revisited: The strategic production and consumption of public and private goods." *British Journal of Political Science* 6 (4): 463–82. http://dx.doi.org/10.1017/S0007123400000855.

Lee, W. 1992. "Read my lips or watch my feet: The state and Chinese dissident intellectuals." *Issues and Studies* 28: 29–48.

Mair, P. 1990. "The electoral payoffs of fission and fusion." *British Journal of Political Science* 20 (1): 131–42. http://dx.doi.org/10.1017/S0007123400005743.

Mayes, B.T., and D.C. Ganster. 1988. "Exit and voice: A test of hypotheses based on fight/flight responses to job stress." *Journal of Organizational Behavior* 9 (3): 199–216. http://dx.doi.org/10.1002/job.4030090302.

O'Donnell, G. 1986. "On the fruitful convergence of Hirschman's exit, voice and loyalty and shifting involvements: Reflections from the recent Argentine experience." In *Development, Democracy and the Art of Trespassing: Essays in Honor of Albert Hirschman*, ed. A. Foxley, M.S. McPherson, and G. O'Donnell, 249–68. Notre Dame: University of Notre Dame Press.

Olson, M. 1965. *The Logic of Collective Action: Public Goods and the Theory of Groups*. Cambridge, MA: Harvard University Press.

Pfaff, S., and H. Kim. 2003. "Exit-voice dynamics in collective action: An analysis of emigration and protest in the East German Revolution." *American Journal of Sociology* 109 (2): 401–44. http://dx.doi.org/10.1086/378342.

Reiter, H.L. 2006. "The study of political parties, 1906–2005: The view from the journals." *American Political Science Review* 100 (4): 613–18. http://dx.doi.org/10.1017/S0003055406062496.

Ross, M.H. 1988. "Political organization and political participation: Exit, voice and loyalty in preindustrial societies." *Comparative Politics* 21 (1): 73–89. http://dx.doi.org/10.2307/422072.

Rusbult, C.E., and I.M. Zembrodt. 1983. "Responses to dissatisfaction in romantic involvements: A multidimensional scaling analysis." *Journal of Experimental Social Psychology* 19 (3): 274–93. http://dx.doi.org/10.1016/0022-1031(83)90042-2.

Rusbult, C.E., D. Farrell, G. Rogers, and A.G. Mainous, III. 1988. "Impact of exchange variables on exit, voice, loyalty, and neglect: An integrative model of responses to declining job satisfaction." *Academy of Management Journal* 31 (3): 599–627. http://dx.doi.org/10.2307/256461.

Salucci, L. 2008. "Left no more: Exit, voice and loyalty in the dissolution of a party." Paper presented at the Annual Meeting of the American Political Science Association, Boston.

Scott, R.J. 1986. "Dismantling repressive systems: The abolition of slavery in Cuba as a case study." In *Development, Democracy and the Art of Trespassing: Essays in Honor of Albert Hirschman*, ed. A. Foxley, M.S. McPherson, and G. O'Donnell, 269–81. Notre Dame: University of Notre Dame Press.

Seyd, P., and P. Whiteley. 1992. *Labour's Grassroots: The Politics of Party Membership*. New York: Oxford University Press.

Spencer, D.G. 1986. "Employee voice and employee retention." *Academy of Management Journal* 29 (3): 488–502. http://dx.doi.org/10.2307/256220.

van Haute, E. 2009a. *Adhérer à un parti: Aux sources de la participation politique*. Brussels: Editions de l'Université de Bruxelles.

–. 2009b. "Party membership and discontent." Paper presented at the Canadian Political Science Association Annual Conference, Ottawa.

van Haute, E., and R.K. Carty. 2012. "Ideological misfits: A distinctive class of party members." *Party Politics* 18 (6): 885–95. http://dx.doi.org/10.1177/1354068810395058.

Verba, S., N.H. Nie, and J. Kim. 1978. *Participation and Political Equality: A Seven-Nation Comparison*. Cambridge: Cambridge University Press.

Voerman, G., and W. van Schuur. 2011. "Dutch political parties and their members." In *Party Membership in Europe: Exploration into the Anthills of Party Politics*, ed. E. van Haute, 203–20. Brussels: Editions de l'Université de Bruxelles.

Weber, T. 2009. Exit, voice, and cyclicality: A micro-logic of voting behaviour in European Parliament elections. Paper presented at the European Union Studies Association USA Conference, Los Angeles.

Whiteley, P., and P. Seyd. 1996. "Rationality and party activism: Encompassing tests of alternative models of political participation." *European Journal of Political Research* 29 (2): 215–34. http://dx.doi.org/10.1111/j.1475-6765.1996.tb00649.x.

–. 1998. "The dynamics of party activism in Britain: A spiral of demobilization?" *British Journal of Political Science* 28 (1): 113–37. http://dx.doi.org/10.1017/S000712349800012X.

–. 2002. *High Intensity Participation: The Dynamics of Party Activism in Britain*. Ann Arbor: University of Michigan Press.

Whiteley, P., P. Seyd, and J. Richardson. 1994. *True Blues: The Politics of Conservative Party Membership*. Oxford: Clarendon Press.

11

Canada's National Parties

From Private to Public Institutions

JOHN C. COURTNEY

Several themes are common in Ken Carty's celebrated body of work. One that many of us find compelling emphasizes the fundamental importance of the local political unit to parties, campaigns, and elections. Dubbed "the trenches" by Carty, the poll, precinct, district, or constituency is central to his argument that party politics is profoundly shaped by what occurs locally. The neighbourhood unit, whether it is "Tecumseh Corners" in Canada (Carty 2002) or the "Parish Pump" in Ireland (Carty 1981), is what gives form and content to much of his distinguished analysis of party organizations and electoral campaigns.

Another of Carty's major research themes interprets the Canadian party system through the lens of its historic development. Together with Bill Cross and Lisa Young, Carty constructs a framework to explain the extensive changes that the Canadian party system has undergone since its inception. More precisely, their analysis points to the fact that it is not one system that has defined Canadian party politics over time but four (Carty, Cross, and Young 2000).

It is within that larger, macro-level framework that I return to a subject I first explored in 1978. In an article entitled "Recognition of Canadian Political Parties in Parliament and in Law" I conclude that legislators had at that point come to accept, grudgingly, the "existence" of parties by custom and in Parliament and that Canadian courts were on the cusp of acknowledging the legal "existence" of political parties (Courtney 1978).[1] What all this would mean for the future of Canadian parties and the party system was then uncertain.

Now, with hindsight, we can see that, since the early 1960s, Canadian parties have moved from being *private* and largely unregulated organizations to being formally recognized *public* institutions operating within a framework of state-sanctioned, court-enforced regulations and laws. Lisa Young and Harold Jansen, among others, describe this shift in Westminster-style political parties as one in which parties moved from being primarily private entities to one in which they have emerged as "public utilities" (Young and Jansen 2011, 12). Comparative studies demonstrate that, as parties in new and established democracies "have come to be perceived increasingly as necessary and desirable institutions for modern democracy ... [growing] direct state involvement in their internal affairs and their external activities" has been legitimated (van Biezen 2004, 702). As will be seen, this has clearly been the case in Canada.

This chapter recounts the developments respecting party recognition that led up to the major legislative changes of the 1970s and picks up the story I left in 1978. Its objective is to see how the question of the legal existence of political parties has played out in Canada. The record shows that, over the past three decades, the regulatory, statutory, and judicial regimes governing parties have cast wide nets – much wider than could have been foreseen in 1978 – and that one of the principal, though not the sole, causes of the change was the adoption of the Canadian Charter of Rights and Freedoms in 1982. The Charter's singular empowerment of the courts to resolve challenges to election laws has meant that what previously had been deemed to be non-justiciable matters concerning private organizations have now become very much a subject of court-adjudicated public law. With the arrival of the Charter, MPs lost their exclusive hold over determining the terms of electoral competition and the statutory responsibilities of parties, leaders, and candidates.

The four Canadian party systems identified by Carty and his co-authors are marked by several variables that distinguish each system and that mark a break with the previous one. Principal among the variables are the number of parties; their organizational features and representative capacity; the measure of inter-party competition, including one-party dominance; campaign styles; and means of communication. With those tools at hand, four systems were identified by historic periods:

1. *Confederation to 1917*: For Canada's first fifty years its party system was a classic duopolistic one in which the two parties competed with one another more or less around the centre of the political spectrum. Both the Conservatives and the Liberals were patronage-dependent, highly localized in organization, with parliamentary caucuses that played a significant role in such party affairs as selecting (and de-selecting) party leaders. Election campaigns and party finance were under the control of the leader, and the absence of a national media reinforced his dominant role in the party.
2. *1921 to 1957*: The electoral success first of the Progressives (1921) and later of the CCF and Social Credit (1935) brought the two-party system to a close, and with its demise the long, practically uninterrupted period of Liberal hegemony began. Brokerage politics among strong regionally based federal ministers diminished the role of the parliamentary caucus in party affairs. The advent of radio and, near the end of the period, of television led the parties to shift their media campaign strategies away from cementing relations with the local print media and replacing that with consultants hired to devise national campaign tours and advertising.
3. *1962-63 to 1988*: This twenty-five-year phase was distinguished by a new record number of minority governments (five of the ten elections of this period) and the end of Liberal brokerage politics. No fewer than three and sometimes as many as five parties were elected to Parliament. The era was marked by a pan-Canadian political agenda, and, at election time, parties turned increasingly to television and paid specialists to get their messages across. The two major parties held highly competitive and expensive conventions to choose their leaders, and Parliament adopted Canada's first election expenses legislation that applied to parties and candidates alike.
4. *Since 1993*: The first three elections of this period produced majority governments, the next three minority ones, and the final one a majority government. Two new parties (Bloc Québécois and Reform/Canadian Alliance) burst onto the political scene with considerable success at the outset. The national vote fragmented to an extent not seen before, and each of the parties (five at the beginning, four following the merger in 2003 of the Canadian Alliance and the Progressive Conservatives, and, along with a tiny remnant of the BQ and the election of the Green Party leader, three following the 2011 election) was disproportionately dependent on a particular regional base of support. Most parties replaced conventions with mass participation direct elections to choose their leaders

and, recognizing the importance of their regional support bases, substituted regional election campaigns for national ones.

The sudden transitions from the first to the second, the second to the third, and the third to the fourth systems were prompted in each instance by the cataclysmic electoral collapse of the governing party: the Unionists in 1921, the Progressive Conservatives in 1962-63 and, again, in 1993. In each case the party that so dramatically fell from grace had won by a landslide in the previous election. And therein lies the explanation for their collapse. The "tents" that the victorious parties had constructed in 1917, 1958, and 1984-88 were simply too big, too diverse, and too conflictual to last.

Robert Axelrod's coalition theory helps to explain such dramatic electoral collapses (Axelrod 1970, chap. 8). Coalitions with less incompatibility of goals among members have a greater likelihood of remaining durable than do coalitions with a greater incompatibility of goals among members. To ensure the least incompatibility of goals, the ideal coalition should be as small as is needed to win and as ideologically like-minded as possible – or, in Axelrod's terms, it should be a "minimum connected winning coalition." The coalitions created by Borden, Diefenbaker, and Mulroney in, respectively, the 1917, 1958, and 1984 elections violated that principle. They eventually imploded when intra-party regional and linguistic conflicts over government policy reached such feverish levels that the various factions could no longer co-habit the same tent. By that measure, one could speculate that the 2011 election victory of the Conservatives gave Harper a winning intra-party coalition, seemingly ideologically connected, and, perhaps most important, with a twelve-seat majority in a 308-member House, only slightly above the minimum threshold.

Although not discussed by Carty and his colleagues, the distinctive party systems that they identified were also marked by important transitions in the development of parties as legal and institutionalized entities. The following account of parties as organizations that were increasingly recognized in Parliament and in law is premised on the notion that the three breaks with the previous party system created conditions for institutional, procedural, legislative, and (later) court-driven changes regarding voters, parties, and elections. Three principal causes for the changes can be identified: (1) the gradual increase in the number of parties in Parliament with each new party system; (2) acceptance and application of the doctrine of agency in setting statutory requirements for political parties, candidates, and interested third parties; and (3) the adoption and application of the Charter.

New Systems, New Parties, New Rules

In its break with the preceding party system each of the three shifts of the twentieth century identified by Carty and his colleagues brought with it electoral success for at least one new party – more often than not of a populist bent. In 1921, the Progressives burst upon the scene with such force that, with sixty-five seats, they secured second place in the House of Commons, and, in 1962, the previously non-existent Quebec wing of Social Credit – the Ralliement créditiste – captured one-quarter of Quebec's votes and one-third of its seventy-five seats. With the spectacular collapse of the Progressive Conservative vote in 1993, the erstwhile Quebec and western wings of the party regrouped, respectively, into two regionally triumphant parties, the Bloc Québécois and the Reform Party of Canada.

The stunning success of the NDP in Quebec in the 2011 election, it could be argued, signalled a significant rebranding of that party into a Quebec populist/protest one along the lines of the *créditistes* in 1962 and the BQ in 1993. Placed alongside the emergence in 2011 of an Ontario-western Canada majority Conservative government and the third-place standing of the Liberals, Canada could be on the cusp of another fundamental shift in party system. This remains to be seen.

To reiterate, a more general proposition can be formulated based on the pre-2011 history of the Canadian party system: with the electoral success of each party newly created at the outset of a system change, questions of electoral and parliamentary institutions relating to election law, electoral administration, and party recognition are thrust to the fore.

The party system shift of 1921 was the first to demonstrate this. It coincided with the introduction of electoral system changes of historic proportions. Two fundamental components of Canada's electoral regime had been added in the Dominion Elections Act, 1920: the extension of the right to vote to women and the establishment of the Office of the Chief Electoral Officer of Canada. The first of these, which effectively doubled Canada's electorate overnight, was a response to changing social values and to the fact that over the course of the previous four years seven provinces had granted the vote to women. The second addition, which created an important public institution now familiarly known as "Elections Canada," was Parliament's answer to the government's brazen manipulation of the electoral process for partisan purposes in advance of the 1917 wartime election. In both cases, advocacy groups such as farm, women's, and temperance organizations called for a fairer and more open electoral system and championed the cause of electoral reform (Courtney 2004, chap. 2; Courtney 2007). Those two developments played to the Progressives' advantage.

There are several lessons to be drawn from the 1920–21 changes to the electoral and party systems that were later repeated in the shifts of 1962–63 and 1993. The opportunity to alter parliamentary institutions and procedures relating to parties, leaders, and members is greater when there is a concurrent change in the party system than when there is not. New players in the field expect the rules of the game to be revisited to accommodate them, and although not all rules will necessarily be changed (to wit, the plurality vote) it is logical that there will be pressure aimed at ensuring that the institutional framework respects the new political realities. Extra-parliamentary advocacy groups can also make a contribution in signalling the importance of an issue and in setting the agenda that politicians will be expected to address. Not least, provincial changes to election laws can profoundly influence federal initiatives with respect to voters and parties. The enfranchisement of women in the provinces between 1916 and 1919; the move in the early twentieth century to turn over the responsibility for party leadership selection to delegated conventions; the replacement, beginning in the mid-1950s, of elected politicians with appointed arm's-length commissions to design electoral districts; and, a decade later, the legislated controls of fund-raising and expenditures by candidates and parties – all of these moves started with the provinces. Collectively, these initiatives demonstrate the utility of the diffusion of innovations theory to explain the federal adoption of provincial changes in electoral system and party management.[2]

The Progressives wasted no time in tackling the rules of the electoral game. They introduced electoral reform as a subject for debate in the House of Commons on several occasions, starting in 1922, with sustained attacks on first-past-the-post elections and calls to replace them with either the single transferable vote or the alternative vote. Although no switch in the method of election was accepted by Parliament – even though the prime minister, Mackenzie King, lent his support to the proposed changes and his government referred approvingly to them in its 1924 Speech from the Throne – the Progressive initiative was to be the first of many, over the course of the twentieth and early twenty-first centuries, from the Opposition benches that pressed the case for proportional representation. At various points over the ensuing decades other Opposition parties, including Social Credit, the Commonwealth Co-operative Federation (CCF), the New Democratic Party, the Progressive Conservative Party (after its 1993 collapse), the Reform/Alliance Party, and, most recently, the Green Party, championed the cause of proportional representation. But, like the Progressives, none had any success.

The 1921 election results meant that Parliament was faced for the first time with a new reality: the presence in the House of three parties, each with a sizable measure of support. The accepted view at that time, and for several decades to follow, in Canada and other Westminster-based democracies was that parties did not exist in Parliament and in law and, therefore, could not be officially or legally recognized. Their presence was not formally acknowledged in Parliament, and, as they were private, voluntary organizations, they had no legal standing in courts of law.

The unwillingness to accept the presence of political parties in Parliament rested on four complementary ideas: first, a view of representation that was inherently individualistic, not group-based; second, a belief that the collective wisdom of individual MPs was preferable to the narrower and more partisan positions of parties; third, a notion that a greater loyalty was owed by the members to Parliament itself than to any political party; and fourth, an understanding, reinforced by court rulings, that parties were private institutions. As late as 1955, MPs accepted the claim, advanced by one of them, that they were "not elected here as parties, we are elected as individuals. The party is only used as the machinery for the election."[3] One CCF MP who shared that opinion expressed his hope "that we shall never change our rules in the House of Commons to the extent that we shall ever give official recognition to the existence of political parties."[4]

But starting in the 1920s, practice had already begun to move ahead of theory. With the success of the Progressives in 1921 (as short-lived as that proved to be, for by 1935 they no longer elected a single MP) institutional and procedural changes were made in the House to accommodate third parties. Separate rooms were reserved for more than the two main parties for the purpose of holding weekly caucus meetings, and an important rule change came in 1927 with an all-party agreement that allowed an amendment to the amendment of a main motion to be accepted by the speaker of the House and voted on separately. This meant that on major confidence votes, such as the Throne Speech or the budget, third parties could present their own position on the government's motion separate from that of the Official Opposition. Such changes brought with them a measure of autonomy in the House for third parties and increased their opportunities to gain public exposure in their own right.

The House of Commons gradually accepted further institutional and procedural changes. Beginning in the 1950s, the printed *Hansard* included the party affiliations of MPs, and parliamentary committees were constructed to reflect the numerical composition of all parties in the House. When televised proceedings of the House began twenty years later, unsurprisingly MPs were identified on the screen by name and party affiliation. Soon after the introduction of television in the House, the party whips persuaded the speaker (Jeanne Sauvé) to replace the practice of the speaker choosing MPs to pose questions during Question Period with accepting lists from the whips of their party members to be called upon to ask questions. Increasingly, according to one MP in 2010, "significant rule changes were made by successive speakers based on agreements reached in private discussions" with whips and House leaders of all parties. All of these changes reflected both the vital role that parties had come to play in determining parliamentary rules and procedures and the attempt by party officers to accommodate the divergent demands of an increasing number of parties in Parliament (Chong 2010, 25).

How 1963 Changed the Rules

What happened in Parliament immediately following the 1963 election (the beginning of Carty's third stage of party development [Carty 1988]) is critical to understanding the impact that an increase in the number of parties in the House and, concurrently, a minority Parliament had on the legislative and procedural recognition of political parties. Four parties were elected to the House when the new Pearson government took over. That in itself was not new, as had been demonstrated by the Liberal, Progressive Conservative, CCF, and Social Credit electoral successes for much of the 1935 to 1960 period. What *was* different was that any one of three in Opposition could ensure the government's survival on confidence votes. The government – lacking an outright majority – moved swiftly and won all-party support for an annual allowance to be paid to the leader of a "recognized political party" in addition to his or her regular parliamentary stipend.

What constituted a "recognized" party became a subject of considerable debate, but the principle behind the initiative followed that established early in the twentieth century. Having, in 1911, been the first country with a Westminster-styled parliamentary system to accord statutory recognition and to award a salary to the leader of the Opposition (McHenry 1954), Canada, in 1963, became the first to grant annual indemnities to leaders of other parties in the House. Two years later all-party committees were formally constituted under these standing orders for the purpose of planning the business of the House, and these committees' extensive powers, together with the regular meetings of the House leaders of all parties, effectively turned over control of the parliamentary agenda to the parties in the House.

The compromise agreement that MPs reached in 1963 on what constituted a "recognized political party" in the House of Commons was a thoroughly pragmatic one, and the number chosen as the basis for recognition (twelve MPs) was selected in a purely arbitrary fashion. Political expediency played a considerable, possibly a determinative, part in the government's decision to press for the adoption of party recognition. As the votes of any one of the three parties in Opposition would be sufficient to sustain the government, the latter was eager to extend an olive branch to the parties early in the new Parliament. It saw leaders' stipends as one way of doing that. The government House leader, J.W. Pickersgill, decided that twelve members would be the appropriate number based on the fact that, of the four parties then in the House, the two smallest ones – the CCF/NDP and Social Credit, with twenty-four and seventeen members, respectively – had first been elected to the House in 1935. He claimed that twelve represented the long-term average parliamentary representation of the two parties. (In fact, the numbers were, on average, fourteen Social Credit and seventeen CCF/NDP MPs elected per election.) The completely arbitrary nature of the choice of the number twelve was made clear from Mr. Pickersgill's admission that had he been more "prescient" he would have chosen the number ten in order to ensure, following the Social Credit split of 1963, that both the Social Credit (with eleven members) and the *Ralliement créditiste* (with thirteen) leaders would have received the allowance (Courtney 1978, 39).

Post-1978 Developments

My 1978 piece argues that the phrase "recognized political party" and the number "twelve" would take on lives of their own and become definitive standards for a variety of parliamentary and legislative purposes. That is exactly what has happened, as several illustrations make clear. The Parliament of Canada Act has been amended on several occasions since 1978 to broaden the list of party officers receiving additional stipends. As matters stood in 2012, if a party met the threshold of a recognized membership of twelve or more persons in the House of Commons its House leader, deputy House leader, whip, deputy whip, and caucus chair were granted annual allowances of between $5,200 and $14,300 in addition to their $157,700 base salary.

Membership on the all-important Board of Internal Economy, presided over by the speaker, is granted only to parties meeting the twelve-member hurdle, and (to choose an extra-parliamentary example) the four members named by the prime minister to the Security Intelligence Review Committee are appointed from outside Parliament only after consultations among the leaders of all parties with twelve or more members in the House.[5] Similarly, membership in the now-defunct Canadian Institute for International Peace and Security (created 1984, dissolved 1992) was based on prime ministerial appointment following consultation with leaders of every "recognized party" in the House (Bédard and Robertson 2008).

Not surprisingly, the number "twelve" and the wide acceptance in parliamentary practice of party recognition have come under attack from parties with fewer than twelve MPs: the Social Credit in the 1960s, the *créditistes* a decade later, the NDP and Progressive Conservatives following the 1993 election, and, most recently, the leader of the Green Party following her election in 2011. Challenges to the application of the twelve-member rule from adversely affected parties have become standard whenever the occasion has arisen. In turn, they have also become the subject of several speakers' rulings. Possibly the best example can be found in the objection raised by the NDP in 1994 to having its members treated as "independents" in procedural matters. Having fallen to nine members in the 1993 election (and the Progressive Conservatives to two), the NDP lost the financial benefits of party recognition and raised an objection with the speaker (Gilbert Parent) regarding having its members treated as Independents in procedural matters. It was unsuccessful in its attempt to have that policy changed (Blaikie 1994; Parent 1994).

A brief reference to other procedural and regulatory practices concludes this account of the influence that an increase in the number of parties, following on the heels of a major structural change in the party system, has on Parliament. Not all of these have been dealt with consistently, nor have all of them had a simple answer when presented to the speaker for a ruling or to an all-party committee for a decision. Some of the thornier nuts and bolts issues common to all members (other than the government front bench) include entitlements to seating arrangements in the House, office accommodation on Parliament Hill, participation in debates, and recognition by the speaker in Question Period. Caucus research budgets, introduced in 1969 and originally intended for recognized parties of twelve or more members, are now routinely assigned to all parties more or less in relation to the respective number of seats they have in the House, but members of parties with twelve or fewer MPs are, as a general rule, not appointed to standing or legislative committees (Black 1972). The whips negotiate the recognized parties' respective numbers, leaving Independents and members of small parties with little option but to attend committee meetings and speak (at a meeting's conclusion) but not vote.

The problems that have surfaced in Parliament since 1963 as a result of having established a fixed number of seats for the official recognition of a party in the House is that numbers come and go. The fate of Social Credit and the *créditistes* in the 1960s, the Progressive Conservatives and NDP in the wake of the 1993 election, and, since the 2011 election, the Bloc Québécois speak to that. At the time the number was agreed upon for party recognition, the object was to determine a membership level mutually satisfactory to all negotiating parties. Since then, the vicissitudes of the party system(s) have meant that over time different circumstances have forced members to revisit the issues with little ammunition to fall back on other than the base number of "twelve." As the record of speakers' rulings and all-party agreements reveals, the application of the rule has been generally consistent but, on occasion – such as research budget allocations – it can be violated for purely expedient reasons.

Registration, Doctrine of Agency, and Elections Canada

The idea of registering political parties was first advanced federally by the special extra-parliamentary Committee on Election Expenses appointed early in the life of Carty's third party period, 1962/63–1988 (Carty 1988). It argues that, in order to encourage "the development of the Canadian democratic system," political parties should be statutorily recognized through changes to the Canada Elections Act. That would mean that they "would not only enjoy legally recognized rights, but would equally incur legal obligations" (Canada, Committee on Election Expenses, 1966, 31–39). The committee's recommendations served as the basis for the historic election expenses legislation of the 1970s. That legislation, in turn, served as the launching pad for the subsequent and significant additions to the regulatory regime that now governs countless party activities.

Party registration started in 1970 and 1974, with the adoption of legislation that set out the terms for the operation and financing of parties. In addition to the registration of parties, the statute included the doctrine of financial agency, the addition of a candidate's partisan affiliation on the ballot, and a requirement that the recognized leader of a political party sign a candidate's nomination papers in order for the candidate to be accepted by the chief electoral officer as someone running on behalf of the party. This last requirement has significantly enhanced the authority of party leaders and central party offices and, on a number of occasions since 1974, has been used (or at least threatened to be used) to deny nominations by overturning a constituency party's choice. The power of the local, voluntary constituency association (Ken Carty's "trenches") to name its own candidate independently of the party leadership has been markedly curtailed with this change.[6]

The list of party, leader, and candidate activities now governed by federal statute is wide-ranging. Accordingly, to oversee the operational and management side of elections and to ensure enforcement of the legal obligations the Canada Elections Act imposes on candidates, leaders, and district associations, the Office of the Chief Electoral Officer has grown in size – a permanent staff of approximately 330 and a temporary one of 160,000 at election time, and cost – an annual operating budget of $122 million in 2010–11 and an estimated $300 million for the 2011 election.

Elections Canada's regulatory responsibilities are considerable. When fully implemented, as they now all have been, they collectively shape the internal procedures and structures of all political parties. Election Canada's responsibilities include the establishment of the Office of the Broadcasting Arbitrator, charged with allocating broadcasting time to the parties during election campaigns; the appointment of and financial and staffing support for the commissioner of Canada Elections, the officer charged with enforcing the electoral rules and investigating allegations of wrongdoings; the selection, following open competition, of a returning officer for every federal constituency; the registration of political parties, electoral district associations, party leadership contestants and third parties – lobby and interest groups; the maintenance of the National Register of Electors; and, together with Statistics Canada, the creation and maintenance of the National Geographic Database used in the design of sixty-five thousand polling divisions and the decennial electoral boundary redistributions.

Collectively, these and other legislatively sanctioned regulations affect parties in several ways. In contrast to the first century of party development, parties now have statutorily established deadlines to be met, reports to be filed, independent audits to be conducted, and financial obligations to be discharged. In the process of establishing this regulatory regime, Parliament has turned parties into organizational and institutional instruments of the state, or, in Young and Jansen's phrase, "public utilities" (Young and Jansen 2011).

For Canada's political parties, no statutory provision has had a greater impact on their operations than the tight regulatory regime governing political finance. For that purpose, extensive oversight and legal enforcement powers have been given to Elections Canada and, since the adoption of the Federal Accountability Act in 2006, the director of public prosecutions. Political parties, constituency candidates, leadership contestants, interested third parties, and party electoral district associations are all required to file financial reports. Contribution and expenditure limits are enforced, and individuals, district associations, and interested third parties are subject to prosecution if the terms of the Canada Elections Act appear to have been violated. To ensure that the necessary legal status is conferred on parties, candidates, and associations, the doctrine of financial agency, proposed first by the Committee on Election Expenses in 1964, has become an established feature of the regime that, perhaps most critically, has been accepted by the courts. Through this doctrine, a party, its candidates, and its associations are deemed to have assumed a "legal personality" whereby they can sue and be sued (Courtney 1978, 50–51). Possibly in no better respect has the "public institution" that parties have become been more obvious.

The Charter, Parties, and Voters

Courts had long been as adamant as parliamentarians when it came to denying the existence of political parties. Like trade unions in the early stages of their development, parties in Canada were characteristically described as private and voluntary associations beyond the jurisdiction of any court of law. A case as recently as 1971 illustrates this fact. An action taken by a Montreal advertising agency against the Progressive Conservative Party of Canada alleged non-payment of a seventy-thousand-dollar contract. Agreeing with the lower court in dismissing the case, the Quebec Superior Court's language echoed that of MPs since Confederation. The suit was said to be "well founded in facts and in law," but the court lacked jurisdiction for "no claim can be drawn up against a political party" as it has no "legal existence."[7]

The adoption in 1982 of the Canadian Charter of Rights and Freedoms, following on the heels of the statutorily established doctrine of agency, changed all of that. My 1978 article had foreseen neither the introduction of a fundamental constitutional document such as the Charter nor its transformative capacity for voters and parties when the courts interpreted it as they did. As seen earlier in this chapter, the rules, procedures, and conventions of the House of Commons had been adjusted in response to shifts within the party system – in particular when the number of parties in the House increased and there was a minority government. But that had all taken the better part of a century.

By contrast, the adoption of the Charter meant that voters and parties were granted standing in legal contests and that a new court-adjudicated framework defined both the party and the electoral systems. The effect was to shift from Parliament to the courts a substantial measure of decision-making power with respect to the status of parties, the requirements imposed upon them, and the framework within which they competed at election time. Carty, Cross, and Young observe that the introduction of the election expense and party finance regime in Canada in the 1970s had established a lever, as well as a claim, for the state to regulate internal party life (Carty, Cross, and Young 2000, 23). With their post-1982 decisions relating to parties, elections, and voters, courts have confirmed that that characterization remains even more apt.

Central to the court rulings in Charter challenges to Canada's election laws has been its acceptance of the proposition that Canadian elections should be fought on a level playing field. Adopting a broad and purposive approach to their interpretation of the Charter's section 3 (the right to vote) the courts have spelled out a doctrine of election law that stresses fairness and equality. The principal subjects of the cases heard to date have been voters and parties, although a handful of other election-related challenges have also figured in the court decisions. A ban on the publication of public opinion polls during the final seventy-two hours of election campaigns has been struck down; a limitation on third party election advertising expenses has been upheld; and a fixed election date law was found not to be an impediment to the prime minister's discretionary power to advise the governor general to dissolve Parliament and call an election.[8]

Claims of constructing a level playing field were part of the justification offered in support of the party finance reforms adopted by Parliament in 2004. Increased reporting requirements were imposed on parties, candidates, and electoral district associations, and, for the first time, leadership candidates were added to the list of those subject to reporting campaign expenses. Lisa Young and Harold Jansen conclude that "the clear intention of [these changes] was to make public funds the primary source of income for the major political parties" (Young and Jansen 2011, 5). With those changes has come a widened circle of the entities and individuals with newly imposed legal obligations (see also Aucoin and Bakvis, Chapter 12, this volume).

Among the voting rights cases decided by the Supreme Court of Canada and the Federal Court of Canada since the introduction of the Charter, there have been two distinctive, but nonetheless interconnected, types. One has expanded the franchise so that it now includes all adult Canadians; the other has equated the right to vote with a citizen's right to cast his or her ballot in an informed manner and, as a related and more general objective, to ensure the citizen's entitlement to effective representation.

Those of the first type resulted from challenges to sections of the Canada Elections Act that had long been in place and that denied the franchise to certain groups or categories of individuals. All were struck down under the courts' reading of section 3 of the Charter, wherein "every citizen of Canada has the right to vote in an election of members of the House of Commons or of a legislative assembly and to be qualified for membership therein." The Supreme Court found that restrictions on the right to vote ran counter to the "movement toward universal suffrage in Western democracies [which] took an irreversible step forward in Canada [with] the enactment of section 3 of the Charter."[9] Accordingly, the three franchise cases that were decided by the courts between 1988 and 2002 extended the vote to judges, the mentally disabled, and prisoners – the only remaining groups that had been barred from voting under Canadian law.[10] As a result of these decisions all Canadian citizens, apart from those under eighteen years of age and resident abroad for more than five years, are now entitled to vote.

Principal among the second type of case have been the challenges to the Canada Elections Act, which imposed spending limitations on third parties and de-registered parties nominating fewer than fifty candidates and stripped them of their net assets. In 2003, the Supreme Court of Canada ruled that de-registration of parties with fewer than fifty candidates denied "a voter's right to be reasonably informed [and] a candidate's right to have a reasonable opportunity to present a position."[11] The 2004 decision in *Harper v. Canada* (2004), upholding a prohibition on third party advertising, echoed that language. In a 6–3 decision, the majority found that "the overarching objective of spending limits is electoral fairness" and that section 3 of the Charter includes "a citizen's right to exercise his or her vote in an informed manner." The right to vote is enhanced when there is "equality of political discourse."[12]

The Supreme Court's explicit reference in *Figueroa* to the purpose of section 3 being to ensure "effective representation" harkens back to language of the Court in *Reference re Provincial Electoral Boundaries (Saskatchewan)* (1991). To date, that early Charter case remains the sole one to have been heard by the Supreme Court on the issue of voter equality and the design of electoral districts. In allowing the Saskatchewan legislation to stand, with its limits in district population size of +/– 25 percent of the average per constituency population, the Court went to some lengths to distinguish Canada's approach to electoral districting – "relative equality of the vote," "better government," and "effective representation" – from its characterization of the American approach – "voter parity" and "one person, one vote." In the words of Madam Justice McLachlin, "effective representation is at the heart of the right to vote" in Canada.

The inclusive and generous interpretation of section 3 on questions of the franchise underscores the importance the Supreme Court attaches to the notion of the "level playing field." At a more general level, the franchise decisions are consistent with the Court's acceptance of its responsibility to protect and to enhance individual rights in non-section 3 challenges. But, given its decision in the *Saskatchewan Reference Case,* the equal right to vote that the Court insisted on in striking down limitations on the franchise does not translate into the right to an equal vote. In the *Saskatchewan Reference Case* the parameters were set, in the Court's words, to take into account different histories, communities of interest, and geographies. Basing its decision, as it did, on "the relative equality of the vote" meant that the Court at least implicitly accepted the notion of "minority representation." This is a not surprising representational concept for a country as mindful of its minorities and its social diversity as Canada.

Conclusion

The world within which Canadian parties operate is markedly different from what it was fifty years ago. Recognition of parties in Parliament was in its formative stage, and in law it was non-existent. By contrast, parties, candidates, and leaders are now subject to court-enforced statutory regulations and requirements that were in earlier times unimaginable. Parliamentarians and courts alike have ushered in the era of parties as public utilities. The changes in the regulatory and public financing scheme of political parties that have marked the period since 1921 have not been without their critics.[13] But for the most part the record of the past nine decades suggests that a large measure of public indifference to the changes has been coupled with a willingness of the principal political players to legislate an increasingly institutionalized and regulated party regime.

Over the course of the post-Second World War changes, Canadian parties moved from the private to the public domain, a fact that is most obvious in the Charter decisions of the fourth party system. That MPs no longer enjoy an exclusive purchase on the franchise and that the courts have the final say over the fundamentals of Canada's election laws can be seen in several key changes of the past three decades. Were it not for the Charter, in all likelihood prisoners, judges, and the mentally challenged would not be entitled to vote; a ban on the publication of public opinion results in the seventy-two-hour period leading up to a federal election would be in effect; and parties running fewer than fifty candidates in an election would be denied the benefits of registration.

Recognition of parties has become an accepted part of Canada's parliamentary and electoral regimes. In Parliament, the opportunities for changes in the rules and procedures of the House of Commons came principally from the electoral success of newly created parties that arrived on the scene with each seismic shift in the party system: 1921, 1962–63, and 1993. If the 2011 election turns out to have been a watershed one in that it represents a break with the previous system, it can be expected that Parliament may once again revisit issues of official party status in the House. Even if a major party system shift has not taken place, the Harper government's move to end per-vote public subsidies for political parties (which will be eliminated entirely by 2015), the Green Party's call for replacement of plurality voting with proportional representation, and questions about the status of the rump BQ contingent in the House have, in the early post-2011 election period, signalled a continued debate over the rules of parliamentary and electoral games.

Election expenses regulations, first adopted in the 1970s, were instrumental in changing the legal framework within which parties, candidates, and constituency associations were required to operate. In both Parliament and in electoral law official recognition of parties became the standard by which important rules and procedures were established. In turn, that statutory framework set the stage for Charter decisions of the next three decades. The courts' interpretation of the Charter produced a doctrine of electoral principles that had been absent from earlier considerations of electoral laws and regulations: "effective representation," "the voter's right to be reasonably informed," "electoral fairness," "the right to meaningful participation," and "equality of political discourse."

Rulings in Charter challenges to franchise provisions, electoral districts, third party election advertising, campaign contribution limits, and number of candidates needed to qualify for party recognition have shaped the discourse over voting rights, parties, and candidates in Canadian electoral democracy. The level playing field that the courts have aimed to ensure for Canadian elections has signalled a fundamental shift in the status accorded parties in Parliament and in law. Over the course of a century parties have been transformed from largely unregulated, voluntary, and private entities into legally accountable public institutions.

Party recognition and party institutionalization have fallen, generally, into the third and fourth stages of party development that Carty, Cross, and Young (2000) laid out a decade ago. Over the course of post-Confederation party history, various sources of regulatory changes – first in the form of parliamentary conventions, then legislated changes, and finally court-ordered directives – accounted for the shift in the rationale for "party" from one that was largely (if not exclusively) electoral to one that accepts parties' instrumental value as state-sanctioned institutions.

Notes

1 My thanks to Gary Levy, editor of *Canadian Parliamentary Review*, for revisiting my 1978 piece and sharing his knowledge of subsequent legal and parliamentary changes.

2 On diffusion of innovation theory, see Walker (1969) and Gray (1973).

3 W.G. Weir, *House of Commons Debates*, 22nd Parliament, 2nd session, March 11, 1955, 1958.

4 Erhart Regier, *House of Commons Debates*, 22nd Parliament, 2nd session, July 12, 1955, 6002.

5 Canadian Security Intelligence Service Act, s. 34 (1).

6 Some parties have expanded that provision for their own purposes. The constitution of the Liberal Party of Canada, for example, now grants the leader or the national campaign committee absolute power to overturn electoral district associations' choices of candidates (Chapter 12, section 49[2] amended 2009). Recent Liberal leaders, notably Jean Chrétien and Paul Martin, combined that section with the authority granted them by the party to name candidates (notably female candidates) of their own choosing.

7 *Young and Rubicam, Ltd., v. Progressive Conservative Party of Canada*, Superior Court of Quebec (March 22, 1971), as cited in Courtney (1978, 36).

8 *Thomson Newspapers Co.* (1998); *Harper v. Canada* (2004); and *Duff Conacher v. Canada* (2010).

9 *Sauvé v. Canada* (2002), para 33.

10 *Muldoon v. Canada* (1988); *Canadian Disability Rights Council v. Canada* 1988; and *Sauvé v. Canada* 2002.

11 *Figueroa v. Canada* (2003), para 2 of introduction.

12 *Figueroa v. Canada* (2003); *Harper v. Canada* (2004), para 2 of introduction.

13 Nothing better captures the criticism of the enhanced regulatory and prosecutorial role that Elections Canada is required to play in a more institutionalized party system

than the Conservative Party's and, especially, Stephen Harper's attacks on that parliamentary office and the legislation it is charged with executing. On this see Heartfield (2013).

References

Axelrod, R. 1970. *Conflict of Interest: A Theory of Divergent Goals with Applications to Politics*. Chicago: Markham Publishing.

Bédard, M., and J.R. Robertson. 2008 [revised version of Robertson 1996]. *Political Parties and Parliamentary Recognition*. Parliament of Canada, Parliamentary Information and Research Service, Law and government Division, Library of Parliament (Background Paper BP-243E).

Black, E.R. 1972. "Opposition research: Some theories and practice." *Canadian Public Administration* 15 (1): 24–41. http://dx.doi.org/10.1111/j.1754-7121.1972.tb01226.x.

Blaikie, W.A. [Bill]. 1994. "The status of small parties in the House of Commons and reflections on the Speaker's ruling." *Canadian Parliamentary Review* 17 (3): 29–32, 36 [see also Parent, G. 1994].

Canada. Committee on Election Expenses (the Barbeau Committee). 1966. *Report*. Ottawa: Queen's Printer.

Carty, R.K. 1981. *Party and Parish Pump: Electoral Politics in Ireland*. Waterloo, ON: Wilfrid Laurier University Press.

–. 1988. "Three Canadian party systems: An interpretation of the development of national politics." In *Party Democracy in Canada*, ed. G.C. Perlin, 15–30. Toronto: Prentice-Hall.

–. 2002. "The politics of Tecumseh Corners: Canadian political parties as franchise organizations." *Canadian Journal of Political Science* 35 (4): 723–45. http://dx.doi.org/10.1017/S0008423902778402.

Carty, R.K., W. Cross, and L. Young. 2000. *Rebuilding Canadian Party Politics*. Vancouver: UBC Press.

Chong, M. 2010. "The increasing disconnect between Canadians and their Parliament." Institute for Research on Public Policy, Montreal. *Policy Options* 31 (8): 24–27.

Courtney, J.C. 1978. "Recognition of Canadian political parties in Parliament and in law." *Canadian Journal of Political Science* 11 (1): 33–60. http://dx.doi.org/10.1017/S0008423900038750.

–. 2004. *Elections*. Vancouver: UBC Press.

–. 2007. "Canada's chief electoral officer: Responsibilities and independence." *Canadian Parliamentary Review* 30 (1): 32–5.

Gray, V. 1973. "Innovation in the states: A diffusion study." *American Political Science Review* 67 (4): 1174–85. http://dx.doi.org/10.2307/1956539.

Heartfield, K. 2013. "What is Stephen Harper's problem with Elections Canada?" *Ottawa Citizen*, 5 October.

McHenry, D.E. 1954. "Formal recognition of the leader of the opposition in parliaments of the British Commonwealth." *Political Science Quarterly* 69 (3): 438–52. http://dx.doi.org/10.2307/2145279.

Parent, G. 1994. "Speaker's ruling: The designation of party status, House of Commons 16 June 1994." *Canadian Parliamentary Review* 17 (3): 33–5.

van Biezen, I. 2004. "Political parties as public utilities." *Party Politics* 10 (6): 701–22. http://dx.doi.org/10.1177/1354068804046914.

Walker, J.L. 1969. "The diffusion of innovations among the American states." *American Political Science Review* 63 (3): 880–99. http://dx.doi.org/10.2307/1954434.

Young, L., and H. Jansen, eds. 2011. *Money, Politics, and Democracy: Canada's Party Finance Reforms*. Vancouver: UBC Press.

Legislation and Court Cases

Canada Elections Act (S.C. 2000, c. 9).

Canadian Disability Rights Council v. Canada, [1988] 3 F.C. 622.

Canadian Security Intelligence Service Act (R.S.C., 1985, c. C-23).

Dominion Elections Act (1920, c. 46).

Duff Conacher v. Canada (Prime Minister), 2009 F.C. 920, [2010] 3 F.C.R. 411; leave to appeal to the Supreme Court of Canada denied, docket no. 33848.

Federal Accountability Act (S.C. 2006, c. 9).

Figueroa v. Canada (Attorney General), [2003] 1 S.C.R. 912.

Harper v. Canada (Attorney General), [2004] 1 S.C.R. 827.

Muldoon v. Canada (Chief Electoral Officer), [1988] 3 F.C.R. 628 (T.D.).

Parliament of Canada Act (R.S.C. 1985, c. P-1).

Reference re Provincial Electoral Boundaries (Saskatchewan), [1991] 2 S.C.R. 158.

Sauvé v. Canada (Chief Electoral Officer), [2002] S.C.C. 68.

Thomson Newspapers Co. v. Canada (Attorney General), [1998] 1 S.C.R. 877.

Young and Rubicam, Ltd., v. Progressive Conservative Party of Canada. Reports of the Superior Court of Quebec, 22 March 1971: 803–933.

12

Canadian Public Funding of Parties and the End of Per-Vote Subsidies

Parties, Strategic Interests, and Decartelization

PETER AUCOIN AND HERMAN BAKVIS

In examining the intersection of rules, society, and the organization of parties and party systems, one subset of rules that deserves special attention is that governing the financing of parties and candidates. Whether an electoral regime limits expenditures by parties, donations to parties, subsidies to parties, or a combination of all three can have a profound effect on the number of viable parties in the party system, the level of competition between them, and, in the case of state subsidies, the degree of cartelization in the system. Rules on financing also have a bearing on the degree of stratarchy in parties, specifically, in the case of the Canadian system, the extent to which parties as franchisors, to use Ken Carty's terminology, have control over their franchisees.

This chapter focuses on one particular state subsidy program, per-vote subsidy (PVS) payments, a program that was launched in 2004 but then phased out in 2015 as per legislation passed in 2011. The last quarterly payment was made on April 1, 2015. As part of a broader package of financial support provided to Canadian federal parties, PVS is unique in that it provided funds to support parties in between elections rather than just during election time and because of its proportional nature (i.e., payments are directly linked to actual votes received in the most recent election). From a theoretical point of view, PVS appears to be the quintessential instrument for promoting cartelization. Examining the reasons, first, for its introduction and, subsequently, for its abolition allows us to test explanations of both cartelization and decartelization. We suggest that strategic considerations on the part of individual parties, specifically the Liberal Party and the Conservative Party, rather than a common collective party interest, either in the form of a cartel (Hopkin 2004) or a syndicate (Jansen and Young 2011a), can account for both processes.

PVS is neither the only nor the most significant source of public funding for Canadian parties. It has, however, been by far the most visible. It caused controversy when the then Liberal government under Jean Chrétien announced it in 2003, to the surprise of other parties. Further, PVS featured in the constitutional crisis of 2008, when the minister of finance proposed that it be abolished (Valpy 2009), thereby triggering a combined effort from all three opposition parties to replace the Harper-led Conservative government with a Liberal-NDP coalition supported by the Bloc Québécois. This opposition initiative was followed by Harper's highly controversial prorogation of Parliament (see contributions to Russell and Sossin 2009). In the May 2011 federal election, abolition of the PVS was a prominent plank in the Conservatives' platform, a commitment on which they made good subsequent to winning a majority.

The significance of both launch and abolition of PVS can be assessed from a variety of perspectives. From one vantage, its abolition can be seen as a major crack in the cartelization of Canadian parties, which, according to some, has existed since 1974 (MacIvor 1996), with the introduction of limits on election expenditures along with subsidies for incurred election expenses and tax credits for political donations. When first introduced the stated intent of these changes was to ensure both a more level playing field and a debate between parties at election time – a debate not obscured or overwhelmed by organizations and interests seeking to affect electoral outcomes by spending large amounts of money. But these changes also had the effect of making it more difficult for newer, smaller parties to gain entry to the system; certainly it favoured the incumbents. With the introduction of PVS in 2004, which, for the first time, provided direct government subsidies in between elections, the cartelization of the Canadian party system appeared complete.

The debate over the extent to which Western parties and party systems constitute cartels has been playing itself out over the past two decades. A party cartel, according to Hopkin (2004, 635), "rather than a party organizational strategy, is in fact a form of collective action between the parties themselves, in that it requires the major governing parties to agree to maintain state party funding for the opposition when in power, and to collude in keeping such a potentially unpopular set of arrangements out of the public political debate."[1] He also makes clear that state finance plays a major role in the development of party cartels. In the Canadian context, Heather MacIvor (1996) has long argued that the Canadian system fulfills all the criteria for a cartel-like arrangement. Lisa Young (1998), on the other hand, argues that there are a sufficient number of exceptions in Canada, including the rise and success of the Reform Party, that lead one to question whether the Canadian system really qualifies. In this chapter we lean towards Young's interpretation. Specifically, with respect to PVS, we argue that one of the putative participants in the cartel was never really on side and, further, while PVS and the preceding public funding measures may have fostered some cartel-like behaviour, that was not its primary purpose or motivation. Nor were the measures terribly successful in this regard. In fact, in some important respects, they probably had the opposite effect. We suggest that the earlier measures in question were in good part motivated by broader purposes, primarily to prevent Canada from going down the US path of unlimited election advertising expenditures on the part of candidates and interest groups and to ensure a reasonably level playing field for parties competing in the electoral arena. We further argue that, in recent years, a number of the innovations in the public funding instruments used to support parties – in particular, the adoption and then abolition of PVS – have a significant strategic component to them whose aim is to promote the specific interests of one party or the other rather than to create a cartel. Currently, the interests of Stephen Harper's Conservative government appear to lie in promoting the creation of a two-party system polarized along the left-right axis rather than any kind of cartel-like arrangement encompassing several parties. And we suggest that this government has succeeded in tilting the financial playing field significantly in its favour through the removal of PVS. We also discuss whether the removal of PVS can potentially lead to the undermining of the broader public financing regime for parties, including perhaps the lifting of limits on party and candidate expenditures, thus making the Canadian regime much more like the American one.

The Canadian Electoral Law Regime

Before tackling PVS, its origins, and how it fits into the larger electoral law and party finance system, it is worth briefly noting the main features of the Canadian electoral regime. Following Peter Aucoin (2005, 1–2), these may be summarized as follows:

- Election spending limits on political parties, candidates, "third parties" (independent groups), and contestants for party-candidate nominations;
- contribution limits with respect to who may contribute, to whom, and in what amounts, and when;
- public funding for qualifying political parties and candidates both directly and indirectly (including partial reimbursement of election expenses, annual grants, and tax credits for contributions);
- disclosure of contributions and expenditures by candidates, political parties, local party associations, third parties, and party-nomination and leadership contestants;
- access to broadcasting time for free-time and paid-time election campaign advertising for political parties; and
- independent and impartial administration and enforcement of the single, comprehensive election law, encompassing all other non-finance dimensions of the federal election regime.

The modern origins of this regime can be traced back to the 1960s, a period, as noted by John Courtney (Chapter 11, this volume), of minority government and a concern with perpetual election campaigns and the consequent heavy financial burdens on political parties. A federal task force (Canada 1966a, 1966b) made recommendations to cap election expenses incurred by parties coupled with limited financial support provided to parties by the state. Most of the recommendations were placed in the Canada Election Act, 1974. Safeguards were incorporated to prevent so-called third parties (interest groups) from undermining the limits placed on spending (and, equally important, to prevent parties and candidates from using third-parties to by-pass the limits) – safeguards that later proved to be controversial because they were seen by many as constituting unwarranted restrictions on the freedom of expression and right to association. It should be noted that the rules applied primarily during election periods and that public funding was related exclusively to election expenses. There was minimal effort to regulate the behaviour of, or provide support to, parties in between elections. On the whole, the Canadian regime took on a character that stood in sharp distinction to the one in the United States. Due largely to the Supreme Court's *Valeo* decision, which construed campaign spending as an extension of the right to free speech and hence was to remain unfettered, the US election finance regime went in a completely different direction. In the early 1990s, the Canadian scheme received an overhaul following controversies over third party spending during elections and a set of recommendations made by the Royal Commission on Electoral Reform and Party Financing (known as the Lortie Commission, after its chair). Legislation in 1992, based on some but not all of the Lortie Commission's recommendations, allowed a limited role for third parties in elections and improved public funding. Along with a permanent voters list, the numerous recommendations had the effect of, in commission chair Pierre Lortie's terminology, refurbishing from top to bottom a basically sound design. Thus the regime's basic structure and philosophy remained intact. While the regime had as its hallmark a level playing field under the rubric of "electoral fairness," achieved largely through placing spending limits on parties and candidates as well as providing limited public subsidies, it also privileged political parties over other political actors. In the words of the Lortie Commission, parties were seen as "primary political organizations." Furthermore, while the playing field may have been on a relatively even keel and the resources available to the parties relatively balanced, there were also enough restrictions to prevent smaller parties from gaining entry to that playing field. In this respect, the regime, as buttressed by the reforms stimulated by the Lortie Commission, had definite cartel-like aspects. Certainly, the parties that were represented in Parliament at the time (and also, incidentally, on the Lortie Commission itself) supported the limited improvements that were introduced by the 1992 legislation.

The 2003 and 2006 Legislative Changes

It was 2003 that saw the edifice constructed in the 1970s and refurbished in 1992 receive major additions in the form of improved public funding, including annual rather than just election-based funding as well as restrictions on individual and corporate contributions. While the former was consistent with the thrust of the Lortie Commission's recommendations, the latter was not. In the Canadian context, limits on contributions had been adopted by only one major jurisdiction, Quebec, which, as well as election expenses, has had since 1977 an outright ban on corporate contributions (i.e., by "legal persons") and a limit of three thousand dollars to the contributions to one or more parties made by individual electors (Bordeleau 2003). According to Peter Aucoin (2005), the adoption of contribution limits in the federal legislation in 2003 (C-24) was probably unnecessary. In the overall scheme of things corporate contributions constituted a relatively small proportion of sources of funding for parties and candidates. For most experts in the area, according to Aucoin, contribution limits would not have been high on their list of priorities. At the same time, the one party that had benefited significantly from corporate contributions is the Liberal Party, the party, ironically, that introduced the legislation. Under C-24, corporate contributions (and contributions from unions and unincorporated organizations) were completely banned only with respect to political parties and contestants in party-leadership selection contests. Candidates, nomination contestants, and local party constituency associations could still receive contributions from these sources, with contributors being limited to one thousand dollars. Individuals could contribute up to five thousand dollars to parties, candidates (including independent candidates), nomination candidates, leadership candidates, and constituency associations.

Given that the Liberals tended to benefit more from corporate donations than did the other parties, it remains a bit of a puzzle why this party introduced restrictions on this funding source. From a strategic perspective it did not make a great deal of sense. The most plausible explanation probably lies with the epic struggle between Paul Martin and Jean Chrétien over leadership succession. Chrétien clearly resented, and found offensive, Paul Martin's use of extensive resources to essentially lock up the leadership mantle well before the formal succession process had even begun. Chrétien made it clear that he was not prepared to relinquish the leadership before he was ready and, no doubt, also believed that the lack of any kind of meaningful contest was not healthy for the party. Paul Martin's successful run for the leadership had been all but concluded by 2003. However, the legislation that year ensured that this would be the last time that someone like Martin could use the same resource-intensive techniques to lock up a leadership contest before it had even begun. The banning of corporate donations in leadership contests was probably the single most effective mechanism for doing precisely that.

The architects of the 2003 changes were faced with trying to figure out what to do about the loss of funding from corporate and better-off individual donors. Here, in addition to the contribution limits, the 2003 legislation provided for more generous public funding. Individual donations received more favourable tax treatment (through credits), with a view to encouraging more individuals to donate. As well, campaign rebates to the parties for election expenses was increased from 22.5 percent of national campaign expenses to 50 percent. For individual candidates the proportion of election expenses reimbursed was raised from 50 percent to 60 percent, and the qualifying threshold dropped from 15 percent of the vote to 10 percent. Finally, the new system of annual funding for parties was introduced, starting at $1.75 for each vote received in the most recent election and indexed to the Consumers Price Index. In 2011, it stood at $2.04, with the proviso that the party receive at least 2 percent of the national vote or 5 percent in all the ridings contested by candidates for that party. The money is paid out on a quarterly basis, and the only restriction is that it be spent on party-related activities. By and large the combination of contribution limits and improved public funding encompassed by the 2003 legislation was intended to be neutral in the sense that parties and candidates would neither lose nor gain significantly in terms of total revenues received (compared to the status quo ante).

The 2003 changes came into effect a year later. In 2006, as part of the new Conservative government's accountability act, further changes were introduced: corporate contributions (and those from other organized entities) were banned altogether, and individual contributions were reduced from five thousand to one thousand dollars. PVS was untouched, even though, as pointed out by Flanagan and Coletto (2010), the Conservatives had not been consulted by the Liberal government back in 2003 when it had been introduced. By implication, the Conservatives would have had grounds for doing away with it back in 2006. The fact of its being a minority government no doubt played a role in its not doing so, and it was much easier to sell the tightening of restrictions on contributions as part of the new accountability act. Still the Conservatives did indicate their unhappiness with the PVS provision, a concern that became manifest with Finance Minister Jim Flaherty's economic update in November 2008. In 2011, having successfully won a majority government in a campaign during which the abolition of PVS featured prominently, the stage was set for the complete phasing out of this part of the public funding regime.

Overall, the strategic calculations on the part of the Conservative Party are clear. In 2006, it successfully hoisted the Liberals on their own petard. The Liberals had broken ground in 2003 by, for the first time, placing restrictions and limits on corporate and individual donations. The Conservatives then simply took this one step further by banning corporate donations altogether and lowering the limit on individual donations from five thousand dollars to one thousand. With the Conservatives drawing most of their donations from sub-one-thousand-dollar donors, the change gave them a distinct advantage. The second stage, doing away with PVS in 2011, took away the main source of funding that the Liberals had originally put in place to compensate for the reduction in donations, thereby making the Conservatives' strategic plan to alter the system in their favour relatively complete, a point to which we return in our examination of the post-PVS era.

One of the features of PVS that Conservatives disliked was that it brought the parties more money than they would have received from contributions under the old regime of no contribution limits. While intended to be revenue neutral, as Flanagan and Coletto (2010, 4) point out, under PVS "the quarterly allowances alone represented an increase of almost $37 million, or 54 percent, in revenue for the parties compared with what they had raised from corporations, unions, and individual contributions over $5,000 in the preceding four years." These allowances represented varying proportions of the total funding available to political parties. For the year 2008, for example, the Bloc Québécois received $5 million in annual allowances and $700,000 in private contributions; the NDP $5.4 million in annual allowances and $5.0 million in private contributions; the Liberals $8.7 million in annual allowances and $5.8 in private contributions; the Greens $1.3 million in annual allowances and $1.6 million in private contributions; and the Conservatives $10.4 million in annual allowances and $21.2 million in private contributions (Elections Canada 2009). Clearly, the Bloc has been far more dependent on PVS than have the other parties, but the Liberals were also dependent on PVS for well over half of their funding (60 percent). These amounts do not include the parties' and candidates' election reimbursements. William Stanbury (2011) calculates the overall cost of the various subsidies for the year 2010 and suggests that, if PVS were to be eliminated, public subsidies to parties would drop roughly by 40 to 43 percent.

PVS and the Lortie Recommendations

When the Liberals announced the 2003 changes to electoral funding, in particular PVS, some people read into them a broader and nobler purpose rather than crass strategic considerations. For example, the chief electoral officer at the time, Jean-Pierre Kingsley, commended them as representing the culmination of the implementation of virtually all of the Lortie Commission's recommendations, primarily to the benefit of strengthening the role of political parties in our democratic system. Some of the changes – the limits on contributions, for example – were definitely not something that Lortie had recommended. Other recommendations, such as the PVS scheme, were implemented in a form quite different from that which Lortie had originally envisioned. Given the perceived centrality of PVS, it is worthwhile exploring the Lortie Commission's original intentions, how they differed from what was implemented, and how the version that was implemented and then later abolished served specific strategic considerations rather than some noble purpose.

PVS featured in the Lortie Report as part of a constellation of measures designed to strengthen political parties as "primary political organizations" (Canada 1991, 1:207). Essentially, Lortie wanted to make parties much more attractive as vehicles for political participation, to move them away from being simply electoral machines that came alive only at election time and in which participation was largely restricted to helping to mobilize the vote. Furthermore, to Lortie it was clear that Canadian parties lacked not only the capacity to absorb interested political participants but also policy capacity: any research or analysis undertaken by party staff was in the interest of short-term partisan advantage. Also, it was clear to Lortie that Canadian parties lacked both interest in and capacity to educate citizens. The Lortie Commission's recommendations were based in part on research in other countries, including those with the largest and richest foundations (Germany) (Pinto-Duschinsky 1991), those with more modest think tank-like operations (Netherlands and Belgium) (Covell 1991; Wolinetz 1991), and the United Kingdom and the United States, where traditionally the links between think tanks, political parties, and individual politicians have been a lot closer than they have been in Canada.

In making his recommendations, Lortie recognized that three provinces already provided annual funding – Quebec, New Brunswick, and PEI – but where the Lortie Report broke new ground was in recommending that, in order to be eligible for direct or indirect annual public funding, parties would need to establish arm's-length non-profit organizations under the Canada Corporations Act, complete with a separate constitution and "specific provisions prohibiting the director and other full-time personnel from participating directly ... in the conduct of election campaigns" (Canada 1991, 1:299). Essentially, for Lortie, the purpose of these party foundations was: (1) to serve as a base for a series of networks extending into different policy fields and drawing on specialists from various sectors to provide sources of advice for the party executives and leadership in order to generate new ideas; (2) to recruit knowledgeable individuals with expertise in specific policy fields and skills needed to support government leaders; and (3) to act as a forum in which party leadership can interact with various party constituents to help chart policy initiatives and to mobilize support in a manner that would not be possible in formal conventions or in government. Neither the premises nor the specific recommendations noted above were ever adopted. Rather, the adoption of PVS in 2003 was a direct consequence of the limits placed on contributions, something that was part of Bill C-24. These limits are very wide-reaching since they affect not only contributions for election purposes (i.e., donations to parties and candidates at election time) but also those donations made in support of candidates seeking the leadership of the party in between elections. As argued above, it is likely that outgoing leader and prime minister Jean Chrétien was keen on preventing someone like Paul Martin from winning a future leadership contest by collecting substantial corporate donations over a sustained period. As mentioned, Chrétien had to face the problem of persuading Liberal caucus members to support legislation that would severely restrict access to donations – money that the party and its candidates would need at election time. Clearly, one of the ways of dealing with this problem was to promise public funding that would compensate for the loss of individual and corporate donations. At the time, the Liberals claimed that the effect of such funding would be essentially neutral.

We would also suggest one further reason that the strategists within the Liberal Party may have had for favouring PVS as a source of party funding. Canadian parties, effectively operating under what Ken Carty (2002; 2004) variously describes as franchise and stratarchy models, are characterized by internal competition over financial resources, primarily between the centre and the actual franchise operations – namely, the constituency associations and local candidates. Donations, for example, can be made not just to the party but also to individual candidates and associations. All parties at various times have experienced a degree of imbalance in funding sources, whereby, for example, the centre may be starved of funding while local associations are running surpluses. Under PVS, the money goes directly to the centre. In other words, PVS would tilt the party's internal power balance in favour of party headquarters, even if a portion of PVS funding ended up being used to support local associations in the form of local or regional campaign advertising. According to Coletto et al. (2011, 113), the changes introduced in the 2003 legislation "contributed to a centralization of power at the level of the national party ... at the expense of candidates and local associations." This evidence appears to be consistent with the fact that the 2003 legislation was planned by a very small group within the Chrétien brain trust and that PVS would have helped address some of the issues arising out of tensions between the centre and the local associations.

One public interest argument either for introducing or for retaining PVS would appear to be an anti-corruption one, or the floor argument: in effect, that PVS helps replace money that parties would otherwise have had to obtain from corporations, trade unions, and the like, organizations that might well influence the policies adopted and choices made by the party should it attain power. Furthermore, it has been suggested that money could also pass under the table as parties and candidates, desperate for funds for campaign purposes, will simply circumvent the elaborate system of rules and regulations. Certainly, this argument has been made in Quebec not only for retaining but also for expanding PVS at the provincial level (Blatchford 2010). A further argument, noted by F. Leslie Seidel, is that doing away with PVS would prevent smaller parties from contributing to debate and "muffle the number of voices in the democratic process" (quoted in Blatchford 2010). In this connection it is worth noting that, since PVS is based on votes received by parties, and given the relatively low threshold (2 percent of the total popular vote or 5 percent of valid votes cast in ridings in which the party has run a candidate), PVS actually does encourage the entry of new parties into the system, something that runs counter to the cartelization thesis. Certainly, the Green Party has been a major beneficiary of PVS.

Neither of these arguments, however, was very prominent when the Liberals announced PVS and related reforms, at very short notice it should be stressed, in 2003. In brief, the introduction of PVS in 2004 can be seen simply as a stratagem to allay Liberal Party backbenchers' fears that contribution limits would reduce the overall amount of funding available to them and the party and to protect them from the Conservatives' much more potent fundraising machine. While there may have been a principled case for contribution limits and restrictions on contributions (though the practical case was relatively weak, as Aucoin [2005] points out), no such arguments were adduced at the time for PVS. In other words, the pragmatic case – to make contribution limits acceptable to the incumbent party – appears to have held sway.

Jansen and Young (2011a, 84–85) make an interesting argument that the 2003 legislation was the product not of a cartel but of a "syndicate," whereby a subset of parties, in this case the Liberal Party, the Progressive Conservative Party, the NDP, and the Bloc, worked together to bring about the changes in question. This argument is certainly plausible, particularly in light of the strenuous opposition of the NPD and the Bloc to the 2008 move by the Conservatives to abolish PVS. However, it appears that it was the Liberals who were, for all intents and purposes, the sole architects of the legislation and that it was a scheme that, primarily, served the internal interest of a small group within the Liberal Party. The other three participants in the putative syndicate were simply happy to go along for the ride. In other words, rather than being a collective party endeavour, PVS was the result of the strategic interests of a specific party.

The one source that did present a well-articulated and well-documented argument for annual subsidies, the Lortie Commission, did so for a purpose – support for arm's-length party foundations – that is distinctly at odds with the essentially untied funding that was adopted in Bill C-24 in 2003. Finally, while support for public funding of parties generally may have been stronger back in 2006, when the Canadian Election Survey showed that of those who had an opinion (about half the sample) 71 percent stated that public financing of parties was a "good thing" (Galloway 2009), by 2011 it was likely weaker. Among the array of public funding instruments PVS was likely the most vulnerable if only because of the sustained attacks on it by the Conservatives, the press, and a number of think tanks. Thus, there is a sense of resignation about the changing tide in public opinion. According to Seidle, "the ability to score some political points by being against subsidies to political parties is probably higher than it was five years ago" (quoted in Blatchford 2010).

To summarize, part of the Chrétien Liberals' strategic considerations applied to the internal dynamics of the party: keeping the caucus on side and strengthening the centre. Vis-à-vis the other parties, the major issue facing the Liberals is that they have always been much more dependent on corporate donations than have the Conservatives. Even the old Progressive Conservative Party under Brian Mulroney had been much more adept at raising funds from individual donors than had the Liberals. And the Conservative Party under Stephen Harper (and, earlier, the Reform Party) was especially skilled at exploiting its support base of individual supporters for small but cumulatively highly lucrative donations. Without a substitute for corporate donations the Liberals would have been at a serious disadvantage. While according to William Cross (2004, 156, 180), parties in jurisdictions such as Quebec, which has had bans on corporate donations and either no or very limited PVS, do not appear to have suffered from financial distress and were able to raise more of their money from individuals, for the Liberals, it would have been a serious challenge to shift to a direct fundraising model dependent on smaller donors.

Strategic Considerations in Unwinding PVS

Given the Conservative Party's position on the issue, the outcome of the 2011 election, and the successful passage of the legislative changes in Bill C-13 in the fall of 2011,[2] the fate of PVS is sealed: as of 2015, PVS was no more. The Conservative Party has been clearly identified as being opposed to the subsidy on a number of grounds, claiming that the money in question helped parties to keep themselves on a permanent war footing, thereby contributing to the acrimonious and highly charged partisan climate of the minority parliaments of 2004 onward, as well as of the majority parliament from 2011 to 2015. According to Harper, who opined during a 2011 election campaign stop, "It is partly in my view this per-vote subsidy – this enormous cheque that keeps piling into political parties every month, whether they raise any money or not – that means we're constantly having campaigns" (*Globe and Mail,* 1 April 2011). Beyond the Conservative Party's concern that PVS was contributing to a climate redolent of a "constant election campaign," it is also worth returning to a question raised earlier – namely: "What strategic considerations did the Conservatives have for doing away with PVS?" First, it is worth noting that, simply on ideological grounds, the Conservative Party has always been opposed to PVS and has always been skeptical about the public funding of parties generally. Second, its predecessor, the Canadian Alliance Party, was not consulted by the Liberals before the 2003 legislation was introduced. As Carty and Young (2012) note, while the Liberals chose to consult with the other parties, including the Progressive Conservatives, they simply ignored the Canadian Alliance Party. Underpinning the Conservative Party's opposition to PVS are two further considerations: (1) its implicit rejection of the Lortie Commission's idea of political parties as privileged political actors; and (2) the idea, which became evident during the course of the 2011 election campaign, that what is needed is a simple two-party system, one in which there is no room for either smaller parties or a party of the middle, such as the Liberals. Ideally, then, a public finance regime that provides a significant payoff for the winning party as well as for the second-place party, leaving remaining parties largely squeezed out, would be the Conservative Party's preferred result. An analysis of what outcomes in terms of financial payoffs for parties we can expect under a regime without PVS will give us some insight into whether such a regime might be consistent with Conservative objectives.

Table 12.1 shows the total public funding received by all five parties before and after the removal of PVS. In this table, 2009 data for PVS are used for both the before and the after comparison. Also included is data on election expenses reimbursement and tax credits received by party donors. (Note that the amount of tax credits attributed to each of the parties is estimated on the basis of the assumption that the amount of individual donations is approximately the same.)[3] For all parties, except the Conservative Party, PVS has been the second most important source of public

TABLE 12.1
Estimated decline in per vote support without PVS

	Conservatives	Liberals	NDP	Bloc	Greens
Per-vote subsidy (PVS) ($M)	10.4	7.2	5.0	2.7	1.9
Tax credits ($M)*	10.5	5.8	2.4	.6	.7
Election expenses reimbursement ($M)	21.4	15.1	12.4	4.8	1.7
Total ($M)	42.3	28.1	12.4	8.1	4.3
Overall per vote support 2009 ($)	8.11	7.75	7.87	5.91	4.59
Overall per vote support minus PVS: ($)	6.11	5.77	4.70	3.94	2.56
(% decline)	(24.6)	(25.6)	(40.3)	(33.3)	(44.2)

* Estimates (see endnote 3).
Source: Elections Canada (2009); Grenier (2011).

funding after election expenses reimbursement. The bottom row (% decline) shows the proportional change for the parties when PVS is removed. The Liberals and Conservatives are affected about equally, dropping around 25 percent. For the NDP, removal of PVS has a more significant impact, bringing with it a more than 40 percent decline. For the Bloc the drop is around 33 percent, while for the Greens the drop is over 44 percent, the highest of all five parties. Note that the data in the table are based on 2009 data. With the 2011 election results, the payout would have been greater for the Conservatives and the NDP and lower for the Liberals and, especially, the Bloc. Nonetheless, especially from a pre-election perspective, when the Conservatives committed themselves to doing away with PVS, the results based on these simple calculations are consistent with what we believe are the Conservative Party's objectives with respect to shaping the future contours of the party system.

Note in particular the manner in which the Greens will be disadvantaged by the changed regime. In 2009, the ratio between the Conservatives and the Greens in terms of per vote support was 1.77; without PVS that ratio is now 2.39 in favour of the Conservatives, a 35 percent change. In brief, in financial terms the changed regime does have the effect of making the playing field much less even. While in various ways, primarily through their attacks on PVS, the Conservatives have implied that public subvention of parties generally is not in the public interest, the net effect of the changes is that the Conservatives will become, relatively speaking, by far the greatest recipient of public funding, enjoying a much greater advantage than they did before the abolition of PVS. If the aim was simply to reduce the overall amount of tax payer subsidies given to each party, then removal of the tax credits for donation to parties would have provided a much fairer result and it would have reduced the overall public funding to parties by almost the same amount ($23.5 million versus $25.2 million, using 2009 data). In effect, removal of the tax credits rather than of PVS would have resulted in a public funding regime more closely aligned with the support the parties received at election time, thereby better reflecting voter preferences, while at the same time reducing the overall amount of public money being channelled to political parties. The fact that the Conservatives chose, instead, to remove PVS reinforces the supposition that their strategy is to tilt the playing field to their advantage.

Some may lament what might have been had PVS been structured more along the lines of what Lortie originally had in mind – that is, in a form that would have made it conditional so that the recipient parties would have been required to use it for specific purposes. Certainly there are arguments aplenty calling for parties to enhance their policy capacity and to focus less on their short-term electoral prospects. The weakness of Canadian parties in this respect is a long-standing theme in the Canadian literature, and not just among students of parties. Robert Young, for example, states that Canadian parties "desperately need a stronger capacity to formulate policy ... In a self-reinforcing cycle, people with genuine policy concerns seek out interest groups to advance their causes, and the parties degenerate further into domination by leaders and their personal entourages, who play the politics of image and strategic vagueness" (Young 1991, 7).

There are two difficulties with this argument, however. First, there is little incentive for the Conservative Party to support such an initiative, if only because it already enjoys extensive links with think tanks and quasi-think tanks that are more or less aligned with it on a variety of issues. These include entities such as the Manning Centre for Building Democracy, headed by former Reform Party leader Preston Manning. As well, the Conservatives already have a small army of at least five hundred political (exempt) staff, whose salaries, benefits, offices, travel, and operating expenses are fully funded by the taxpayer.[4] Second, there is scant evidence, either inside or outside parties, of general support for such bodies. According to Baier and Bakvis (2001, 111): "Party foundations have popped up, but they have never been of much consequence. Often these organizations appear after a particularly demoralizing defeat in the polls, or after a change of party leadership.

They are usually an attempt to revitalize or reinvent a party in the short term rather than a genuine effort at party education." There is no evidence to suggest that this pattern has changed over the fourteen-year interval since those words were written. In fact, given that none of the parties that received PVS over the past seven years invested even a small portion of those funds into something like an in-house institute suggests that the basic attitudinal problem is well entrenched and unlikely to change.

The End of Public Funding?

When PVS goes, it has been suggested, the rest of the public funding regime will follow. As with many things associated with the Conservative Party and Stephen Harper, it is difficult to pin down concrete plans or an agenda. PVS was clearly highly vulnerable to political attack, an attack that has clearly served the Conservative Party strategy of undermining the Liberals and of fostering a two-party system. PVS was also exclusively party focused. The other components in the public funding regime are less so. Reimbursement for election expenses benefits both the party and the candidates running on their behalf. The same holds true for political contributions. To reduce or take away either of these benefits would mean spending considerable effort to keep Conservative backbenchers on side. Even with the Conservative Party's highly centralized management of caucus, that would be no easy feat (Radwanski 2011).

By far the most critical component in the Conservative Party's cash flow, as is evident in Table 12.1, is the donations received from its base. Using techniques originally pioneered by the old Progressive Conservative Party and the Reform Party, the present Conservative Party has become a past master at raising significant amounts of money in the form of small donations from a relatively large base. Yet those donations are, in good part, contingent on the very generous tax treatment that they receive: donations up to four hundred dollars results in a tax credit or refund of 75 percent of that amount. Also evident in Table 12.1, and noted earlier, is that the Conservative Party is far ahead of the other parties in exploiting this particular vein of public funding. Removal of the tax credit, therefore, will likely hurt the Conservative Party far more than the other parties. In their paper, Flanagan and Coletto (2010) do not address the question of how the contribution rate of Conservative donors might be affected by reducing or eliminating the tax credit for political donations. To be sure, it would be tricky to test these hypothetical scenarios, but the results would certainly be interesting. It is conceivable that the Conservatives could structure a campaign targeting their support base to make a virtue out of eliminating the subsidy, thereby persuading their supporters to contribute more to compensate. On the other hand, the pragmatic side of Stephen Harper might well kick in, leading him to decide that discretion may be the better part of valour. In summary, complete dismantling is a possibility, but it is not a strong possibility.

Conclusion

This chapter examines the ill-fated PVS component introduced by the Liberal government in 2003 as an addition to the public funding regime for federal political parties in Canada. PVS was later abolished by the Conservative government under Stephen Harper in 2011.

We begin by asking whether the case of PVS, both its introduction and its subsequent dismantling, could be best understood within the cartelization thesis or, conversely, could have negative implications for this thesis. By and large, while cartelization is useful in framing a set of questions, we reject the supposition that PVS had both the intent and the effect of promoting it. While PVS, like other components of the public funding regime, may have been conducive to a degree of cartelization, some critical elements are lacking, foremost being the fact that one of the parties not only never agreed to the scheme but was adamantly opposed to it and, subsequently, oversaw its demise. Furthermore, since PVS was vote-based with a relatively low (2 percent) threshold, it in fact encouraged newer parties that were able to garner votes, if not seats. Both the launch, and the subsequent abolition, of PVS can best be understood in terms of strategic considerations, both internally and externally, on the part of political parties. For the Liberals, PVS was a way of compensating for the loss of funding resulting from the restrictions placed on both corporate and individual donations introduced at the same time as PVS. These restrictions were imposed by an outgoing Liberal leader wishing to leave a legacy to ensure that internal party leadership contests could not be won primarily on the basis of money and resources. PVS also served the purpose of redressing the balance of power within the Liberal Party by giving more control over funding to party headquarters. These particular developments are by and large consistent with the party franchise and stratarchy models as developed by Ken Carty and others.

For the Conservative Party, both the funding restrictions and the removal of PVS represented an ideal strategic opportunity to place the Liberal Party at a disadvantage and to foster a regime more conducive to a two-party rather than a multi-party system. By tightening considerably the restrictions on contributions, including an outright ban on corporate contributions, and then, subsequently, abolishing PVS, the new regime played to the Conservatives' strength, which is raising funds through relatively small donations from a large pool of donors.

It is these strategic explanations that best account for why PVS was initially adopted and then abolished rather than introduced to promote further cartelization of the Canadian party system. We also reject public interest arguments, which hold that PVS was adopted in order to fulfill the Lortie Commission's recommendations for strengthening the policy capacity of Canadian parties or limiting the corruption of elected officials. Even if the Lortie Commission proposal to use a PVS system to support party think tanks or foundations played a role in the subsequent adoption of PVS in 2003, PVS as introduced by the Liberal Party made no effort to force parties to use these funds to strengthen policy capacity. Furthermore, we suggest that the parties have little appetite for a form of PVS that would tie public funding to something like party foundations or think tanks.

Focusing on motives and party strategies also leads us to predict that the abolition of PVS is unlikely to lead to further or wholesale dismemberment of the public funding model. The party most likely to contemplate such a move, the Conservative Party, would face considerable pressure from its own caucus should election expenses reimbursements for candidates be eliminated. Furthermore, more so than any of the other parties, the tax credit for political donations is extremely lucrative for the Conservatives. Among the advantages of this credit, aside from the fact that the Conservatives are currently much better positioned to exploit this feature of the public funding regime, is that it represents an indirect subsidy and is thus partially hidden from public view. Pragmatism, among other considerations, will suggest to the Conservatives that the tax credit component is the one element of the regime that they would prefer to retain.

Finally, it is worth reminding ourselves that partial dismantling of the system of public funding for parties means that other parts of the overall Canadian electoral law regime will become more decisive in preserving what is generally considered a hallmark of the Canadian system – electoral fairness in the form of a level playing field with a basic floor and ceiling on what parties have available and what they can spend. And the most critical part by far is not public funding but the relatively low spending limits imposed on not only parties and candidates but also on so-called third parties (interest groups). Here we know that Mr. Harper, at least in the past, has had a visceral dislike of the limits, pejoratively referred to as the gag law, on third parties in particular (see Bakvis and Smith 1997). Since becoming prime minister, Harper has made no comments and given no indication as to whether he would seek their removal – in the event no easy task given that they have survived the test of a Supreme Court challenge, albeit with a split decision. Nonetheless, should a similar challenge come forward again, it is conceivable, given his experience as leader of an incumbent party, that he will recognize the strategic advantage of maintaining centralized control over advertising spending on behalf of the Conservative Party and favour maintaining current restrictions on third-party advertising.[5]

Notes

1 See Katz and Mair (1995) on the conceptualization and evolution of the cartel model. For critiques and debates, see Katz and Mair (1996), Kitschelt (2000), Koole (1996), and Pierre et al. (2000).

2 "An Act to implement certain provisions of the 2011 budget as updated on June 6, 2011 and other measures," House of Commons of Canada, first session, forty-first Parliament, 60 Elizabeth II, 2011. Among the provisions in C-13 are those for phasing out PVS over a three-year period, beginning in 2012.

3 Tax credits are, in effect, tax expenditures, not direct cash payments to parties. Given that the federal Department of Finance only releases information on the overall value of the tax credits (foregone tax revenue) and that the tax credit value of each donation varies with the size of the donation (the proportionate value of the tax credit decreases as the size of the donation increases), calculating the value of these credits for each party poses a challenge (Jansen and Young 2011b). In the case of the estimates presented in Table 12.1, these were calculated by Grenier (2011), who assumed that the size of the donation was the same for all parties and then divided this amount into the amount in donations raised by each party to arrive at the estimated value of the tax credits that can be attributed to each party. Given that the limit on the maximum credit value of small donations (75 percent) was raised from one hundred dollars to four hundred dollars in 2004, combined with the overall limit on donations of one thousand dollars introduced in 2006, Grenier's assumptions appear reasonable if not ideal.

4 Each minister and minister of state is allowed up to eight exempt staff. Plus a minister is eligible for four more if she or he has regional responsibilities (Canada 2011). The Prime Minister's Office alone has over eighty-five staff members (Rana 2008).

5 This advantage should be seen in the context of the Fair Elections Act of 2014, which greatly expanded the opportunity to spend more. If an election campaign exceeds 37 days, parties can spend an extra $685,000 per day. For the 2015 election, Prime Minister Harper triggered a 78-day campaign period, allowing parties to spend twice as much ($50 million rather than $25 million). The Conservatives, with funds at both the riding and national levels exceeding that of the Liberals and NDP combined, were thus much better positioned to take advantage of the expanded limit at the start of the 2015 campaign.

References

Aucoin, P. 2005. *Political Party and Campaign Financing in Canada*. Washington, DC: OAS Unit for Promotion of Democracy.

Baier, G., and H. Bakvis. 2001. "Think tanks and political parties: Competitors or collaborators." *Isuma* 2 (1): 107–13.

Bakvis, H., and J. Smith. 1997. "Third-party advertising and electoral democracy: The political theory of the Alberta Court of Appeal in *Somerville v. Canada (Attorney General)* [1996]." *Canadian Public Policy* 23 (2): 164–78. http://dx.doi.org/10.2307/3551483.

Blatchford, A. 2010. Tale of two approaches: Quebec's idea for political financing opposite of Harper's. *Canadian Press*. November 4.

Bordeleau, F. 2003. *Political Financing and the Control of Election Expenses in Québec: Past and Present*. Montreal: Directeur général des élections du Québec.

Canada. Committee on Election Expenses [Barbeau Committee]. 1966a. *Report of the Committee on Election Expenses*. Ottawa: Queen's Printer.

–. Committee on Election Expenses [Barbeau Committee]. 1966b. *Studies in Canadian Party Finance*. K. Paltiel et al. for the Committee on Election Expenses. Ottawa: Queen's Printer.

–. Royal Commission on Electoral Reform and Party Financing. 1991. *Final Report*. Ottawa: Royal Commission on Electoral Reform and Party Financing.

–. Treasury Board Secretariat. 2011. *Policies for Ministers' Offices*. Ottawa.

Carty, R.K. 2002. "The politics of Tecumseh Corners: Canadian political parties as franchise organizations." *Canadian Journal of Political Science* 35 (4): 723–45. http://dx.doi.org/10.1017/S0008423902778402.

–. 2004. "Parties as franchise systems: The stratarchical organizational imperative." *Party Politics* 10 (1): 5–24. http://dx.doi.org/10.1177/1354068804039118.

Carty, R.K., and Lisa Young. 2012. "The Lortie Commission and the place of political parties as agents of responsible government." In *From "New Public Management" to "New Public Governance": Essays in Honour of Peter C. Aucoin*, ed. H. Bakvis and M. Jarvis, 105–27. Montreal and Kingston: McGill-Queen's University Press.

Coletto, D., H.J. Jansen, and L. Young. 2011. "Stratarchical party organization and party finance in Canada." *Canadian Journal of Political Science* 44 (1): 111–36. http://dx.doi.org/10.1017/S0008423910001034.

Covell, M. 1991. "Party foundations in Belgium." In *Working Papers for the Royal Commission on Electoral Reform and Party Financing*, vol. 2. ed. H. Bakvis. Ottawa: Royal Commission on Electoral Reform and Party Financing.

Cross, W. 2004. *Political Parties*. Vancouver: UBC Press.

Elections Canada. 2009. *Quarterly Allowances to the Registered Political Parties (2008)*. Ottawa: Elections Canada website.

Flanagan, T., and D. Coletto. 2010. "Replacing allowances for Canada's national political parties?" *SPP Briefing Papers* 3 (1): 1–13. Calgary: University of Calgary, School of Public Policy.

Galloway, G. 2009. Per-vote subsidies still provoking debate. *Globe and Mail*, January 6.

Grenier, É. 2011. Per-vote subsidy but a fraction of taxpayer support for political parties. *Globe and Mail*, January 23.

Hopkin, J. 2004. "The problem with party finance: Theoretical perspectives on the funding of party politics." *Party Politics* 10 (6): 627-51. http://dx.doi.org/10.1177/1354068804046911.

Jansen, H.J., and L. Young. 2011a. "Cartels, syndicates, and coalitions." In *Money, Politics, and Democracy*, ed. L. Young and H. Jansen, 82–103. Vancouver: UBC Press.

–. 2011b. "State subsidies and political parties." *Policy Options* (Institute for Research on Public Policy) (October): 43–47.

Katz, R.S., and P. Mair. 1995. "Changing models of party organization and party democracy: The emergence of the cartel party." *Party Politics* 1 (1): 5–28. http://dx.doi.org/10.1177/1354068895001001001.

–. 1996. "Cadre, catch-all or cartel: A rejoinder." *Party Politics* 2 (4): 525–34. http://dx.doi.org/10.1177/1354068896002004005.

Kitschelt, H. 2000. "Citizens, politicians and party cartelization: Political representation and state failure in post-industrial democracies." *European Journal of Political Research* 37 (2): 149–79. http://dx.doi.org/10.1111/1475-6765.00508.

Koole, R. 1996. "Cadre, catch-all or cartel? A comment on the notion of the cartel party." *Party Politics* 2 (4): 507–23. http://dx.doi.org/10.1177/1354068896002004004.

MacIvor, H. 1996. "Do Canadian political parties form a cartel?" *Canadian Journal of Political Science* 29 (2): 317–33. http://dx.doi.org/10.1017/S0008423900007733.

Pierre, J., L. Svåsand, and A. Widfeldt. 2000. "State subsidies to political parties: Confronting rhetoric with reality." *West European Politics* 23 (3): 1–24. http://dx.doi.org/10.1080/01402380008425381.

Pinto-Duschinsky, M. 1991. "Party foundations and political finance in Germany." In *Comparative Issues in Party and Election Finance*, ed. F.L. Seidle, 179–250. Toronto: Dundurn.

Radwanski, A. 2011. How Tory rush to kill per-vote subsidy could backfire. *Globe and Mail*, April 25.

Rana, A. 2008. PM's new chief of staff Giorno to shake up Cabinet's chiefs of staff, too. *Hill Times*, July 14.

Russell, P.H., and L. Sossin, eds. 2009. *Parliamentary Democracy in Crisis*. Toronto: University of Toronto Press.

Stanbury, W. 2011. Comparing the per-vote subsidies to all federal political subsidies. *Hill Times*, January 20.

Valpy, M. 2009. "The crisis: A narrative." In *Parliamentary Democracy in Crisis*, ed. P.H. Russell and L. Sossin, 3–18. Toronto: University of Toronto Press.

Wolinetz, S. 1991. "Party foundations in the Netherlands." In *Working Papers for the Royal Commission on Electoral Reform and Party Financing*, vol. 2. ed. H. Bakvis. Ottawa: Royal Commission on Electoral Reform and Party Financing.

Young, L. 1998. "Party, state and political competition in Canada: The cartel model reconsidered." *Canadian Journal of Political Science* 31 (2): 339–58. http://dx.doi.org/10.1017/S000842390001982X.

Young, R.A. 1991. "Effecting change: Do we have the political system to get us where we want to go?" In *Canada at Risk? Canadian Public Policy in the 1990s*, ed. G.B. Doern and B.B. Purchase, 59–60. Toronto: C.D. Howe Institute.

13

Electoral Reform and Parliamentary Legitimacy in Canada

CAMPBELL SHARMAN AND KYLE ATTANASIO

Whatever the vagaries of partisan politics in Canada, until the 1990s there had been little public debate on the process through which parties were represented in Parliament. Changes could be made to electoral rules by the governing party with little discussion beyond complaints by opposition parties. It is true that there had been some academic discussion prompted by Cairns's (1968) analysis of the distortion of national party representation produced by a single member plurality system in a regionally diverse federation (note Johnston, Chapter 2, this volume), but there had been no broad-based expression of the need for electoral reform. With the exception of the Liberal Party in Quebec, no governing party since the 1960s had given serious thought to championing the principle of greater electoral proportionality and the changes in partisan representation that this would entail.

Yet, in the period between 2001 and 2010, there was an extraordinary upsurge in proposals for electoral reform in Canada, followed by an equally dramatic decline. Five of Canada's ten provincial governments initiated comprehensive proposals for modification of their electoral systems, and the national government toyed with various schemes for institutional change. The defining characteristics of this reform activity were (1) the use of public inquiries as precursors to electoral change and (2) recommendations for some form of proportional representation. But, by 2010, all proposals for voting system change had either been defeated at referendums or abandoned by governments.

Much of the explanation for this failure can be found in the resistance of the usual suspects hostile to electoral reform (Rahat and Hazan 2011), chiefly governing parties and those political interests that benefit from the existing system. But an explanation for the original impulse for electoral reform is more elusive. As Carty points out, "there is no easy or obvious answer why Canadians are now seriously debating electoral reform" (Carty 2006, 22). By the 1990s, a growing number of voices had begun to complain about the way party control subordinates the role of local members to the dictates of government or opposition policy, the arbitrary use of executive power, and the generally unresponsive and error-prone behaviour of government. There was extensive evidence of public disillusionment with the governmental process (Nevitte 2002; Putnam et al. 2000) and an increasing use of the term "democratic deficit" to describe a malaise with parliamentary representation. The problem is that the suggestion that some generalized democratic deficit in Canada's political institutions prompted an interest in electoral change can say little about the timing, content, or style of government proposals for reform. This is especially the case given that the moves for electoral reform were initiated by governing parties rather than as the result of widespread popular complaint.

From our perspective, the mode of recent attempts at changing electoral systems in Canada is more interesting than the substance of the proposals for reform, and it provides more potential for explaining the interest in electoral change. Previous government involvement with the adoption of different formulas for turning votes into seats – the alternative vote and the single transferable vote – sprang predominantly from the partisan interests of government without any felt need to ask for extensive prior public consultation.[1] Such voting systems were used for varying periods in Alberta, British Columbia, and Manitoba from the 1920s to the 1950s (Jansen 2004) and were dispensed with in a similar summary fashion. While the element of partisan gain has been of varying significance in recent proposals for electoral reform, the concern with providing formal avenues for public discussion, and of linking electoral reform with broader issues of democratic representation, were new.

Apart from examining the five major attempts at electoral reform in the Canadian provinces, we note that, early in his prime ministership, Paul Martin expressed interest in "democratic renewal," but there was no commitment to electoral system change of the kind recommended by the Law Commission of Canada (2004), and his interest had evaporated by the time of his defeat at the 2006 federal election (LeDuc 2009, 23). Five provinces, however, developed comprehensive proposals for electoral reform, all of which involved broad public consultation, ranging from conventional requests for public submissions to highly innovative procedures for citizen involvement in the design of the electoral system. While, in some cases, partisan interest has been important in precipitating the initiative for electoral reform, it is the search for public approval that has been the distinguishing feature. What was it about provincial politics that prompted the need to involve the public? Our answer is that these efforts at citizen involvement can be seen as the provincial governments' response to a series of challenges to the legitimacy of their parliamentary governments, some contextual and some springing from the enhanced role of the judiciary following the adoption of the Canadian Charter of Rights and Freedoms in 1982.

Five Initiatives for Electoral Reform

Before pursuing this theme, some background is required. All five provinces pursuing electoral reform after 2001 had used public consultation as a component of their deliberations over proposals for a new electoral system, but the extent and mode of this public involvement varied widely.

The case of Quebec is the most conventional in that parliamentary institutions played a more important role than in other provinces. The Parti Québécois had an ideological commitment to proportional representation since the 1960s; however, when in government, it made only sporadic and half-hearted attempts to implement this policy (Massicotte 2007, 252–54). Following the setting up of parliamentary hearings on electoral system reform in 2001, a Parti Québécois government established the Estates General on the Reform of Democratic Institutions in 2002 (the Béland Commission), which was to tour the province and to take evidence from the public on a wide range of issues related to the structure of provincial government, including the shape of the electoral system. After holding twenty-seven public hearings around the province, the commission reported in 2003 and, among many other recommendations, offered a proposal for a form of proportional representation.

This was taken up by the Liberal government of Premier Jean Charest, which was elected later in 2003, and another round of parliamentary considerations of electoral change ensued. A parliamentary committee was appointed in 2005 to study a draft bill setting out a new electoral system, assisted by an eight-member citizens' committee, which, in turn, undertook public consultations across the province in 2006 (Library of Parliament 2009, 11). This process eventually resulted in a detailed legislative proposal for a form of proportional representation whose final shape was to be accepted by the National Assembly (Massicotte 2007). The impulse for electoral system change, however, came to a halt with the re-election of a majority Charest Liberal government in 2008.

In the case of New Brunswick, the government set up the Commission on Legislative Reform late in 2003 after the Progressive Conservative government of Premier Bernard Lord had been narrowly returned to office in an election in which the issue of democratic renewal had not played a significant role. Nonetheless, a comprehensive study of citizen involvement in the political process was foreshadowed in the government's election platform and was seen by some as a complement to the Lord government's previous policies on the delivery of health and education services (McLaughlin 2007, 24). The nine-member commission was chosen to accommodate the linguistic and regional communities in the province and to achieve a gender and political balance, the latter posing some difficulty because of the hostility of the Liberal Party opposition in Parliament.

The commission was given twelve months to undertake an extensive schedule of consultations and to make recommendations on a wide range of issues, including the relationship between the legislature and the executive, the conduct of elections, the process of redistricting, and an appropriate electoral system for the province. In its final report (New Brunswick 2004), the commission provided extensive recommendations on these topics and proposed a binding referendum to be held on the adoption of a mixed member proportional (MMP) electoral system. After a period of a year and a half, Premier Lord released a formal response adopting most of the commission's recommendations, including those for a referendum on the proposed electoral system (McLaughlin 2007, 37). But, within three months, the Lord government was defeated at a general election, and the new Liberal Party government declined to proceed with all but a few procedural reforms.

In contrast to the sudden appearance of the issue of electoral reform in New Brunswick, Prince Edward Island had a long history of debates over its parliamentary representation and the difficulties of lop-sided majorities produced by a majoritarian electoral system in a small parliamentary assembly (Cousins 2002). Although a committee of the Legislative Assembly had requested information on proportional representation in 2001, the formal process of investigating proposals for electoral change was initiated early in 2003 with the appointment of a former chief justice of the Supreme Court of Prince Edward Island as a one-person commission of inquiry (the Carruthers Commission). The Commission on Electoral Reform took evidence from a wide range of sources, held public meetings around the province, and produced a report in December 2003 (Prince Edward Island Electoral Reform Commission 2003). Earlier in 2003, a general election for the assembly had returned the Progressive Conservative government but produced another highly disproportionate result.

The Electoral Reform Commission report suggested that a change from the existing first-past-the-post electoral system was desirable but recommended yet more public consultation, the need for a referendum to settle the issue, and the use of a citizens' assembly procedure to devise the referendum question. A year later, the Legislative Assembly set in train the process of appointing the eight-person Commission on Prince Edward Island's Electoral Future, which began its work early in 2005 (Library of Parliament 2009, 8–9). The recommendation of a citizens' assembly process was ignored, and the task of canvassing the public and devising a clear referendum question was given to the new commission. In November 2005, a referendum on an MMP system for the province was soundly defeated, with only 37 percent of the voters favouring change.

The remaining provinces of British Columbia and Ontario followed a different route, choosing a citizens' assembly process as the focus for involving the public in electoral reform. This process, pioneered in British Columbia, involved the setting up of a body of citizens drawn from the voters' list in the province and chosen by a combination of random choice and self-selection. The citizens' assembly then acquired information on electoral systems, invited public submissions and expressions of opinion, used the information to deliberate on the merits of various electoral systems, and, finally, made a recommendation on an appropriate electoral system that was to be submitted to a referendum.

A great deal of interest has been expressed in both the details of this process and in its implications for deliberative democracy (see generally British Columbia 2004; Carty et al. 2008; Fournier et al. 2011; Warren and Pearse 2008). From our perspective, citizens' assemblies represent an attempt to give citizen involvement an autonomous role in the choice of an electoral system and to distance the process from partisan politics. Governments still set the institutional framework of the assemblies, and government approval would have been required if change were to be implemented, but the nature and content of the debate over electoral reform was shaped by the citizens' assemblies.

Two questions arise: What prompted government interest in electoral change in these two provinces, and why was a citizens' assembly process adopted? As outlined by Fournier et al. (2011, 22–28), the answer to the first question is that the premiers of British Columbia and Ontario had come to believe, when leaders of the opposition, that aspects of the parliamentary process in their respective provinces were seriously impaired and that, among other things, a review of the electoral system was an important component for the restoration of a healthy parliamentary process. This had less to do with a concern over any perceived democratic deficit than with a sense that norms of political fairness and due process had been breached (note Cutler and Hooper, Chapter 14, this volume). The answer to the second question varies by province.

On winning office in 2001, Premier Gordon Campbell of British Columbia had considered some form of citizens' assembly as part of his election platform in 2001, but the idea needed to be refined before the institution was finally put in place, a process that resulted in the creation of the British Columbia Citizens' Assembly on Electoral Reform in 2003. The assembly completed its work by the end of 2004 in time for a referendum on its proposed electoral system, which was to be held with the general election in 2005. The referendum failed to gain the required 60 percent support for the adoption of the assembly's proposed electoral system; however, at 58 percent, the support was high enough for the government to arrange a second referendum on the proposal to be held in 2009. This also failed, with only 39 percent in favour of change (Fournier et al. 2011).

On winning office in Ontario in 2003, Premier Dalton McGuinty shared misgivings about representative institutions in his province that were similar to those of Premier Campbell. Following the lead of British Columbia, in Ontario a similar citizens' assembly process for electoral reform was set up in 2006 (Fournier et al. 2011; LeDuc 2009). It reported in 2007, with a recommendation for a new electoral system that was submitted to voters at a referendum held at the same time as the general election in 2007. The referendum gained only 37 percent support, far short of the required 60 percent.

In comparing the experiences of the five provinces, Table 13.1 summarizes the characteristics of public engagement used in each. The first column shows the period from the start of the inquiry into electoral reform to the

TABLE 13.1
Comparing the process of public involvement, five Canadian provinces, 2001–09

		Public involvement				Process ended by rejection of reform proposal by:	
		Submissions to:					
Province and period of public inquiry*	Process initiated by government decision to:	Parliamentary committee	Commission or citizens' assembly	Regional hearings	Citizens' assembly process	Negative referendum result	Executive inaction
BC 2003–09	Establish a citizens' assembly		✓	✓	✓	✓	
NB 2003–06	Set up a commission of inquiry		✓	✓			✓
Ontario 2006–07	Establish a citizens' assembly		✓	✓	✓	✓	
PEI 2003–05	Set up a commission of inquiry		✓	✓		✓	
QC 2001–08	Hold parliamentary hearings	✓	✓	✓			✓

* See text for explanation.

rejection of its recommendations through either government inaction or the failure to gain sufficient public support at a referendum. Both citizens' assemblies, however, were active for a period of fewer than eighteen months, and the six-year period shown for British Columbia includes the four-year gap between the first and the second referendum on the proposed BC-STV electoral system. Without the second referendum, the period for British Columbia would be two years.

The periods shown in the table for provincial inquiries also mask variations in the context of the inquiries. For British Columbia, New Brunswick, and Ontario, the process was initiated by the commitment of a premier to institutional change, with little previous public discussion of the topic or partisan debate. For the provinces of Prince Edward Island and Quebec, the issue of institutional reform had been in play for a longer period and had more partisan overtones.

The process of electoral reform had a clear termination date in those provinces that used referendums to gauge public support, although British Columbia needed two referendums to put the proposal to rest. For the remaining provinces, the closing date represents an assessment of the removal of the topic of electoral reform from the government agenda. For New Brunswick, the electoral defeat of the initiating government by the opposition party signalled the end of reform efforts, and for Quebec, the return of the Liberal government of Jean Charest (with a comfortable majority) provided the opportunity to shelve what had become a divisive issue both within and between political parties.

With these caveats aside, Table 13.1 shows that all inquiries had a broad commitment to public involvement. All inquiries invited submissions and expressions of opinion, and all held hearings at population centres around the province. Three inquiries resulted in referendums on proposals for electoral change, and this could be increased to four if the original recommendation for a referendum by the New Brunswick Commission on Legislative Reform is included. Quebec is an outlier not only for the lack of a proposal for a referendum but also for the role played by the National Assembly and the variety and number of stages in the process of public consultation. But for all provinces, the public was to be a major player in the process of electoral reform.

The Loss of Legitimacy

This returns us to the question of why governments felt that the public needed to be involved. The short answer is that, since 1982, the traditional model of governmental legitimacy through popular endorsement of parliamentary democracy had been challenged by the Canadian Charter of Rights and Freedoms. Mass politics and the majoritarian assumptions of parliamentary government based on partisan competition for votes were faced with the politics of individual rights and judicial review.

At the end of the 1970s, Canada and all its component provinces enjoyed a system of parliamentary government dominated by the executive and free from constitutional checks, except those related to the creation, structure, and operation of the federal system.[2] While there was some scope for judicial review of governmental action, most elements of the governmental process were not subject to constitutionally based checks through the courts. If a consensus element in the Canadian polity was provided by federalism and the judicial review of a federal constitution, majoritarianism reigned supreme in the parliamentary realm, untroubled by constitutional challenge.

But the adoption of the Canadian Charter of Rights and Freedoms as part of an entrenched national constitution in 1982 (the Constitution Act, 1982) radically changed the balance. The list of individual and group rights in the Charter provided an avenue to strike down legislative provisions and to limit government action in a way that, to this point, had not been possible. This has given Canada a much larger degree of consensus politics by greatly increasing the scope for minority veto of government action through the use of the courts to question a wide range of public policy issues.

This change has had a number of effects on the legislative process at the provincial level: the monopoly of legislative and executive authority in areas of social policy has been broken; the visibility and political salience of the judiciary has been increased; and, to the extent that the Charter is a national instrument whose final interpretation rests with a national Supreme Court, there has been a transfer of power from parliamentary politics in the provincial sphere to judicial politics in the national sphere (Morton 1995; but note Kelly 2001).

The biggest loser has been the executive branch of government. It is not that judges were constantly looking over the shoulders of provincial premiers – only a minute proportion of governmental activity was scrutinized by the courts – but that there was a rival institution to speak to the public on behalf of citizen voters and to claim constitutional legitimacy. After over thirty years' experience with the Charter, it is clear that the settled pattern of majoritarian parliamentary politics has been disturbed: the scope for mass politics and political parties that rely on public endorsement through elections is now more limited. Even if the Charter had done no more than change the way governments consider the consequences of legislative action (Hiebert 2005), it is hard not to see both it and the potential for judicial involvement across the whole ambit of public policy as major contributors to the sense of uncertainty and loss of legitimacy felt by parties, governments, and parliaments.[3] Where it could be deployed, the politics of individual rights could trump the politics of collective choice (note Lusztig 2010).

Institutional Responses

If one of the attractions of the Charter of Rights and Freedoms is that it requires the government to recognize the importance of due process in both the mode and the goals of decision-making, why cannot the parliamentary system respond by adopting similar characteristics? What is to stop provincial governments from adding extra vitamins to the parliamentary process by setting up a committee system free from government veto and by enhancing the autonomy of the legislature by greatly expanding the opportunities for opposition parties and interest groups to become involved in the scrutiny of government and its legislation? This could be supplemented by a range of provisions that constrained the discretion of the executive by limiting the scope of delegated legislation, by mandating parliamentary approval of all regulations made under an enabling act, and by requiring Parliament to meet more frequently.

To list the requirements for the Canadian provinces to achieve more limited government and consensus democracy is to show why the likelihood of such change is remote. The idea of reducing the practices of a British-derived parliamentary executive to constitutional provisions would be regarded by governments as both redundant and dangerous; even worse, it might give the courts entry to an aspect of the governmental process from which they are now excluded. This is quite apart from accepting changes that would reduce executive control over the parliamentary process, change the career structure of members of Parliament, and severely limit the extensive network of executive patronage outside Parliament, which characterize the current system. It is, in short, hard to imagine the circumstances under which constitutional amendment to enhance the procedural legitimacy of Parliament could be achieved.[4]

Nevertheless, governments had become dimly aware that some kind of change was required and there was a growing realization that some kind of reform would win them kudos and enhance the public acceptance of their role.[5] For a period in the 1990s, some suggested direct democracy as a way to improve the process of government: if the institutions of representative democracy were not working to limit the excesses of government, why not bypass them so that the people could express their views directly? Bending to this pressure, the government of British Columbia passed the Recall and Initiative Act, 1994, but set the requirements for citizen-initiated recall of members of the Legislative Assembly (and for initiating the review of legislation) at a level that was very hard to meet.[6] The populist recourse to the institutions of direct democracy was circumvented by procedural obstacles put up by those who saw recall and initiative not as a remedy for party domination of the political process but, rather, as another strategy that parties could use to embarrass their partisan opponents. As a consequence, electoral reform began to be seen as the only way of enhancing the legitimacy of Parliament because it could be used to change the dynamics of representation without constitutional change.

The modification of the electoral system can spring from a wide variety of motivations and can be studied from many perspectives (see generally Leyenaar and Hazan 2011). We argue that, in the cases under review, the focus on the electoral system is the consequence of an institutional structure that precludes other choices for altering the style of parliamentary representation. The only avenue of structural change that remains is the process of representation itself. The Charter points the way: section 3 provides that "every citizen of Canada has the right to vote in an election of members of the House of Commons or of a legislative assembly and to be qualified for membership therein." This section and others in the Charter, which can be held to relate to the electoral process, have been the basis for constitutional challenges to the composition of legislative assemblies. But the courts have been cautious in their interpretation of this section (Courtney 2004, 61–63). In the *Carter* decision of the Supreme Court of Canada,[7] the Court declined to use section 3 to limit the discretion that governments have in varying the number of voters in electoral districts as long as there was a measure of "effective representation." While the process of judicial review is likely to remain important as litigants invite the courts to modify the increasingly complex set of rules that regulates election campaigns (Katz 2011), the registration of parties and election finance – the basis of representation – are left predominantly to legislatures. In particular, if the goal is to change the dynamics of the parliamentary process, something more is needed: what is required is electoral change that breaks down the neat dichotomies of majoritarian representation. This explains the interest in systems of proportional representation.

Bringing In the Public

Being aware that proportional representation might be a way of altering the parliamentary process to satisfy the critics of the existing mode of government is a long way from taking action to change the electoral system. But any move in this direction would be greeted with profound suspicion on the part of most politicians precisely because it would threaten existing partisan and parliamentary norms, quite apart from the uncertainty that such a move would generate for MPs and political parties.

This is the dilemma faced by governments: altering the electoral system might induce changes that enhance the legitimacy of the parliamentary process, but the political costs for governing parties might be high. Of course, if the political costs were seen to be low, then the move to a proportional electoral system might be acceptable. It is plausible to argue that, initially, Prince Edward Island was in this position as both its political parties displayed some acceptance that the current system had produced dysfunctional parliaments.

Quebec also fits this category, but with some caveats. The Charest Liberal government might have benefited from a proportional system, even though the process of reform began with the Parti Québécois. By the end of the period under review, the Liberals had shelved any consideration of reform, presumably after an assessment indicating that the partisan benefits of change were too uncertain and the costs too high.

It is no accident that, for both Prince Edward Island and Quebec, consideration of reform began with parliamentary inquiries. Both governments saw benefits in canvassing the issue of electoral reform – sanitized to a greater or lesser extent by including a range of other issues related to government – within a parliamentary context within which governing parties had control over the process. But both governments also set up extra-parliamentary commissions to invite wide public consultation. Two explanations can be advanced for this subsequent move. The first is that the governments genuinely wanted more information on the possibilities of reform and the way in which interested publics might respond to proposals for changing the electoral system. The second is that there was dissent within the governing parties, with public involvement functioning not only as a stalling tactic but also as a way of demonstrating the government's concern with democratic representation and reforming the parliamentary system without having to take any further action. Either way, the government would gain political approbation for bringing the public into the discussion pertaining to the legitimacy of the existing system of parliamentary representation.

In the final stages of the process, Prince Edward Island chose to refer the question of electoral reform to a referendum, an indication that it was struggling with how to bring closure to a complicated process that had raised fundamental questions about parliamentary democracy. It can also be seen as an indication that the political costs of change were not perceived to be so high as to preclude the public from having the final say, even though the context of the referendum and the threshold of 60 percent were likely to preclude change.

For Quebec, the many stages through which the reform process had passed indicated that differing assessments of partisan costs and benefits within the governing party could not be resolved and that the issue had to be shelved. This was not a matter on which the government wanted to risk a referendum, especially in a province in which referendums were identified with highly contentious issues of sovereignty. The public had been consulted through other processes: the expectations of popular involvement had been fulfilled, and electoral reform could be left for another day.

For the remaining three provinces – British Columbia, New Brunswick, and Ontario – partisan gain did not figure as a major component in the initiation of the electoral reform process, at least in the form of clear partisan advantage for the governing party. It is true that, in the preceding elections, all three premiers of these provinces used the commitment to some form of institutional reform to bolster their claims for electoral support. But all three premiers appeared to have been motivated (1) by an awareness that parliamentary government had suffered a loss of legitimacy that electoral reform might help to restore and (2) by a belief that extensive public consultation was an integral part of this process. Aware of possible criticism that consideration of change was driven by partisan and institutional self-interest, all three set up public inquiries that were neither extensions of Parliament nor conventional commissions. The citizens' assembly process used in British Columbia and Ontario was the most adventurous, but the composition of the New Brunswick inquiry was designed to cancel out partisan, regional, and linguistic differences. All three inquiries were to be followed by referendums on a proposed new electoral system, although the change of government in New Brunswick precluded the holding of a referendum in that province.

For all three provinces that held referendums – this includes Prince Edward Island, which did not use the citizens' assembly process – the proposal for a new electoral system had to gain a qualified majority of 60 percent of those voting. While, after the recommendations narrowly failed to gain the necessary support in the first referendum in British

Columbia, there was some debate that this requirement was too restrictive, it was generally accepted that recourse to a referendum was an appropriate procedure for such a serious matter as changing the electoral system. Electoral rules were, it was widely assumed, an important component of the Constitution and deserved a procedure consistent with the amendment of key constitutional provisions (Levinson 2001).

The requirements for the success of the referendums were, however, entirely at odds with the constitutional tradition of the Canadian provinces. Provincial constitutional documents have never been submitted to the voters at a referendum and there are no special procedural requirements for legislative change to constitutional laws. And there have been many changes to provincial electoral laws and procedures, none of which has been submitted for direct public approval.

The use of the referendum process is symptomatic of changes in the way governments see their authority. It is true that governments can use referendums to avoid having to make decisions on highly contentious topics; however, in the case of the electoral change process, other considerations were at work. One reason for the use of a referendum – and the 60 percent threshold for success set by British Columbia and copied by the other provinces – was that it was the price exacted by government party caucuses as a poison pill against the success of electoral change. This amounted to an admission on the part of governments that they could not persuade their own supporters to enact electoral change but were willing to leave such decisions to a referendum – a process that looked like an exercise in public consultation but was, in fact, nothing more than a populist device that functioned to ensure that governments could avoid the blame for a failure to enact electoral change.

Consequences

The spasm of attempts at provincial electoral reform in Canada can be seen as the result of a series of coincidences that brought to a head concerns with the legitimacy of parliamentary government and, to a lesser extent, the nature of partisan representation in the legislature. In each of the cases examined, shortcomings in the process of representation, whether principled or partisan, led to broader questions about the ability of parliamentary government to respond to the preferences of citizens. While it is tempting to concentrate on the fact that all five provinces considered some form of proportional representation as a vehicle for parliamentary reform, we argue that it is the interest in public consultation that has been the most significant development.

This is not simply because some provinces used new and adventurous forms of public deliberation but, rather, because all provinces felt that public involvement in the process of reform was required. Even in those provinces in which public consultation was limited to the making of submissions, the fact of consultation reinforced the belief that electoral reform has some quasi-constitutional significance that is more fundamental than a simple issue of party representation. This elevation of the electoral system to the status of an organic law was reinforced by those who opposed change. Their strongest argument was essentially a constitutional one: that the nature of the partisan choice offered to voters under proportional electoral systems would fundamentally alter the way in which governments are formed and operate (Sartori 1997).

It can be argued that provincial governments have responded to the challenge of the Charter of Rights and Freedoms by accepting two things: (1) that parliamentary legitimacy – and hence the authority of provincial governments – can be enhanced through electoral reform and (2) that changes to the process of partisan representation can only be legitimate if they are grounded in broad-based public involvement and consent. Those who argued for public consultation and referendums as a way of deferring or countering electoral reform may have created a result they might have been keen to avoid – a guarantee that any future discussion of electoral change will, of necessity, generate a public debate about the nature of parliamentary government and the appropriate role of parliaments. The more governments talk about public consultation, referendums, and de facto entrenchment of the electoral system, the more they elevate the debate above a concern with party politics and transform it into a discussion about governmental legitimacy, the style of parliamentary government, and constitutional change.

If this is the shape of future electoral reform in Canada, the consequences for political parties are substantial because questions of electoral change will be removed from the ambit of purely partisan debate. This will pose an awkward dilemma for governing parties if the dictates of partisan advantage suggest modifications to the electoral system or if resentment about lack of representation generates pressure for electoral change (see Cutler and Hooper, Chapter 14, this volume). If the changes are made without some process of public consultation, the government will be open to charges of partisan manipulation of the electoral system. In the past, this might have been taken for granted, with only opposition parties having grounds to complain, but now governments can be accused of evading public consultation on a key aspect of parliamentary representation that has Constitution-like status. Yet, from the evidence above, if governments engage in some process of popular involvement with regard to proposals for electoral reform, this may have the effect of greatly reducing the likelihood of change. In this area, as in others, parties have, in effect, been co-opted as a formal component of democratic representation (see Courtney, Chapter 11, this volume): the process of electoral reform has been transformed from a question of partisan convenience into one of parliamentary legitimacy.

Notes

1 In Renwick's (2011) terms, a case of "elite majority imposition."

2 These include some specific provisions relating to the use of the English and French languages and the status of educational institutions in some provinces (Constitution Act [Canada] 1867, ss. 133 and 93).

3 On the nature of an implied dialogue between courts and legislatures in Canada, see Webber (2009).

4 Even serious constitutional crises appear unable to generate parliamentary change in this direction. See Sharman (2002).

5 For an optimistic view of the extent of this process, see Docherty and White (2004).

6 But not impossible – the Recall and Initiative Act was used successfully to force a referendum in 2011 on harmonized sales tax (HST) legislation in the province, a referendum that led to the repeal of the tax.

7 *Reference re Provincial Electoral Boundaries (Saskatchewan)*, [1991] 2 S.C.R. 158.

References

British Columbia. Citizens' Assembly on Electoral Reform. 2004. *Making Every Vote Count: The Case for Electoral Reform in British Columbia – Technical Report*. Vancouver: BC Citizens' Assembly for Electoral Reform.

Cairns, A.C. 1968. "The electoral system and the party system in Canada, 1921–1965." *Canadian Journal of Political Science* 1 (1): 55–80. http://dx.doi.org/10.1017/S0008423900035228.

Carty, R.K. 2006. "Regional responses to electoral reform." *Canadian Parliamentary Review* 29 (1): 22–26.

Carty, R.K., A. Blais, and P. Fournier. 2008. "When citizens choose to reform SMP: The British Columbia Citizens' Assembly on Electoral Reform." In *To Keep or to Change First Past the Post? The Politics of Electoral Reform*, ed. A. Blais, 140–62. Oxford: Oxford University Press. http://dx.doi.org/10.1093/acprof:oso/9780199539390.003.0006.

Courtney, J.C. 2004. *Elections*. Vancouver: UBC Press.

Cousins, J.A. 2002. "Electoral reform for Prince Edward Island." *Canadian Parliamentary Review* 25 (4): 22–31.

Docherty, D.C., and S. White. 2004. "Parliamentary democracy in Canada." *Parliamentary Affairs* 57 (3): 613–29. http://dx.doi.org/10.1093/pa/gsh048.

Fournier, P., H. van der Kolk, R.K. Carty, A. Blais, and J. Rose. 2011. *When Citizens Decide: Lessons from Citizen Assemblies on Electoral Reform*. Oxford: Oxford University Press. http://dx.doi.org/10.1093/acprof:oso/9780199567843.001.0001.

Hiebert, J.L. 2005. "Interpreting a bill of rights: The importance of legislative rights review." *British Journal of Political Science* 5 (2): 235–55. http://dx.doi.org/10.1017/S000712340500013X.

Jansen, H.J. 2004. "The political consequences of the alternative vote: Lessons from Western Canada." *Canadian Journal of Political Science* 37 (3): 647–69. http://dx.doi.org/10.1017/S0008423904030227.

Katz, R.S. 2011. "Democracy as a cause of electoral reform: Jurisprudence and electoral change in Canada." *West European Politics* 34 (3): 587–606. http://dx.doi.org/10.1080/01402382.2011.555985.

Kelly, J.B. 2001. "Reconciling rights and federalism during review of the Charter of Rights and Freedoms: The Supreme Court of Canada and the centralization thesis, 1982 to 1999." *Canadian Journal of Political Science* 34 (2): 321–55. http://dx.doi.org/10.1017/S000842390177792X.

Law Commission of Canada. 2004. *Voting Counts: Electoral Reform for Canada*. Ottawa: Law Commission of Canada. http://publications.gc.ca/collections/Collection/J31-61-2004E.pdf.

LeDuc, L. 2009. "The failure of electoral reform proposals in Canada." *Political Science* (Wellington, NZ) 61 (2): 21–40. http://dx.doi.org/10.1177/00323187090610020301.

Levinson, S. 2001. "Designing an amendment process." In *Constitutional Culture and Democratic Rule*, ed. J. Ferejohn, J.N. Rakove, and J. Riley, 271–87. Cambridge, UK: Cambridge University Press. http://dx.doi.org/10.1017/CBO9780511609329.009.

Leyenaar, M., and R. Hazan. 2011. "Reconceptualising electoral reform." *West European Politics* 34 (3): 437–55. http://dx.doi.org/10.1080/01402382.2011.555974.

Library of Parliament. Parliamentary Information and Research Service, 2009. *Electoral Reform Initiatives in Canadian Provinces*. Ottawa: Library of Parliament, Canada. http://www.parl.gc.ca/Content/LOP/ResearchPublications/prb0417-e.htm.

Lusztig, M. 2010. "Charter creep: Creeping precommitment and the threat to liberal republicanism." *Canadian Journal of Political Science* 43 (3): 689–709. http://dx.doi.org/10.1017/S0008423910000673.

Massicotte, L. 2007. "Towards a mixed-member proportional system for Québec." *Representation* 43 (4): 251–69. http://dx.doi.org/10.1080/00344890701574898.

McLaughlin, D. 2007. "The New Brunswick Commission on Legislative Democracy." In *Democratic Reform in New Brunswick*, ed. W.P. Cross., 23-38. Toronto: Canadian Scholars Press.

Morton, F.L. 1995. "The effect of the Charter of Rights on Canadian federalism." *Publius* 25 (3): 173–88.

Nevitte, N., ed. 2002. *Value Change and Governance in Canada*. Toronto: University of Toronto Press.

New Brunswick. Commission on Legislative Democracy. 2004. *Final Report and Recommendations, Commission on Legislative Democracy.* Fredericton: Commission on Legislative Democracy. http://www.electionsnb.ca/content/dam/enb/pdf/cld/CLDSummary-e.pdf.

Prince Edward Island Electoral Reform Commission. 2003. *2003 Prince Edward Island Electoral Reform Commission Report.* Charlottetown: Prince Edward Island Electoral Reform Commission. http://www.gov.pe.ca/photos/original/er_premier2003.pdf.

Putnam, R.D., S.J. Pharr, and R.J. Dalton. 2000. "Introduction: What's troubling the trilateral democracies?" In *Disaffected Democracies: What's Troubling the Trilateral Countries?* ed. S.J. Pharr and R.D. Putnam, 3–27. Princeton, NJ: Princeton University Press.

Rahat, G., and R.Y. Hazan. 2011. "The barriers to electoral system reform: A synthesis of alternative approaches." *West European Politics* 34 (3): 478–94. http://dx.doi.org/10.1080/01402382.2011.555976.

Renwick, A. 2011. "Electoral Reform in Europe since 1945." *West European Politics* 34 (3): 456–77.

Sartori, G. 1997. *Comparative Constitutional Engineering: An Inquiry into Structures, Incentives and Outcomes.* 2nd ed. Houndmills, UK: Macmillan.

Sharman, C. 2002. "Governmental crises and constitutional reform: The case of WA Inc." In *Power and Freedom in Modern Politics: Essays in Honour of Patrick OBrien*, ed. J. Moon and B. Stone, 117–28. Perth: University of Western Australia Press.

Warren, M.E., and H. Pearse, eds. 2008. *Designing Deliberative Democracy: The British Columbia Citizens' Assembly.* New York: Cambridge University Press. http://dx.doi.org/10.1017/CBO9780511491177.

Webber, G.C.N. 2009. "The unfulfilled potential of the court and legislature dialogue." *Canadian Journal of Political Science* 42 (2): 443–65. http://dx.doi.org/10.1017/S0008423909090362.

14

Winners, Losers, and Electoral System Change

FRED CUTLER AND GRAEME HOOPER

Perhaps the most fundamental tenet of democracy is that citizens' votes are equal. The objective, of course, is not mere technical equality but, rather, equality of effective representation. In practice, though, voting equality is never perfect. No electoral system currently in operation effects a perfect conversion of votes into representation. No system has equally sized districts. And there can be no perfect way to divide a territory into geographic districts for the purposes of local representation. Every system systematically advantages some groupings of citizens and disadvantages others, with the result being that at least some citizens justifiably feel that their votes "don't count" as much as do those of other citizens. Importantly, this feeling extends beyond the victories and losses of election day: it involves the connection between voting on election day and the identity of one's representative and government until the next election. Saying that some votes "don't count" as much as others implies a fundamental inequality not just in citizens' capacity to determine electoral outcomes but also in representation, and this latter inequality may ultimately be the most important. Many theorists contend that citizens' views about their system's ability to properly represent them over a lifetime are even more important to the health and legitimacy of democracies than are turnout in elections and ephemeral post-election feelings of democratic satisfaction (Pitkin 1967; Dahl 1956; Anderson et al. 2005).

In every modern democracy there is at least a little contention over issues of equality of representation, and in most they are a fixture in the high courts. Democratic theory, democratic constitutions, and legal systems all want votes to count equally towards effective representation so that each citizen can be said to possess an equal say in her/his own governance and that governments can have a legitimate claim to representing their citizens (Sharman and Attanasio, Chapter 13, this volume). In systems with local representation, the role of parties is to represent voters from the districts upwards (Carty, Cross, and Young 2000), but this role will be hollow to the extent that districts are safe and that those citizens perpetually voting for local losers feel no connection to their representatives. But what about citizens themselves? Do they notice if their votes don't elect representatives? Do they care if their votes can be connected to symbolic and effective representation? If they do care, will they act to make their votes count when they get a chance to change electoral institutions?

Many commentators and scholars argue that the most serious threat to democratic stability comes from citizens who are not temporarily, but perpetually, on the losing side of election outcomes (Norris 1997; Anderson et al. 2005). The logic is that seeing oneself as being effectively represented is a necessary condition for regime support, and so a citizen who cannot see herself ever being effectively represented will reject the political regime. In other words, we assume that, over and above the correspondence between voters' preferences and government outputs, citizens have an interest in feeling represented. These arguments take many forms, referring variously to geographic, ethnic, or interest-based groups whose members are not denied their right to one-person-one-vote but who go to the polls knowing the candidate or party of their choice will not hold executive or legislative positions in government. These citizens, despite the formal right to vote, are legitimately labelled disenfranchised. Controversies over redistricting are a natural result. Some advocate consensus-oriented institutions of government to mitigate the threat to democracy. Others argue that electoral institutions can be engineered to give more voters, more of the time, the feeling that someone or some party they have chosen is in a position to affect government policy (Lijphart 1984). For instance, the effectively minor difference between single-member first-past-the-post (FPP) and alternative vote (AV) electoral systems, whereby voters in the latter use a preferential ballot, is thought to have a substantial effect on citizens' beliefs that they are represented in government and, ultimately, on overall levels of regime support (Farrell and McAllister 2006). Accordingly, questions about the degree to which voters understand and care about the quality of representation can be answered by comparing citizen attitudes and behaviour within and across different electoral systems thought to have different effects on voters' feelings about the quality of representation.

The recent explosion of work on the link between satisfaction with democracy and voters choosing winners or losers provides circumstantial evidence that voters notice and care about how their votes count in terms of representation (Anderson et al. 2005). The research establishes that voters who choose winners at national and/or local levels are more satisfied than losers. And it shows that satisfaction with democracy is higher in countries with more proportional electoral systems and preferential single-member systems than in FPP systems, all else being equal. Also circumstantial is evidence that proportional electoral systems have higher levels of turnout than do majoritarian ones, ceteris paribus (Blais and Carty 1990; Blais and Dobrzynska 1998; Blais 2000). Recently, Selb (2009) has provided strong evidence that, in majoritarian systems, turnout varies across districts according to competitiveness (see also Johnston, Matthews and Bittner 2007). Turnout, however, is a fairly indirect indicator of the degree to which voters think and care that their votes count.

While the evidence from these two strands of research is clear, it does not allow us to say with certainty that voters care that their votes count. Winning and losing in one election, especially when measured only at the national level, is an imperfect indicator of long-term feelings of satisfaction with representation. And satisfaction with democracy is a diffuse indicator measured by very vague survey questions the interpretation of which must take into account much inter-respondent variability. Competitiveness and turnout are certainly linked, but this link may involve candidate quality, differential mobilization, and other factors unrelated to voters' feelings about the benefits of turnout (Selb 2009). Moreover, winning and losing may affect turnout both negatively and symmetrically as voters on either side of the ledger, winners and losers, feel their votes are "wasted." In what follows we distinguish votes that "don't count" from wasted votes for the simple reason that only the former are implicated in shortfalls in representation.

Specifically, we test whether votes that don't count matter to the health of democracy. Voters whose votes objectively don't count as much as do others should act to solve the problem by choosing to change the electoral institution. We ask whether voters who are likely to feel that their votes don't count at the local level want to change their electoral system. Evidence comes from British Columbia, where voters were asked to vote in binding referendums on whether they wanted to change from an electoral system in which ineffectual votes were common to a system in which nearly every vote counted directly towards local representation. In 2005 and then again in 2009, voters in British Columbia had an opportunity to choose whether or not to jump from the FPP system to a much more proportional single-transferable vote (STV) system. High-quality academic surveys are available to us, and vote choice in the two referendums is our dependent variable. We use the BC case to ask whether voters care about votes that are counted but that, effectively, don't count. We do this by examining the link between vote choice in the electoral reform referendums and the local competitiveness of a voter's preferred party.

Votes That Count and Votes That Don't

There are many ways that votes in general can be said to count or not to count. Analogously, there are many ways in which voters themselves might feel the satisfaction of their votes being important. The most obvious of these is that a vote counts when it makes a difference to the outcome (Downs 1957; Riker and Ordeshook 1968; Cox 1997). By this standard, no citizen can reasonably imagine her vote counting, except in very small districts (or Florida in November 2000). Votes "counting" in this sense drive turnout according to a strong rational choice theory of turnout, whereby "closeness" – the voter's expectations about the margin of victory – affects the probability of a voter's being decisive. While difficult to detect at the individual level, there is an unquestioned aggregate link between closeness and turnout across districts and across elections (Blais 2000; Johnston, Matthews, and Bittner 2007; Brockington 2004). Scholars infer that incentives to pay the cost of voting are lower when each vote is less likely to count decisively; we might reasonably conclude that some voters, some of the time, at the margins, care that their votes are decisive.

Nevertheless, most voters continue to vote with virtual certainty that their vote will not decide the outcome. So what else might voters and the media mean when they speak of votes counting or not counting? Many attempts to resolve the "paradox of voting" (Ferejohn and Fiorina 1974; Dowding 2005) turn to various "expressive" motivations for turnout, whereby the benefit of voting is determined by the degree to which voters feel positive about going to the polls and marking the ballot (Schuessler 2000). Some accounts focus on the emotional benefit of being on the winning side, perhaps congratulating oneself for the "right choice" or being part of the largest group. Even committed rational choice theorists go down this road, as with Hinich's "contributions model," which "rests on the key assumption that a voter gains a bit of utility for voting for the winner, or loses some utility for voting for the loser" (Hinich 1981, 140). Similarly, Scheuessler (2000) and others liken the positive side of the ledger to cheering for a sports team knowing that doing so will have no effect on the result but deriving some pleasure when the team wins and knowing full well that one will suffer negative feelings if it loses (Ashworth, Geys, and Heyndels 2006; Brennan and Buchanan 1984, 186–87). The so-called "bandwagon effect" (Simon 1954) is taken to be another possible manifestation of the psychological inclination to identify with winners rather than with losers.[1] If all of this is true, voters might be said to have purely emotional reasons for caring that their votes count: voting for a winner feels good and voting for a loser feels bad. But note that this would be a fairly ephemeral effect, strong on election night but waning quickly.

Unfortunately, neither the strictly rational account nor the emotion-based account provides a satisfying basis for the common-sense notion that voters care if their votes don't count. While a deeply socialized duty to vote is responsible for much turnout and rational factors operate at the margins (Blais 2000), there is surely some middle psycho-political ground that explains many of the findings that link competitiveness, expectations, and turnout and that, by implication, defines what is meant by votes counting or not counting. Without attempting to solve the thorny issues in the turnout literature, we want to suggest that this middle ground is something more rational than a blind sense of duty but less rational than the calculations that motivate the voter in strict formal models of turnout (Riker and Ordeshook 1968). The reasoning would be that voters want to experience the benefit of feeling represented, and they imagine that, even if their party's candidate is elected, they will not feel as satisfied with her/his election if they have not actually voted.[2] To the extent that voters think this way and that this motivates them to vote, this process should be moderated by the chance that their vote will connect them with a representative. Something like this is behind hypotheses that connect large margins of victory to district turnout, but these hypotheses do not distinguish between winners and losers, the implication being that wasting a vote on a big victory is as depressing as is preferring a no-hoper candidate. We argue that votes that count and don't count can be defined in terms of representation rather than in the more rational terms of affecting the outcome. A vote that doesn't count involves marking a ballot knowing that doing so is almost certainly not connected to who becomes one's representative; a vote that counts involves marking a ballot knowing that doing so has a decent chance of helping to elect one's representative (even if the vote for that person is nowhere near decisive).

Our focus on the relationship between voting choice and the experience of representation after and between elections points towards the need to consider a richer set of motivations, with deeper implications for the institutions of democracy, than is considered by either the rational account or the analogy of cheering for one's home team. Despite the enthusiasm for the sports analogy and the nebulous "bandwagon" concept among those who use the public choice tradition to explain turnout, politics is, in an important sense, decidedly *not* a game. The uncertainty of electoral outcomes is quite different from the uncertainty of a sports match or season. While politics may generate psychological effects similar to those visited upon die-hard fans, there is a great deal more to a citizen's relationship with politics and its institutions. At the national level, in the extreme case of one-party majority government, the views of losers are not obviously represented in the policy process. At the local level, it has been shown that supporters of local losers feel less fully represented, their interests less well looked after, than do supporters of candidates who get elected (Anderson et al. 2005).

One might ask whether votes counting or not counting will have any effect on the overall operation of the system if some votes count but others don't. Might the net effect of local winning and losing be zero? Not if the behavioural effects of winning and losing are asymmetrical, and there is good reason to believe that the behaviour of citizens who are underrepresented political losers will be qualitatively different from the behaviour of citizens who are political winners (Anderson et al. 2005). This qualitative difference is manifest in the scholarship on the reactions of citizens who support losing parties at the national level. Losing apparently leads to dissatisfaction with democracy and then, potentially, to behaviour aimed at changing institutions. The link is particularly vivid in the context of democratization, but even in established democracies losers are, as Riker (1983, 64) suggests, the "instigators of political change." For example, Anderson et al. (2005, 173) show that supporters of the party not holding the US presidency are more likely to support a relatively minor change in electoral institutions than are supporters of the party holding it. But there, and in similar research, losers are mere short-term losers. After all, major-party supporters in the United States can expect that their party will return to the White House before too long. In truth, effects on short-term losers are probably ephemeral: returning to the winning side will dampen voters' enthusiasm for change and, lo and behold, it will arise among supporters of the other party. So, in fact, short-term losing is unlikely to lead to sustained and predictable behaviour aimed at changing institutions in mature democracies.

Part of the genius of democracy, of course, is that losing is meant to be temporary. And this is certainly the case under appropriate institutions; however, under certain institutions, losing can be perpetual. The sports analogy, connecting winning and losing to turnout, breaks down here as there are no teams who lose every game, year after year, as do certain political parties in certain districts. The eternal hopelessness of the Conservative supporter in West Ham (UK) cannot be matched by the hopelessness of the fans of West Ham United (one of the authors being among them). Losing in politics, at least in terms of local representation in single-member district electoral systems, can be perpetual (unless one votes with one's feet). These are voters whose votes will never count, and surely many of them know it. Tolbert, Smith, and Green (2009) call these voters "representational losers" to distinguish them from short-term "electoral losers." And being perpetually shut out of representation is toxic for regime support, as has been seen in democratic revolutions throughout history. According to Anderson et al. (2005, 11-12): "If citizens expect to keep losing – as ethnic minorities do in many US states, for example – then this might well generate long-term and deep-rooted disaffection from politics." Smith, Tolbert, and Keller (2010, 510) argue that this situation entails "long-term structural conditions under which 'losers' find themselves to be underrepresented." They argue that the effect of long-term losing involves more than simply not enjoying the feeling of winning or suffering the short-term disappointment at losing. Disaffection and support for institutional change are rational responses to a lack of ongoing symbolic representation as well as to a lack of tangible benefits of effective representation. While other work is equivocal on the question of whether, in fact, representatives actually favour their supporters (e.g., Hurley and Hill 2003; Clinton 2006), what matters for overall democratic satisfaction and preferences for electoral system change are citizens' feelings about the fairness of the institutions of representation currently in operation.

Evidence is now piling up on this score. Anderson et al. (2005) entitle one of their chapters "Losing and Support for Institutional Change." In this chapter they hypothesize that voters who support losing parties and candidates are "attempt[ing] to change the rules of the game" (170). They cite numerous examples of elites who push for change because they feel perpetually shut out of power (e.g., Bowler, Donovan, and Karp 2002). Various pieces of evidence are used to show that supporters of parties disadvantaged by existing systems are less likely to vote and are more likely to support changing those systems (Anderson et al. 2005, 170–80). For example, supporters of minor parties were much more likely to support electoral reform in New Zealand (Vowles et al. 1995, 202), and Indiana voters who thought they would vote for a losing candidate "most of the time" in future congressional elections were more supportive of proportional representation for the US Congress. According to Anderson et al. (2005, 174), "even after controlling for several other possible and powerful explanations, it is possible to see large effects of winning and losing status on the willingness to change institutions." These and other examples suggest that citizens have rational, instrumental responses to losing, if losing implies that their views are not likely to be represented.

We concur with Anderson et al. and with Tolbert, Smith, and Green that citizens want their votes to count, meaning that they want their votes to determine representation, even if only marginally. Basically, we ascribe to citizens a self-interested desire to contribute equally, in effective rather than merely in formal terms, in the totality of political representation in the polity. We assume that, while self-interested, the desire to contribute equally is due to a preference for equality rather than for advantage. Citizens want their votes to count, but they do not want them to count more than those of their fellow citizens. We are able to assess this latter claim by specifying an asymmetry in the effects of winning and losing (see below).

We add to this theory of self-interested desire for equal representation that, in systems of indirect election (most commonly in single-member district parliamentary systems), local-level votes are more interesting than national-level votes. This is because national governments alternate with at least minimal regularity. In what follows, we test our theory in the context of two binding referendums on changing from a single-member plurality (SMP) system to an STV system. For quite a few voters in SMP systems, changing the rules of the game is the only way, short of moving to a different district, to make their votes count.

Local Representation and Electoral System Change

Most of the research cited above, particularly Anderson et al. (2005), assumes a great distance between the act of voting and the determination of winning or losing (but see Tolbert, Smith, and Green 2009). That is, it focuses on the national level, where individual votes disappear into the national soup that produces a government.[3] For example, supporters of minor parties in New Zealand (Alliance, NZ First) realized they would be perpetually shut out of power under an FPP system but that they might well be influential small-party powerbrokers under an MMP system, and so they were massively supportive of change (Vowles et al. 1995). In the electoral systems in which change is most likely, however, voters vote only within single-member districts with FPP or AV rules. That is, their votes only count *directly* if they vote for the local winner; they count *neither at the local nor the national level* if they pick a loser. Winners and losers at the national level, the subject of most of the research on losing, are, by contrast, determined by an aggregation process that is often opaque to voters in a district, even if the counting rule is simple.[4]

Most important for this chapter, local losers are much more likely to be long-term losers than are national losers. Because few national-level parties survive in these vote-wasting electoral systems if they don't get a sniff of power (Cox 1997; Duverger 1959; Grofman, Blais, and Bowler 2009), few voters will think of themselves as perpetual national-level losers.[5] By contrast, in these systems many local districts are safe enough seats for one party that supporters of other parties can reasonably conclude that they will never vote for a local winner. Their votes will not "count" locally, and, thus, they will never have an effect on the higher-level outcome. To add insult to injury, even their own party will ignore them, rationally devoting its mobilization resources to competitive districts (Johnston, Hagen, and Jamieson 2004; Cox 1997). In more proportional electoral systems with some kind of local representation, such as STV or MMP, there are far fewer voters who can reasonably see themselves as losers. Local losers in SMP systems, therefore, are likely to prick up their ears at talk of changing the electoral system.

Who are local losers? We start with voters' preferences for a party since, in these systems, voters are far more likely to base decisions on parties and national leaders than on local candidates. What matters with regard to what effect losing has on preference for change is that voters think that the candidate whose party they prefer is almost certain not to win the district. Long-term election results in such districts are the obvious referent, but, of course, the measurement of safe seats over time is often confounded by redistricting.

The best indicator then, to voters and scholars alike, is simply the margin of victory in the most recent election. There may be more accurate measures that factor in the length of the incumbent party's tenure in the district, national swings, and redistricting, but the margin of victory is probably the clearest indication of the information voters use to judge whether or not their votes count. Voters who prefer a party that loses by a wide margin are likely to remain losers as the bulk of districts see relatively small vote shifts from election to election. Only in rare cases are there dramatic local swings that elect previously locally uncompetitive parties.

This study, then, complements Tolbert, Smith, and Green's (2009) study of referendums in California and Ohio regarding redistricting reform. Their article is the only published study of behaviour at a referendum vote that defines winners and losers at the local level as a determinant of choice. Together, their article and our chapter paint an important picture of voters who do indeed care that their votes don't count, even in fully democratic systems.

Winning versus Losing: Asymmetry and Functional Form

Despite our study's similarity to Tolbert, Smith, and Green's (2009) study, we propose two innovations, one of which involves the asymmetry of winning and losing. Tolbert, Smith, and Green theorize that representational losers should want to change the status quo, while winners should not want to do so. The other innovation involves our emphasis on the strength of the feeling of being a perpetual loser as a function of the vote margin in the local district. Tolbert and her colleagues seem to assume that voters who win or lose by small margins are no different than those who win or lose by large margins.

In politics, as Riker (1962) points out, winners and losers are not two sides of the same coin. We take advantage of this obvious asymmetry. In the voter turnout literature, wasted votes are usually defined as symmetric around a tied result. That is, in uncompetitive districts the many supporters of the winner are just as likely to feel their votes are wasted as are the few supporters of the losers. Aggregate turnout is a function of the winner's margin of victory. While that may be a reasonable assumption for turnout, and fits well with rational models of that behaviour, it does not correspond with either a more emotional, expressive theory of voting or with concern about electing a sympathetic representative. An asymmetric theory is required. In other words, we want to distinguish *wasted votes*, which matter for turnout and are symmetric in winning and losing, from *votes that don't count*, which apply to losers alone due to a lack of representation and may therefore affect support for changing electoral institutions. We need to theorize not only how perpetual losers compare the status quo with a different system but also how perpetual winners do so.

Winners, even if their candidate wins by a large margin, can at least say that their vote contributed to the election of the representative. More important, these voters-for-big-winners benefit from the utility of a like-minded representative in the legislature and a symbolic feeling of connection to that representative. For these reasons, we argue that winners should estimate that they will derive no greater utility from their party winning a seat by thirty-five points as winning by five. Thus, the relative safety of the seat of a preferred party should not affect the utility voters derive from the existing electoral system.[6] If they know enough about the alternative system, in this case STV, voters will realize that a candidate from their party will be even safer if the system is changed. It may well be true that their party benefits from the disproportionality of the system at the national level, but this is an independent influence on preferences for a new system, and there are plenty of local winners in safe seats whose party suffers at the higher level from disproportionality.

As we have argued, voters who vote for a non-winning candidate are likely to feel very differently than voters who vote for a winning candidate. Even if the election is fairly close, the immediate experience of losers will be that their vote had no effect on the outcome. The voter may well say to herself: "I didn't elect my representative AGAIN!" The voter's estimate of the likelihood of this experience of disenfranchisement continuing in the future is a function of the safety of the seat. Almost any alternative electoral system would be likely to overcome this feeling of one's vote not counting, but the most effective would be the STV, which has relatively proportional outcomes within districts.[7] In the case examined here, the proposed alternative system is STV, with district magnitudes between two and seven. Our guess, based on distributions of support in existing ridings being combined into the larger STV districts, is that, among the supporters of the two major parties (90 percent of the electorate), almost *every voter* would see her first choice elected and therefore feel adequately represented between elections. Even Green Party voters, who might not elect a Green member, would probably see their second preference as contributing to the election of an MLA.

The winners/losers asymmetry leads to two clear predictions:

1. For supporters of losing candidates: The less likely a citizen considers her party's candidate is to win her district, the more likely she is to vote for a more proportional electoral system.

2. For supporters of winning candidates: The degree to which a voter thinks her party's candidate is likely to win the district *will not* affect her likelihood to vote for a more proportional system.

The second departure from existing work involves attempting to operationalize, with objective, exogenous contextual data, a subjective estimate of the chances the voter will ever vote for a winning local candidate. Some scholars ask direct questions in experimental and survey settings to make this estimate. Bowler and Donovan (2007, 462) rightly point out that simple measures of voting for or against the party in power are "largely unable to capture the subjective effects of perceptions of long-term electoral losses, or expectations of future losses," a critique that applies to the Tolbert, Smith, and Green (2009) study. Bowler and Donovan ask respondents whether the "candidates they support usually win or usually lose elections." They do this separately for the presidential arena and the congressional arena. These questions get at the long-term component of perception that can affect preferences for institutional change, but using them as a causal influence on referendum choice is fraught with endogeneity as such questions may provoke those who have decided that they like the new system for other reasons to infer that they are likely to continue losing under the current system. Tolbert, Smith, and Green propose using partisanship rather than vote choice because being a "representational loser" requires that the voter be at least minimally committed to the party that always loses in the district. And they avoid endogeneity by marrying the individual-level data to objective indicators of which party holds office. But their operationalization ignores the long term by categorizing voters as "district losers" if their party identification does not coincide with at least two-thirds of their representatives (state House, state Senate, or Congress).

We put these two ideas together, using party preference and district-level contextual data from the previous election to calibrate winners and losers. We assume that the margin of victory and of loss of a voter's preferred party is a good proxy for the information voters use to figure out if they are likely to be a long-term loser or winner. The bigger the margin, the more likely the voter is to continue as winner or loser, represented or unrepresented.

Finally, we contend that political information, specifically information about the proposed electoral system, is a necessary condition for the positive effect of losing on support for reform. A voter who feels her vote does not count is unlikely to jump from the existing system if she does not know and cannot imagine how an alternative system would make her vote count.

In the referendums examined here, it is demonstrated that knowledge about the systems has a powerful direct effect on support (Fournier et al. 2011), and some of that may involve perpetual losers realizing that they would be better off under a more proportional system. Indeed, this proposal was made by a citizens' assembly whose final report, mailed to every household in the province, was entitled *Making Every Vote Count*. We therefore expect an interactive relationship between political information and the margin of loss. If we observe that the effect of the margin of loss is moderated by political information, our confidence in the theory will be bolstered. Our final prediction is, therefore:

3. Support for electoral system change should increase with the margin of loss only in the presence of political information.

Data and Model Specification

The data come from surveys conducted prior to two referendums on electoral reform held in British Columbia in 2005 and 2009, respectively. Voters chose between the FPP status quo and a new system called BC-STV. The proposal was for multi-member districts ranging in size from two to seven, with members elected by STV, as in Ireland. In the first referendum, the threshold to change the system was placed at 60 percent approval, and the proposal fell short of this by a slim margin. In response, the government scheduled a second referendum to coincide with the 2009 provincial election. This time the proposal fared much worse, with only 38 percent voting to change the system (see Fournier et al. 2011; Cutler et al. 2008).

Our dependent variable is the survey respondent's reported vote intention, yes or no, stated in interviews conducted in the months before the referendum. The main data source comprises the full-scale academic surveys fielded to measure voters attitudes and choices in the BC referendum.[8] Both surveys were campaign rolling cross-section telephone surveys (Johnston and Brady 2002). We include only those voters who had decided yes or no (eliminating "don't knows") because our study period began four months before the vote and we had too many respondents who were simply unaware that a referendum was being held.

We are forced to measure the voter's partisanship with party feeling thermometer differentials because the traditional partisanship question was not asked. We operationalize party preference as the party rated highest on the thermometers, and we exclude respondents for whom the two highest-ranked parties are tied. For each respondent, we calculate the margin by which her or his preferred party won or lost the local district (electorate, constituency) in the 2005 election. Respondents are located precisely in constituencies by linking postal codes to electoral districts, using, for 2005, a correspondence file provided by Elections BC, and, for 2009, GIS correspondence procedures.

Our measure of party preference represents measurement of winning and losing at the province-wide level, which is required to control for feelings of policy representation in government. For the information measure, respondents were asked six questions about the proposed electoral system. From these we created an additive index, rescaled to the 0–1 interval, to test for the interactive effect of margin of victory/loss conditional on information about the new system.

No other survey variables are required for the estimation model because any formative attitudes, like the fairness of the current system or the need for strong majority governments, are probably a result of experience with winning and losing. That is, we treat our measure of local winners and losers as completely exogenous, implying that the causal effect is represented by a coefficient relating the size of the voter's preferred party's victory or loss to the probability of voting for electoral reform.[9] Formally, in our model: $h(p_i) = f(\text{margin}_i, u)$ where $h(p_i)$ is the logit transformation and p_i is the probability of a vote to change the system, for voter i. This probability is a function of the win/loss *margin* of the voter's preferred party in her district and u, error, distributed identically and independently of margin. The only control variable required, therefore, is a measure of winning or losing at the higher level because this likely has a causal effect of its own (Tolbert, Smith, and Green 2009) and is probably correlated with the margin at the local level. (The average margin for supporters of the national/provincial-level winner may be higher than the average margin of supporters of losing parties, particularly minor parties.)

In each of the two cases, we estimate separate logistic regressions of referendum vote on margin alone, on margin and party identification, and then add an interaction with knowledge of the proposed system.

The margin variable does not enter the estimation as a continuous variable from −100 to +100. We argue above that losers should be more willing to change electoral systems as their prospects for representation get more and more hopeless – that is, as the margin of loss increases – but that winners' margin of victory will have no effect on support for reform. We therefore include separate measures of the losers' margin and the winners' margin, where the losers' margin is set to zero for winners and vice versa (see Brambor, Clark, and Golder 2006).

The form of the full estimation model is:

$$\text{logit}(p_{\text{VoteYesi}}) = \beta_0 + \beta_1(\text{lossmargin}) + \beta_2(\text{winmargin})$$
$$+ \beta_3(\text{lossmargin} * \text{information}) + \beta_4(\text{winmargin} * \text{information})$$
$$+ \beta_5(\text{PID}_{\text{gov}}) + \beta_6(\text{PID}_{\text{opp}})$$

Results

To begin, Table 14.1 shows descriptive statistics for average margins of victory and loss for survey respondents in our two referendums. The medians here, for instance, are median loss margin among those preferring losing candidates *in these samples.* In 2005, the median margin of victory was sixteen percentage points. Readers can be assured that there is plenty of variation across the categories of provincial winners and losers. The point is that there are plenty of provincial winners that were big local losers, and plenty of provincial losers that were big local winners.

TABLE 14.1
Margins of local victory and loss, BC, 2005 and 2009

	Percentage point margins	2005	2009
Winners	10th, *50th*, 90th percentiles	6, 16, 40	3, 23, 48
Losers	10th, *50th*, 90th percentiles	2, 18, 43	3, 32, 50

The second preliminary is to use the 2009 data to examine the link between objective margins of victory or loss and voters' perceptions of whether their preferred candidate is competitive. Respondents (only in 2009) were asked: "How often does the local candidate you vote for win?" and we coded this from 0 (Never) to 1 (Always). The estimated OLS regression is *W* in = 0.53 + .002 ∗ margin, with a *t*-statistic above 7. And the effect is three times stronger among the best informed about STV than it is among the uninformed. So, for example, a 30 point loser is predicted to be about .12 away from a 30 point winner on average, and about .20 apart for the best informed. Clearly, perceptions are related to reality: forecasts about future representation are almost certainly informed by the history of voting for winning or losing candidates. But we refrain from using perceptions in order to avoid endogeneity, as we mention above.

FIGURE 14.1
Yes vote and margin, BC, 2005

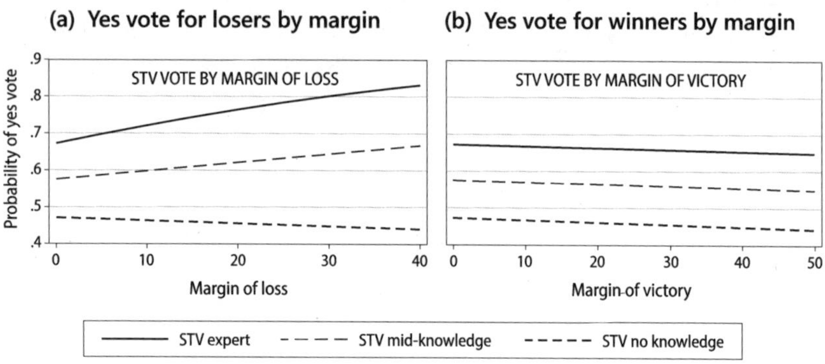

Note: Vote variables set to Liberal voter.

We now present our logistic regression results in graphic form, showing predicted probabilities of voting for electoral change across the range of margin of victory and loss from 0 to 40 percentage points (50 points in 2009). Two tables (14A.1 and 14A.2) are provided as an appendix for readers interested in inspecting coefficients. In brief, the results indicate both different effects for winning and losing *and* an interaction with knowledge of the alternative system. Figure 14.1 shows one graph of predicted probabilities by margin of loss (panel a) and another by margin of victory (panel b) for 2005.[10] Three lines appear on each graph, depicting the probabilities for 3 points on the 0-to-1 scale measuring information about the proposed STV system (0, .5, 1). The hypothetical respondent in these graphs is a Liberal voter, to show the effects even on the provincial-level winners.[11]

These 2005 results show two things clearly. First, the losers' margin and the winners' margin figures are not mirror images. The bigger the loss, the higher the support for institutional change (left figure), while the margin of victory has no significant impact on the vote (right figure). Second, knowledge of the proposed system is required for the losers to understand the appeal of the proposed system in relation to the hopelessness of their cause. Comparing a 2005 referendum voter in a highly competitive riding (margin = 0) to another in a riding with a huge loss (margin = 40), we see support in the best informed group (top line) rising from 67 percent to 83 percent (16 points). At the midpoint of information the difference is nine points,

FIGURE 14.2
Yes vote and margin, BC, 2009

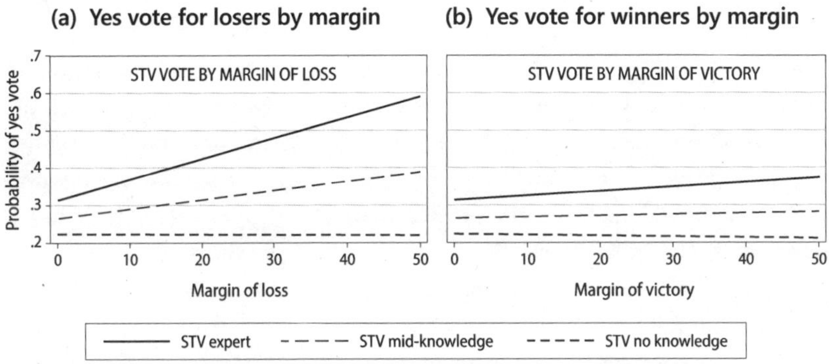

Note: Vote variables set to Liberal voter.

while among the totally uninformed, support is utterly unaffected.[12] These are very large effects indeed considering that they are truly exogenous and that we control for election (i.e., party) vote choice.

We conducted our initial analysis after the 2005 campaign, and so the 2009 referendum provides a true test case for the theoretical model (but, for caution on this approach, see Clarke and Primo 2012). Graphs analogous to those above are presented as Figure 14.2. Despite the drop in overall support for the Yes side, the figures are essentially identical to those for 2005, but the effect is stronger: approximately twenty-five points for the best-informed and eleven points for the moderately informed. Again, for winners, the lines are flat, indicating that big winners are not more likely to reject the new system because they like being big winners.

These patterns leave little doubt that losers are distinct from, and more important than, winners with respect to electoral system change, but it is the combination of the winners/losers pattern and the increasing effect of losing when having political information that is so striking. Voters who are likely to vote for local winners perpetually have no special attachment to the system. Voters whose local choice loses narrowly, and by implication has a decent chance to win in the future, are no more likely to push for change than are marginal winners.[13] Substantively important preferences for change are found only among citizens who find themselves in safe seats for the party they reject and who are likely to know this and to understand that the alternative electoral system will give them a very good chance of voting for an elected representative.

Conclusion

Voters less likely to consider that their votes count towards representation are more likely to take action to make them count when presented with the opportunity to do so. Our findings fit this theoretical argument extremely well: a large effect for losers, none for winners, and the losers' effect conditional on knowledge about the proposed system. Proponents of STV in BC stressed the fact that most voters would vote for a winner under the proposed system. We can assume this message was heard by those at the top of our information scale. Losers who hear this message would be gratified to have their votes count, whereas winners would see little change: their votes would still elect a representative, maybe more than one.

It is important to emphasize that a theory of winning and losing and electoral change predicated on the psychological satisfaction of winning and losing would predict that big winners would be jealous of their advantage (i.e., the thrill of being champions) and thus more inclined to reject the new system than winners and losers in close districts. That they do not suggests to us that citizens are not simply cheering for their ideological and partisan team but, rather, that they want to be represented by the candidate they prefer, whether or not their party wins overall. As the literature on democratic satisfaction contends, it is losing, particularly losing that persists, that threatens democratic stability. We provide evidence that clearly demonstrates that even citizens in stable advanced democracies want change when they are shut out of representation.

Patterns like these are squarely in line with the only comparable study, that of Tolbert, Smith, and Green (2009) on redistricting reform in American states. They conclude, as do we, that "objective representation at the subnational level matters: individuals who are ... district-level losers are significantly more supportive of institutional change, regardless of their partisan leanings" (105). And these results help to provide a deeper account of why voter turnout is higher in proportional systems, as Blais and Carty (1990) showed two decades ago. Voters' approach to electoral institutions thus involves a form of self-interest, though hardly an anti-social one. Partisan self-interest is usually cited, pejoratively, as a determinant of voters' and elites' attitudes towards institutional change, even though additional factors may be in play (see Sharman and Attanasio, Chapter 13, this volume). Tolbert,

Smith, and Green lean towards this interpretation when they characterize citizens' behaviour as "strategic." A more charitable, and perhaps democratic, interpretation is that, when voters foresee a future in which their vote will never go towards choosing a representative, they will, if able to do so, choose an electoral system that ensure that their votes count.

Appendix

TABLE 14A.1
Referendum vote, BC, 2005

Dependent variable: intend to vote yes	I	II	III	IV
Margin of preferred party's loss	0.008 (0.005)	0.006 (0.005)	0.006 (0.005)	−0.003 (0.006)
Margin of preferred party's win	−0.004 (0.005)	−0.003 (0.005)	−0.003 (0.005)	−0.003 (0.007)
Vote Liberal (winner)		−0.57 (0.135)	−0.614 (0.138)	−0.608 (0.138)
Vote NDP		−0.161 (0.152)	−0.222 (0.155)	−0.237 (0.155)
Vote Green		0.09 (0.259)	0.153 (0.262)	0.186 (0.264)
STV knowledge (0 to 1)			1.053 (0.157)	0.848 (0.227)
STV know * lose margin				0.025 (0.013)
STV know * win margin				0.001 (0.013)
Constant	0.593 (0.082)	0.825 (0.112)	0.418 (0.127)	0.491 (0.141)
Observations	1,395	1,395	1,395	1,395

Notes:
Table entries are logistic regression coefficients.
Standard errors are in parentheses.

TABLE 14A.2
Referendum vote, BC, 2009

Dependent variable: intend to vote yes	I	II	III	IV
Margin of preferred party's loss	0.015	0.000	0.001	−0.013
	(0.005)	(0.006)	(0.006)	(0.009)
Margin of preferred party's win	0.000	0.002	0.003	0.001
	(0.005)	(0.006)	(0.006)	(0.009)
Vote Liberal (winner)		−0.58	−0.555	−0.574
		(0.203)	(0.206)	(0.207)
Vote NDP		0.331	0.379	0.352
		(0.197)	(0.199)	(0.202)
Vote Green		0.894	0.948	0.979
		(0.204)	(0.208)	(0.209)
STV knowledge (0 to 1)			0.918	0.429
			(0.215)	(0.369)
STV know * lose margin				0.03
				(0.013)
STV know * win margin				0.005
				(0.015)
Constant	−0.244	−0.172	−0.694	−0.438
	(0.130)	(0.241)	(0.274)	(0.309)
Observations	713	713	713	713

Notes:
Table entries are logistic regression coefficients.
Standard errors in parentheses.

Notes

Originally delivered at Parties as Organizations and Parties as Systems conference in honour of R. Kenneth Carty, UBC, May 19–21, 2011. The research reported here was supported by the Social Sciences and Humanities Research Council of Canada and the Centre for the Study of Democratic Institutions at the University of British Columbia. We thank Richard Johnston, Ken Carty, Patrick Fournier, André Blais, Mark Warren, Stuart Soroka, and Campbell Sharman for collaboration on the data collection. David Northrup and his colleagues at the Institute for Social Research, York University, were indispensable, providing unparalleled expertise and responsiveness. This projected originated in a master's thesis by Hooper in the Department of Political Science at UBC, supervised by Cutler, and with Ken Carty as reader. We thank Ken for comments on that work. Thanks to the editors and to John Aldrich for comments on a draft of this chapter. None of the aforementioned is responsible for errors herein: these are the authors' business alone.

1 Evidence for bandwagon effects is scant, and attempts to link it to a psychological motivation to support winners are unconvincing.

2 We see some affinities between this view and the group basis for voting proposed by Uhlaner (1989; Morton 1991).

3 Anderson et al. (2005, 168) do use a Canadian election study to predict the intention to turn out to vote with voters' own expectations of their preferred party's chances in a district. They find a significant but very small effect, and this does little to convince us that local losing really affects feelings of representation and support for change. This surely reflects both a large degree of wishful thinking, even among supporters of parties well out of the running, and limited variation in the dependent variable.

4 For example, in multi-party systems with widely varying levels of support, such as are found in Canada, understanding and interpreting the aggregation of the behaviour of voters across the country is not easy and occupies experts for weeks following an election.

5 Of course, Canada's New Democratic Party and the New Zealand parties mentioned above are prominent exceptions to this rule. The UK Liberal Democrats, however, are now no longer an exception.

6 Contrast this with Tolbert, Smith, and Green (2009), who see the effects of winning and losing as symmetric: we suggest that many citizens who voted against the measures – even if they supported redistricting reform in principle – did so because they were representational winners under the status quo. The subtle difference here may be in the relationship to the ballot question: winners under status quo districting in the United States may indeed lose and become losers with reforms, whereas changing from FPP to a more proportional system is unlikely to produce loss for the existing winners.

7 STV results in many more voters voting for a local winner, as long as the district magnitude is not uncharacteristically low (e.g., Japan); MMP at least gives local losers the benefit of fully compensatory proportional party votes; and list proportional representation systems, while diluting the voter's vote in a larger pool, still allow the voter to point to members from her preferred party and say: "I voted them in."

8 Full details of the surveys and question wording for questions employed here can be found in Fournier et al. (2011).

9 Voting with one's feet strikes us long-time residents of British Columbia as so rare as to be legitimately ignored.

10 These graphs do not show confidence intervals because this would make them too cluttered. See the tables in the appendix for standard errors. Suffice to say the effect of the losing margin on voting yes is significant at normal levels for voters in the top half of the information scale.

11 In order to avoid cluttering the graph, we do not graph the standard errors around these predicted probabilities. Suffice to say that the 95 percent interval for the effect for the best informed does not overlap zero.

12 Among those who said they knew even a little about the proposed STV system (and were thus asked the STV information questions) the mean on the 0-to-1 information scale (built from six factual questions) is 0.63, while the overall mean is .29 if we set the know-nothings to zero correct responses.

13 We conclude this not from the estimates showing in this chapter but in unreported estimates of a generalized additive model (Beck and Jackman 1998; Hastie and Tibshirani 1990), which suggests that the effect declines rapidly from the maximum loss margin to a loss of about 10 points, where the effect flattens out at 0, exactly as the theory would predict.

References

Anderson, C.J., A. Blais, S. Bowler, T. Donovan, and O. Listhaug. 2005. *Losers' Consent: Elections and Democratic Legitimacy*. New York: Oxford University Press. http://dx.doi.org/10.1093/0199276382.001.0001.

Ashworth, J., B. Geys, and B. Heyndels. 2006. "Everyone likes a winner: An empirical test of the effect of electoral closeness on turnout in a context of expressive voting." *Public Choice* 128 (3/4): 383–405. http://dx.doi.org/10.1007/s11127-005-9006-8.

Beck, N., and S. Jackman. 1998. "Beyond linearity by default: Generalized additive models." *American Journal of Political Science* 42 (2): 596–627. http://dx.doi.org/10.2307/2991772.

Blais, A. 2000. *To Vote or Not to Vote? The Merits and Limits of Rational Choice Theory*. Pittsburgh: Pittsburgh University Press.

Blais, A., and R.K. Carty. 1990. "Does proportional representation foster voter turnout?" *European Journal of Political Research* 18 (2): 167–81. http://dx.doi.org/10.1111/j.1475-6765.1990.tb00227.x.

Blais, A., and A. Dobrzynska. 1998. "Turnout in electoral democracies." *European Journal of Political Research* 33 (2): 239–61. http://dx.doi.org/10.1111/1475-6765.00382.

Bowler, S., and T. Donovan. 2007. "Reasoning about institutional change: Winners, losers and support for institutional reforms." *British Journal of Political Science* 37 (3): 455–76.

Bowler, S., T. Donovan, and J.A. Karp. 2002. "When might institutions change? Elite support for direct democracy in three nations." *Political Research Quarterly* 55 (4): 731–54. http://dx.doi.org/10.1177/106591290205500401.

Brambor, T., W.R. Clark, and M. Golder. 2006. "Understanding interaction models: Improving empirical analyses." *Political Analysis* 14 (1): 63–82. http://dx.doi.org/10.1093/pan/mpi014.

Brennan, G., and J. Buchanan. 1984. "Voter choice: Evaluating political alternatives." *American Behavioral Scientist* 28 (2): 185–201. http://dx.doi.org/10.1177/000276484028002003.

Brockington, D. 2004. "The paradox of proportional representation: The effect of party systems and coalitions on individuals' electoral participation." *Political Studies* 52 (3): 469–90. http://dx.doi.org/10.1111/j.1467-9248.2004.00491.x.

Carty, R.K., W. Cross, and L. Young. 2000. *Rebuilding Canadian Party Politics*. Vancouver: UBC Press.

Clarke, K.A., and D.M. Primo. 2012. *A Model Discipline: Political Science and the Logic of Representations*. New York: Oxford University Press. http://dx.doi.org/10.1093/acprof:oso/9780195382198.003.0001.

Clinton, J.D. 2006. "Representation in Congress: Constituents and rolls calls in the 106th House." *Journal of Politics* 68 (2): 397–409. http://dx.doi.org/10.1111/j.1468-2508.2006.00415.x.

Cox, G.W. 1997. *Making Votes Count: Strategic Coordination in the World's Electoral Systems*. Cambridge University Press. http://dx.doi.org/10.1017/CBO9781139174954.

Cutler, F., R.G. Johnston, A. Blais, R.K. Carty, and P. Fournier. 2008. *Deliberation, Information, and Trust: The BC Citizens' Assembly*. New York: Cambridge University Press.

Dahl, R.A. 1956. *A Preface to Democratic Theory*. Chicago: University of Chicago Press.

Dowding, K. 2005. "Is it rational to vote? Five types of answer and a suggestion." *British Journal of Politics and International Relations* 7 (3): 442–59. http://dx.doi.org/10.1111/j.1467-856X.2005.00188.x.

Downs, A. 1957. *An Economic Theory of Democracy*. New York: Harper and Row.

Duverger, M. 1959. *Political Parties, Their Organization and Activity in the Modern State*. 2nd English edition. London: Methuen.

Farrell, D.M., and I. McAllister. 2006. "Voter satisfaction and electoral systems: Does preferential voting in candidate-centred systems make a difference?" *European Journal of Political Research* 45 (5): 723–49. http://dx.doi.org/10.1111/j.1475-6765.2006.00633.x.

Ferejohn, J.A., and M.P. Fiorina. 1974. "The paradox of not voting: A decision theoretic analysis." *American Political Science Review* 68 (2): 525–46. http://dx.doi.org/10.2307/1959502.

P. Fournier, H. van der Kolk, R.K. Carty, A. Blais, and J. Rose. 2011. *When Citizens Decide: Lessons from Citizen Assemblies on Electoral Reform*. New York: Oxford University Press. http://dx.doi.org/10.1093/acprof:oso/9780199567843.001.0001.

Grofman, B., A. Blais, and S. Bowler, eds. 2009. *Duverger's Law of Plurality Voting: The Logic of Party Competition in Canada, India, the United Kingdom and the United States*. New York: Springer.

Hastie, T.J., and R.J. Tibshirani. 1990. *Generalized Additive Models*. New York: Chapman and Hall.

Hinich, M.J. 1981. "Voting as an act of contribution." *Public Choice* 36 (1): 135–40. http://dx.doi.org/10.1007/BF00163775.

Hurley, P.A., and K.Q. Hill. 2003. "Beyond the demand-input model: A theory of representational linkages." *Journal of Politics* 65 (2): 304–26.

Johnston, R., and H.E. Brady. 2002. "The rolling cross-section design." *Electoral Studies* 21 (2): 283–95. http://dx.doi.org/10.1016/S0261-3794(01)00022-1.

Johnston, R., M.G. Hagen, and K.H. Jamieson. 2004. *The 2000 Presidential Election and the Foundations of Party Politics*. Cambridge: Cambridge University Press. http://dx.doi.org/10.1017/CBO9780511756207.

Johnston, R., J.S. Matthews, and A. Bittner. 2007. "Turnout and the party system in Canada: 1988–2004." *Electoral Studies* 26 (4): 735–45. http://dx.doi.org/10.1016/j.electstud.2007.08.002.

Lijphart, A. 1984. *Democracies: Patterns of Majoritarian and Consensus Government in Twenty-One Countries*. New Haven: Yale University Press.

Morton, R.B. 1991. "Groups in rational turnout models." *American Journal of Political Science* 35 (3): 758–76. http://dx.doi.org/10.2307/2111565.

Norris, P. 1997. "Representation and the democratic deficit." *European Journal of Political Research* 32 (2): 273–82. http://dx.doi.org/10.1111/1475-6765.00342.

Pitkin, H. 1967. *The Concept of Political Representation*. Berkeley: Berkeley University Press.

Riker, W.H. 1962. *The Theory of Political Coalitions*. Cambridge: Yale University Press.

–. 1983. "Political theory and the art of heresthetics." In *Political Science: The State of the Discipline*, ed. A.W. Finifter, 47–67. Washington DC: American Political Science Association.

Riker, W.H., and P.C. Ordeshook. 1968. "A theory of the calculus of voting." *American Political Science Review* 62 (1): 25–42. http://dx.doi.org/10.2307/1953324.

Schuessler, A. 2000. *A Logic of Expressive Choice*. Princeton: Princeton University Press.

Selb, P. 2009. "A deeper look at the proportionality-turnout nexus." *Comparative Political Studies* 42 (4): 527–48. http://dx.doi.org/10.1177/0010414008327427.

Simon, H.A. 1954. "Bandwagon and underdog effects and the possibility of election predictions." *Public Opinion Quarterly* 18 (3): 245–53. http://dx.doi.org/10.1086/266513.

Smith, D.A., C.J. Tolbert, and A.M. Keller. 2010. "Electoral and structural losers and support for a national referendum in the U.S." *Electoral Studies* 29 (3): 509–20. http://dx.doi.org/10.1016/j.electstud.2010.04.017.

Tolbert, C.J., D.A. Smith, and J.C. Green. 2009. "Strategic voting and legislative redistricting reform." *Political Research Quarterly* 62 (1): 92–109. http://dx.doi.org/10.1177/1065912908314201.

Uhlaner, C.J. 1989. "Rational turnout: The neglected role of groups." *American Journal of Political Science* 33 (2): 390–422. http://dx.doi.org/10.2307/2111153.

Vowles, J., P. Aimer, H. Catt, J. Lamare, and R. Miller. 1995. *Towards Consensus: The 1993 Election in New Zealand and the Transition to Proportional Representation*. Auckland: Auckland University Press.

15

Parties and Party Systems

The Imperatives of Integration

RICHARD JOHNSTON AND CAMPBELL SHARMAN

By juxtaposing problems and analyses, this book is intended to provoke further integrative thinking. This chapter responds to this provocation, returning to the four themes mentioned at the outset in order to identify further connections and the tensions among them. It also identifies where individual chapters address more than one theme. It concludes by identifying possible future directions.

Brokerage: Parties and Systems

Although brokerage as a political concept is North American in origin and seems to be a special preoccupation for Canadians, it should have analogues in other systems with a dominant, centrist party. In Chapter 1, Carty takes us some distance down this road by comparing the Canadian case with the handful of others in which a single party has been dominant for many decades. One of his critical contributions is to clarify what a brokerage party is not. It is not a variant of the "catch-all" party described by Kirchheimer (1966). It is not enough that a party has a "big tent," that it tries to recruit widely. Even a catch-all party starts from somewhere – rooted in the labour movement or among Roman Catholics, for example – and it cannot venture too far from this base. Catch-all parties typically come in pairs, with one side building out from the labour movement. Although it may not be the polar party on the left, its link with organized labour makes it a coordination point for voters or coalition partners. The other party of the catch-all pair typically has a more chequered history (Lipset and Rokkan 1967; Boix 2009). It may not start out on the right, but the logic of competition usually puts it there, eventually if not immediately.

The brokerage party, in contrast, attempts to reconcile opposites. The spectrum of interests or tendencies it aggregates need not be wider than those assembled by catch-all operations. The key is that it draws from opposing tendencies and does so with a very broad goal: building the nation or preserving the constitutional order. And, if most party systems have a dominant player, brokerage parties take dominance to an extreme. Indeed, longevity in office may be a necessary condition for the brokerage system to be maintained: a broker that is small or that has a weak grip on office seems like a contradiction in terms.

The conditions for brokerage align with those identified by Sartori (1976) for polarized pluralism: the existence of an abiding existential threat. One type of threat comes from credible anti-democratic parties or movements. The clearest cases are Christian Democrats in Italy and the Liberal Democrats in Japan, facing relics of authoritarian politics on one flank and a communist party on the other. Another existential threat targets the political community's territorial integrity. Canada is the clearest case of this, being a "deeply divided" society (Furnivall 1948; Rabushka and Shepsle 1972) with the Liberals as the historic party of national unity. India before 1990 faced both kinds of threat: there were armed insurgencies in some states, state-specific parties in others, and the ongoing dispute over Kashmir as well as threats to the secular, liberal constitution from Hindu nationalists on one side and Soviet-backed communists on the other. The Irish case seems like shadow boxing: the long-lived Fianna Fáil defended both a Republican constitution and a united Ireland. Neither the Constitution nor the territory it covered seemed really under threat, but the physical proximity of the old conqueror and colonizer – especially its Ulster legatee – kept the existential pot on the boil. And, like the others, Fianna Fáil faced competition on both flanks.

The fact that brokerage may be a functional requisite for a polity offers no guarantee that brokerage will actually occur. Johnston (Chapter 2) takes up the specific case of Canadian parties, the Liberals in particular (but not only the Liberals), and outlines the necessary and sufficient conditions for electoral victory. He shows that seats in Quebec have regularly been pivotal to the formation of national governments. This is true even though Ontario has always had the largest bloc of seats. The pivotal position of Quebec was based on the concentration of its seats on one major party only and the mobility of that concentration between parties. Critical to this pattern was

Quebeckers' focus on their subnational interest and the mobilization of the province's political elite around a particular party. Much remains to be explored, however, and the swift evaporation of the pattern remains a mystery.

Both the Canadian and the Irish examples provoke us to wonder whether brokerage – or the claim to be engaging in it – is as much a clever stratagem as a response to necessity. This certainly was Cairns's (1968) view of Canada. Even if Johnston's chapter differs from Cairns on mechanistic details, it is not incompatible with his scepticism regarding motives. The Canadian Conservatives acquiesced in the game and occasionally benefitted from it. And they did so in spite of their followers' views (Johnston et al. 1992).

Brokerage unravelled in each place. One might ask whether brokerage is indefinitely sustainable in principle. If it corresponds to Sartori's polarized pluralism, the system should be vulnerable to competitive outbidding on the flanks, which, in turn, should lead to attrition of the broker's vote share. The more this happens, the less the putative broker can discharge its self-appointed task. To the extent that brokers rely on patronage, as opposed to programmatic appeals, an electoral reverse can begin an irreversible downward cycle. In this respect, Thelen (1999) contrasts the now-defunct Italian Christian Democrats with the resilient Swedish Social Democrats. The evidence in Carty's chapter bears her thesis out.

In any case, the fading of fascist legacies and the end of the Cold War removed threats from the right and left extremes. In the Italian case, as elsewhere in Europe, recent threats from the New European Right may be ethnocentric and may threaten a real or perceived elite consensus, but they are not obviously anti-democratic. The absence or weakness of threat on the left flank gives competing parties of the centre-left and centre-right room to manoeuvre, sometimes to accommodate the threat on the right, sometimes to marginalize it (Meguid 2008). Quarantines on parties of the New Right seem quite permeable as some have now been accepted in coalitions, even if with reluctance and distaste. If India remains deeply divided, ethnic outbidding, which Rabushka and Shepsle (1972) argue to be the dominant ethno-religious dynamic, has moderated (Chandra 2004). With the end of the Cold War, the Congress Party was able to slide leftwards and shift from a brokerage to a catch-all party. In Canada, Quebec stopped playing the game in 1993: the province's electorate deconsolidated and a large fraction moved to a party with no interest in controlling the federal executive. How a pattern of such long duration and such benefit to Quebec can suddenly end remains a mystery. On the other side, in the decades before 1993, the

Progressive Conservative leaders' neglect of the anti-brokerage tendencies of their followers provoked a fracture in the party's base. The ultimate reconstitution of the right side of the spectrum produced a party that has been mainly indifferent to Quebec and that is uncomfortable with catch-all status, much less with brokerage.

If we face a future without brokerage, Stewart and Sayers (Chapter 3) give us a glimpse of it. They show that the new Conservative Party is ideologically quite coherent and certainly opposed to the old way of doing business. The 2004 election shows that a party distinctively committed to social conservatism and individualism can be palatable to a large proportion of electors. That proportion is well short of a majority, but Canada's electoral institutions bring the party close to or just over the threshold for a majority in seats. The rise of the NDP to Official Opposition status in 2011 completes the picture. NDP supporters are about as distant from the median voter as are Conservative voters. However, the lesson of other systems indicates that this is cold comfort for the still-centrist Liberal Party. In the long run, the Conservatives and the NDP may be forced into a catch-all mode, but – to circle back to Carty's opening statement – this would leave neither party as a broker.

Keeping the Team Together

The need for cohesion is thought to follow from the dependence of governments in parliamentary systems on majorities in the confidence chamber. But merely contesting elections may suffice. For instance, the "reputational premium" identified by Sniderman and Stiglitz (2012) stems from reflection on the US case. A similar intuition animates Bardi, Katz, and Mair (Chapter 7). Just as Caramani (2004) found that merely extending the franchise induced European parties to push for nationwide contestation, so might the creation of the European Parliament produce Europe-wide coordination. Bardi and his colleagues detect evidence for an emergent pan-European party system, notwithstanding the complete detachment of the selection of commissioners from the makeup of the EP. Bardi, Katz, and Mair propose circuitous pathways by which EP electoral politics might tend towards the creation of a responsible EU executive. Should this come to fruition, it would reverse the usual causal sequence between party cohesion and executive responsibility: party cohesion might create cabinet government rather than emerge as its functional requisite. But then, pursuit of the phantom of a European cabinet might undermine parties' already visible first steps towards EU-wide coherence. Ironically, if EP party alliances were to seek control of the executive the price might be to turn them into brokerage parties.

So far, the focus is on end states: parties are disciplined to support governments; parties are coherent so as to earn a reputational premium. The arguments gloss over how parties actually reconcile the competing imperatives of collective coherence and local responsiveness. Indeed, they seem to preclude such reconciliation: local autonomy and collective accountability are treated as poles in a trade-off. The possibility that they can be reconciled, that the game might be positive-sum, is not taken seriously.

Farrell, Mair, Ó Muineacháin, and Wall (Chapter 5) directly challenge this zero-sum presumption. Even though Ireland's single transferable vote formula is quintessentially open (in Carey's sense), and candidates court local opinion shamelessly, legislators are nonetheless highly disciplined. Evidently, the collective accountability of parties does not necessarily preclude some version of individual accountability. This apparent contradiction is highlighted by survey information from Irish *Teachtaí Dála,* which shows that members put greater stress on the importance of representing the voters in their constituency than on the interests of their party, even though in the Dáil TDs rarely choose constituency over party. The authors suggest that the existence of a majoritarian parliamentary tradition in Ireland based on members who are more concerned with local matters than national policy may undermine effective scrutiny of the government and, to that extent, weaken the overall process of parliamentary accountability.

How is any of this actually accomplished? The literature on parties suggests that one solution is "stratarchy" (Eldersfeld (1964), whereby local entities are essentially independent of the centre and of each other. Wolinetz (Chapter 4) systematizes this intuition and explores its terminological history, starting with Carty's (2002, 2004) extension of stratarchy to the idea of a "franchise" party. Carty began by reflecting on the extreme coordination challenge faced by brokers. Subordinate units may be independent within their spheres – primarily local recruitment and campaigning – but the party leadership also needs to operate essentially independently of the local units. Carty sees franchising as a solution to brokers' coordination challenge, but he also suggests that franchise arrangements are inevitable in spatially dispersed societies, at least those with candidate-focused elections. (And big polities do tend to feature single-member districts. According to Reynolds et al. [2005], 70 percent of the citizens of established democracies and 44 percent of all persons with some experience of democracy vote in single-member districts.) Moreover, to the extent that the number of intense activists is shrinking, franchise parties may be the wave of the future.

Wolinetz sees the challenge identified by Carty as more general: all party organizations represent vertical bargains. The bargains vary widely, with the critical variance resting in how open the top is to influence from below. Conditioning this variance are institutional constraints, the most important, perhaps, being federal. At one extreme are strict and bounded hierarchies, where local manifestations seem to have no autonomy. Eldersfeld's (1964) stratarchical parties are an intermediate type: the direction of the party is set centrally but local entities have considerable autonomy over organization and recruitment. In confederative parties the local components are next to impossible to discipline. Notwithstanding reforms to nomination procedures initiated in 1972, US parties continue to exemplify this type. Clientelist parties may not actually be more decentralized than confederative ones, and, indeed, clientelist arrangements may typify the lower-level units of a confederative party, as with traditional US urban machines. In this classification, Carty's franchise system emerges as a type that includes stratarchy as a defining feature.

The bargain may also be conditional on factors within a given party, such that different bargains prevail in different places at the same time. Cross and Young (Chapter 9) show that the individualization of campaigns is conditional on the locus of candidate recruitment. The key fact is whether a candidate was recruited locally or by the national party. Locally recruited candidates tend to run campaigns that are locally resourced and locally themed, and, by implication, constituency campaigns are individualized. Although national campaigns are the major source of information for voters, local campaigns are critical to electoral success, for it is this level that drives the turnout of partisans and that attracts new supporters. But the extent of national involvement in candidate recruitment is surprisingly great and may be growing, and this, in turn, can shift the relative balance of local and national campaign resources, issues, activities, and personnel.

If keeping the team together is a ubiquitous challenge, parties have devised alternative routes to this objective. For instance, Hazan and Rahat (Chapter 6) start with a variant of the dual-mandate story: candidates are chosen first by the party and only then by electors. But what is the party that does the choosing? It seems natural to suppose that the more inclusive a party's "selectorate," the weaker the party leadership's ability to maintain a disciplined public face. An inclusive selectorate privileges the mass media, campaign professionals, interest groups, and financial backers – all, we might suppose, with centrifugal effect. Empirically, however, the correlation between decentralized candidate selection and overt discipline is weak. It appears that, as the base for selectorates has broadened, the individuals who make up that base have become more party-oriented.

But then, what do we really know about those individuals? Van Haute (Chapter 10) argues that we have studied parties with the wrong optic. Although we talk about parties as organizations, we commonly study them as sites for political participation. Our reliance on the survey method leads to an emphasis on ex post reflection rather than on the dynamics of joining, much less on the dynamics that follow the initial participatory moment. Van Haute argues for greater emphasis on social psychology and on studies rooted in labour economics and management. We also take her chapter to be a call for participant observation, as exemplified by Nielsen's (2012) brilliant study of US congressional campaign organizations.

Principals and Agents

Parties seem extraordinarily adaptable. One result of this is that they can confuse accountability even in their own ranks. For example, Hazan and Rahat raise the possibility that the expansion of a party's selectorate in the name of democratic accountability offers only a pretense of inclusion. The lower reaches of the rank and file may actually be quite docile, and their docility is a weapon to be used by leaders against the truly feisty actors – intermediate elites. Patronage may be a weapon in this squeeze play.

If Hazan and Rahat hint at agency for MPs, Koop (Chapter 8) comes right out and ascribes it. Like others, Koop conceptualizes MPs as caught between leaders and voters, but, in both relationships, he sees them as agents. The fact that MPs rely on constituency associations for their very selection as candidates makes them eager to shape those associations to maximum personal effect. Associations are also called upon for assistance with the tasks expected of a local member. Koop examines the involvement of constituency association executives in the second of these functions – helping the member by recruiting party members, raising funds, responding to the requests of constituents, and generally maintaining the local association in working order for the next election. In delegating these tasks, the MP must ensure that these party volunteers – the MP's agents – discharge their tasks in a satisfactory manner. Even though many of the resources available to traditional managers are not available in the voluntary context of the constituency association, MPs can still call upon a variety of strategies to minimize agency loss.

Institutional Fragility, Institutional Resilience

In Chapter 4, Wolinetz places an institutional bet. He emphasizes institutions as the primary condition for intra-party structures. Courtney (Chapter 11) qualifies this logic by showing how a single-member electoral equilibrium can sometimes be self-undermining. Weak Liberal minority governments in the 1920s, 1960s, and 1970s were responsible for the most consequential shifts in Canadian election law. Most important has been election expenses legislation, which was passed under the impetus of a fractionalized electorate and Parliament and which may have encouraged further fractionalization. The initial legislation also shifted the financial balance within parties, to the disadvantage of the centre.

Pulling the opposite direction was another central feature of the 1960s-70s changes: formal recognition of parties and a doctrine of agency. The smaller parties that appear on the fringe of the electoral battle naturally crave recognition for themselves, but such recognition can also be useful in a divide-and-conquer game played by the governing party: recognition of small parties enables a downgrading of the Official Opposition. Arbitrary choices can then become self-reinforcing, as for instance with regard to the number of MPs necessary to qualify for official party status. Recognition of parties in law facilitated the acquisition of formal rights for leaders to veto local nominations. But recognition also converted parties into public utilities. As a yet further complication, legal recognition interacts with the Canadian Charter of Rights and Freedoms (especially through section 3, which states that, as a democratic freedom, "every citizen of Canada has the right to vote in an election of the members of the House of Commons or of a legislative assembly and to be qualified for membership therein") to make parties the objects of external regulation. Given that public money – tax deductions and subsidies – are involved, further regulatory incursions are inevitable.

Courtney's account naturally makes us ask if Canadian election law replicates a pattern identified for European party systems by Katz and Mair (1995). They propose the notion of "cartelization," in which parties react to global decline in grassroots involvement by seeking state support. This further attenuates their links to civil society even as it erects a barrier to the entry of new political formations. MacIvor (1996) takes this view for Canada, although her perspective was never shared unanimously (see Young [1998] for a contrary position). MacIvor's focus is on outcomes rather than on motives. But the strategic element in Liberal governments' acquiescence to initial cartel-like moves suggests that the system might still be subject to narrow party calculations.

Aucoin and Bakvis (Chapter 12) make precisely this point, with a focus on the per-vote subsidy (PVS), enacted in 2003 and subsequently repealed. Like Courtney, they offer an account of legislative history, including a survey of the circumstances and motives for change. The PVS ostensibly embodied a proposal by the Royal Commission on Electoral Reform and Party Financing (the Lortie Commission) that was intended to create policy capacity outside the pressure of elections. As implemented, however, the PVS was a substitute for corporate and union donations, which were restricted by the 2003 legislation and later banned. Once again, however, the timing seems to have been driven by fractionalization of the party system, although this time with a different logic. Whereas in earlier episodes, Liberal minority governments responded to parliamentary fractionalization, now a Liberal majority government (its leader, at least) hoped to maintain the electoral fractionalization that enabled the party to turn a modest popular vote plurality into a comfortable parliamentary majority. It was never popular with the newly reconstituted Conservative Party, and the 2011 election result gave it the opportunity for repeal. It seized it, suggesting that party-specific interests trump system-wide ones. So much, it would seem, for cartel theory in Canada.

Both the Courtney and the Aucoin-Bakvis chapters remind us that, even in hung parliaments, the prime agenda setter remains the governing party. How that party uses its agenda power differs according to the parliamentary situation, but now it must also react to the courts. This is a key point for Courtney, but the pattern is thrown into even sharper relief by Sharman and Attanasio (Chapter 13). The legitimacy of parliamentary institutions has declined. Citizens seem less persuaded than before that majority rule is appropriately channelled through dominant executives as opposed to representative parliaments. But executives are naturally reluctant to enhance parliamentary processes. At the same time, the courts have emerged as a rival power centre. Their starting point may be the Charter, but the critical point for Sharman and Attanasio is the growing legitimacy of institutions that challenge simple majoritarianism. For executives, one stratagem is to circumvent the floor of Parliament and to make populist appeals of their own. Critical examples of this are the British Columbia and Ontario citizens' assemblies. Each seemed designed to fail as they were required to refer their proposals to the electorate at large in a referendum with a high threshold. Accidents were possible, of course, and in British Columbia the accident almost happened. Either way, the focus on electoral reform was appealing because it promised to change the dynamics of representation without altering the Constitution. In fact, broad public consultation works to constitutionalize representation issues in any case. At the same time, the expressed hope is that the legitimacy of the public consultation will enhance that of Parliament itself. The animating notion is that the public transcends narrow partisan considerations. This combines with the common-sense view that players should not revise the rules in the middle of the game. Merely to say this, much less to commit to act on it, is to "constitutionalize" the object of deliberation – in this case, election law. But if election law is now sanctified as constitutional it will be harder than ever to change.

If this is so, it might only deepen discontent, at least in some parts of the electorate. Recent work (notably, Anderson et al. 2005) does not take voters' support for electoral institutions as a given. It is not obvious why losers should just accept the result, and in many places they do not. Even in consolidated systems of long standing, Canada being a prime example, the vein of discontent runs surprisingly deep. Worrisomely, the evolution of the party systems – not just in Canada – has narrowed the popular bases of parliamentary majorities: collectively, losers typically outnumber winners – and by growing margins. If most voters have little sense of the alternatives to the status quo, those in British Columbia and Ontario are exceptions. Each was treated to the deliberative spectacle of the citizens' assembly and then given the opportunity to choose a specific alternative formula. Cutler and Hooper (Chapter 14) show that losers support change in the direction of a proportional representation system as a direct function of the magnitude of election loss they typically experience. On the other side, it suffices merely to win: supporters of winners reject change, but this rejection does not increase as the margin of their side's victory increases. The effect on the losers' side is amplified by substantive understanding of the alternatives. Indeed, information is a necessary condition for voters to make the connection between magnitude of loss and choice of an alternative electoral system. Critically, losers express not so much a crude desire for the spoils of victory as a sharp awareness of enduring inequalities in representation.

Conclusion

The closest link between organization and system comes out of reflecting on the implications of the breadth of a party's appeal for intra-party power. The extreme case is the brokerage party, challenged as it is to reconcile opposites. But catch-all parties face a challenge only slightly less extreme. The response in these situations has been to tolerate considerable local flexibility in organization and recruitment in return for freedom of action at the top. It turns out that parties seem able to square this circle in a wide variety of contexts, including variation in the size and inclusiveness of their rank and file. It helps that power relations within parties are not necessarily zero-sum. So one call is for a conversation that forces students of party organization, whose modus operandi is basically ethnographic, and scholars of parliamentary forms (and non-parliamentary ones, for that matter), who work deductively, to confront each other. Are positive-sum games ubiquitous or can we set boundaries on their relevance?

Institutionalists have adopted principal-agent relations as the analytic starting point. This gets us to sort institutions for their implications for moral hazard, on the one hand, and adverse selection, on the other (Strøm et al. 2003). Additional texture comes with the recognition that individual parliamentarians are agents with two principals. Those familiar with the workplace know that, for an employee, having more than one boss can be a good thing: as the saying goes, to have many bosses is to have no boss. This becomes startlingly visible when one descends into parties' engine rooms: there we find a confusion of principals and agents. Certain political actors can clearly be both principal and agent and not simply occupy an intermediate position in a unidirectional chain of accountability.

Institutionalism broadly conceived is a theoretical battleground, and this book shows why. Rational choice institutionalists typically emphasize the stability of institutions and, accordingly, give priority to constitutional forms in shaping the structure and behaviour of more fluid entities such as parties. The example of the nascent European party system should give pause, however. So should the recent history of Canadian election law. That history shows both the fragility and the resilience of the electoral framework. On the one hand, it is susceptible to tinkering even in the absence of political crisis or sociological rupture; on the other hand, in the long run, the tinkering may work to make the framework *less* susceptible to change. Inadvertently, strategic manouevres by political executives may have raised institutions formerly open to statutory revision to the level of entities that can be revised only by extraordinary majorities or even by majorities over which the political class has no control and, thus, are unlikely to be invoked.

Bringing together a distinguished body of party and election researchers reveals how little we know about electoral campaigns and about the dynamics of party organization. Students of elections work hard at draining the objects of their study of strategy and contingency – of politics, in short. Some initiatives have been ventured in survey research, but these barely scratch the surface and are most relevant for the so-called "air war." For the "ground war" we need to focus on parties as organizations, all the while attending, of course, to the electoral objective. But for organizations, we rely on questionnaires or depth interviews with key personnel, usually outside the heat of battle. Indeed, the last thing studied for the party organization seems to be its electoral function. A clear lesson of this book is that both kinds of scholarship – on elections and on parties – need a recommitment to ethnography. This is not to say that we abandon theory or turn our backs on the critical advances made by methodologically sophisticated scholars. Such scholars are represented in the pages of this book, after all. We need to take the principles articulated in recent work on the case study (Brady and Collier 2010) – how to select cases, what constitutes causal process observations, and the critical deployment of counterfactuals – and get inside parties. And we need to get inside them for extended periods.

References

Anderson, C.J., A. Blais, S. Bowler, T. Donovan, and O. Listhaug. 2005. *Losers' Consent: Elections and Democratic Legitimacy*. Oxford: Oxford University Press. http://dx.doi.org/10.1093/0199276382.001.0001.

Boix, C. 2009. "The emergence of parties and party systems." In *The Oxford Handbook of Comparative Politics*, ed. C. Boix and S. Stokes, 499–521. Oxford: Oxford University Press. http://dx.doi.org/10.1093/oxfordhb/9780199566020.001.0001.

Brady, H.E., and D. Collier, eds. 2010. *Rethinking Social Inquiry: Diverse Tools, Shared Standards*. Lanham, MD: Rowman and Littlefield.

Cairns, A.C. 1968. "The electoral system and the party system in Canada, 1921-1965." *Canadian Journal of Political Science* 1 (1): 55–80.

Caramani, D. 2004. *The Nationalization of Politics: The Formation of National Electorates and Party Systems in Western Europe*. Cambridge: Cambridge University Press. http://dx.doi.org/10.1017/CBO9780511616662.

Carty, R.K. 2002. "The politics of Tecumseh Corners: Canadian political parties as franchise organizations." *Canadian Journal of Political Science* 35 (4): 723–45. http://dx.doi.org/10.1017/S0008423902778402.

–. 2004. "Parties as franchise systems: The stratarchical organizational imperative." *Party Politics* 10 (1): 5–24. http://dx.doi.org/10.1177/1354068804039118.

Chandra, K. 2004. *Why Ethnic Parties Succeed: Patronage and Ethnic Head Counts in India*. Cambridge, Cambridge: Cambridge University Press.

Eldersfeld, S.J. 1964. *Political Parties: A Behavioral Analysis*. Chicago: Rand McNally.

Furnivall, J.S. 1948. *Colonial Policy and Practice: A Comparative Study of Burma and Netherlands India*. Cambridge: Cambridge University Press.

Johnston, R., A. Blais, H.E. Brady, and J. Crête. 1992. *Letting the People Decide: Dynamics of a Canadian Election*. Montreal and Kingston: McGill-Queen's University Press.

Katz, R.S., and P. Mair. 1995. "Changing models of party organization and party democracy: The emergence of the cartel party." *Party Politics* 1 (1): 5–28. http://dx.doi.org/10.1177/1354068895001001001.

Kirchheimer, O. 1966. "The transformation of the Western European party systems." In *Political Parties and Political Development*, ed. M. Weiner and J. LaPalombara, 177–200. Princeton, NJ: Princeton University Press.

Lipset, S.M., and S. Rokkan, eds. 1967. *Party Systems and Voter Alignments; Cross National Perspectives*. New York: Free Press.

MacIvor, H. 1996. "Do Canadian political parties form a cartel?" *Canadian Journal of Political Science* 29 (2): 317–33. http://dx.doi.org/10.1017/S0008423900007733.

Meguid, B. 2008. *Party Competition between Unequals: Strategies and Electoral Fortunes in Western Europe*. Cambridge: Cambridge University Press. http://dx.doi.org/10.1017/CBO9780511510298.

Nielsen, R.K. 2012. *Ground Wars: Personalized Communication in Political Campaigns*. Princeton: Princeton University Press.

Rabushka, A., and K.A. Shepsle. 1972. *Politics in Plural Societies: A Theory of Democratic Instability*. Columbus, OH: Merrill.

Reynolds, A., B. Reilly, and A. Ellis. 2005. *Electoral System Design: The International IDEA Handbook*. Stockholm: International Institute for Democracy and Electoral Assistance.

Sartori, G. 1976. *Parties and Party Systems: A Framework for Analysis*. Cambridge: Cambridge University Press.

Sniderman, P.M., and E.H. Stiglitz. 2012. *The Reputational Premium: A Theory of Party Identification and Policy Reasoning*. Princeton, NJ: Princeton University Press.

Strøm, K., W.C. Müller, and T. Bergman, eds. 2003. *Delegation and Accountability in Parliamentary Democracies*. Oxford, UK: Oxford University Press.

Thelen, P.K. 1999. "Historical institutionalism in comparative politics." *Annual Review of Political Science* 2 (1): 369–404. http://dx.doi.org/10.1146/annurev.polisci.2.1.369.

Young, L. 1998. "Party, state and political competition in Canada: The cartel model reconsidered." *Canadian Journal of Political Science* 31 (2): 339–58. http://dx.doi.org/10.1017/S000842390001982X.

Contributors

Kyle Attanasio was a graduate student at the University of British Columbia where he completed a Master's thesis on the differences between private members' bills in the Canadian House of Commons and the Senate. He is currently director of Legislative and Communications Services for the County of St. Paul in Alberta.

Peter Aucoin, FRSC, was a professor emeritus of political science and public administration at Dalhousie University and director of research for the Royal Commission on Electoral Reform and Party Financing (Lortie Commission), 1989-91. He passed away in July of 2011. In 2012 he was awarded posthumously the Donner Prize for excellence in public policy analysis and the Donald Smiley prize for best book in Canadian politics for *Democratizing the Constitution: Reforming Responsible Government* (2011), co-authored with Mark D. Jarvis and Lori Turnbull.

Herman Bakvis is a professor of public administration at the University of Victoria, Canada. He was research coordinator for the section on political parties and voter turnout for the Royal Commission on Electoral Reform and Party Financing, 1989-91. He is the author of *Regional Ministers: Power and Influence in the Canadian Cabinet*, co-author of *Contested Federalism: Certainty and Ambiguity in the Canadian Federation* (with Gerald Baier and Douglas Brown), co-editor of *Canadian Federalism: Performance,*

Effectiveness, and Legitimacy (with Grace Skogstad), and co-editor of *From New Public Management to New Political Governance: Essays in Honour of Peter C. Aucoin* (with Mark D. Jarvis).

Luciano Bardi is a professor of Political Science at the University of Pisa, where he teaches courses in comparative politics, European Union politics, and international relations. He is also co-director of the European University Institute's Observatory on Political Parties and Representation (OPPR). Between 2009 and 2012, he was chair of the Executive Committee of the European Consortium for Political Research (ECPR). He has published extensively on EU parties and party systems.

R. Kenneth Carty is a professor emeritus of political science at the University of British Columbia. His work is primarily concerned with the structure and character of political parties and party systems. Recent books include *When Citizens Decide: Lessons from Citizen Assemblies on Electoral Reform* (OUP, 2011) and *Big Tent Politics: The Liberal Party's Long Mastery of Canada's Public Life* (UBC Press, 2015).

John C. Courtney is a professor emeritus of Political Studies and Senior Policy Fellow of the Johnson-Shoyama Graduate School of Public Policy at the University of Saskatchewan. He is the author or editor of ten books and numerous articles and book chapters on electoral boundary delimitations and representational and electoral systems. His recent books include *The Oxford Handbook of Canadian Politics* (OUP, 2010, co-edited with David E. Smith) and *Elections* (UBC Press, 2004).

William Cross is professor and Bell Chair in Canadian Parliamentary Democracy at Carleton University. His work focuses on questions of intra-party democracy and party organization. His recent publications include *The Challenges of Intra-Party Democracy* (OUP, 2013) and *The Politics of Party Leadership: A Cross-National Perspective* (OUP, 2015).

Fred Cutler is an associate professor of Political Science at the University of British Columbia. He holds a PhD from the University of Michigan. He has published on voters' responses to federalism, electoral choice, context and public opinion, and regionalism, and is a principal investigator of the Canadian Election Study, 2011–15.

David M. Farrell holds the Chair of Politics at University College Dublin. A specialist in the study of parties, electoral systems, and parliamentary representation, his most recent book (co-authored with Russell Dalton and Ian McAllister) is *Political Parties and Democratic Linkage* (OUP, 2011). In 2012–14 he was the research director of the Irish Constitutional Convention.

Reuven Y. Hazan is professor and chair of the Department of Political Science at the Hebrew University of Jerusalem. His research interests include parties and party systems, elections and electoral systems, and legislative studies. His most recent book (with Gideon Rahat) is *Democracy within Parties: Candidate Selection Methods and Their Political Consequences* (OUP, 2010).

Graeme Hooper was a graduate student at the University of British Columbia and was honoured to defend his Master's thesis before Professor Carty in 2006. Following his graduate studies, Graeme became a lawyer and now practises in the areas of administrative law, constitutional law, and legal research.

Richard Johnston is Canada Research Chair in Public Opinion, Elections, and Representation at the University of British Columbia. His primary research focus has been on elections in Canada and the US. He was principal investigator of the 1988 and 1992–93 Canadian Election Studies and research director of the National Annenberg Election Survey 2000–08 at the University of Pennsylvania.

Richard S. Katz is professor of political science at Johns Hopkins University. He was co-editor of the *European Journal of Political Research* (2006–12), and of the *EJPR Political Data Yearbook* (1996–2006). He is a member of the Executive Committee of the European Consortium for Political Research and chair of the OSCE/ODIHR Core Group of Experts on Political Parties.

Royce Koop is an associate professor in the Department of Political Studies at the University of Manitoba. His research focuses on political parties, representation, and Canadian politics. He is the author of *Grassroots Liberals: Organizing for Local and National Politics* (UBC Press, 2011).

Peter Mair, at the time of his death in 2011, was professor of comparative politics at the European University Institute, having previously served as professor of comparative politics at Leiden University. His books include: *Representative Government in Modern Europe: Institutions, Parties, and Governments* (with Michael Gallagher and Michael Lever); *Political Parties and Electoral Change: Party Responses to Electoral Markets*, (with Wolfgang Müller and Fritz Plasser); *The Enlarged European Union: Diversity and Adaptation* (with Jan Zielonka); *Party System Change: Approaches and Interpretations*; and *Identity, Competition, and Electoral Availability: The Stabilisation of European Electorates 1885-1985* (with Stefano Bartolini), which received the ISSC/UNESCO Stein Rokkan Prize.

Séin Ó Muineacháin holds a PhD in political science from Trinity College Dublin. His thesis examined the institutional and party-based determinants of the persistence of factionalism in political parties. He previously worked as a consultant to an Irish parliamentary committee on electoral reform and currently works in public policy analysis and evaluation in London.

Gideon Rahat is a professor in the Department of Political Science at the Hebrew University of Jerusalem. His research interests include political parties, candidate selection, the politics of electoral reform, and political personalization. His most recent book (with Reuven Hazan) is *Democracy within Parties: Candidate Selection Methods and Their Political Consequences* (OUP, 2010).

Anthony M. Sayers is an associate professor of political science at the University of Calgary. His research interests include political parties and elections. He is the author of *Parties, Candidates and Campaigns in Canadian Elections* (1999, UBC Press), as well as numerous chapters in edited volumes and articles in journals such as *Party Politics* and *Electoral Studies*.

Campbell Sharman is an adjunct professor in political science at the University of British Columbia and a senior honorary research fellow in the School of Social Sciences at the University of Western Australia. He has had a long-standing interest in electoral systems and parliamentary government.

David K. Stewart is a professor of political science at the University of Calgary. His research interests focus on political parties and political leadership. He is the co-author of *Quasi-Democracy: Parties and Leadership Selection in Alberta* and *Conventional Choices: Maritime Leadership Politics.*

Emilie van Haute is a lecturer at the Université libre de Bruxelles (Cevipol). Her research interests focus on party membership, intra-party dynamics, factionalism, elections, and voting behaviour.

Matthew Wall is a lecturer in politics at Swansea University's Department of Political and Cultural Studies. His research interests include Vote Advice Application (VAA) websites, online politics, electoral campaigns, and electoral system effects. He has published research articles in journals, including *Electoral Studies, Party Politics,* and the *British Journal of Political Science.*

Steven B. Wolinetz is professor emeritus in political science at Memorial University of Newfoundland. He has written widely on political parties and the politics of smaller European democracies.

Lisa Young is professor of political science and vice provost and dean of graduate studies at the University of Calgary. Her research interests include women's participation in public life, political party organization, and electoral finance. She is the author of *Feminists and Party Politics,* co-author of *Rebuilding Canadian Party Politics* and *Advocacy Groups,* and co-editor of *Money, Politics and Democracy.*

Index

Note: Page numbers followed by (t) indicate tables and (f) indicate figures.

Printed and bound in Canada by Friesens
Set in Segoe and Warnock by Artegraphica Design Co. Ltd.
Copy editor: Joanne Richardson
Proofreader: Dianne Tiefensee
Indexer: Lillian Ashworth